OUR SOUL MUSIC JOURNEYS

BOOK 2

I0141608

A collection of personal soul stories

Author - John Warren

Foreword

by Dennis Locantore, collector & musician

Our Soul Music Journeys is a chronicle of the worldwide brotherhood of a variety of producers, artists, collectors from different backgrounds united in their mutual love of the honesty, good vibes, and power of that which we lovingly call Northern Soul.

May their personal stories enlighten and entertain the uninitiated! Read forward and be amazed at the unity of love of soul music lovers from throughout the world! May we get more converts to our beloved artists who in many cases toiled in obscurity and out of the limelight except to those whose stories are included herein. Enjoy it.

Soul bag image © Stephen Bardsley

Dedication

To my daughter Ethan Elizabeth Warren R.I.P, who inspires me every day to be the best I can be, until we meet again!

This publication is a collection of individual stories about the lives of the contributing writers assembled and authored by John Warren. The views expressed herein do not necessarily reflect the views of the author, publishers, editors, illustrators or their production companies. Images have been supplied by individual story contributors who indemnify and hold harmless the publisher, author, editors and production companies. Every effort has been made to identify the use of content and copyright holders and if any errors or omissions have been made the publisher will be happy to rectify in future editions. Some corrections, restoration and retouching of images have been applied to the original material to prepare images so as to be suitable for reproduction, images have not been altered to reflect any adverse change to their content.

Introduction

by Stephen Bardsley

Author John Warren came up with the concept for the "Our Soul Music Journeys" book series to assist soul artists not in the best of health, who were unable to pay their medical bills & struggling to make ends meet, or who had already passed away, but did not even have a recognisable grave, this because some died virtually penniless and their families have been unable to afford a headstone for their grave. John did not know how important his books were to be, as other soul artists would pass away even before proceeds from Book 1 were available. This is of course what makes Book 2 and future books so important, the harsh reality of life is there will be others for which proceeds from the books will be needed. We should all be grateful for small mercies such as the proceeds from these books, a small but so important contribution. Many thanks to John Warren, all who wrote Chapters and who contributed to, and/or helped make Books 1, 2 and possible. Each book will make a difference to those in need and for this all involved can be proud.

I do however now wish to mention not only those who have unselfishly contributed to the books and help soul artists in need, but also a small minority of detractors on the Australian soul scene, who contributed nothing to any of the books, but took it upon themselves to announce Book 1 would never be published. When Book 1 was published they didn't admit they were wrong, but instead attempted to convince others not to buy the book, suggesting it was not worth reading and Author John Warren only came up with the concept of the books to line his own pockets. What will they say now Books 1 and 2 have been published, Book 3 is in production, proceeds from the books will be distributed to artists and John is out of pocket for his efforts?

The detractors should hang their heads in shame. Although they will not be named in this book, or indeed elsewhere, they know who they are, as do those who may have heard or seen their comments on social media or elsewhere, the detractors will be judged accordingly.

John Warren, all the contributors and purchasers of the Book's in the "Our Soul Music Journeys" series will continue the good work, this to help the artists and those connected with them who may be in need, for this all who have contributed to and supported the books can be very proud.

Enjoy this book, it's another cracking read to which so many on the soul scene have contributed out of the goodness of their hearts and it shows. If you have contributed to, or purchased any of the books we thank you sincerely.

The more books are sold, the more soul artists and their connections can be helped, it's what we do together that actually counts. If you have enjoyed any of the books, a review on Amazon would be appreciated and will be beneficial to all.

Until Book three, let us all not just keep the faith, but spread it around.

Best wishes and many thanks
Stephen Bardsley

Contents

Chapter 1

Eulogy Chapter for Jan Lisewski by John Warren

My heart truly bleeds writing this Eulogy, as Jan Lisewski, my soul brother and the editor & publisher of Book 1 "Our Soul Music Journey" sadly passed away on the 4th April 2021. I truly feel he is with me as I communicate "In Spirit". I know Jan would want this project of books, which he was so very passionate about to continue and I will try my hardest to make that happen. Jan had so many dreams and ambitions for an Ebook and an Audio book to be spoken by passionate soul lovers in their own voices and unique accents. This would enhance the cause, of which many Artists and their connections truly need the support of, so hopefully we can make this happen!

I first met Jan Lisewski in Orlando in 2011, at my 3rd soul trip to the USA organised by the fabulous couple Kev & Sam Roberts, who through their iconic events have enriched my life because I have met so many lifelong mates from those events, for this I will always be truly grateful. Jan Lisewski was assisting Kev and Sam Roberts, his passion and professionalism were quickly apparent and I immediately saw in him what he saw in me "Moths Around a Light ", a term he coined & mentioned to me only a few weeks before he sadly passed. I spoke to Jan a week before he left us, he told me was eating a little, the antibiotics were helping and he believed he had food poisoning, mentioning the hash browns he had eaten several weeks before had tasted 'Soapy', he also told me a recent Covid test returned negative. Richard Lisweski, who was Jan's very close brother, related that to me on Easter Saturday, Erica who was Jan's wife messaged him to say Jan was very ill and had collapsed, she gave him CPR and he was immediately admitted to hospital. On Easter Sunday, Erica messaged Richard in the afternoon saying he had deteriorated. At 8.00 pm I had a video message from him saying, "He knew I was there, but was too heavily sedated to speak". Just before 10.00pm Erica messaged Richard to say he had passed away. Jan had lots of projects going on, he thought he was going to live a long life and not pass at the young age of 69. The world and the soul scene are weaker place for his passing. Due to the Orlando soul trip I have met many life-long friends, too many to mention but you all know who you are, some like Jan etched in my heart forever.

Robert Paladino is without a doubt one of my closest soul brothers and a true soulmate. In Book 1 he relates how we met in a hotel lift and a more humble and extremely talented man I have never been prouder to know. Jan also touched me in a similar way and our mateship grew over the years, when I needed an editor & publisher of my book his name sprung out at me like a Belisha beacon. We then commenced 3-hour phone calls twice a week, often Jan would laugh and joke "You burnt my Phone down again John" & bless him he would only get in one word to my five, because I am renowned to waffle, it is a weakness I truly need to fix!

My spirit guide Ethan Warren, my daughter who passed over 22 years ago often reminds me of this and the message is slowly being taken on board. Jan would comment that you can talk underwater John, it's now been 8 months since his passing and the tears still flow and I do not think they will stop any time soon. Some people touch my inner soul but very few as much as Jan did. He truly thought he was going to live to be a 100, and had so much planned to do. So my personal motto is to live in the "Second" because are we going to be next? They say only the good die young, sadly with Jan this rings true. Jan's incredible talents and humbleness is a major characteristic of all my true friends, no "Willy Wangling" from them, about how many rare records they have which some people always seem to want to mention, which just annoys me! Jan will now be in the company of so many of our soul idols that it makes you dizzy and in Timmy Thomas, Jan related he was like a second dad! I met Eugene Thomas at the Orlando soul event so I can also relate to that for him, Eugene R.I.P. In Book 1 "Our Soul Music Journey" there is a photo of Eugene Thomas and I that tells the story of the bond we had, this at first sight when we met in Orlando! I have included it in this book as well. In October 2021 Simon Bayliss with the help of Robert Paladino brought out a new version of "You Don't Love Me" on a 45, by Jamie and the Numbers on the New Zealand label Deltaphonic, to honor Eugene Thomas.

Timmy Thomas was also to be Chapter 1 in Book 2 but has not been well, so sadly this did not eventuate. I have recently spoken to Timmy's wife, she told me Jan Lisweski was the best manager Timmy ever had. I personally feel a eulogy chapter to honor and remember our mate Jan Lisweski is very important because, in reality, the formatting and structure if our first book was his structure and formatting, as were the incredible drawings of Betty Wright and the Radio Caroline pirate ship & the iconic drawing on the front cover and idea he and Steve Bardsley came up with.

Jan and my great mate Steve Bardsley also met at the Orlando soul trip & together worked on the graphics in Book 1 and they did an incredible job that made a reader want to open the book in my humble view! Steve has agreed to be the go-to man to do all the graphics in all books going forward and that is such an asset, as the covers really help sell the book's, with their eye-catching graphics, colours which jump off the page including the photograph of Steve's original Adidas bag and soul patches from the early 1970's which he still has and which we will use for Book 2 and beyond. This is because in July 2021 we revised & changed the Book 1 cover because I had to republish because the original artwork was under Jan's copyright. Jan during the years would mention to me about soul artists in need, that he was working with those who were down on their luck and needed help with their medical bills, and often died in a pauper's grave and that for me is beyond sad! Jan was also working with Ric Patterson, who also wrote in Book One. Ric and Jan had BMI licensed a lot of songs over 20 years that are currently unreleased and they are more than good, in fact some of Jan's unreleased songs are great. I hope Ric Pattison gets them released in the future because they will do very well.

Timmy Thomas song "Wings Of Change" is a peace anthem similar to the iconic one of his from the 70's with the title "Why Can't We Live Together" of which there is also an updated version 40 years on, which will also do well. I know Timmy Thomas has had tough times over the last few years and hope things improve for him. I feel Jan's passing will have hit Timmie very hard. Jamie & the Number's from New Zealand want to record "Wings Of Change", sadly I am unable to get a contract accepted due to Timmy being in hospital much of the time recently, so being unable to speak to him and secure a license.

Tina Valdez is an extremely talented lady who lives in Miami and has written some brilliant tracks including "Love Destiny " with Jan & my personal favorite "I Dreamed You Into My Life" with the superb intro of thunder and rain and then the pan pipes kick in, a true masterpiece! I truly hope it comes out on a 45 because I really feel it will do extremely well as a double A sidder! I have been fortunate to chat with Tina Valdez on messenger, and she is a delightful talented singer and like me very religious, as also like a lot of my close friends, and to name a few they are Robert Paladino, Pat Gwinn, Dennis Locantore, Eugene Thomas R.I.P. & Bart Mazzarella.

11

Matt Lucas has two brilliant blues R&B style off tracks called "Yolanda" and "I'm Hearing Stories" which are really fabulous and they would sell out in my humble opinion. Many other of the tracks that Jan was working on with Ric Patterson I have yet to hear, but Ric has mentioned some are more than good, so I look forward to hearing them in the future! Ric related he and Jan worked long hours together so they developed a very close relationship and Jan's passing has hit Ric very hard, and recently in July 2021, Ric did a song called "You Didn't Say A Word" and when you listen to those lyrics it's very obvious he was doing it in memory of Jan Lisewski! That was the ilk of the man, Jan was to move people to write a song in their memory!

Some of the other tracks that I have been fortunate to hear which were written over 3-4 years ago include these! "New Girl In The City", "On An Empty Street", "Our Time", "Hey Mister" & "Downtown Train" Jan also owned a studio acetate of a Jerry Butler song called "It's A Parade" which is as good a beat ballad, I have heard in many many decades and Jan would have loved to have released it on a 45, we tried so very hard to get a license to do so. Jan was very much a dot the I's and dot the T's man and when we published Book 1 the legal publishing contract between Jan and I ran to nine pages, which sadly I will need as the book proceeds are tied up in litigation, as Jan sadly died without a will! Sadly, a lot of Jan's songs, some of which he wrote, never saw the light of day because of many reasons, including Covid and trying to post worldwide.

Jan felt it was not a good business decision at that time and this has proved to be smart, as recently I had to do several refunds as my 45's arrived melted and warped when posted to the UK. So sadly Jan had the release of 45's on the back burner, waiting for the right time, which for him was sadly "Too Late" and that is beyond sad! I personally found Jan was very cautious with business music decisions, and often rightly so, he often would start so many projects at the same time, he had brought out his own book in 2019 called "The Australasian Vinyl Record Guide", it has a complete list of vinyl record stores & record shows in Australia and New Zealand. The book is very well done with the usual diligence we all loved and is available on Amazon worldwide. I now truly understand Jan's reluctance to pull the trigger on some of the projects. We were recently talking about releasing some records on a label we registered as "Our Soul Music Journey" and hopefully in the future, I can make this a reality.

There are many incredible ideas as Jan was always thinking left field and outside the square, a proper free thinker he was. The "Soul Music Journey Book" project started 3 years ago with an epiphany, a truly spiritual moment, and a motto that I now utilize is KISS "Keep It Simple Spiritually". I quickly found out that Graham Rogers, a dear mate who I met in Thailand who was doing the editing at the time, was honestly being overloaded with my workload, so I then passed the baton on to Jan who went off to the races with it and brought about a book we were all very proud of. Jan's talents were in so many areas, especially drawing, as he was a fabulous graphic artist having done his apprenticeship in Derby, UK. He told me when he started in year one there were a lot in the class, but by the end of the four years there were only a few left, and they all went on to excel in their career paths. For Book 1 Jan drew the stunning piece on the front cover and also the picture of Betty Wright when she performed at Wigan Casino. Incidentally Jan was at Betty Wright's funeral with Erica, he told me often when he attended soul music artist's funerals, they were often the only white people there showing their respects to the artists that had moved so many of us in our lives through the love of soul music. Jan also draws the radio Caroline pirate ship in Book 1 and this saved the book many hundreds of dollars in license fees, but it was very time consuming for him, but he was a true believer, a giver and hoped that those who seem to feel money is their god, would be converted by the generosity of his time, given to help the artists that were his friends.

Jan had planned to do many more drawings in the books in the future because drawing was a passion he truly loved. He also related to me about going to Jackie Moore's funeral, and those other artists he got to know on a personal basis, their passing hit him extremely hard! He had helped Jackie Moore perform at the Las Vegas Soul Trip USA in 2019, which I sadly missed as suffering from Aspergilloma, a lung condition, a fungus ball (mold) growing in my left lung. I was truly devastated to have missed that event in Vegas, which I heard was great and which my good mate Steve Bardsley & his lovely wife Elizabeth attended and brought me souvenirs from.

It always disappoints me that more Australian soul lovers did not attend many of the five Soul Trips which were put on in Los Angeles, New Jersey, Chicago, Orlando and the final farewell in Las Vegas, which sadly for many of us was also a final farewell to those beautiful artists. Too many to mention have passed away, but to have seen some of them, like Francis Nero, who I was fortunate to have shared a lunch table with in Detroit and with who I bonded spiritually, Eugene Thomas in Orlando, Weldon McDougall 111 in Philadelphia and who could ever forget that other man with the smiling face, Ronnie Walker in New Jersey, Mel Britt in Detroit & Eugene Thomas in Orlando.

I owe Jan so very much and these words cannot in any way explain how much he impacted and enriched my life with his passion, humbleness & his many talents, he was a rare breed of man, intelligent, a straight shooter like myself, we can upset some of the fickle half glass full type people that pervade the soul scene, it's worth remembering all too frequently it's the good who die young, so maybe we gotta put up with these cretins for a while yet, who will probably live to be 120, but life could be described as "Hell On Earth" so maybe there is a reason why they live so long! Me and Jan did clash occasionally, such is our passion for "Soul Music", but we soon got over it, as life is far too short, as it sadly proved for him! With music and books, Jan would say, "John this is not a 'Dress Rehearsal", look at Berry Gordy, he surrounded himself with the best of the best, very wise words, which I will try to utilise. Jan was always teaching me new skills, I will miss his wisdom & mateship. We at the book project will all miss Jan in so many ways, hopefully we can continue the high standards he set and after you have read this Book No 2 you may agree we have achieved that end, we are open to suggestions to improve, we gladly listen to constructive critique.

Jan was very proactive before he became ill, after finishing a construction project he would go to record fairs. He enjoyed that and also the selling of our book. He had so much energy, getting up early while I struggled to fire on one cylinder due to a multitude of health issues. I am currently firing on four cylinders as acupuncture has helped relieve my chronic fatigue which has plagued me in recent years, no doubt due to having suffered lung disease. I will end this now as I am waffling, but I really loved you, my true friend Jan and I hope you guide me "In Spirit" to do a grand job with these books. My dedication song for you Jan Lisewski, and my Father, John Warren Snr, and my daughter Ethan Elizabeth Warren who is in heaven, is Lee Roye's "Tears Nothing But Tears". I would like to thank Jan's partner Erica Woodard for the photos on the next page.

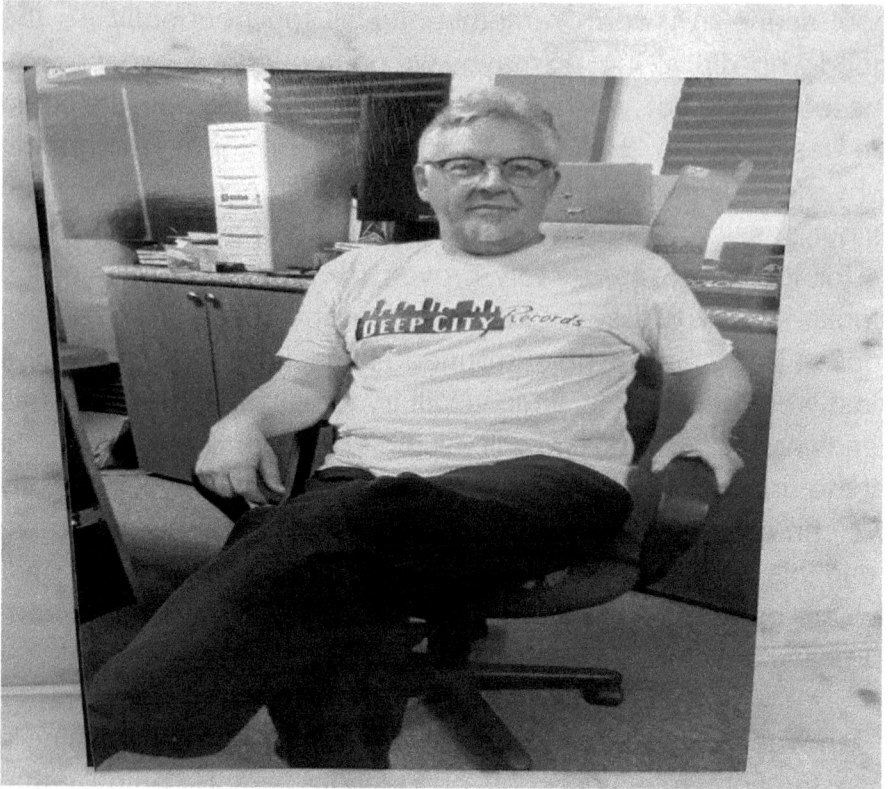

Jan Lisewski chilling © Erica Woodard

Jan as a youngster © Erica Woodard

Top - 1972 College photo: left to right: Alan Fernihough, Jan Lisewski, Adrian Wood, Ian Clarke © Alan Fernhough
Bottom - Pub photo: Alan Fernihough, (man standing unknown), Adrian Wood, Jan Lisewski, © Alan Fernhough from personal archives

Chapter 2

'One Can Have A Dream, Baby!'

Paul Stuart Davies' personal memories of the 2015 'Northern Soul Survivors Weekender'

Northern Soul Survivors Weekender had started life in September 2013 as Wigan Casino's 40th anniversary celebration, starring Martha Reeves, Brenda Holloway, Chris Clark, Dean Parrish, Sidney Barnes and Tommy Hunt. The weekender was held at the unlikely venue of Butlins' holiday camp in Skegness and was organised by Russ Winstanley, the same man responsible for founding the now legendary all-nighters at Wigan Casino between 1973 and 1981. The event was attended by thousands and when the acts came together on stage for a rousing Sunday night finale of Frank Wilson's 'Do I Love You (Indeed I Do)', Dean Parrish told the audience: "This is something that we will remember for the rest of our lives". It was apparent that the fans felt the same way. Plans were made to make the weekender an annual event, Northern Soul Survivors was born.

After announcing my decision to step down as lead singer of 9-piece band 'SoulTrain', I saw footage from the 2014 Northern Soul Survivors event online. Somebody suggested that I get in touch with Russ Winstanley through Facebook (oh, the power of Facebook!) and the following day Russ called me. Impressed with my recordings and my endorsements from Marvin Gaye's former wife, Jan, who when asked on radio to make a comparison between my voice and Marvin's had said "Well, he comes just about as close as you can get", Russ invited me to perform at Northern Soul Survivors 2015 event that September. For its third year the weekender was billed as 'A Salute to Motown' with performances lined up from Motown stars The Velvelettes, The Contours, Brenda Holloway and Chris Clark.

I would be well paid and have a ten-piece band provided who would learn my choice of songs. I couldn't believe my luck and quickly accepted Russ's invitation before he could change his mind, although he did say that he would like to come and see me perform live before any commitment was made. We first met in person that May when I was a guest on Russ's show on Sunshine Radio. We also met his sound engineer, Di Herring who was one of the DJs at Northern Soul Survivors. Russ advised due to illness, Chris Clark was unable to join us in Skegness, she would be replaced by Kim Weston, he suggested I join her on stage for 'It Takes Two'. Wow! To sing one of my hero's songs on stage with the lady he sang it with for their 1966 hit! Unbelievable.

Kim Weston recorded for Motown from 1961 but it wasn't until 1966 she saw notable success, after being paired with Marvin Gaye for the duet album "Take Two". By the time the lead single was a major hit, Kim had already left the label. As September drew nearer, I emailed Russ to ask if he had spoken with Kim about his idea of us singing together. He hadn't, and I got the impression Russ's original suggestion was just Russ thinking out loud and I would have to wait and see if the opportunity arose when we arrived at Skegness.

 was booked in for a rehearsal and sound check with the backing band when we arrived on the 25th September. I was already enjoying the musical freedom of personally selecting every song in the setlist. I tried to balance Northern Soul favourites with Motown classics, aware the audience enjoyed many of the rarer tunes over the biggest hits. I included Marvin's 'Little Dar-lin', The Dells' 'Run For Cover' and Edwin Starr's 'S.O.S.' and the band had done a wonderful job preparing these and another 7 songs for my arrival. The rehearsals took place in REDS; the Butlins venue that would be hosting the live acts (there were several other large venues that were to host DJs). The schedule showed Kim Weston's name below mine, she was in right after me so, after running through my songs, I took a seat at the back of the room alongside another singer called Johnny Boy to watch Kim rehearse.

Kim came into the room looking very tired after travelling from the States and she stopped the band mid-way through almost every verse as she listed what they were doing wrong. What a diva! I was later to realise that, as an artist who had travelled the world, first singing these songs 50 years ago, you would know immediately when something isn't right. I was just happy to be there, I spent my rehearsal politely nodding and thanking the band without suggesting any changes to the arrangements. Unlike me, Kim had no need to prove herself, after her frustrat-ing years at Motown (the label shelved what would have been her debut solo album) Kim had recorded some excellent solo LPs between 1966/1970 for MGM, Volt and People Records, as well as a duet album with Johnny Nash.

Kim taught me that day to speak up and say how you want things to be – otherwise how can you ever be in complete con-trol of the performance? Towards the end of Kim's rehearsal, the band asked if 'It Takes Two' was going to be part of her setlist. Kim replied: "I'll sing it if someone's here to sing it with me?!" This was my chance! I approached the stage and caught Kim's attention, telling her about Russ's suggestion that we sing together. She asked me if I knew the song (of course I did) and I joined her on stage for a run through.

20

Mid-way through the song Kim changed. Until this point in her rehearsal she had seemed unhappy and had been seated throughout. But then she stood up, beamed at me and put her arm around me as we swayed and sang our way to the end of the song. She even asked the band to applaud me at the end which, given the tough time they had been given, I don't think they were too enthusiastic about! Someone else who didn't look too pleased was Johnny Boy, the singer we had been sitting with at the back of the room. It turned out that Russ had also mentioned the possibility of the 'It Takes Two' duet to Johnny and his badly timed men's-room break meant that it looked to him that I had stolen his chance to sing with Kim. He must have returned to his seat to see me on stage and after the rehearsal told me: "I was supposed to be doing that one, mate". I felt a little guilty, as I know how I would have felt had it been the other way around. Johnny had been on the show the previous year and here was the new boy coming in and spoiling things (albeit accidentally). Johnny and I have since worked together many times. He's a great singer and we soon became good friends once I learned to ask around a little more before I threw myself in head first! It was Friday afternoon and thousands of fans started to arrive on site with their suitcases and their many matching t-shirts: the iconic black fist encircled by the words 'Northern Soul Keep the Faith'.

I first met Brenda Holloway at dinner, a few hours before she was due to provide the opening performance of the weekend. She was lovely right from the start, although she looked very surprised when I introduced myself and told her that I was one of the UK artists on the show. I didn't exactly fit the bill: a little white guy from Lancashire who was surely too young to be sing-ing these songs. Although the same description can be said of Johnny Boy, I was the newbie here. It became apparent that I was going to have to prove myself on this scene, especially with the fans - I was the wrong colour, the wrong age and the wrong nationality. Brenda's performance that night was my first taste of the live shows at Northern Soul Survivors, and she blew the roof off REDS. Then the Velvelettes took to the stage for their own wonderful show, the atmosphere was electric and the audience clearly in their element. Trying to get to sleep was difficult that night, thinking about my upcoming performance with Kim less than twenty-four hours later. We were given an apartment next to Russ and directly above Kim, although once she had rehearsed that afternoon she retired to her apartment, closed the curtains and wasn't seen again for the rest of the day. The following morning, I was awoken at six am by DJ Di Herring who had invited me for an early morning walk with Brenda. I was keen to mingle so didn't mind being tired and on our walk around the site got to know Brenda a little more. We later went for breakfast where she told me how she had at times filled in as Marvin Gaye's singing partner when Tammi Terrell had fallen ill. I was mesmerised. On my way back to our apartment I noticed that Kim's curtains were open and there she was, standing with a big smile on her face and wishing us "Good morning!". Kim had overcome her jet lag and was ready for her show that evening. I ended up spending the rest of the morning in Kim's apartment, talking and meeting some of her UK friends who had bought tickets to the event. After lunch there was a scheduled 'Meet n Greet' panel with the weekend's artists where we were to make ourselves available for photographs and sign photos, books and records. I sat next to Kim feeling very awkward. Why would anybody want my autograph? They hadn't even heard me sing yet! I think most of the fans must have assumed I was Kim's assistant – the white boy sat in between Motown legends Kim Weston and Brenda Holloway, I hardly looked like one of the stars of a weekender that celebrated sixties soul music. After sitting through three hours of watching fans ask Brenda for photos and autographs before skipping past me to see Kim, I felt embarrassed that Russ had put me on the meet 'n' greet, although it had been lovely of Kim to tell everyone who I was and that I'd be singing with her that night. By my third year on the event I was joining fans for photographs and selling many signed records. I realised that if Russ hadn't thrown me in at the deep end, I would still be seen as an unimportant part of the shows and I am grateful for the indirect lessons he gave me. That evening we met Kim at her apartment whilst we waited for our ride over to the backstage area of REDS. Kim was running over her lyrics. Although these were Kim's songs, she released them 50 years ago and doesn't sing them so often anymore. Many of Motown's less successful acts are largely forgotten in the States and when the artists are invited to perform for the UK's Northern Soul scene, they're often the biggest shows they have performed in years.

An hour later Kim was on stage and I was waiting in the wings for the moment in the show when Kim would announce 'It Takes Two'. "I want you ready after I've sung 'A Thrill A Moment'", Kim told me. I couldn't get that wrong. 'Thrill' was one of my favourite records. But just as the song was coming to an end and I was ready to walk out onto the stage, Kim walked off! Had she forgotten? Was this my moment gone? It turned out that Kim had become too hot under the stage lights and needed to cool down for a few minutes. I had heard a similar story from the previous year when Tommy Hunt had fainted on stage, falling from his stool. These are artists in their seventies and eighties, don't forget! Around ten minutes later Kim returned to the stage; we sang 'It Takes Two' and she finished the show like the professional she is. She made sure that the audience all knew my name and it gave me the opportunity to remind the crowds about my upcoming solo show the following day. We took Kim back to her apartment and I sat up listening to Kim's music quietly, reflecting on having just sung on stage with one of my idols in front of thousands of people. My solo show didn't feel like anything to worry about now.

On Sunday afternoon it was time for me to take centre stage. There were noticeably fewer in the audience than there had been for Kim's show, but that was no surprise. I wasn't a soul legend and Sunday afternoon was hardly a prime-time billing, given that the majority of the fans had danced long into the early hours. One person watching was John Rhys Eddins; the writer of 'Time Will Pass You By' – a song originally recorded by Tobi Legend and that I had recorded in a more intimate style earlier in the year. My recording of the song had played a part in Russ's initial interest in me and he brought me back to the stage after my show, insisting that I perform my version in front of its writer, whilst at the same time asking me if I would return to perform again the following year. In my recording of 'Time Will Pass You By' my voice was backed by just piano and strings in an effort to enhance the emotive lyrics. Recording with just a piano was also an easy way to get good results in my small studio at Darwen School of Music. I certainly didn't have the space or the budget for a full band. Fortunately for me, John Rhys Eddins liked my take on his song and we had a long talk when I left the stage. Our paths would cross again, in Detroit, after a little more time had passed us by. It was Sunday night. The weekender was almost over, but not before The Contours and their band brought the house down with their polished show. Nothing much had been said about the grand finale. I knew that at the last two events many of the weekend's artists had joined together on stage for an impromptu performance of 'Do I Love You (Indeed I Do)'. It didn't look likely to happen this year, as Brenda Holloway and The Velvelettes had already returned to the States and Kim was getting an early night before her flight home early the next morning. But just as we were ready to wind things down, Russ invited me to the stage, along with Prince Philip Mitchell, Johnny Boy and The Contours to join Diane Shaw and her band in performing the song that I had sung so many times before with SoulTrain.

Nobody wanted the weekend to end, and the song lasted for at least four or five times the length of the recorded version before we all finally said goodnight.

My First Northern Soul Survivors Event Was Over!

Paul Stuart Davies & Brenda Holloway © Paul Davies.

Kim Weston & Paul Stuart Davies © Paul Stuart Davies

Paul Stuart Davies Live ©Paul Stuart Davies

Top: Paul Stuart Davies with The Original Vandellas in Studio A at Hitsville USA, Detroit. © , Middle. The Original Vandellas, Kim Weston and Tobi 'Legend' Lark in a recording session at United Sound, Detroit. © Paul Stuart Davies, Bottom. Sidney Barnes, Paul Stuart Davies, Tommy Hunt, Dean Parrish on stage at Skegness.

Chapter 3

Ronnie Canada By Paul Mason

I first met Ronnie in 2012 when he called my phone and shouted "Where's my money", imagine that in a deep growly soul voice, it seemed false, an American in the UK, phoning me and shouting! My response was, is this one of my black friends winding me up? 'No' was his response, "It's Ronnie Canada", "Ronnie from Canada?", "NO.... RONNIE CANADA!" Well this misunderstanding went on for another 5 minutes and then he said," I sang at your events and you haven't paid me". The penny dropped, like me he did some event work for a con artist and both of us got ripped off . He was then incensed on my behalf, we chatted for 3 hours, from that point forward we became great friends. When we finally met for the first time, he was a very small guy, much shorter than his voice implies, he was wearing a big Parka jacket, Beanie hat, glasses and builders boots, he was so welcoming and so pleased to see me, we spoke that day for hours, I took him for an Italian meal, which was complimentary from my colleague who owned the restaurant. He had so many stories which included so many well-known artists that he knew or had connections with. At the time I was doing some marketing for a new Italian restaurant not far from where he lived, so Ronnie got a New Year's eve gig, free food and good drinks. He was awesome, a proper soul man, what a voice and a fantastic entertainer, a tiny guy on 5ft 2" tall, but in his red jacket, cool shoes and his custom 'RC' logo glasses, he definitely looked like a star. He performed with such ease and engaged with the audience, he really knew how to work a crowd and get them involved with him. And of course, the voice, he had that rasping soulful voice that could break glasses at the top end and then low to give a sorrowful tone to deliver strong lyrics. He knew songs I hadn't heard before, one in particular was "Put your hands together" by the O'Jays, one

I will never forget as it was joyous yet meaningful, a real song about peace and love, which Ronnie advocates that we are all joined and should live in peace and understanding. I realised he gave up a career in Spain to come to the UK to live with his partner and found a home in Watford, he joked, it is the closest town like Cleveland in the UK. So I proposed a campaign to get him back in the limelight, I built a new website www.ronniecanada.com , I did a set of photos, with his pride and joy, the Caviar album. We discussed his history which is littered with highs and lows, he seemed to be a go anywhere and perform kind of guy, and that's what he lived for. The new website along with my online marketing got him some good response and enquiries started coming in, you could see a real lift in his demeanour and we started getting invites to gigs, parties and places to network. We met so many interesting people and Ronnie was back being noticed and the centre of attention.

He had so many stories, met and worked with so many artists and producers and had performed at so many venues. He actually performed in Las Vegas, and with Hank Ballard, The Platters, The Ink Spots to name but a few then, 'Sly, Stick & Wicked' where he got his first professional break as a singer, recorded a record entitled: "All I Want Is You " on epic sweet city records 1979 and it's since been re-released twice on expansion records. He was one of the main group members of Sly Slick And Wicked which had 3 album releases. Sly Slick had already had three top albums under its belt and had been managed and produced by the legendary godfather of soul Mr. James Brown. Who had also been produced and managed by the legendary O'Jays and a major band - 'Omari', this was the group that he first got his passport to travel with to play in Bogota and Medellin Colombia and he also performed on the biggest national television show there called the: "Jimmy Salcido" show.

He knew many contemporaries like Little Anthony, Tommy Hunt, Betty Wright, Bobby Blue Bland, Edwin Starr (cousin), Billy Hunt among many others and was always conversing with many US artists regularly. He was always helping connect people with business or production ideas. He was a real livewire and loved being out with people and being interested. In the car he would often react to my playlist, mostly Northern Soul, while driving, and he would scream out, a la James Brown singing along with the songs, then he dropped a bombshell.... One of my favourite songs is 'Time' by Edwin Starr, he sang along, word for word, in perfect tune and pitch. Wow, it was like a concert in my car, then..... "Edwin is my cousin" he declared, "He was the reason I came to the UK, to perform in his shows" I couldn't believe it, my favourite soul artist, and now his cousin is in my car! Ronnie actually began a concept album as a tribute to Edwin Starr with Edwin's ex-manager Dr. Marlon Mac-Nicholls, out in the USA on which he performed a few songs and helped bring artists into the project.

His history as a vocalist took him to many bands and collaborations with some amazing artists, he joined The Bluenotes when Teddy Pendergast departed, they rehearsed a new album, but due to legal wrangling with Harold Melvin, they had to change the band name, which became 'Caviar' and released the album, it was a shame that is it was not released under the name The Bluenotes, it could have been a hit. The album was released in May of 1982 on Survivor Records Miami Florida Caviar was Ronnie and the original Harold Melvin and the Blue Notes members John Sweet, John T. Atkins & Mr. Lawrence Larry Pop Brown, Tony Sharp, Maxx Goodie and Valarie Rouse. He then was approached by Bobby Ruffin who was putting a band together to go out on tour, so he joined the 'American Drifters' and toured Europe, later settled in Spain, then the UK. He performed a duet with Betty Wright as Omari. His cousin Edwin Starr got him to leave Spain where he was currently living and came to the UK so that he could perform with his touring band; they performed at many of the clubs and venues around the UK. It was the tonic Ronnie needed and gave him the spirit to set up his own band with a set of UK musicians who could deliver the brand of new brit funk that was sweeping the country. He had many iterations of bands under several names. He actually was invited to perform live on British TV with his 'Ronnie and the Revelations' band on the James Whale Show in 1995. Destined for the big time, it fell apart mostly due to relationships, so once again back on his own.

Ronnie became a solo vocalist and put himself out there as an American living in the UK had a vocal skill which was quite rare in the UK, it was at the time that the DJ producers were beginning to create music that was unique to them. His vocal style, growling and JB style screams became iconic and in demand, his notoriety was growing and the offers to work as a studio vocalist were flooding in. So many music producers were embracing the new media and computer programs that helped them create their own tracks. This was a fruitful time, anyone with an idea could actually create a track, but what they needed was a singer, in that period so many vocalists became famous with their contributions to the backing tracks. Ronnie was getting great interest and allowed him to move into a different direction as a house artist performing on many of the UKs dance tracks being played at new clubs opening all over the country like Ministry of Sound, The Limelight and many more. The DJ producers were becoming the stars of this new musical genre and dance music was now a major part of the UK music industry with million selling albums. Ronnie had been booked as a vocalist for many of the DJ producers, like Mario Tosti, Scott Lees/Groove Technicians, Victor Simonelli, a New York based producer who recorded with Ronnie as the vocalist several times, but heard him sing before employing him. He told me he couldn't believe there was someone currently with such a powerfully controlled voice with that classic soul man voice and now he had to have him vocal a set of tracks he had in production. Some of these songs were so iconic, "I Just Can't Get Enough Of Your Love", "We've Got To Believe" and "It's So Good", all well-known House/Dance tracks. These came out on several of Victor Simonelli's labels like West Side Records (USA), Stellar Records and Criminal Records.

Another high profile producer was the famous Judge Jules where he lived in his London residence and recorded vocals for many of his tracks, He has appeared on two of the legendary superstar DJ, producer and former A&R man Judge Jules 2009 albums entitled: "Bring The Noise Singing" the first track on the album entitled: "Got to Be Heard" released on Maelstrom Records, And also on the Gatecrasher 1993-2009 compilation album. Ronnie also wrote and performed the vocals for Paul "Trouble" Anderson's swan song track, "Greedy T" which was a homage to James Brown and a reflection on his life released just before Paul sadly died. In conversations with Paul, he had a great respect for Ronnie and the project 'Greedy T' was not a track designed for profit, but to help with cancer awareness and Paul's suffering, which Ronnie was only too happy to oblige, and of course delivering a vocal which James Brown himself would have been proud. Ronnie had the pleasure of working closely with Solar Radio presenters and DJs, Ash Sethi and John Jules and regularly performed on their soul nights to a really appreciative audience of 80s and 90s dance music. In fact, searching on Google, Ronnie features in so many listings for music, he should have been a megastar! In 2010 Ronnie is the lead vocalist of "Baby Squeeze Me" by Blazing Black Fire who also had a world cup anthem out earlier this year from April 15th with Blazing Black Fire's, welcome to the 2010 South African world cup. During my collaboration period, Ronnie was approached to perform at The Soul Weekender to perform a duet with Maxine Brown, taking the part of Chuck Jackson on the track 'Hold on I'm Coming', who was already booked as the main artist, we went to the rehearsals, and hung with Maxine and her band and the organisers, later met up again at the 'Weekender' venue in northern England and spent the weekend with Maxine, her entourage and the organisers, we were treated like royalty, a great weekend. Ronnie got to perform his Caviar songs on the Sunday and certainly didn't disappoint. He knew how to work the audience, I guess from his club days touring the casinos and stages around the UK and Europe, he just knew what the audience wanted and delivered, time after time.

He had several private party bookings, which we attended as a team and set up his show. He was so accommodating and made the night swing, I also filmed and photographed all the events. I arranged an interview on soul music.com which gave an insight into his whole career, he did several small venue gigs, performed many times with The Drifters - Ray Lewis and made guest appearances at soul clubs. One club was set up by myself at a venue in High Wycombe, which I had several house DJs and guest DJs designed as a Northern Soul night, but featured Ronnie Canada performing to the crowd, it was special to have him at my own event, guests came from all over the UK and even Safy, a DJ from France came. We were invited to several of Leee John's music launches, especially as Ronnie met Leee in Paris when recording a song out there, with Lee we met the British Collective, a group of amazing UK soul artists, described as Godfathers of UK Soul, featuring Don-E Junior, Noel Mckoy and Omar. We got to see and meet The Four Tops and The Temptations which was such a blast for me, being a fan of both bands and of course `Motown', but who isn't? Ronnie was re-acquainted with some of his European associates and had regular shows in Holland through Dicore Artist Management, In Zaandam at The Bevrijdings festival and other events around Europe with these promoters. He was also invited to participate in The Voice, Holland's version, in which he didn't get any seats turned, but a standing ovation from the audience. It was pointed out that they really only want the newer style of artists and he may have been too old school. He was also quite well known in France and was invited to work with Ammerine Safy, a Rouen/Paris based DJ/producer and whilst Ronnie performed in Paris, he recorded a track, 'The Party Song' a 80s style disco track. Safy knew of Ronnie as a fan of 80s dance music and 'Caviar' and their album was big in France. Ronnie managed to get regular boxing events with the BBA (British Boxing Association) and attended events, opening the night and of course mixing with past and present boxers. One of his finest achievements was at Dingwalls in London where a new talent show was being set up and he was the opening act each night before the talent acts, the main final was classic where he performed "Georgia on My Mind" by Ray Charles, a move from his normal soul and R&B, then of course his main opening gig track, "In the midnight hour" Wilson Pickett, which he made his own 1, 2, 3, 4, 5 Aargh! Among the guests and judges were Ray Lewis, The Drifters, Lee John - Imagination, Paul Young and many more. Not long after the Dingwalls sessions, Ronnie split from his partner and was forced to leave his home, I managed to get him housed in High Wycombe, 30 miles west of London, with an accommodating friend, Kenny, I think this was the start of his health downfall, he was heartbroken, he couldn't eat and started to feel depressed and began to shake. It was sad to see him go from a healthy bubbly guy to a low level of sadness, even desperation. We locals kept him focused and tried to keep his positivity up, he did some sales work with Kenny's company and started to feel appreciated again. He made a big mistake by cancelling several gigs in the UK and agreed to perform with an old band who performed upbeat gospel songs, 'The Les Humphries Singers' who gave the big story and had him traveling to festivals across Europe, which turned out much less than promised, he couldn't get the gigs in the UK back which could have meant a theatre tour. I wonder whether the gospel band was a way of trying to build his religious roots again, being a god-fearing Christian and wasn't afraid to declare his beliefs. But that did lead to an offer to join up with the 'New Bluenotes', a band with apparently a financial backing, recording contract and 50 shows lined up, what could go wrong? Well it did! After a promising start, the band leader left, leaving the remainder of the band high and dry, and although they went on to finish their EPK, the die was cast and Ronnie was left living with a friend and band member and over the years became quite disheartened by this band.

In January 2020 I went to Paris to see Ronnie perform on a party boat on the Seine 'Le Nix Nox', we had a great day with the organisers, met many lovely people and stayed until the early hours partying, Ronnie's performance was strange, he was so tired and actually short of breath so he sat for the last song while he performed, it was hard to watch him in this state, he still had the voice and soulful growl, but fading it seemed. In what became the final throw of the dice, he was offered a gig in Holland with The Drifters, where he got the band together with friend Ray Lewis and his vocalists and took the contract. He arrived in the UK in October and I took him with me to Harrogate, a beautiful town in Yorkshire where he met up with one of his daughters, who lives there. He was also spotted by an audio engineer who worked with him over 15 years previously, that was a nice touch. But Ronnie looked awful, very thin, his face was drawn and he was so tired, which at first seemed to be jet lag. I took him directly to the airport for a 6am flight to Holland, that was the last time I saw him. We did speak on the phone a few times. I have a studio booked for Ronnie to record vocals for a song I was working on, but from his hotel room he told me that he was feeling too weak to come over, I actually asked him to see a doctor as it was unlike him to refuse the chance to sing. I now realise his condition was worse than expected and he sadly died in December 2019. It's sad to think that he, like so many artists, died a poor man.

I now run Metro Jam Productions www.metro UK, and we produce and promote music shows and artists, plus run an open stage night in London. Ronnie would have been part of this and the tracks we were planning. A lot of the thanks for my involvement in music was down to Ronnie for which I will always be grateful.

Ronnie will be fondly remembered as the person who got me into the music industry, he was an emotional guy who had a heart of gold and stood up for the injustices of the world, produced songs with meaning and I think he left me with a song called 'Die Trying' which I found on our shared drive, which I hadn't been aware of. I guess this summed him up perfectly... I'm always trying!

He died trying !

Top: Paul Mason © Paul Mason
Bottom: Ronnie Canada © Paul Mason

Chapter 4

Who Threw The Whiskey In The Well?

Lisa Boogaloo – My Journey

This is my journey, I am Lisa Lane, alias DJ Lisa Boogaloo, born in Hammersmith London in 1965. I have been DJing Soul & 60's RnB for only 7 years, but during this time have learnt so much about the scene, the people, the hate and most importantly of all the amazing music that has set my heart and soul on fire. So here we are and here we go... I want to dedicate my journey to my late Dad who gave me the utmost encouragement to chase my dreams and aim high.

STOP AND LISTEN......

My Soul journey started very briefly at the tender age of about 11 / 12 years old, sharing a bedroom with my elder sister Jill. She loved Philly Soul / Disco and Reggae, she first introduced me to the likes of Harold Melvin, The O'Jays, The Trammps etc, etc. We had an orange and white Dancette record player and when my sister went out I played those albums repeatedly. She also had an amazing collection of Jazz Funk & Disco 12"s - which I so wish she still had as she had some pretty valuable gems. The 1980's for me was a pretty bad era for music, there was the odd dance tune, but generally it was over synthesized rubbish to me. In 1984 I landed my dream job in Our Price Records, a tiny store in High Wycombe, Bucks. It was shabby, it only sold Vinyl and tapes and I loved it. It was mind opening working with people with such different music tastes it really was an education. I learnt so much, I knew what tunes were on which albums, I knew the catalogue numbers, the years they were released and when customers hummed me a tune I would find it....

I was young and had a good memory back then! I used to compile the 12" Dance chart every week - I loved doing that as I could put in any tune artist I liked, it was not dependent on the national charts. Record shops seemed to attract some very dubious characters, one in particular had a small scale and exact model of the starship enterprise strapped around her body with rope, she was apparently married to Captain Kirk, many a time I was threatened with being beamed up! But she had an amazing taste in music, Soul music and her knowledge was extraordinary, I learnt quite a bit from Mrs Captain Kirk. My years with Our Price Records took me to many different stores, thankfully I got moved to the Uxbridge Branch in Middlesex and there is a reason why I was so pleased. The journey from where I lived with my parents was pretty horrendous – buses and coaches – leaving the house at 6.15am & getting home at 8 / 8.30pm was no joy which meant my social life was non-existent, so it made sense to stay at my sister Jill's who had a flat just between Chiswick & Acton, it was a tube journey from Uxbridge well handy and the start of my life changing music journey.

The Warehouse

One Saturday night we decided to hit a club called (back then) The Warehouse, it is now known as the Electric Ballroom, in Camden Town. It was this night that changed my life, all down to the music and the vibe, this would have been about 1984, and I was 19 years old. It was probably about 11pm, we parked up, my sister always drove, she had a metallic brown Vauxhall Cavalier Sport, my god that motor flew! I remember many times hurtling down the Marylebone Rd laughing my head off on route to Camden, one time coming home at 3am she got overtaken by all of things, a Reliant Robin. OMG! She wasn't having that …so she floored it and eventually overtook it …straight up the A40 at that time of the morning was less busy back then.

So here we are outside the Warehouse, in the queue wondering what sort of night and place it would be. I walk in, it was quite a big entrance lobby , we walk down a couple of steps and there is a pretty big bar area and on the left , a huge wooden dance floor, it was scruffy, old posters peeling off the walls, it was dark and hadn't changed since the 60's, the music was a mix of old soul and Motown and I loved it, the DJ was Jay Strongman . People were dancing already, that floor was heaving... we thought we would have a look upstairs as apparently there was another room, there was an enclosed balcony with windows so you could look down on the main dance floor and thankfully there was another bar upstairs too. I remember getting to the top of the stairs and seeing these mega sleek dressed Guys and Girls dressed in vintage 50's clothing, looking cool as hell. I felt rather inferior in my wide jeans, deck shoes and t-shirt and bleached blonde hair in a rather poor quiff. There were some small double doors that led into the 2nd room, so I went in! I was immediately hit with a thick mist of smoke (as you could smoke in venues back then couldn't you) amongst the thick smoke was couples jiving flat out to some of the most amazing music I had ever heard, it was thumpin' and I didn't know any of it. I could not take it all in, I stood there listening and gawking as if I had been put in a time machine and gone back to 1955, my first introduction to R&B and I fell madly in love. These tunes actually made me shake with excitement and gave me ice-cold goosebumps despite the heat! All I needed to do now was learn how to jive to them so I could lose myself even more on that floor! That's another story! So after that first night we got our membership cards and this became our regular Saturday night haunt for about 2 years, Tom Ingrams Record Hop at The Warehouse ...it was top drawer I met some amazing people, one guy Nicky, this giant black dude who could jive like a dream offered to show me , so several vodkas later, in a dark corner he tried, I say tried as I literally had no coordination after spinning and hurtling into a column near the dancefloor we thought best forget it before I caused him and myself injury.

From regular nights at these "hops" it led to other fabulous places, Silks in Shepherds Bush which was another dinghy club in the middle of a shopping centre, I think that was Wednesday nights, then on Sunday nights we would hot foot it to The Clay Pigeon Pub in Eastcote (I think it was there!) where it was just DJ's spinning the coolest and best R&B, we were going out almost every night, sometimes getting in at 6am as we always ended up back at someone's house for more tunes then having to be up at 7am for work, working Saturdays was a pain in the ass! All I can say is thank goodness for Pro-plus which was part of my staple diet back then. I wanted to be wherever that music was. It buzzed me so much that I didn't care about lack of sleep. I would try and track down these tunes at work, no computers then it was all paper catalogues. There was one tune in particular I really wanted, I knew the title but not the artist, I found it in a catalogue from Making Waves, a vinyl importer and thankfully we dealt with them. I wasn't chasing 7" then, I wanted the LP's, so I ordered this LP to wait about 2 weeks for it to arrive, beyond excitement I took it home, put it on and damn it, it's not the version I heard or wanted I was gutted ! I'd spent my booze money on that album! Still, one bad purchase didn't deter me, I did discover Wynonie Harris, LaVern Baker, Wynonia Carr, Louis Jordan, Etta James & the list is endless. I scoured the catalogues from Charly R&B and Ace records and built up my R&B LP collection.

THE UPS, THE DOWNS AND A NEW JOB!

Like most of us, I left the club scene, normal life began, I was 23, got married and moved away from my home town area and all my friends. Things didn't work out, but I did find out a lot about myself and what my strengths are. I was young and a bit naive at the time & I was living in the marital home which I hated in Farnborough, was in debt up to the hilt, I was paying the mortgage, everything and my husband turned out to be a compulsive liar so I filed for divorce. I eventually gave up the house and moved to Basingstoke where I was working as Branch

Manager still at Our Price Records and with no money, paying back debts, was literally sleeping on my mates office floor at their house with just a hold-all of personal belongings. I couldn't hack that for long and was having a pretty rough time at work with a complete tosspot of an Area Manager, who, after knocking him back, became an even bigger tosspot. I got offered a room at a mates flat in Reading so I swiftly took it. I was now 27, divorced, skint and going through hell at work. I fought back (long story but I took on WH Smiths as they now owned Our Price Records and was about to take them to court. I won my case single handedly out of court with just the help and advice from my Dad, no solicitors. After 10 years at Our Price I started a new job working at the new Virgin Megastore which was opening in Reading. I soon met my 2nd husband, he was into very different music and was in a band, I managed them, it was great fun touring round the Country, it was tough as you never got paid, we slept in transit vans or on promoter's floors, would not have changed any of it, met some great people and it was a great experience and got on some good tours sometimes! I left Virgin Megastore after several months as I was headhunted by a friend who worked at Plastic Head Music Distribution, who were looking for a Label Manager, I had no idea what that meant, but I wanted out of retail, customers were just getting ruder and ruder so I went for an interview and got the job. I was there for 25 years from 1995, for 10 of them I was Production Manager, we manufactured vinyl, CD's and merchandise. It was a fantastic job, went abroad, met loads of great characters, bands, musicians.

I also experienced arrogance and sexism of the highest order! I still hankered after my R&B and 50's nights and managed to persuade my husband to go to a night in Guildford. I was excited these clubs were opening again. Eventually I managed to convert him! I finally learnt to Jive! The nights were brilliant albeit not the same as when I was 19 but it was somewhere to go and hear those tunes again. We went to weekenders, it would have been about 2009 which were something else, the Rhythm Riot

Weekender at Pontins Camber Sands, every November was my favourite, grotty chalets, freezing cold, but amazing music, clothes, cars and original artists saw so many from the US (Young Jessie, the Teenagers, Clarence "Frogman" Henry to name but a few) & made a new round of friends. I just lost myself totally at those weekenders, everyone looked cool, we all dressed impeccably and danced to amazing DJ's. The tunes were truly awesome. This particular weekender had been going for 20 odd years, I could never afford to go to them when I was younger and I never had transport. At the ripe old age of 49, I started to think about what I was doing with my life, it was all work, work, work and no play. I was supporting my husband's band wholeheartedly as that was his life, but then I was being left at home more and more at the weekends on my own, so I asked him to buy me some record decks and a mixer, which he kindly did.

TWO DECKS, A MIXER AND AN IRONING BOARD

So here I was, itching to play my new found tunes with nowhere to set up my brand new Numark Record decks. I was in a state of despair, so out came the ironing board, which seemed a much better use for it. I set up my decks and my mixer connected my speakers. It was good to go and watch the world, here I come! I bought my first few records, I was just so excited to get the tunes that I only just heard and loved. One of my first tunes was an original T.D. Valentine " Love Trap" is still a big favourite of mine. So with about 5 records purchased as money was still tight even then, I bought my first DJ record box, a small orange Swanflight. I would rush home from work like an excited teenager to play my new 45's, thankfully my husband was at his studio most nights till about 8pm, so I would switch those decks the minute I got home. This every night, I didn't even put the kettle on, it was always decks first. It was my escape, I was discovering new tunes and a new genre that made my heart race just as it did when I went to the London Clubs in the 80's.

I could not believe at my age this could happen again, I felt re-born! I felt sorry for my neighbours as we lived in a Semi, but thankfully they were into Mod and Northern Soul, so I'm sure they enjoyed my tunes as much as I did. I practiced DJing every night, Tim showed me how to prevent slurring starts and that was it, I was ready for my first gig with my little box of tunes! The feeling it gave me behind those record decks was quite un-believable. It was a feeling I hadn't had before, I had found something I could do for myself, I didn't need anyone, I could play what I wanted, I was 18 at the age of 49! I had a great marriage and great times with Tim, he taught me a lot, he was an extremely talented musician and songwriter, he did some banging techno tunes as he had his own studio and I would sometimes sing on them or play some keyboards. It was great fun. Sadly like all good things it came to an end after 20 years together, we were going in different directions.

FIRST NIGHT NERVES, A CHANCE MEETING & NORTHERN SOUL

In December 2014 I put on a Vintage Fair at our local pub and in the evening a cocktail Party with music from the 40's, 50's R&B & 60's. My first time playing out, I spun the 40's & 50's tunes, I was so nervous, it was a busy night, the chairs and tables were moved so we had a dancefloor, this was it! This was really IT! My mate Pete stood beside me and showed me how to cue a record again as I was in a state of complete panic! So my first tune spun, people jiving it was just awesome. Pete told me he had invited a mate to come and play some 60's soul, I didn't have enough Soul 45's to do a set. Halfway through my first set the door of the pub flies open and in crashes this bloke with a load of record boxes and he walks right into my heart! Peter Baker hit the decks after me and played some fantastic Soul tunes, something inside went boom and the rest as they say is history.

A few months passed before I bumped into Peter again in our local pub. I was slowly building up my Soul collection and I was telling him about it, I had been doing a couple of slots at the pub and Peter got me a slot at Bare Groove, which was a brilliant Northern Soul club in Reading, we double decked and it was great, I was nervous, I loved it and wanted more. I went to those nights as often as I could after that as there were some great DJ's and many tunes I had never heard in my life before, amazing! I would dance my feet off! This is where the real addiction and obsession to DJ truly began. Peter would tell me all about Ian Levine as he was buying a lot of records from him back then and visiting his studio listening to fabulous big tunes. He took me to Acton, West London to Ian's soul night in the function room at The Windmill Pub , he told me Ian wanted to meet me, I was completely gobsmacked! ME! this DJ, this legend, wanted to meet a little ole me, wow! It turned out to be one of the best nights I had had for a very long time. We went in and Ian was sitting on a sofa behind the decks he summoned Peter (as Ian does) to the decks and I went up and met him, I felt rather honoured to be honest. He then dedicated another favourite tune of mine, Jeanette Wade Flemons, to me. I could not believe it! I danced and I really do not think I came off that floor for well over an hour nonstop, only to go for a quick pee and have a slurp of a drink, I was pretty fit back then and the tunes were so mind   blowing   so   I   could   dance   nonstop.

After a few months Peter took me to Ian's House to buy one of his Soul Packs. Usually you just get the box and what you are given but he went through every single 45 and literally sang them all to me all 500 of them! His memory and knowledge was awe inspiring. It really was a privilege to have sat there with him picking and choosing what I wanted and what I didn't like. We had some disagreements, but I stuck to my guns, but still, I considered myself very lucky that day.

A NEW CLUB , A NEW LIFE AND A
NEW RECORD DEALER

With my 2nd divorce finalised it was now Aug 2015, I moved out of the marital home and rented a flat in Caversham (outskirts of Reading). I set my decks up and it was like being a teenager and leaving home for the first time. I also started to buy some seriously good vinyl and I don't know how I "met" John Dunne of Honest John's Records, but I started buying a lot of my tunes from him and still do. I trusted him, as I was new to this DJ game and buying decent legitimate Soul / R&B 45's and he soon became a good friend and supporter. John knew the kind of tunes I liked and he always gave me the heads up before anyone else and still does, I was super chuffed about that. John introduced my ears to some fabulous tunes and artists, one of which was Marva Whitney, who blew my mind. I truly thank him and respect him for that. Having support from a DJ as brilliant as John is an absolute honour. A lot of what I have in my record boxes are from John and I could never thank him enough for that. Dealing with John led me to get a slot at his WHAT IS SOUL 5TH ANNIVERSARY in Dublin alongside top notch DJs, some of Ireland's finest, I was bowled over. It was one of the best nights of my DJ career so far, I loved every single minute. I know when John messages me with tunes and says "I think this is right up your street Lisa ", he is generally right, so my original Soul & R&B vinyl collection grew rapidly! Sadly, Bare Groove NS Club announced it was ending. We knew Paul and Andy so we approached them and asked if we could take on the nights at the venue as they had secured dates for several months.

We didn't want a stand-alone Northern Soul Club, we wanted a Soul club so it was across the board and I could spin my beloved R&B, I bought myself a pair of Technics 1210's which were my dream decks and all I ever wanted, my mate who runs a DJ equipment shop had a pair arrive in his shop and he called me right away, so lucky.

I was more than delighted as they were in great condition and I wanted decent decks for the Soul club. The Right Track was born, we launched it in June 2016 and had Alan King as our guest DJ. We met Alan at The Northern Soul Survivors weekend at Skegness and he soon became a very good friend and actually gave me away at my wedding to Peter. We did the club once a month for about 2 years, we had guest DJ's, Ian Levine came and did a rare and underplayed set, it was just incredible. We had good nights and we had quiet nights. It was hard work, setting up at 4pm, going back for 8pm then not getting home till 3.30am, but it was a great experience. The venue was not ideal as there were two rooms, the large room had the wooden dance floor, but it was a big room to fill, the smaller room that we had the floor was tiled so not great for dancing. We fell out with the venue after I had an argument with them, we had the large room booked for another night with Ian Levine guesting and the venue cancelled me 24 hours before the date, it was major stress and luckily we knew Ian and we managed to cancel him but it was just awful, a lot of people were coming, it would have been one of our busiest nights, the irony being the venue said we were not taking enough money over the bar! Yet they never put our nights on their Facebook page, the venue didn't have the greatest reputation, it was a bit shabby and the floor in the small room was not good for dancers. The Right Track Soul Club ended September 2017, we had some great guests and I'm so glad we did it, it wasn't a failure, it was just one of those things. Peter and I are doers and very determined.

MORE THAN SOUL RADIO

Peter and I were asked to do a Northern Soul show on Twilight Soul Radio, a local internet Radio station. We did a Northern Soul show on Sunday afternoons, I was absolutely bricking it! Our first shows were a bit shaky, but we soon got into it and it was fun. This lasted only a few months, Lee the owner said he was going to close it down as the other DJ's were too unreliable and it was too stressful for him.

He asked us if we wanted to take it over, we talked it over with a friend of ours who used to run a local radio station, he said, why don't you start your own station? Don't take on someone else's Radio station, do your own thing. I asked him how on earth we do that! Simple he said, I'll sort it for you. So in June 2017 with PPL license sorted, our very own Radio station was born. It was nerve racking but we launched it at one of the Right Track Soul nights live, it was brilliant. From then on we did a show on Sunday afternoons and one on Wednesday nights, we also had a friend Jim B. Donovan who did a couple of shows in the week, fabulous DJ with a wealth of knowledge and experience. Once we got over our initial nerves and teething problems, things ran pretty well, of course some of the haters came out of the woodwork slating it as they do, but hey at least we were doing something and we are still here doing it! We decided as Sunday shows were Northern Soul, Mod and R&B, we wanted to do a midweek smooth and mid-tempo soul show, so Wind Down Wednesday was created. We did various solo shows as we didn't want to keep being booked as a double act as we had different "soul" tastes and I was more into my R&B style tunes so double decking was always a little stressful.

When we moved to Wigan in 2019 we continued with the Radio Station, we relaunched the Wind Down Wednesday Show and it has proved to be a very popular show. We have a great listenership and have made some lovely friends through this. We do our Underplayed and Rare Soul/ R&B tunes on Monday nights, I love this show as it gives me a chance to play those special tunes that REALLY blow my mind. On Friday nights we have our Living For the Weekend show, this is basically Top 500, classic Northern, Mod, Ska across the board really and it's a request show, it really is great fun and listeners get really involved. We feel so lucky that we have kept this going, during Lockdown owing to the Covid Pandemic we were doing 4 shows a week, sometimes 5 if we did a solo show, it kept us sane and many others. We also set up Mixcloud so we could stream on both platforms, this led to more listeners worldwide which is fantastic. Everything we play on the Radio Shows are all vinyl and it's generally chaos on Fridays when we have all our record boxes out everywhere! Between us we have around 8000 45's, so that's a lot of boxes you need access to. The Radio station is going from strength to strength and we are looking forward to having guest DJs to come and join us to do shows again. The feedback and our regular listeners really lifted our spirits too, especially through this pandemic, it brought people together and friendships formed in our chat rooms, just brilliant. We just keep going and we are so glad we have brought people together through great music.

STICKS AND STONES

Yes, I have only been DJing properly for 6 years, I got some great slots, just by being me, I did it purely off my own back, I have not been "in" with anyone to help me progress, I just got gigs without asking or begging, despite what some DJ's have claimed. I have never lied about being "there" back in the day, I was at my own "there" in London as stated earlier in my chapter. This is my story, my true story and I will always be true to myself. I have really enjoyed DJing at some superb venues, Chesham Soul Club, Bassetlaw Soul Club, the Pelirocco Brighton, the Holborn Aberdeen, Kevesten Soul Club, Lincoln, the Spitfire Soul Club, Farnworth and various venues in Brighton, Scunthorpe, Worthing, London. Peter and I were asked to run the DJ Room at March Of The Mods Reading in 2019, it was truly amazing and a much talked about night, we are hoping to bring MOTD to Wigan in the near future. I don't really know where I fit in as a DJ and yes, I state DJ and not female DJ, as why should your gender affect where you play, but sometimes I feel it does. A pet hate is when there is an all-female DJ night you don't see flyers stating all male DJ night, I am by no means a feminist I just want to be booked because they think I am good, not just because I am female.

What I had not prepared myself for was the spitefulness and flack I got when I started getting spots at good clubs it was quite overwhelming sometimes and more often than not it came from other DJ's spreading awful rumours and complete lies and they didn't even know me, so there was absolutely no truth in what they were saying. Rumours spread that we only moved to Wigan to further our DJ Careers, hilarious beyond words, I had plenty of gigs in the South so why would I think that moving to Wigan was a good move as a new DJ, laughable. Our move was for personal reasons, it was life changing and no-one's business but ours. I have been hounded to the point I could not look at my mobile phone anymore. I was sick of it and really didn't know the best way of dealing with it. I got to the point of requesting to meet them somewhere so we could have it out, but then realised it was not worth the effort as they were never going to change. I blocked them and others but it didn't stop there, promoters where I was booked were getting phone calls / texts asking them why they were booking me as I play bootlegs (YAWN! I wish I had £1 every time I heard that one!) It got so bad that one promoter actually told me to call the Police, he was absolutely disgusted at what this person was saying and texting, he offered to show them what was in the message.

All of the promoters have thankfully supported me and taken no notice, but still they were pretty shocked. I have had to take legal advice from my solicitor when threats of violence were made to myself and Peter and more lies were put up on Soul Group pages. Well once violence is threatened then that takes it to a new level, I won't tolerate that from anyone so the police were notified and our complaint has been registered. I don't get it, I am simply playing tunes that I am passionate about and YES they are originals before anyone gets on their high horse. What is in my record boxes is no concern to anyone but me, I have nothing to hide and I am very proud of what I play and what I own. I have kept those reissues I purchased in my early days, I won't play them out, but I won't throw them away either, they are part of my journey.

I have my opinions, but I most certainly do not air them. I could name and shame quite a few, but I simply cannot be bothered to give them a second of my time. Thankfully my time working at PHD Ltd taught me how to deal with arrogance of the highest order, I'm not phased by Billy Big ball DJ's, I'll spin my tunes next to any of them anytime as we definitely would not have the same records. I have developed a very thick skin, some might say I'm too cocky for my own good, but I think they are mistaking this for confidence and my passion. It's of no consequence how much I have paid for tunes, I have some that are £400 and some that are £10, they are all cracking originals, I don't claim to be a Northern Soul DJ. I don't chase those tunes, I have a few NS tunes, but I simply purchase the tunes that make my heart race like we all do. It would be nice to see more new DJ's in the all-nighter scene, as there are some cracking new DJs coming through, sadly like myself, we just get overlooked and that's such a shame this scene should be embracing more new DJ's and welcoming them all with open arms, not slating them and putting them down, it's so hurtful and unnecessary. It would be lovely to play alongside those big names, the DJ's I look up to for their experience, knowledge and amazing tunes, there must be room for all of us.

DJ LISA BOOGALOO – I AM JUST ME

I think, despite my memory being so bad, my DJ name was created when doing a gig with my ex-husbands band, he wanted me to spin some Northern Soul / 60's Soul before and after their set, so for the poster I just came up with the title Lisa Boogaloo, I have no idea where that stemmed from, it was a bit of fun, but it kind of stuck so The Boogaloo was born! I have met some fabulous people through DJing. I have made some fabulous friends and some fabulous enemies too. It really has been an amazing journey for me which I am still on and will only end when I am 6ft under. I love discovering new tunes. There are just so many. It's just wonderful and just how it was when I first stepped through those doors of Tom Ingrams Record Hop all those years ago. I usually fall in love with a tune within the first few seconds, it honestly just blows my mind. So you see, to most, I have only been DJing 5 minutes but to me, it's been 7 glorious years of discovery, some shocking and some amazing, I have loved every gig I play and I plan for days what I am going to take with me, I turn up early so I can hear and support the other DJ's and treat every slot and my tunes with utmost respect. Playing these wonderful tunes and seeing people dancing to them is just the best feeling in the world. I totally lose myself when I am behind those decks. So the question is, who threw the whisky in the well? There is a story behind this tune by Wynonie Harris, which as a new DJ to the Soul scene resonates with me during my journey, it's a personal thing. I won't forget what has been said about me and who said it, I don't need or want them in my life. Whether I ever forgive them is a different matter altogether, but in all honesty the answer to that is probably never. There are many positives and what I am grateful for are my believers and those who have supported me, especially Peter who has put up with my anger, venting, cursing, crazy ideas and also shared the hatred aimed at me which came at a particularly stressful time in our life.

To be asked to write my story has been an honour, who am I (as the song goes), I am Lisa Boogaloo, I am passionate about my tunes, I have tried things and succeeded and I have tried things and they have not worked out through no fault of My own, but at least I tried. Thankfully I have inherited my Dad's determination so I will never give up, I simply want to play my tunes, I'm not seeking large venue gigs, I don't play those big floor filler tunes and I don't want to, I prefer the small niche clubs where there is a buzz in the air and they are open minded to new tunes and something a little different. Many do not know much about me or my background and they will never ask, they just assume or listen to the lies but I am headstrong and thankfully have the sense of humour that gets me through the tough times being a "Female" DJ.

Well you certainly know a bit more about me now, the real truth and where it all started for me, I had the best times and I hope those times will continue. My Soul journey is ongoing, my tune searching for my want's list is ongoing, my passion for DJing is ongoing and that's all part of this wonderful journey for me. For my supporters and especially my haters, I thank you as you have made me even more determined to try and be one of the best.

Thank you for reading and Toodleoo.

Lisa Lane 1985 © Lisa Lane

Lisa 1986 © Lisa Lane.

Ian Leroy Seabrooks Jr, Lisa Lane & Spyder Turner © Lisa Lane

Peter Baker & Lisa Lane © Lisa Lane

Chapter 5

"SOUL TRAVELS" from our wee hoose in Fife, Scotland
by George and Maureen Wallace

I'll have to make this a shorter version than was originally planned as things like Covid-19 and Maureen being unwell and having to have an operation this year have slowed things down a little. Who would have thought that in my 70th year it will have been over a year since my last soul outing which was the Tyneside Soul Weekender in March 2020!

Where did this all begin? Well the main part of my upbringing was in a village called Wilmslow in Cheshire, not far from Manchester airport. I had a sister called Lynn Wallace whom some of you on the scene in the early days may remember. She was out and about with her pal Sue Ogden and Lynn eventually got married to Howard Yates, another early soul man. They split up after a few years and during a strange talk to someone many years later I found out that Howard was living in Australia. I was born in 1950 and so growing in the 60s was a musical dream. You had groups like the Rolling Stones and the Beatles but then along came this sound from America: Tamla Motown, the Four Tops, Temptations etc. No prizes for guessing which direction I went in and that has been the same for now over 55 years. I left school in mid 1966 and after looking at loads of jobs and apprentice offerings, I decided to join the Royal Navy. How did that happen? Well, one day I was in Manchester city centre and found myself going into the RN careers centre, speaking to them about jobs and a career and came away thinking "Well that will get me away from here and possibly be more exciting than standing in a factory". That night my dad asked where I had been so I told him and said that I was thinking about joining the Royal Navy. His answer was "You wouldn't last five minutes!" Well we'll see about that is what I thought, and so in

September 1966 I got on a train and headed for HMS Raleigh in Torpoint, Cornwall.

Now if you want to grow up quickly, learn to smoke and drink lots of alcohol, that's what the first few years in the Navy were like. After training, I was drafted to HMS Intrepid and off we went for nearly three years based out of Singapore and I was just 17! Far better than standing in a factory in Manchester, also I was able to start the dreaded habit of buying records not knowing that this would be a lifetime pursuit.

I still have pictures of me in the barracks in Singapore surrounded by a whole pile of Soul LPs that I had bought in Singapore along with a small portable record player. I can also remember having an early reel to reel small tape player and recorder that, when anything decent was on the radio, I would try and just tape the sounds I wanted. Whenever I was on leave, I would go home and in the late 60s and early 70s my sister Lynn would go upstairs and in her bedroom she had a record player, the type that you could put a stack of 45's on and when one finished the next one would drop, or you could just having it playing one record over and over again. How my mum loved that! One record that always stood out in those early days was "The Shakers "One Wonderful Moment". After hearing it about 30 times on the run it's no surprise mum was fed up! Lynn was born with heart defects and she eventually settled in Bristol but sadly passed away in the late 80s. I still have a copy of Blues & Soul No 125 from December 21st 1973 in which she is mentioned in the Frank Elson page after getting up on stage at Wigan to meet him. With my love of all things soulful and my sister providing the early Northern Soul, it was always going to be my future path.

In 1972 I was posted to HMS Nubian which was having a refit in Rosyth Dockyard, Fife, Scotland. Little did I know then that I would marry Maureen, have four daughters, six granddaughters and two grandsons and would be living in what was an ex Royal

Navy married quarter that we bought in the late 90s. That was a quick 50 years! I met Maureen not long after I came to Scotland and can always remember being at the Bellville in Dunfermline where some commercial Northern sound was being played. There was a beautiful young girl dancing as if she had been to many Northern Soul nights, and it turned out that she'd been on a few trips south to The Twisted Wheel in Manchester and Up The Junction in Crewe. We started dating and then in August 1974 on Maureen's 21st birthday we got married. We still go to lots of Northern nights and Maureen is well known as being the first on the floor and the last off. In the early days in Scotland we had lots of small venues and clubs playing soul music such as The Forth Bridges Motel, The Northern Roadhouse, The Well and Kinema Ballroom in Dunfermline. We also travelled up to Dundee every Sunday to the Angus Hotel Soul nights. I used to take some records with me which the DJs would play and eventually after someone didn't turn up, I was asked to DJ myself.

This was the start of many years behind the decks and we had some great nights up there. The Marryat Hall in Dundee was an iconic venue promoted by Tony Cochrane who also ran the nights in the Angus Hotel, a big venue which was part of the main Caird Hall. We had many great all-nighters and dayers with people travelling from far and wide. There were also clubs in Aberdeen, Glasgow, Arbroath and Edinburgh with Clouds and Tiffanys and a few years later Allanton Miners Welfare Club near Shotts. There were many more but I'm just picking out some of the venues that always come to mind. Even back then we used to travel around and we both have lovely memories of The Sombrero Club in Chester-le-Street and I also DJ'd at Dunelm House which was at Durham University. Over the years things have changed and bringing up a family got in the way of attending lots of places that might be familiar to others but we still had a lot of great nights going to places like Wigan Casino, Nottingham Palais, Tony's Empress Ballroom in Blackburn ,The Ritz Manchester, Winsford, Keele, Nantwich and later Kings

Halls in Stoke. All this was followed by weekenders in the late 90's at places such as Cala Gran Fleetwood the caravan site, followed by all the great weekenders at Blackpool Tower Ballroom and Cleethorpes.

These days you can go to a weekender nearly every weekend and not only in the UK, there are lots of places to go abroad as well and we have been lucky enough to attend a few over the years. I DJ'd in Bologna and also Gothenburg and have attended Rimini in Italy, Dusseldorf in Germany and also a ferry weekend from Tyneside to Amsterdam which included a trip into Amsterdam and a spot on the decks in a club there. On the way back the weather was a bit nasty and there were several people looking a bit green. This didn't stop Maureen and Sue Moffat dancing! We have always been blessed to have great DJs up here in Scotland. Too many to mention them all but we lived close to Kenny Burrell and travelled with him many times either in a group of cars or would hire a people carrier and go to events such as The Manchester Ritz, Bretby and The Griffin Hotel in Leeds. Our trip to Bretby was some journey, about 350 miles just to get there so you can imagine when you are talking to people and they ask "so where did you go at the weekend?" "Oh I just travelled 700 miles to go to an all night dance, then drove straight back home". When you think about all these places and trips that we all made over the years, meeting in some places that didn't have the finest of décor or facilities but who cared about that? Nobody (well maybe a few), some of the best places were always the worst as far as décor was concerned, yet they just worked. Lots of like-minded people listening to great DJs playing the music that we loved. It was never a fashion show either, remember Wigan where loads of guys went topless all night.

So things move on, people get married and have kids and we were no different. We married in 1974 and had our first two daughters in the late 70s.

We were the same as a lot of other couples in the 80s and raising our children was our main priority.

I remember bumping into Kenny Burrell on the odd occasion and he would tell us about a soul night and if we could get baby sitters then off we went. The love for the music was still there, but children came first. Ten years after our first two girls we decided that the time was right to increase our family and we had two more daughters in the late 80s. One of the good things with this was that by this time we had some extra babysitters so we managed to get out to soul nights more often. Scotland has always had soul clubs since even before I came up here in 1974, speaking to guys like Lenny Toshack who was always involved with the Edinburgh scene and the other guy that has to get a mention is Brian Joyce.

The following article is from an interview Maureen and I had with Brian about the East of Scotland Soul Club which was held in The Grosvenor Hotel, Edinburgh. Many years later this was used again by Graham (Shaz) Shanley and James (Jolly) Rogers for nights that ran under the banner of "Bumpin and Stompin". Needless to say, "Bumpin" was the main room featuring Disco and Modern and the smaller "Stompin" room was Northern.

EAST OF SCOTLAND SOUL CLUB ESSC)
EDINBURGH 1974 – 1980
(From an interview with BRIAN JOYCE)

There can't be too many people on the soul scene north of the border who didn't visit the East of Scotland Soul Club when it first started back in 1974 at The Grosvenor Hotel in Edinburgh, so it was with great pleasure that Maureen and I went over to meet Brian Joyce who it has to be said is one of the main reasons that Soul Music took off in such a big way in 1974 when he had the vision and the nerve to stage the event.

Remember that in those days you also had the restriction of the licensing laws which dictated that you could only be open for drinking up to 10pm and on Sundays it had to be in a Hotel! So what did Brian choose? Yes, a Sunday at The Grosvenor. How did Brian get into Soul Music? Well, he used to meet some of the US guys that were posted to Kirknewton in the 60s and found himself at a few parties and invariably some of the guys from the USA were bringing over with them their tastes in soul music and the rest as they say is history. A great story that Brian told us was when he was in London in 1966 and Otis Redding was at Tiles club on Oxford Street. Brian had just moved into a bedsit in Notting Hill Gate and, along with some like-minded people, went along to see Otis perform. It was pay on the door and upon entry he really wanted to meet the great man. Brian saw a guy from the USA doing interviews which were going to be sent back to the States, so he approached the guy and told him that he had travelled all the way from Scotland to see Otis. This clearly impressed the guy so much that he began to interview them. "Have you really come all the way from Scotland?" Towards the end, Brian said that it was one of his great wishes to meet Otis and get his autograph, so the guy took them over to Otis's dressing room and told him how these guys had come all the way from Scotland just to see him. "Come on in" said Otis and Brian spent about ten minutes in his dressing room before having to leave. Great story and one that makes me slightly green with envy! Brian had been working in London for many years and returned to Edinburgh in 1974, looking for his fix of soul music to satisfy his love of dancing. He went to places such as the Fire Island in Princess Street and the Forth Bridges Hotel where Bob Malcolm of Radio Forth fame years later was a DJ at what was called a "disco night", playing a mix which included some soul records. This wasn't enough for Brian as he wanted soul music from the start of the night to the end, so as promoting was part of the skills he had collected down in London, he started to look at the possibilities of running something in Edinburgh. Brian had been at The Grosvenor Hotel for some reason and found that The Rosebury Suite was empty.

He saw the manager and everything went well. It was left for him to organise things and also make assurances to The Grosvenor that this was being organised properly, door staff hired, no under-age drinking or drugs would be tolerated and anyone caught would be thrown out and banned. They were not allowcd to ohargo an ontranco foe thon so to get around that there was to be a donation to Club Funds of 40 pence (how times have changed!) On some occasions, a late licence would be granted, by promoting the night as a fancy dress party! Music policy in those days was simple, if it was a black soul star and it was music that you wanted to dance to then play it. Not much different to today. The Soul Nights at the Grosvenor Hotel lasted from late 1974 through to 1980 and was on every week on the Sunday night from 6pm until 10pm with the resident mobile disco of Ronnie Cowan from Dunfermline as the supplier of both equipment and also DJ expertise. Occasionally, other special nights were held at different venues, one that I can remember being at Stewart's Ballroom in 1975. Following the closure of ESSC at The Grosvenor, it re-emerged as the 3B's Club at the same venue but only lasted about another year, then following that there were a few revival dances held between 1981 and 1985. Brian's major bucket list trip was to visit Macon, Georgia to see the Otis Redding museum and Memphis, Tennessee to see the Stax museum. This would be followed by Hitsville, Detroit and throw in Chicago and New York to round it all off. Some trip and happy to report that this has since been done. Brian, in my mind, was one of the main people in the early days of the scene here in Scotland, even though if he had not done it then someone else might have stepped in. I know that, but at the end of the day Brian got off his arse and ran what was to this day one of the great early Soul clubs in Scotland and I thank him for that.

Moving on into the 90's, one of the clubs that started and had a great following over the years that it was open was "The Spider's Web" near Haymarket Station in the middle of Edinburgh. Kenny Burrell and Derek Robertson started the club in 1996 and it ran through to the 18th anniversary in 2015. What was it like? Well, it was in the basement of a well-known old man's type pub, you went down the stairs inside to the function room. To be honest, just like all the other clubs that seemed to work well on the Northern scene, it was a bit of a dive - a bar area, small dance floor, low roof, lovely sticky carpet, dodgy toilets! Having said that, it was just the right place at the right time; stick in 60 people and you had a great night but stick in 100 which was our maximum and the place was bouncing and hot and sweaty. Remind you of anywhere? Below is an article written by Kenny Burrell, who started the club.

SPIDERS WEB "The Early Years"

Following the end of the soul venue at the Claremont Hotel, (itself a small basement venue) which I attended regularly with Billy Ramsay in the early 90s, meeting lots of like-minded soul fans, there was a gap in the market. I really enjoyed its "up front" music policy and one night I was talking with Derek Robertson who suggested that he and I should start up a regular soul night. Derek sourced the Spider's Web as a venue and when I saw the basement layout with low ceilings and several alcove recesses, it came across as an intimate layout where a potential great atmosphere was the likely outcome, all things being equal. First night this was in January 1996 and was more or less advertised by word of mouth. I had decided from the start to take everyone's names & addresses on arrival, the rationale being we were starting what I perceived as a "club" and these details would come in useful. It's important to note at this point that 60 attendees would make the venue feel pretty busy and with 90 - 100 it would be totally rammed.

FLYERS & MEMBERSHIP CARDS

I arranged to have these produced in colour (coordinating both for "brand awareness") and given the numbers above I had 2000 x A4 size flyers printed and 300 membership cards done in credit card size and material. These were used until the flyers ran out, by which time most of the membership cards had been distributed. In those days remember, unlike today, nobody could advertise on Facebook, very few people had personal email facilities, and for group texting to mobile numbers we would have needed to go "back to the future." Every month therefore, I'd print address labels for members, type onto blank paper specific date and DJ details, photocopy onto the pre-printed coloured flyers, pop them in envelopes, apply stamps, address labels and post them! This was the protocol rather than "dump" flyers at various venues.

DJ'S & MUSIC

In the early days Derek would mostly arrange the DJ line-up where 3 guests plus him and I would grace the decks between 8pm-1am. It was always a given to rotate guest DJs from Glasgow, Dundee, Aberdeen, Edinburgh etc (bringing new members from all over) and the word spread pretty quickly. After a few months I latched onto what I thought was a clever idea which was to hand out C60 cassette tapes to the first 30 people through the doors containing either lesser known records and/or new acquisitions by myself. The idea was to play a lot of these records the following month when they'd be more familiar to more people. This I did for around 7 months culminating in the 1st Anniversary tape and it also helped with "club" loyalty and big "family feel". As well as all the fabulous sounds played that year by all our guest DJs and Derek, I included the following (selection only) from the aforementioned tapes again all played in 1996: Dennis Edwards "Johnnie On The Spot", Jesse Davis "Gonna Hang On In There", Jimmy Gresham "This Feeling I

63

Have ", Anderson Brothers "I Can See Him Loving You",Silhou-ettes "Not Me Baby", Arin Demain "Silent Treatment", Johnny Hendley "My Baby Came From Out Of Nowhere", Rita & The Tiaras "Gone With The Wind Is My Love", Cajun Hart "Got To Find A Way", The Magnetics "Lady In Green", Romona Collins "You've Been Cheatin, Dreamettes "That's Not Love", Yvonne Vernee "Just Like You Did Me", Fascinators "In Other Words", Sea Shells "Quiet Home", Hytones "You Don't Even Know My Name'

Going forward from the second year we'd also have guest DJs from England and even in the early years we had, for example, Terry Davies, Mick H, and Arthur Fenn (twice). I smile at Ar-thur's first appearance because he and Maria simply turned up as punters having come to Edinburgh for the weekend and then heard the Spider's Web was on. Not to miss an opportunity I "coerced" him to DJ from my record box. (It was the best spot he ever played ha-ha).

AWAY TRIPS

Once we were pretty established, I arranged a couple of bus trips which left from the Web to go to The Griffin in Leeds having arranged with Pat Brady a Scotland v England DJ line up. The 45 seater buses were full on both occasions with Spiders Web members and absolutely fantastic music was played. The buses' sound system also blasted out our compiled tapes on the 4-5 hr trip.

MY 50th BIRTHDAY (2003)

Nearing the end of my tenure with the Web, (I was working down south a lot and had precious little spare time) I decided to celebrate my 50th birthday and have our monthly night as a "freebie" with no admission cost, plus I stuck £1200 behind the bar as a thank you to our members to cover their drinks (the monthly bar take was normally £1000). I'd hand out vouchers to people on arrival: 6 if they arrived early, reducing to 3 at 11pm. The music digressed that night to mainstream oldies from all the DJs and it was jumping (even my kids were there aged 17 & 20). The Web would then continue to go from strength to strength over the next 15 years with George at the helm and I would make occasional guest DJ appearances, normally at an anniversary. So that was the start of The Spider's Web and over the early years a few other people also had a hand in running the place, namely Alan Mckenzie, Div Miller and Shug Robertson to name a few. Eventually, rather than lose the venue, I agreed to take it over. I used to seek out DJs all the time and one day I got a message from a guy called Ray Parker who at the time was living down in Ayrshire running a pub. I sent a message back and asked him to send me a tape so that I could have a listen to what he had in his box. Well after a quick listen I got in touch and made him a resident DJ, as he had now moved to Cowie near Stirling so it was a bit easier for him to reach us. The funny thing was it emerged during conversations that we had already met at Tony's Empress Ballroom when Ray was living in Rochdale and had a side line of selling t-shirts and polo shirts with logos on and I had ordered a blue one with a Scottish badge on. One of the best things about the Spider's Web was the fact that it was minutes from Hay Market Station near the centre of Edinburgh. You would not believe the people that would either get in touch and ask when was the night on, as they were coming up for a weekend or even some that just turned up on the night. I always remember one night there was this guy sitting in the bar and I thought he looked like someone familiar but could not place him. Turned out to be Ady Croasdell from the legendary 100 club in London. These sort of things just kept on happening. Mark and Amanda Garcia from San Diego who were on a Euro visit a few years before getting married. Christian Ostlund (Punky) from Gothenburg came walking down the stairs one night just to surprise us! We never had any problems attracting DJ' and our anniversary nights were always the best, having local guys like Kenny Burrell, Derek Robertson,

Keith Money, Fraser Dunn, Andy Dennison, Des Crombie, Jim Sim and Charlie Watson (now living in Turkey) to choose from, not to mention all the top guys from England. To do a full list would go on for sometime but if I mention Nige Brown, Ted Massey, Mick H, Ginger Taylor, Dave Ferguson, Derek Mead, Pete French, Eddie Hubbard, Sean Chapman and Sean Tasker you can see that we always managed to get the premier DJs to come up and the anniversary nights were always all tickets and sold out well in advance. Did we ever have any problems I hear you say? Well you know what small clubs are like with strange drunk people sometimes wandering in. One night that comes to mind, we were very busy and it was brought to my attention that some chap was going around the dance floor and bar area making unwanted advances to the ladies. Next thing I know this chap was out cold on the floor. Someone who shall remain nameless got to him before we did and gave him something to think about! Needless to say he was carried up the stairs. We made sure that he was ok then once all was well he made off to the next drinking establishment, with some choice words ringing in his ears. Who else did we have? I can remember one of our friends Graham Shanley (Shaz) from Edinburgh gave me a call one night and said that he had a friend coming over from Australia and as we had a soul night on the same night could we look after him? Shaz said that he was also a DJ and could he bring his records? Yes, no problem, just get him to come along, he'll get a spot and can stay with us as well. What's the guy's name I asked? Johnny "Redpants" Warren answered Shaz, he used to live around Rushden, Northamptonshire and moved out to Australia some time ago, currently living in Scarborough village near Brisbane . Great, look forward to meeting him! Now that was many years ago and we looked forward to another special night. The highlight was Johnny turning out in his trademark red pants and I have to say that he also wore red shoes and a black Queensland 1st Anniversary Soul Scene T-Shirt. Safe to say he pretty much blew us all away with both the records that he played and also just being Johnny. A great guy and he got on very well with Maureen as they are both very spiritual people. I remember we even took him on a River Forth sightseeing mini-cruise under the rail and road bridges. I have to say though that I don't think he liked the Scottish weather that day, let's just say it was a bit cold compared to Brisbane! We have remained friends ever since and even though he is on the other side of the world I always keep a close eye on what he is up to, which most of the time is something to do with soul music. It's a shame that he is so far away in Australia as it means we don't get to see him on our travels but he does phone and always keeps in touch. Great guy and I hope that these books we are all helping with get published for us all to read and also help some of the great soul music stars who aren't doing so well, it can't be easy when your health is not the best and basically we are all not getting any younger.

The Spider's Web kept on ticking along on the first Saturday of every month, it was always something to look forward to and to get organised. Eventually I was told by Kenny Burrell that he was going to stop DJing as the time spent going around the country was too much and he wanted more time to himself, most probably so as he could get on his road cycle bike and do 100 miles a weekend, which he is still doing to this day. He mentioned also that there was only one place that he would finish off at and that was The Spider's Web, seeing as he had started the club all those years ago, so between me and other residents, Ray Parker, Lenny Toshack and John Reid started to organise the night. We decided that his last night as a DJ would coincide with our 15th Anniversary to be held on Saturday 5th February 2011 and what a night that was. We managed to get the lovely and also brilliant DJ Barbara Grassi over from Italy, our good friend Eddie Hubbard came up and of course last spot of the night (and ever as far as Kenny was concerned) eventually started and wow, he played all the big sounds that he was known for: Frank Wilson, The Mellow Souls and finishing off with Timi Yuro "It'll Never Be Over For Me". It turned out to be just one of those nights that will never be forgotten. Below is a review of the night that went into "Soul Up North" No 71 in

Spring 2011, written by Andy Bellwood (York) . I travelled up from rural North Yorkshire for the weekend and boy was it worth it, one of those memorable nights for all the right reasons. The venue was oozing with charm and atmosphere, a throwback to those legendary 60s vaulted basement mod/beat/jazz club venues. I managed about 7 of the 10 hours on offer and caught most of the excellent sets from the residents (Ray Parker, John Reid, Lenny Toshack and host extraordinaire George Wallace). I sadly missed Roddy Brass, but word was that it was outstanding. It was floor filling stuff throughout, including: The Broadways "You Just Don't Know" Clifford Binns "You've Got To Help Me" Alma Faye "Believed" and the then current favourite at The Spider's Web judging by the whoops of delight, Lou Rawls "Time Will Take Care Of Everything". Some particularly nice tunes were spun by Eddie Hubbard (standing in for Mick H), including the Denise LaSalle version of "The Right Track." I was also blown away by Barbara Grassi's set (all the way from Italy), varied with lovely rarities and the occasional golden oldie, well crafted and flowing like a dream. Lots of stand out tracks for me, such as Mark 1V "Sounds Of Dying Love" Nate Evans "The Look On Your Face" and Sandra Wright "Midnight Affair" just pipping it.

The grand finale was of course (King) Kenny "Do I Love You" Burrell, being his last ever DJ appearance. Uptempo and a floor packing reaction tune after tune, a simply wonderful tribute to the man who has embraced and contributed so much to the Northern Soul scene over the years. Brought a tear to the eye when Kenny played Katie Briggs "Last Time Around". I exchanged a few CDs, extended the "wants list" and on Kenny's recommendation had the best Indian meal ever. Big thanks to all who made us so welcome and nice to see a few from Yorkshire (especially Steve Crawshaw & Lydia) and from across the Pennines, Greatstones' Pete & Lady Best & Andy Bellwood .That sums up the whole day and Kenny's last DJ appearance back in 2011, a great occasion with wonderful DJs that you just won't forget.

I couldn't remember what Kenny's last record was and having spoken to him today, neither can he, though he did give me a few options which were Darrell Banks "I'm The One Who Loves You", Velvelettes "These Things Will Keep Me Loving You", Timi Yuro "It'll Never Be Over For Me", Jimmy Wallace "I'll Be Back".

The End Of "The Spider's Web"

So what happened to "The Spider's Web?" Well the guy who owned it all the time we used it was called Peter and he was not in the best of health, also because of the pub's location in Edinburgh he was most probably being pushed to sell up by the bigger chains. Early in 2014 we were being told that this would be the final year, so we asked Peter if we could have the whole pub for the 18th Anniversary night which was to be on Saturday 1st February 2014. We had two rooms, upstairs in the main bar was Modern Soul and downstairs was the usual Northern and as usual the place sold out by ticket only and it was another excellent night. Guest DJs on the night were Nige Brown, who showed us his other DJ side by doing both rooms, all round nice guy and avid record collector Dave Ferguson (who we were lucky enough to have on our decks twice over the last few years) and Des Crombie from near Aberdeen, one of Scotland's finest.

We kept going with our normal 1st Saturday of each month and we even spoke to the people that had bought the place to ask if they could renovate it. They seemed fine and promised us that downstairs would carry on and that they wanted us back when it reopened after what would be nearly a 1 million pound overhaul. We got through to May 2014 and then due to work not starting were asked if we would like Saturday 7th June 2014. We assumed that this was to be our last night ever at The Spider's Web, a sad night indeed.

After a while, I got word that what we were being told about returning once all the work was complete was incorrect, so we went over and had a meeting with the new owners. It turned out that they had indeed decided to refurbish the basement so that was that. The next time it opened was as The Jolly Botanist, a typical Edinburgh city centre bar with gin as its theme drink and needless to say I have never been back since we left, though I have on a few occasions been told that the downstairs function room is still there and just left as it was and never reopened. Strange but sounds about right. We did have a look at some places in Edinburgh but some were too big, others some too small, and the one thing that they had in common was they were very expensive. We did try a venue called The Park Hotel in Leith and held a 19th anniversary event there with Ted Massey and John Vincent but that also came to an end as it was a bit too big and like all places in Edinburgh, just too much money. After that we tried a local place in Rosyth that had not been used for a while, an upstairs function room in an old converted cinema called CJ's and before that The Palace here in Rosyth about a mile from home. It was good and I think given the chance it would have worked, but then as usual the man that owned it along with a few others in the local town decided that it was too dark in the function room so just closed it so after all the years we basically just called it a day.

The man that stood by my side as co-promoter at The Web for all those years and long term friend was Ray Parker. Ray was a great record collector and DJ and always amazed me with some of his tales of how little he paid for some big sounds. I think he must have been on every country's eBay website in the world and also had people looking out in markets in 3rd world countries just to hunt for some of his records. Sadly in 2016 Ray was told that he had pancreatic cancer. Following some major surgery he was good for a while but then very sadly he passed away on 9th May 2017. A big loss to all that knew him all over the UK and also overseas. We organised a large tribute night to him in which all the proceeds would go to Macmillan Cancer

Support. The night was held at The Corn Exchange in Edinburgh and it was a very touching night, a lot of his friends came along from all over and we even got Kenny Burrell out of retirement to play a few tunes along with George Hunt from Carlisle, the same place that Ray grew up in. Following that, Ray's wife Christine asked me if I could help to sell his record collection which, along with Ian McKenzie, we did for about 6 months before giving her back what was left. It was an honour to have him as a friend and he is still missed. I would like to end by thanking Johnny for asking me to write this and be a small part of his great idea and also just to say a big RIP to all those soul stars who are no longer with us. Also many thanks to all the soulies that have been part of my life over the last 71 years and have sadly passed away. Maureen and I hope that we can keep on doing what we have been doing for so many years, maybe for a few more yet.

Groove City Soul Badge © George Wallace

The Spider's Web Badge © George Wallace

George & Maureen Wallace © George Wallace

Johnny Redpant's Warren © G Wallace

The Spider's Web Edinburgh © George Wallace

"THE SPIDERS WEB"

THE SPIDERS WEB PUB, MORRISON STREET,
HAYMARKET, EDINBURGH, EH3 8DT

PRESENTS

15th ANNIVERSARY ALL-DAYER
SATURDAY 5th FEBRUARY 2011

3PM TO 1AM - 10 HOURS OF GREAT SOUL

TICKET ONLY @ £8 : Only 100 On Sale

FEATURING GUEST DJ's

EDDIE HUBBARD (Oxford)

BARBARA GRASSI (Italy)

KENNY BURRELL (Fife)
KENNY'S LAST EVER DJ APPEARANCE

RODDY BRASS (Edinburgh)

• RESIDENTS (SEE US AT "THE WEB" FOR TICKETS OR CALL)
RAY PARKER (07983 388 898) / LENNY TOSHACK (07738 209 440)
JOHN REID (07969 811 608) / GEORGE WALLACE (07767 775 796)

Check the web site @ www.groovecitysoulclub.co.uk

Spider's Web Flyer © George Wallace

SCOTTISH SOUL SOCIETY

ALLNIGHTER

Marryat Hall, Dundee — Friday, 8th July, 1977

10.30p.m. – 7.00a.m.

(STRICTLY NO ADMISSION AFTER 11.00p.m.)

TICKET £1.50

Marryat Hall Dundee Flyer 1977 © George Wallace

SOUL CLUB

Groove City

MY WORLD IS ON FIRE

JIMMY MACK

SPIDERS WEB

(SATURDAY 6TH April 1996)

Do not miss the next Groove City soul club event. It will be packed with all the latest (60T's & 70T's) rare northern soul sounds.

8pm-1am Haymarket Edinburgh
Admission only **£3**

GUEST DJ'S
**Alan Mckenzie...........
Charlie Watson............
Keith Money................**

Derek & Ken.

GOOD-BY CRUEL LOVE
LINDA GRIMER
M-1037

SOUTHERN ARTISTS

YOU DON'T EVEN KNOW MY NAME
THE HY-TONES

GONE WITH THE WIND IS MY LOVE
RITA & THE TIARAS

NOT FOR SALE

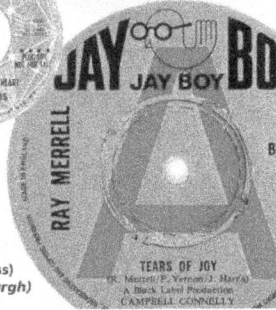

Promoters:
Derek Robertson 0131 665 9600
Ken Burrell 0131 553 4300 (business)
Sponsored by Ideal Windows (Edinburgh)

JAY BOY

RAY MERRELL

TEARS OF JOY

Groove City Flyer © George Wallace

75

Chapter 6

Joan Bosson "Never Been To Wigan"

An Aussie's Northern Soul Experience

I was born in New Zealand but left when I was only two months old and have lived in Australia ever since, almost fifty five years. My mum was Australian and my dad was Welsh and I was not brought up listening to any kind of Motown or soul music. My dad loved the big bands like Glenn Miller and my mum liked Perry Como. I grew up a shy Aussie kid who was tubby and had a stutter so I wasn't really one of the popular kids, more one of those kids that would be listening to and being exposed to other musical styles other than the pop charts of the day. I moved out of home as soon as I left school and started going out to the pubs and clubs in Perth, meeting all types of people at places like The Red Parrot, The Underground, The Old Melbourne Hotel and The Railway Hotel. During the early to mid-eighties I heard some tunes that I later found out to be Northern Soul tunes. At the time I was into the local mod and scooter scene here in Perth. We had great times wearing all the sixties clothing and hanging out. I even rode my own scooter and still do. I guess you could call the tunes we were listening to "Pop Northern" songs like "Skiing In The Snow", "Out On The Floor", "Bongo Rock" and yes, you guessed it, "The Snake". I loved them all and still do. We heard the term "Northern Soul" from some expat Poms who hung out with us. I eventually drifted out of the mod and scooter scene which was full of the usual conflicts and mix of personalities. I just did not want to be a part of all that but I still loved my music and dancing so went out looking for it elsewhere and in early 1999 I attended a Motown night at the Woodvale Tavern, hosted by Robbie and Larraine Burns.

As well as the usual Motown pop tunes being played, there were a few dance numbers I hadn't heard before. On one occasion after dancing with my hubby all night, just doing what came naturally, as I left the dance floor a very tall bloke came up to me and said, "You look like you know how to dance to Northern Soul". That bloke was Pete Fowler who was at the night with some mates who I now know to be Keith Collett, Kev McCord and a few others. Pete suggested that I should go to his Northern Soul night at The Irish Club in Subiaco. I had noted Keith dancing earlier in the night and was amazed at how the guys were dancing like they did. I was used to my very conservative, two left-footed Macedonian husband's wobbling and so seeing these lads dancing solo, shuffling and spinning, was a bit of an eye opener. I was intrigued and was certainly going to go to the Irish Club and find out more about this Northern Soul stuff I'd been hearing about.

My first night at the Irish Club was in July 1999, and I have never looked back. On that first night everyone was so nice and welcoming and the music was awesome. I stayed in my corner and danced all night, watching everyone else dancing and generally soaking it all in. At one point a guy called Steve Parker came over and gave me a compilation tape. I played that tape over and over, I loved every song and was hooked. I managed to get hold of a video of Wigan Casino footage and WOW, I was blown away. I must have watched it over a hundred times. We continued to go to the Irish club, sometimes I would go with another friend as my then husband and his Macedonian country wobble dance just didn't really fit, plus the Irish Club was full of Poms with only a few token Aussies, one of them an old friend from my mod scene days, "Karl The Mod". National weekenders had just started so in October 1999, I attended my first all-nighter at the Embassy Ballroom in Carlisle. I was so excited. I remember as we drove up being confused as I thought I heard Fat Boy Slim "Funk Soul Brother" playing. Ha I soon learnt it was the Just Brothers "Sliced Tomatoes".

I was so thrilled to be there and be a part of this scene and learn more and more about it. The dance floor at the Embassy was huge, full of happy smiling faces, people enjoying themselves. I danced and danced, rested, had snacks and danced some more. I had never been so tired in my life, but I was definitely in a happy place. Tired but happy . Not to dwell on it but I was having some domestic problems and the Perth Northern Soul scene and the people in it who quickly became some of my closest friends was my happy place. The music helped me forget my problems and I could get lost on the dance floor. I continued to go to the Irish Club on the first Saturday of every month. I made sure it was my priority to go, even by myself. The scene was my world away from a crappy life in the suburbs. I was not allowed to go interstate to the now developing annual "Nationals" (The Nash). I was always envious of those that went and who would come back and tell me of the wonderful times they had and how great the weekend was. I made the most of my monthly northern Soul nights at the Irish Club. I made sure I had a nap in the afternoon before going out, so that I could dance all night. I very rarely left the dance floor. There were special events every March to commemorate the anniversary, normally all-dayers. I would pack a spare change of clothes, some snacks and frozen cordial to keep me going. Also, each September there used to be a "Wigan Anniversary" do but that has stopped now. I would go to whatever I could. My next big all-nighter was in 2003, WOW it was fabulous; dancing, dancing and more dancing, meeting more people and soaking up the vibe. I was now a part of the Perth soul crew. For me, the way I felt about my soul nights and the way I looked forward to them was similar to the way that some of the original soulies would describe looking forward to going to Wigan or some of the other clubs, I loved it and lived it. At the all-nighters people were taking stuff (mainly Dexys) to help them last till the morning, I would be fibbing if I said I never, but my main trick was to just never sit down. If you did sit, that was it - goodnight Vienna. I didn't drink that much back then as it made me sick sometimes and I didn't want to ruin my night.

While at the 2003 Perth Nash, the all-nighter which was at "The Talk Of The Town" in Malaga, just dancing away in my own little world as usual, the music stopped for some announcements and to give a thumbs up for the best dancers. I was blown over when they called my name out for "Best Female Dancer". Who, me, this little Aussie chick just doing her own thing, dancing the way she always dances? I had never won anything in my life so to win an award for doing something I just love to do was out of sight, especially from my soulie peers and mentors. I look at the award now and then and remember what a fabulous night that was. I know it's a silly award, but it means the world to me and to top it off the picture and presentation was published in the "Manifesto" magazine for all the soulie world to see, my fifteen minutes of fame haha. At the next Irish Club I remember Boyne Callanan joking with me saying "They are setting up a table for people to sit and watch you dance"….haha, it still sounds funny. The monthly Irish Club nights continued, and I would never miss one.

I gotta love it more and more and it became an escape for me from a controlling marriage. I got this feeling every time, arriving at the door, the anticipation of hearing all my favourite tunes being played and just dancing all night. I wasn't much of a talker but still in between songs I would chat and meet people. I had made some good friends by now and would carpool with the likes of Van & Les Astbury and Denny & Clare Johnson. In 2005 I was allowed, (yes allowed) to go to my first interstate Nash which was in Sydney, only for one night though. This was only because my ex-husband and I were visiting his family in Melbourne on the Thursday and Friday before. We flew up to Sydney on the Saturday afternoon, did the all-nighter and left Sunday morning but it was fabulous, I loved being part of the National scene. I think Debbie Taylor won the best female dancer that year. She is such a lovely soul who, like me, just loves to dance and dance. Little did I know that also on the dance floor that Saturday night, only a foot or two away from me and almost brushing hands as we danced was my future (2nd) husband.

It was a great night, one I will never forget as we all waited outside the Marrickville Bowling Club for the bus back to the hotel. Back in Perth and it was back to the monthly Irish Club, hearing more and more tunes as peoples' collections grew bigger. I was loving it just as much as ever and couldn't get enough. My next all-nighter was Adelaide 2007. I was starting to take more control of my private life and managed to be allowed to attend the full weekend by myself. The whole weekend was great. I loved it except for the concrete floor in the café venue, it has stuffed up my feet to this day and I have to cover my feet in band aids every time I go dancing now. On the other end of the scale, the dance floor at the Adelaide Polish Club was like a skating rink, so slippery I even poured water on to the carpet and stood in it to wet my shoes before going on to the dance floor but still felt like I was going to go Arse over Tit, haha.

I remember feeling exhausted after that night but got a lift back to my hotel from fellow Perth soulie Eric Pearson, what a top bloke. After Adelaide it was back to my boring life back in Perth's northern suburbs just hanging out waiting for my monthly Irish Club fix. I would get through my day to day life by looking forward to my next soul night. If I could, I would go to the odd night at the Fly By Night Club in Fremantle with Denny and Clare and a few others, it was mostly Motown but they played some Northern and a bit of Modern Soul.

The next Nash I went to was the 2008 event here in Perth. I loved these weekends away from home. Great music, great people, a great scene and just doing what I liked to do: dance to top tunes. I loved it and I loved the feeling it gave me and it made me reflect on my marriage. In 2009 I left my very controlling husband and oh what a relief, it is hard to explain but at the first Irish Club I attended after that horrible time with my ex was like going home to family, everyone was so supportive and it felt like the chains had been taken off me. The months that followed opened up new friendships and a whole lot more Northern Soul.

Although due to money now being very tight I could no longer go to interstate nationals, however I never missed my monthly Irish Club nights. I went with the same sense of excitement as always; the thrill was still there.

In 2013 after finding myself and coming out of my shell a little thanks to the support of my soulie family and friends I met and chatted up this guy, Thomas Bosson , remember the guy I mentioned on the dance floor in Sydney? He was recently separated and back in Perth and I was divorced. We caused a stir when we were seen holding hands at the Perth Nash 2013, haha, and even more of a stir when people found out we were sharing a hotel room! We are married now thanks to the Northern Soul scene. I have been going to the Irish Club Northern Soul nights now for 22 years. It has been the best time. I went every month except for when I was in hospital or too poorly to dance. I have met lots of lovely people who I am proud to call my friends including my soulie soul mate, my now hubby. The Irish Club has changed a bit over the years, there have been scandals, loves lost and found, people coming and going, new faces and people still just discovering this Northern Soul thing. Not so many people going these days compared to the early years and all-nighters are now all half-nighters, but it is still my happy place.

I was devastated when it closed because of Covid 19, then when it returned they had stuffed up the dance floor. It had taken 24 years to get the dance floor the way we wanted it, 22 for me and then they varnished it with thick sticky stuff. I still plan my work schedule around the Irish Club nights and will continue to go to as many as I can, and I still stick to my rule of "don't sit down". I'm going to just keep on keeping on, I LOVE MY NORTHERN SOUL and my Aussie Northern Soul experience. A Big Thank You to Pete Fowler for coming up to me that night at The Woodvale Tavern and inviting me along to The Irish Club. Also to all the soulies along the way, some of whom made my time at the Irish Club even more special, sadly some have now passed away, some pop in every now and then and some are still hard core "every-monthers" like myself, and lastly thank you Johnny "Red Pants" Warren. I always loved watching you DJ here in Perth whenever you are over. You never stand still even dancing through your sets.

Joan Bosson Australian Dancing Champion © G Williamson.

Thomas Bosson & Joan Bosson © Joan Bosson

General Justice, Keith Collet, Van Astbury (RIP), Pete Fowler, Kev McCord, Steve Parker © Joan Bosson

Perth Nash 2003 – Eric Pearson, Joan Bosson, Maxine Fowler, Bobby Millard, Clare Johnson, Ian Astbury, Paul Feeny, Gill Feeny, Les Astbury, Peter Fowler © Joan Bosson

Chapter 7

Paul & Gill Feeney's Northern Soul Story

My interest in soul music started in 1971 as a 14 year old in and around Huddersfield doing the youth club rounds. This is where I met Gill Hirst, as she was known those days, to those that know us now Gill Feeney. Our first full on Northern Soul night was 1973 upstairs in the function room at the Royal Swan in Huddersfield and the DJ was local boy Ian Dewhirst, known on the scene as Frank. He and local soulie Les Hall started northern soul nights at the Starlight Club above Burtons Tailors, which was also attended by Keith Sutcliffe from Halifax who now resides in Melbourne and has become a good friend. Two of Keith's mates, Pete Flynn and Clint Bennett, were also mates of mine , It's a small world. Next came the Taurus Club, again run by Frank and Twink down on Venn Street, the red light district of Huddersfield. This took place in The West Indian Club and the punters there weren't too impressed with white boys dancing to Northern Soul in their beloved reggae club.

In 1974 I passed my driving test and my boss gave me a van as I was an apprentice plumber. That was the turning point; me, Gill (who was the only girl in our group) and the guys were Wigan bound, the then holy grail of the scene. Visits to other big venues followed; Manchester Ritz ALL-Dayers, Coalville Tiffanys and a few visits to the Highland Room at the Blackpool Mecca. Gill and I were now married and attended other local nights around West Yorkshire such as Halifax Tiffanys (mentioned in Blues & Soul magazine as the only northern night on a Monday night), Mirfield Pentagon and Raquels in Wakefield to mention just a few. Some years later we decided to emigrate to Australia and after having our 2 daughters life was pretty normal being mum and dad, paying the bills and mortgage etc. That was until one Sunday in November 1999 when we were in an old second hand vinyl store in Fremantle, promising our girls if they were good whilst mum and dad looked through records, we would take them to McDonalds! Then Gill saw a flyer on the wall "Perth Northern Soul Weekender " at The Embassy Ballroom. We rang the contact number and spoke to a guy called Pete Fowler whose first question was "Did you ever go to Wigan?" The answer was of course yes. A couple of weeks later we rocked up to the event and were greeted on the door by a rather tall dude, who greeted us with the old soul brother handshake (Mr Fowler). I said straight away to Gill "This ain't no handbag night, this is the real deal"! 20 years between drinks and dancing to some of our favourite tunes was surreal. I remember Steve Parker introducing himself, saying we had been noticed rushing to the dance floor each time a favourite record came on. We also got talking to a guy at the bar, who we couldn't believe had come all the way from Adelaide, yes you've guessed it, Pete Feven. We became regulars at the Perth Irish Club and Australian Nationals and Gill used to do a few DJ spots in the early days. We went to Pete Feven's Duke of York 4th Anniversary in Adelaide in 2001 where Gill did a spot. It was there where we first met former Warrington resident Ainsley White after his old mate Denny Johnson introduced us. 12 months later we were back in Adelaide for the 5th Oz National, where Gill did a spot at the Sunday all-dayer in the Enigma Bar, that was the first time we met the man behind this book Johnny "Redpants" Warren.

In 2004 we had a 6 week holiday to the U.K. where we went to my home town's famous Brighouse Ritz for the Friday soul night run by Roger Banks. All our old soul mates turned up, people we hadn't seen in 20 years: Pete Flynn, Kenny, Mick Waddington, Andy Lawson, Fred and Bob Ward to name but a few. Lowton and Prestwich were also visited, and in case you hadn't guessed, we were hooked again. In 2006 and we were back for another 6 weeks, Roger Banks had unfortunately passed away and Ginger Taylor had taken the reins, so the Ritz was in safe hands. We extended our horizons and visited Middleton all-nighter, probably the best gig we have ever attended, also 2 visits to Sheridans all-nighter, not far from Brighouse. We were now being exposed to some of the rarest tunes on the planet, a lot of them are new to us and very exciting! We had our first visit to Whitby weekendor with Nell Goddard and his mate Yocky. We met so many great people but all good things came to an end and it was time to go home. However, we just couldn't stay away so in 2007 we returned for another 6 weeks and attended Whitby again with our new mates Nell and the gang, also the first Bridlington weekender at the 3B's ballroom, before it moved to the Pavilion. We also made our first trip to the famous King George's Hall in Stoke, along with Pete Fowler and Mark Heaney who were both back in the U.K. The following week we attended an all-nighter at the legendary Cleethorpes Pier with Pete Fowler and Denny Johnson and a couple of weeks later, me and Gill had done a soul night at another iconic venue, Cleethorpes Winter Gardens before it got demolished. For the third time in 4 years it was time to say our sad farewells and go home! Later that year I had a light bulb moment: why not go back on a working holiday and stay as long as we want? Now all I had to do was sell it to Gill. She was a bit hesitant to say the least and said it was another of my crack-pot schemes, but with my girls both on board, we swung her around. We sold our small collection of records, mostly U.K. issues, and made about A$7,500 which wasn't bad seeing as most were bought in the 70s for 85 pence each. This money helped to fund a 15 month soul pilgrimage so in 2008 the Feeneys flew back into the unknown.

Most of our Perth mates were thinking we had totally lost the plot except Pete Fowler who said to me "Brilliant! How did you manage to pull that one off"? The first few weeks were quite stressful because we had to buy a car, look for jobs in a recession and even try to recover our National Insurance numbers, but then it all started to fall into place. My mate Dennis McAuliffe said we could live in his attic conversion, we bought an old Saab for £600 and both found work. This was the beginning of the most exciting 15 months of our lives. We became great friends with my old mate, Colin Wood and his wife Shirley, who both helped Howard Earnshaw with his "Soul Up North" fanzine. I don't think there was an all-nighter, weekender or soul night we didn't visit. We became regulars on the nighter scene and became friends with everyone: my old mate Steve Cato, Spot & Gail, Trevor Wright, Mike & Jan Coghlan, Dave Rivers, Mick H, the list is so long! Saw so many live acts on 2 visits to Prestatyn and bumped into Johnny Redpants who was also spending a lot of time in the U.K.

At the end of our holiday, we had the privilege of being invited to Steve & Lydia Cato's wedding reception all-dayer in Manchester, again with so many familiar faces in attendance. A couple of highlights were me and Gill DJing for Mouse at the Wilton all-nighter, and Gill DJing for Yocky and Nell at the Mexborough bank holiday all-dayer. We saw Melvin Davis at the Cleethorpes weekender, another highlight. I could go on forever, but after 15 months we had to go home. It was so hard and sad to say goodbye to everyone, so many tears on our last all nighter in Crewe. If it wasn't for our daughters, we may never have come home! Trying to settle back into the Perth lifestyle was hard, but we had no choice and knuckled back down into work and normality. 2014 and guess what? Jetting back to Manchester and that familiar drive over the Pennines to Yorkshire, "God's Own Country". Another great 6 weeks of soul and catch ups, the highlight of this trip being the Newquay weekender which was brilliant, well worth the 7 hour drive down there. The weekend was spent with Dave & Janet Ferguson and Ady Heaney, Mark's younger brother. We all got a big surprise when our new mate Mick H rocked up Saturday night with Eula Cooper, they quickly rigged up a mike and she treated us to a couple of her classics. The 6 weeks went by all too quickly, and we were back to reality. The next 3 years we worked hard and saved for another trip, so in 2017 we packed our jobs up and were off for 4 and a half months.

I got to see my beloved Huddersfield Town go up to the premiership with fellow fanatic Steve Cato. We went to Wembley with 42,000 other Town fans and it was magic. We also got to see the first few premiership games with Steve and other lifelong friends. Next it was off to Benidorm for the International Soul Fiesta, where Pat Lewis was the main act.

Dave & Bev Moore put on a great event which went for 5 days and where we met up with fellow Aussies Pete & Maxine Fowler, Denny Johnson and Una Hanlon. Back to England and the next big event was the Bridlington weekender at the Spa which was voted the best ballroom in Europe, 5 rooms of music, something for everyone. Another mate from Oz, Keith Collett was over for this event, so with Col & Shirl Wood and Gill's old best mate from Huddersfield, Sue Duncan (nee Spray), a great time was had by all.

The following week was the much anticipated Manchester weekender. We spent 3 days in this fabulous city, the weather was warm and sunny, the whole city was buzzing and the bars and beer gardens were packed. I knew this small boutique weekender would be different with fellow Huddersfield fans, Steve Cato and Darren & Mandie Sykes, at the helm helped by Neil Higson. R&B, rare soul, gospel, soulful funk and very underplayed oldies made for a great and very different event. No rest for the wicked, the week after we were off to the Burnley Kestrel Suite all-nighter, affectionately known as the Bat Cave, and run by our friend Sean Haydon, who had kindly put us on the guest list. Nothing better for a Yorkshire couple than free entry. We had a great 4 and half months with many other venues visited for the first time. If you add up all our trips since 2004, Gill and myself have spent a good 2 years on the U.K. soul scene, which if I say so myself, is not a bad effort considering we live over 9000 miles away! For us, we still love the all-nighter scene where DJs and punters are still searching for different and underplayed tunes, and it still has that truly underground feel and the special vibe we all fell in love with.

A few of my favourite venues are Middleton, Sheridans, Mirfield, Bidds Stoke, Kestrel Suite Burnley and my mate Mouse's Wilton, the longest running gig after the 100 club. All of those nights and many more like Winsford and the Stables in Wolverhampton, have disappeared due to old ballrooms, civic centres and town halls being demolished or turned into apartments or shopping centres. To me this is one of the biggest threats to the scene, keeping these iconic buildings going. I wrote my ramblings because of my respect for what our mate Mr. Redpants is trying to achieve. Writing does not come easy to me so I hope this hasn't been too boring. There is really too much to write about, and too many people to include, too many funny anecdotes, which were only funny if you were there. Anyway, hopefully see you all on a dance floor somewhere soon when all this Covid crap has disappeared! Hope you have enjoyed this little read.

Paul & Gill Feeney KTF

Paul & Gill Feeney © Gary Williamson

Gill Feeney behind the decks © Gill Feeney

Gill Feeney Out On The Floor © Gary Williamson

Chapter 8

A Mixtape Memoir by Dana Smart
Soul for the Heart!

Lou Ottens died in March. His obituary featured a photo drawn from his company's archive: a respectable man in a muted-patterned suit with deep set eyes. He wore a warm smile, quizzical, a superficiality befitting a pose for a corporate photographer. It nevertheless exuded an intensity, a mischievousness, even. He knew something we didn't.

I grew up in New York City, where the exchange of pop culture ideas flowed easily between it and the UK. "London and New York are suburbs of each other" a former boss would fondly point out when we reminisced about the City in our L.A. office. I bought the Kent compilation Gems, my first bona fide rare soul purchase, around 1986 at Sounds, an upstairs record shop on St. Mark's Place on Manhattan's Lower East Side. Sounds had a healthy selection of imports; my friend Gene walked his fingers across the top spines of the shop's Kent section, hearty enough to warrant its own bin card. A fellow Mod from New Jersey, Gene was only three years older than I, but his musical knowledge was lightyears ahead and encyclopedic. He was friends with all the ska and mod bands in the Tri-State Area. He knew about the Mod Revival. He knew Two-Tone and Trojan. And he knew Northern. "This is a good one," he said matter-of-factly, looking at the back of the Gems jacket. "Get this." I bought it blind, but my eyes—and ears—were blown wide when I got home. The drum pick-up and gutsy horns that open Carl Carlton's "Competition Ain't Nothin'' electrified my spine. I stared at my speaker's slack jaw. I was hooked. I needed more. Northern was arguably underground but understood in the UK, it was virtually unknown in the indifferent US. In the land of Stax and Motown and Atlantic, the records exalted by Northern were the never happened and failed-to-launch & no one cared. I picked up as many Kent LPs as I could find and afford at import prices but even in New York City, the LPs were scarce.

Lou Ottens was a Dutch mechanical engineer who joined the European electronics powerhouse Philips in 1952. By the early '60s, he was the head of product development. Vexed by a reel-to-reel tape deck's poor behavior at home one night, so the story goes, Mr. Ottens gathered his team at Philips the next morning with a mission: develop a medium where both the tape and take-up spools are encased. The clincher: make it portable. Philips Museum director Olga Coolen told the New York Times that Mr. Ottens carried a small wood block in his jacket that approximated the dimensions of his vision. In 1963, the final product was introduced: the cassette. Portable, playable, recordable, the cassette "was a big surprise for the market," Mr. Ottens told Time Magazine in 2013. Portrayed as a pragmatist, Mr. Ottens saw the cassette as a solution to a problem, a developmental advancement; for me as for so many cassettes were much, much more. Mr. Ottens' invention kept me nourished.

I was completing my senior year of university in St. Louis, Missouri. Maniacally lazy, I never dared transport my records halfway across the continent for school, I committed vital sounds to tape. Cassettes were easier to carry and it ensured that my precious platters didn't sit in the back of a friend's hot car for the thousand mile one-way drive to campus. Late autumn 1990 was unseasonably cold. The rhythms of the Kent albums acquired that summer and of my respectable but embryonic singles collection that were once so fresh were soon beat. I grudgingly listened so that there was something to listen to on the walk from campus to my apartment. But the familiarity bred disdain; the songs no longer ignited my soul. I was bored and thirsting. A small padded envelope was in my mailbox in my building's entryway, just inside from the chilling wind that chugged down Delmar Blvd. I recognized Gene's penmanship. Mindful of postage, all extra weight was stripped, it contained only a cassette

93

and handwritten double-sided index card; no case, no J-card, no note. Northern '60s Newie's. I popped it in my Walkman. Sparks. Chills. I'm certain my pupils dilated. High, noble horns soared through my head. Soon the track opened up to a sensuous, swaying midtempo underpinned by a breezy Hammond and propelled by mellow congas. A man in love entreats. The tape fed and fueled. A bounce returned to my step. The tape rarely left my Walkman, providing my St. Louis soundtrack. I was schooled in beat ballad courtesy of Timi Yuro's smoky, potent "It'll Never Be Over For Me" and Gene Stridel's cosmopolitan "Tomorrow Is Another Day," in the savage propulsion of Luther Ingram's "If It's All The Same To You" and its vocal less "Exus Trek," the grit of Tony Middleton's "Paris Blues," the sweet spite of Carolyn Crawford's "Forget About Me." But the opening cut eluded; it was omitted from the index card. I asked Gene about it. "That's a version of Darrell Banks' 'Open The Door To Your Heart' by Joe Young. It's on the UK Toast LP." I embarked, paraphrasing Francis Ford Coppola, on an idiot odyssey. I returned to New York City following graduation. Freed of senior-level classwork, living at home with entry-level employment provided just enough time and money to continue building my singles collection. My own mixtapes soon followed. My tastes in the early '90s gravitated to the dance sounds of the early- to mid-'70's latter-day soul and proto-disco, when it itself was underground and distinctly Black. My friend Alden traded tapes of disco and funk, when we were not sitting around with the freshly released James Brown Star Time box set dissecting hip hop samples. Our friend Greg, one year our senior at university, had also settled in New York and gleefully shared his discoveries from trolling the city's backroom and basement record shops. But like all good mixtapes, many of mine soon headed west to California, to a girl I had fallen in love with, the drum patterns, the heaven-bound background "oohs" and the beggin', pleadin' and shoutin' on the C-90s expressed my heart better than my words ever could. The Chi-Lites' "To Change My Love," The Van McCoy Strings' "Sweet & Easy," The Vontastics' "Lady Love," The Fiestas' "Think Smart."

The background refrain of Edward Hamilton & The Arabians' "I'm Gonna Love You"—I'm gonna love you forever and a day ,became the closest of every letter I wrote. The title of Jackie Wilson's "Nothing But Blue Skies" is inscribed on her wedding ring. I would eventually follow my tapes and move to Los Angeles. Planning to travel by train, Gene gave me a stack of seven cassettes: Burpin' sax cuts from Detroit essentials from L.A.'s Mira, Mirwood and Keyman imprints; the Northern: Cheap to Obscure trilogy. But Volume 3, Detroit: Ed Wingate's Empire / Unreleased Motown, proved pivotal. Passion, persistence and a healthy scoop of favor from above blossomed after a few months in the City of Angels, I secured an internship at Motown. A bright-eyed but precociously ardent 23-year-old advocate for the company's catalog, I was elevated to the fledgling Catalog Development department after paying my dues answering phones and filing. A campaign celebrating the legacy of Marvin Gaye was planned for 1994. I offered up to my boss the searing "This Love Starved Heart (It's Killing Me)," which I bathed in from that cassette during my transcontinental journey, as a candidate for a collection of unreleased recordings to accompany Marvin's three vital early to mid-'70s studio albums. "Love Starved Heart" was not only selected but became the title track. As a promotional piece, we issued a seven-inch of the song in a picture sleeve that used The Temptations "Beauty Is Only Skin Deep" as the style guide. The following year, I put forth another Marvin cut from that cassette, the original take of "Lonely Lover," for consideration for the career box set. It made the cut, joined by a reprise appearance of "Love Starved Heart" on that retrospective. In time, other cuts from that cassette would see proper release. The Marvelettes' "Boy From Crosstown" and The Lollipops' "Look What You've Done Boy" were boosted to a various artist year-by-year exploration series. I compiled and supervised a Ric-Tic / Golden World retrospective; my heart quickens to this day when I recall seeing the tape box spines labeled "GOLDEN WORLD" in the Motown vault. Tentatively titled Moonlighting, I parted ways with the company before the project was completed.

In the midst of the Marvin Gaye campaign, Kent's Adrian Croasdell visited Los Angeles. During lunch, I asked, "Are you familiar with 'Open The Door To Your Heart' by Joe Young? A friend put it on a tape for me once but he didn't have much info on it. "Yeah, Joe E. Young & The Tonics," he said. "a group of West Indian kids, they were on the Toast label." In the mid-nineties I was on the online record marketplace gemm.com looking for reference sources for a project. A thought struck: Search = Joe E. Young & the Tonics Results... Joe E. Young & The Toniks Soul Buster Toast. Adrenaline sparked through me. I emailed the seller in a fury: "Does this album have 'Open The Door To Your Heart' on it?" The reply from the UK lagged in the time zones. An unread email awaited when I logged in the next morning: "Yes it does."

References : Genzlinger, Neil. "Lou Ottens, Father of Countless Mixtapes, Is Dead at 94." New York Times online edition, March 11, 2021.
https://www.nytimes.com/2021/03/11/arts/music/lou-ottens-dead.html?searchResultPosition=1   Puckett,   Jeffrey   Lee. "Mixtapes Are the Original Playlists, All Thanks to Lou Ottens." Discogs   Blog,   March   15,   2021.
https://blog.d

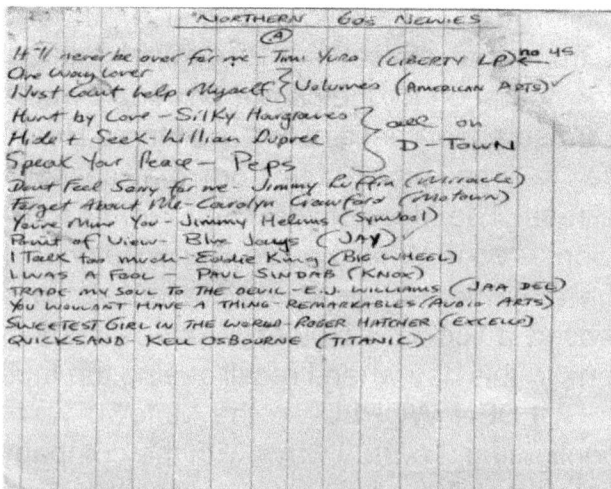

The Original Tracklist card © Dana Smart

The Magnificent Seven © Dana Smart

97

Chapter 9

Steve Trindall's 55 Year Northern Soul Journey

In this chapter I can offer the odd story about my journey through Northern Soul, never sure how to start stories like this so let's go straight to the beginning. I was born in the Scunthorpe area to the Jollands family in September 1951. I was named Barry Anthony Jollands and within nine months had been adopted by my present family who lived in Cleethorpes and gave me a good life and my present name, Stephen Bradley Trindall. We were not poor but definitely not rich, I would say we were "hard up" and a family living week to week. Through good luck and good fortune my adoptive parents were made an offer from a family friend which enabled us to move to Humberston, a country village where we had a chance to own a place of our own. I think I was around five or six at that time. I had some good mates in Humberston and still have contact with many of them today. Forgetting the years of playing out with my mates between the age of four and twelve, I now bring my story forward to when I was around thirteen or fourteen years old and had an insatiable appetite for music. I played trumpet and trombone in the local band and started listening to pirate radio but couldn't find anything with the "pull" to make that my genre. One of my friends had an older brother called Mike who worked on the Humber Bank (Laporte's I think) and was into what we now term as Northern Soul. When he was at home, he had lots of music blasting out from a reel to reel tape machine and would play it for us when we got to his house. As time went on, the music he got from his mates who had portable tape machines (we all remember them) became nearly impossible to remember as the volume they had was overwhelming. I asked where they got all this music from and he mentioned a couple of places they went to, also recorded off the radio and some of the people they met shared their tapes. When they shared these record-ings he made playlists for us which was very technical for those days. He advised me to listen to pirate radio to hear alternative types of music which I told him I did.

Mike told me to tune my little transistor radio with tho hearing aid earpiece late at night to Radio Luxembourg and begin writ-ing down the tracks that I really liked and he would record them for me. Not that many were written down at first as they had to be played right through for me to decide and by then I lost track of the artist. I had to wait until they came round again partly due to the poor reception on those early transistor radios. It really started in earnest for me like I said around late 1964 early 1965, not sure of the exact date, with my best mate's brother (yes, I know a familiar story!) who was into this music that got you off the couch. It was fascinating and seemed to grab me right from the soul (pardon the pun).

As I said they were playing a lot of sounds that I had not heard and I spent many hours listening to what he had on tape (reel to reel) and trying to find that style on radio, usually without suc-cess.

This was 1965 and, being just fourteen, I was like a sponge for any information I could get my hands on. After some time prov-ing myself by looking after the tapes and returning them on time, I was eventually asked if I wished to go with him and his mates at weekends to venues they visited. Having an extra person to split the costs with made sense. Over the coming months and years I managed to go with them starting once a month then once a fortnight then every week so I got a job at Tates super-market to pay my way. One journey we took in an old Morris Minor should have taken two hours and ended up taking six. It was snowing and the car had a faulty fuel pump and kept stop-ping, so by hitting the glove compartment it started to tick again, it was stop start, stop start, but we got there in the end.

On the way home we mastered the art of keeping the pump going by hitting the glove box in just the right place. But then the clutch went! The driver managed to get us home just using the revs to change gear. By the end of 1969 I had an apprenticeship and was able to contribute more. We visited venues in Manchester, Stoke, Wolverhampton and Bolton. Then came the seventies and we went to venues such as Wigan, St Ives, Blackpool, Nottingham, Cleethorpes, and Stafford. These trips developed over the years to what we called "roulette weekends'', never knowing where we were going until we all set off and chose the venue by majority vote. The country was our oyster, we had ideas where to go as we had our regular haunts. This included Samantha's on Friday night, Sounds Manchester on Saturday evening, Wigan Casino on Saturday Night, Wigan Baths on Sunday morning and Cleethorpes Pier on Sunday. By now, the original group had gone their separate ways and a new alliance was formed with others more my age. I was still travelling to the same venues just with different people. There were many variations to these weekends as I said, with the venues usually decided at the last minute. I frequented the Pier more when the Saturday all-nighters got underway, rather than travelling so much. Here are a few memories I have from the various clubs we frequented.

VA VA's

I remember one time at Va Va's when Richard Searling was playing a track on the British Philips label by Frankie & the Classicals called "What Shall I Do?" I only remember this because of the buzz it caused on the night. The breaking of many Northern Soul classics happened there, the most famous one of which was "Tainted Love" by Gloria Jones, a song covered by Soft Cell in 1981 reaching the top spot in the pop charts. Other Northern Soul classics that I remember being spun inside that small venue included "My Dear Heart" by Shawn Robinson, "I Got To Find Me Somebody" by the Vel-Vets,

"Slow Fizz" by The Sapphires and "Stranger In My Arms" by Lynn Randell, which I believe was one of the last tracks to be played there. The interior of the venue at Va Va's was certainly different. The DJ pit was below floor level and we had to bend down to request a track. The walls had mirrors on them making anyone who was "chemically enhanced" freak out when seeing themselves!

THE CATACOMBS (aka "CATS")

The Catacombs club lasted a short time but it was brilliant. It was in a former Wolverhampton smelting works, helping to grow Northern Soul from the earliest days. I only went twice and don't remember why. It was commonly known as "The Cats". The club began playing Northern Soul around October 1968 and was one of the earliest Northern Soul venues on the scene. The dance floor was on the second floor but it looked more like a cellar. Horrible condensation would drip down the walls, generated by the heat of enthusiastic, often amphetamine driven dancers. The song that reminds me most of the Cats is "Psychedelic Soul" by Saxie Russell as this track just blew me away at that time and also went massive at Cleethorpes. The way it echoed down the passages still plays in my mind. The Catacombs as a Northern Soul club ranged from the sublime to the downright dangerous. They served orange squash by the pint and had a fire escape made of wood. It was not what I thought of as a Northern Soul club being a teenager but I went only a handful of times and did not have a lot of experience.

THE GOLDEN TORCH

The Torch was more like a theatre than a nightclub in the early days. First opened in 1965 in Tunstall, used to host music groups such as Black Sabbath and T-Rex before becoming a Northern Soul club.

101

By the time 1970 came around, Colin Curtis & Keith Minshull approached Chris Burton, the owner of the Torch, with the idea of starting an all-nighter based on soul. The growing attraction of Northern Soul, popularised by venues such as the Twisted Wheel, which hosted many live acts including Edwin Starr & the Stylistics, ensured the Torch all-nighters quickly turned it into a sought after venue. Still today it is spoken about fondly by soul folk old and new.

BLACKPOOL MECCA

Not one of my most favourite of places, I went a few times but preferred Cleethorpes and Wigan in all honesty. Still, it was a very popular venue indeed with the then unusual feature of an escalator taking you to the first floor. I have blurred memories of my times there with Kev Hildreth but seem to remember that the people who went to the Highland Room from Cleethorpes were those who later started to turn first to what was termed "Modern Soul" as that seemed to be the way the Highland Room was heading. Again, I was not a regular so maybe I have blinkered recollections?

WIGAN CASINO

Wigan allnighters were another type of beast altogether, from the "Squaddies" outside, the Beachcomber in the downstairs swamp, rowdy queues and a yelling bouncer (Mick) to the magic of the ballroom and just the feel of the place from the start to the finish. The smell of Brut , the floor covered in talc, the spinners, the acrobats and the footwork were all brilliant. Mr M's, a room within Wigan Casino, was in my opinion, the place to be with the best music. Even though we had danced all night when the famous "Three Before Eight" was played in the ball-room it brought much sadness to know the night was coming to an end. I found some of the oldies nights were sometimes sparsely attended but still great for those there.

When Dave Critchley came with me we used to divert to New-ton-le-Willows to pick up two girls whose names elude me. After Wigan Casino we then went off to the Wigan Baths to wake up. I don't know if anyone who went to Wigan can remember my cars. The first one was a black Hillman Hunter Estate with the "Talk of the North " badge painted on covering the bonnet. The second was a VW Beetle with a huge black fist on the front. They were always parked at the side of the Casino.

THE TWISTED WHEEL

The Wheel was a dark, sweaty, basement club close to Pic-cadilly Station. It had grown to be the garden of a whole new music scene and its name, The Twisted Wheel is still known today. It really took off around 1965 when it moved from Bra-zennose Street to Whitworth Street. A great deal of artists played there bringing a range of genres but that night of nights, the grand opening of Whitworth Street brought the Spencer Da-vis Group, Ike & Tina Turner, Jimmy Ruffin, Edwin Starr & Ben E. King and others performed to crowds who packed a venue which only held a couple of hundred people.

LINCOLN DRILL HALL

At Lincoln Drill Hall, I remember Dave Godin, who coined the term "Northern Soul ", playing sounds sometimes from Emidiscs (purpose cut lacquer discs). At that time, DJs played Emi Discs as the "real ones' ' (original recordings) were too hard to find and too good not to hear in a big venue. In my opinion the scene would not have got as big without pressings, Emi Discs etc. In fact a famous DJ sold me an Emidisc with "Sitting in my Class" by Ronnie McNeir on one side and "Beyond 2001"by Rufus Wood on the other hand. The playing of these discs didn't detract from the success of the venues as all the people wanted was the music, they didn't care about where the music came from. They just wanted to dance!

At that time there was no standard way of dressing. Everyone was "smartish" but Northern Soul was not yet established as a universal movement with a lot of ex-skinheads and mods taking the leap. It seemed the mods brought their smart dress code with them. The mix of clothes in those days was very interesting and catered well for me being on the large side and not having to buy a whole new wardrobe. Later in the early seventies a different look came in with sweatbands, v neck t-shirts and "baggies' ' with broad waistbands and lots of pockets & ideal for sweaty dancing. By now a lot of the soul kids were wearing "Keep The Faith" badges either on their shirts or the very popular "Nighter Bag". They were also adorned with Wigan and Torch badges. Although the seventies were blessed with a plethora of venues and magic times, they also saw the slippery slide to commercialisation through Wigan opening its doors to the TV. This altered the Northern Soul movement and did seem to slow it down, but in a good way in my opinion, also during that time some venues closed their doors. In those that remained nothing altered. Out came the talcum powder and the dance floor came alive with gyrating bodies and acrobatic dancers. I was a big lad but found I was good at dancing because of my feel for the music. The fact was, outside of all-nighters, all-dayers etc., blokes often refused to dance. Everyone would point and laugh as most did not understand. I guess this is what makes our "soul family" so special as no one judges a dancer (unless in a competition). They dance where and how the music takes them. For me as time moved on after sampling many venues, I settled on only four venues for all-nighters but still travelled more for dayers. In those formative years I had to rely on others to get around until I passed my driving test and bought my first car which was a blue Austin A35. This little car gave me the freedom to go anywhere, any time. It also served as a bed for four when we were too tired to travel, and believe me you had to be tired to sleep four in a small car like that. It didn't take me long to upgrade to my Hillman Hunter and later my VW 1500.

CLEETHORPES PIER

Because of the lack of Northern Soul music in Cleethorpes and surrounding areas and having to contend with all the travelling, I was getting really tired driving here, there and everywhere every week. It was at least 140 miles there and 140 miles back so it was a relief when Colin and Mary Chapman (Mary later became known as "The Queen of Northern Soul") arrived and started the soul scene in Cleethorpes. I didn't go to the Duke of Wellington as I was otherwise engaged but I was there at the start of upstairs in the Winter Gardens. It was a great venue with a small crowd at first but equally as good as other places and more than welcoming. I know at first there were doubts around the longevity of the venue but the people were genuine so the numbers grew and grew quickly each week. Although I still travelled, it did cut down on the mileage every weekend. Mary and Colin were credited with multiple venues such as the Duke of Wellington, Cleethorpes Pier, Winter Gardens and Lincoln Drill Hall. People were hiring buses from everywhere to go to the Pier All-nighters and the Gardens. All-nighters were on somewhere every weekend and people spent their last pound to get there. This was the start of an era never surpassed with venues putting on all-nighters, all-dayers, regular evenings and weekends. The Pier was so popular in its day with crowds awaiting entry right along the pier and onto the promenade itself. The Pier, in my opinion, was the greatest all-nighter and the most frequented in that era, rivalling Wigan Casino, to the point that the Casino hired the Winter Gardens on the same night as the Pier, bringing their best DJ crew and playing to about six people hoping to get the "Soulies" back. On the Pier, the crowds, the noise and the incessant "stomp stomp stomp" on the wooden decking was an experience no one could forget and nowhere else could rival in my opinion. It could even be heard at the Winter Gardens and walking between the two venues was like being inside the Pier all the way. Records such as "So Is The Sun" by World Column, "The Champion" by Willie Mitchell, "Manifesto" by James Lewis, "The Age Of The Wolf" by Susan Coleman and many many more may have contributed to the Pier sinking in the sands. If you were late to the Pier, that stomping from inside almost made you stay in the night air on the approach and listen outside to the stomping echoing around this seaside resort. Eventually the Winter Gardens dayers had a "Modern Room" upstairs where Soul Sam continued to flourish.

Mary and Colin never received the kudos they deserved from the Northern Soul community as a whole but they did everything to make it a great venue. They were first in line to help anyone who came their way in need. They paid DJs well but expected the best progressive records where possible. Mary and Colin gave up a great deal of their time and money helping people and are never mentioned in articles and programmes with the reverence they truly deserved. Mecca, the Wheel, the Torch, Wigan Casino, etc., all seem to be mentioned before Cleethorpes and yet, in essence, many considered it the best all-nighter in that era. Mary and Colin did a lot for the scene, the DJs and the people helping everyone that needed it with no regard to how it affected them personally. They were good people without a doubt. As a supplement, when not travelling or when we were broke, a great friend of mine of some forty seven years (Nick Borst & still mates to this day) had a gig as a DJ at the holiday camp in Humberston near Cleethorpes (the Beachcomber). This was for visiting people from all over the country. Within the boundary was a place called "The Boathouse" where we could dance and listen to a variety of music. The room was almost a mini Wigan without Mr M's. We went in at the front to the dancefloor and it had a balcony all around. After that closed in the evening it was Nick Borst's turn in his upstairs room above the main ballroom called "The Flightdeck". This was where he played a great variety of music and I used to give him a hand now and then. He played Motown and Northern when the right people were in and always filled the floor which was constructed of stainless steel and very small but good. Lots of locals were there too, I will name a few but after some forty nine years since

I last went there my mind is getting misty. If I have forgotten anyone, please don't be offended. Here goes.. Nick Borst, myself, Debbie Shum (nee Ridlington), Dean Daly, Lizzie Foster (nee Gray), Bob Watson, Gary Lee, Pete Burke, Kev Muse, Gary Muse (Passed on, he was a great guy), Lynn Vince, Lynn Raynor, Miko Simpson, Dawn Fenty (nee Smith), Elaine Denis, Ross Machon, Wayne Townsend, Martin Johnson, Ray Oxley, Phil Newton, John Todd, Graham Bemrose, Gino Pavone and Lesley Newton.

One of today's most popular DJs and a friend from many moons ago, Sean Chapman, used to come to our venues before he started his journey through the Northern Soul jungle. Nick wouldn't like to be reminded of this, but we went on holiday to Norwich in a caravan and I took a box of records to play in the caravan. We were out and about and got invited to a soul dance in a venue in Norwich, the name of which I've forgotten. It was such a long time ago but because I had records they invited me to DJ and it was a great night , great times & great people. As stated, during the week we had great soul nights at Tiffany's on a Monday which helped keep the weekend going in our minds. We both had a gig at St. John's Hall (circa 1972/3) where we had the freedom of no politics or "soul police" and we were able to please the audience by request. I must point out that in those days it was easier to play to the crowd as the volume of sounds was small compared to today. This night was mainly for the locals but I am hazy about that. I have a couple of old photos but not of printable quality. Another venue was the "Orchard Room" with Dave Raistrick on a Wednesday night in sunny Mablethorpe. I believe Terry Coates was there too? I would just like to move briefly forward to 2021. Colin has passed away and Mary is ill. She could have made lots of money and walked away, but ask any DJ or person that was close to either of them and they will tell you they were the best!

SCUNTHORPE

One of the Cleethorpes resident DJs, Rick Scott, along with his girlfriend Linda Lewis (not the singer), started a soul night in Scunthorpe on a Friday night and they invited me down ("Soul Scene") to help monitor behaviour and that became a regular thing for a while. It was a good night, supplying a broad taste of soul music for those unable to get to the dayers or nighters. You have to remember that, as the months and years passed and more Northern Soul records were found, the more diverse the tastes became and the more factions formed. As time moved on, the Cleethorpes DJ roster grew from a few locals such as Rick Scott, Dick Jervis, etc., to include a wider variety of names such as Rick Todd, Chris Dalton, Poke, Bub, Soul Sam, Dave Appleyard, Pep, John Manship and myself in a small way (very honoured) which brought a larger crowd to each event. My apologies to the unmentioned as I have not included the newer group of DJs! During that time, I still travelled to Blackpool, Wigan, Notts Palais, Samantha's, Sounds etc. I took many people with me over time because it was difficult to get to the venues from Cleethorpes or Grimsby and all these people wanted to do was widen their knowledge and experience. During these times, we didn't have a great deal of money between us. We used Hartshead Moor truck stop to change and get ready for Wigan, also on the way back after we had gone swimming at Wigan baths. This was to get changed for Cleethorpes and share a bacon butty and cup of tea because we couldn't afford one each after paying fuel, entrance fees, paying to go swimming and sometimes buying records. I mostly went with Dave Critchley, Big Rod (forgot his surname) and Chris Sparkes. Although there were many others such as Kev Hildreth, Pete Burke, Dawn Smith (now Dawn Fenty) and Mandy Heywood (Spike). I remember being so hard up that when I blew a tyre on my car I couldn't afford to buy a new one. Then when I stopped and looked underneath I saw that the other side was showing the wire too so that was two needed.

So when we got to Manchester late in the evening we found a scrap yard, climbed the fence, dodged the dogs and got two second hand ones off the scrapped cars with the two dogs going crazy. We managed to trap them inside a van otherwise we would have been dead meat. We all loved the trip although it was tiring. We loved the venues, the DJs and most of all the people we met, many became friends for life.

Interestingly, I meet people here in Australia who went to Wigan but I cannot say I remember them. This shows the density of the crowds that were there and the sheer amount of people wandering around. In fact, people I knew from Cleethorpes went to Wigan and I didn't see them either. The DJs in those days were great. Most of the time they were willing to share their knowledge and what records they had played because they were really rare and they knew they were safe because the ordinary soulie couldn't afford that kind of money or even dream of finding another copy. There were many "cover ups" too in those days, done to protect the true identity of the latest rarity and preserve exclusivity for that DJ. The DJs also played Emidiscs when they couldn't buy the original. Most DJs did this (I say this as I saw many playing those heavy discs) and there were no "Soul Police" knocking them for it either. The audiences were just appreciative of the music. The record bar at Wigan was like a wrestling ring. People clamoured to buy the 50 pence release of the week before it sold out, whereas others were busy rummaging through those record boxes trying to find the elusive monster hit or completing a collection they had started.

The Cleethorpes DJs were a great mix and played a wide variety of sounds. One of those DJs, Rick Scott along with his girlfriend Linda, used to put a mini-bus on every two weeks to go to an all-nighters at Cleethorpes known as "The Talk of The North". There they would turn the sound down part way through a record, for example " The Champion" or "So Is The Sun" and all we could hear was the shoes stomping and hands clapping, it was fantastic.

109

You have to remember that all the dancers were mostly wearing leather soled shoes which contributed to the sound they made. Someone with short hair, 30 inch bottom bags with lots of pleats, school ties and cardigans, flat caps and brown/black brogue shoes seemed to have the dress code of the day. These new types of shoes were flat with leather soles to aid dancing, but deadly on a talcum patch. A guy called Tony used to make trousers to order at the Wintergardens and they were ordered one week to get them the next. They had sewn in pleats, bags, or whatever was specified! I saw a young man outside the all-nighter at Wigan where there was a disturbance with older men of about thirty years of age going up to the younger ones and saying "DS" (Drug Squad) "empty your bag". The lads did as they were told and the false Squaddies took all of their gear (amphetamines) off them. Strangely enough, that (fake) DS member and his girlfriend were dancing really fast at the front of the stage inside as it was all just a scam to get free drugs. With these being older, none of the younger ones dared say anything to them. I must just mention a young man called "Woody", a friend of Dave Critchley, who would swallow any-thing pill-wise you put in front of him. I believe he is still with us but I don't know how. Cleethorpes Winter Gardens was a sea-side show bar ,dance hall , wedding venue and they had eve-rything going on there. Record fairs, ”bags ball” & “ a grab a granny night” on Wednesday, brass bands and even scooter gatherings. All good soul clubs were of varied condition inside except this one. The Winter Gardens had a bit of class but was transformed when the right people and the right music turned up. I used to work there as a bouncer four nights a week & great times. I was not in the UK when the Gardens closed but it still made me extremely sad. DJs, promoters and record dealers such as Ian Levine, like him or not, were the very backbone of early days Northern Soul. Ian would often go on record hunts to the States to buy demos and rare records that had never re-ally seen their day after their first release in the US. It gave a DJ kudos to play a new discovery at a club, which is why DJs would always be on the hunt for the next biggest soul tune, digging deep into US warehouse archives. Other DJs leading this charge were Richard Searling and Colin Curtis. Moving forward in time again to address social media comments, it would be nice to sign into Facebook one day without the sanctimonious few trying to run the Northern Soul scene. Don't play this, don't play that, this is shite, played too many times, I have a demo, well I have a WHITE demo, you can't play a boot, I went to Wigan so I know it all! Some of these so-called 'soulies' history only start at Wigan or later. About 30 million people now claim to have been to Wigan and some are now undermining the scene. Some of these people were barely out of nappies when they claim to have been out and about, get real people we do what pleases us and the crowd. If we wish to play an Emidisc 40 times in a session, it is the individual's call and better still if people dance. I have been around the scene for some 55 years now and have never been so disappointed in all that time with so few. If you own a box of vinyl carvers and it makes you happy, good on you, forming a group, being an administrator or owning an incredible set of OV (original vinyl) does not make you an expert or a DJ and although I have been around many years I do not claim to have a full box of OV either although I have had success as a DJ. I wish for the clock to turn back as I yearn for the times when there was no judgement, just friendship. I believe prices of OV are pushed up just because of these people, yes they are rarer now but prices are astronomical.

I now move on to modern times as I emigrated to Australia in 1990 with my wife and two children and landed in Perth. As we settled and found our way around, I missed the music but still had my own to play. It would have been around 1995 when I saw an ad for the Irish Club playing Northern Soul music. I went to it in the early years but it would be a few years later when I returned and started to DJ there. This venue was started by Pete Fowler, originally from Chorley and has lasted twenty four years to date. It is a good venue with DJs rotating every month but there are too many now to cope with. I was known for my

100 mph stompers and oldies only. I had a distinct aversion to a lot of "Modern" music. It didn't grab me like the oldies. I also DJ'd on the yearly National Weekenders in Queensland, Sydney, Perth etc. but the Irish Club is the longest running venue & kudos to Pete Fowler for the longevity, during those times, I got to collect some magic records. sold a few, swapped a few and of course bought more. I also met hundreds of wonderful people, all like-minded with regards to the music.

There are people that I am still in contact with from that humble beginning right through my journey to now. I do not attend these venues any more due to medical problems and the fact I live in Perth, Australia, but the sounds still resonate around the house and in the car. I still own a substantial amount of vinyl and I am happy to play them at home now. My years being into Northern Soul now are clocking up fifty five this year from discovering the music to today. K.T.F. to all readers. I would like to add as an addendum to my story that these recollections are mine. Only seen through my eyes. If I have forgotten someone or you think something is not accurate I am now sixty eight going on sixty nine and it was an awful long time ago. So my abject apologies.

RICK SCOTT, CHRIS DALTON, TOM PADDERSON © Steve Trindall

Lady's unknown with Bub a well loved DJ © Steve Trindall

Nick Borst & Steve Trindall © Steve Trindall

PAUL ROWAN UNKNOWN OTHERS © S Trindall

NORM PILLAY © S Trindall

PIER DJ's EARLY DAYS L TO R CHRIS DALTON, POKE, JOHN MAN-SHIP, SOUL SAM, RICK TODD AND RICK SCOTT. FRONT AND CEN-TRE MARY CHAPMAN © Steve Trindall

CHAPTER 10

How A Collector Stumbled On To Northern Soul

By Nay Nassar

Back in 1956 when I was fourteen years old, I bought my first record, it was The Penguins doing "Earth Angel" on DeTo Records for the princely sum of $1.25. In the following seventy five (75) years, I have evolved from a kid who just wanted 'The Hits' to a collector who appreciates and enjoys music from the 1950's right up to current musical trends. I have come to understand and appreciate the fact that categorizing music by genres is not an exact science and musical genres don't just change overnight but evolve. Vocal Group records did not just begin in 1954 and end in 1963. Many great local groups had releases before 1954 and beyond 1963, but when you meet other collectors and inquire what they collect, you will generally hear: Groups, Soul, Rhythm and Blues, Rock, Northern Soul etc. I stumbled upon 'specialized' record collecting first when I met my old friend from Rhode Island who went by the name "The Duke of Doo-Wop" (the late Steve Rothwell). When Rocky (as he was called) and I would go to Val Shively's or Clifton Music, we were never competing for the same records. Rocky always favored the up-tempo groups and I would always lean towards the ballads. This was the first time that I realized record collecting was a specialized hobby and records other than the hits were focused on and collected. During my working life in the Insurance profession, I was fortunate to travel the U.S. and on many occasions visited way out places that an ordinary collector, based locally, may not get the chance to see.

There was no Internet and barely working telephones at some record shops so calling ahead only became worthwhile if you had formed a physical relationship with a store. More often than not you would be surprised or dismayed depending on the luck of the draw in finding a shop. Many of the better sources were well known among collectors, yet some were guarded secrets, until the dam broke so to speak. One of the earliest recollections I have, even before my job afforded me to travel, was buying records for pennies then selling them on. This became a source of education over and above the collecting bug and to realize that some records could be worth small fortunes always left one with the anguish to flip a record, swap it or keep it. Fortunately (even though I sold my entire collection twice) I was able each time to amass a collection of beauties I was proud of. Outside of certain genres like Northern Soul, many group collectors would also strive to be "completionist", buying every single record by a group, sometimes even if they did not like it! I have met many record collectors over the years who only collected: Beatles, Rhythm and Blues, Black Groups or only White Groups. I thought this to be crazy when I heard some collectors tried to run certain Record Labels.

When I first met Jan Lisewski "Soul Man Jan" in 2004 or so, I began to appreciate there were collectors who specialized even more by delving into some sub-genres that many of us never knew existed. Jan was born and raised in the United Kingdom and his musical interests started in the mid 1960's as a teenager. He started out as a soul music enthusiast and was never interested in the British Invasion artists, but instead he preferred the soul sounds coming from the United States via the offshore pirate radio stations. Our chance meeting was a curiosity in itself, when we were introduced by a mutual friend Alan, a former colleague of mine from the insurance business and he was also one of Jan's clients in his marketing and graphics business. Alan knew we both had a passion for collecting records but never assumed or realized we were working in different genres, but that did not matter.

After our initial meeting I think we both came away learning something about our respective genres and soon we both realized that it was a thin line between Doo-Wop and soul in many instances. I learned that as a teenager Jan made the weekend trek from his hometown of Derby to the clubs in the North (Wigan Casino etc.) This was where the northern soul phenomenon was born and named "Northern Soul." From the videos I've seen the songs were predominantly up-tempo and the dancers would dance in a modified "Line Dance" style (as we would term it in the U.S.A.). Anyone who grew up in Rhode Island would know what Line Dancing is. These dances would begin late and run all night long.

Most 'Group Collector's like myself had a difficult time getting our heads around exactly what defined the "Northern Soul Sound". Most of the 'Vocal Group' collectors that I knew favored Black groups or White groups and looked for harmony, some like myself liked both. I considered the entry of the Beatles on the scene (1963-64) as the death of the 'group sound.' Many in the U.S.A. like myself continued collecting groups beyond 1964 or so, but a large percentage of the early group collectors either died, got married or for a variety of reasons left the hobby. At this point, the late 60's and early 70's, the British invasion and Soul music was dominating our charts. Many of the early Doo-Wop groups also had to make the transition from simple vocal group harmony top more orchestrated and 'pop' leaning compositions so as to survive developing audiences and I believe at this time during the mid and certainly late sixties a lot of songs were 'transitional' in nature, neither Doo-Wop, nor pure soul which had exploded into the new generation of young Americans.

Indeed as Motown professed it was "The Sound Of Young America." Also, at this point in time, the Europeans were coming to the U.S. in search of vinyl records and they were looking for Soul music and this new 'upbeat' sound that they called "Northern Soul." Since the Group collectors in the U.S. had picked the stores clean of 50s and early 60s records, the majority of the records still readily available were records from the mid 60's and later on the major as well as indie labels that group collectors either passed on or were just lying around there for the picking. When the Brits, Germans, & Japanese etc, came to our shores looking for these records they cleaned out our inventories and dominated the markets for soul and this new thing called "Northern." Collectors like myself shifted easily from groups to soul music without a glitch. "Northern" however, was a little more difficult for me to appreciate. Early on, I realized there were records that I liked as a group record but they were also coveted by the "Northern" crowd!

If we could split a record down the middle along its thinnest edge you could often peel off one side for the group collectors and the other side for "Northern" collectors!

Back in the mid 1970's I used to receive weekly packages of records from Val Shively (owner then and now of R+B Records). Since Val did not collect or appreciate white 'Group' records (that has since changed), he would send me records all priced between $3 - $10 each and I could keep what I wanted and return the rest with my payment check. These records were almost entirely white 'Group' records. Among these records were: The Steinway's on Oliver, Johnny Maestro on Scepter etc., just to name two. Most of the later releases were on labels like Jubilee, Josie, Parkway, Cameo, Columbia and other labels that continued to put out records into the late 60's and early 1970's, were checked over very carefully by our " Foreign Invaders" who were looking for that up-tempo sound that was good to dance to and readily available. The shocker to me was that a high percentage of the songs that fit the Northern sound were actually by white artists, like Paul Anka "I Can't Help Loving You."

As a radio "Oldies" Disc Jockey (1972- Now), I had occasion to meet many artists who were caught up in this thing called

"Northern Soul." Back in 1989, whilst in Baltimore, Maryland on WTMD, I put a record on by an artist by the name of Leroy Taylor. My phone immediately lit up and as I answered, the caller said "Hey Nay, you're playing my record!"

The record that I played was "Hey You" on Columbia from 1963. I think I said something like "Glad you liked it, and it's your record." thinking it was his favorite. "No," he said, "that's my record, I made it!" I invited Leroy down to the show the following week and he brought down several of his releases. He shocked me with a ballad on the Tan label called "If I" which is a great group sound that I'm still looking for. He also whipped out a copy of "I'll Understand" on Shrine by Leroy Taylor and The Four Kays. It was too rough to play and I didn't like it anyway. Every release on Shrine is in my understanding a Northern Soul Monster. Once whilst getting a fitting for a new business suit at a Boston tailor's I noticed some rather distinguished black individuals being measured for some exotic suits. I inquired about who they were and was told this is the group to be relaunched as the Tavares. I went over and spoke with them briefly and after introducing myself as a record collector we made the connection. I knew them as a much earlier group after the disbanding of Linda and the Del Rios, named Chubby and the Turnpikes. In fact, I have had the fortune to meet a number of groups and artists through my radio shows and by writing for "Echoes of the Past" magazine. In fact, to continue the story of my friendship with Jan we still at the time of writing hunt for records together today (RIP Jan). Jan and I hosted a radio show in our hometown of Sarasota for 10 years, The Doo-Wop 2 Soul Show, after that stint we syndicated the show and it still airs on "Remember Then Radio" (Internet only) and WGCH in Greenwich, Connecticut. As a lifelong Group Collector, I'm still on the hunt for elusive sounds like "If I" on the Tan label by Leroy Taylor, but when I come upon a record which has that "Northern Sound " I know that I face stiff competition for it. My only hope is that more of the remaining Group collectors will give up the ship and that this 'Northern' thing will only be a passing fancy.

120

If I live long enough, I may find out. When Soul Man Jan and I would go record hunting we are seldom in competition with each other. He will like one side and I will like the other. Long live the 45 RPM recording.

Nay Nasser © Nay Nasser

Chapter 11

My Soul Music Journey by Tony Gallagher

When you talk about a musical journey it's not just a journey of discovering music, it's a trial of endurance especially if you just happen to drop on a music scene that not only captures your imagination, it drags you through one of the most exciting turbulent times of my teenage life and beyond. Never in my wildest dreams did I think that at the young age of fourteen would I be dancing to Dobie Gray "Out on the Floor" in a local Youth Club deep inside my home town of Wigan. I had seen my Mum and Dad dancing together to Frank Sinatra, Bing Crosby and all those wonderful heroes of past generations, but for me a mere boy dancing solo and not knowing or caring who, or what was watching, it was my space, my emotion, my heart, my soul, my music that drove me on to this very day 50 years later. The Music I discovered was not your white Caucasian although in later years I did realise that some of the Musical Soul Artists where actually white, not the people what drove me to a new discovery where Black Soul Music was hitting the United Kingdom in the sixties, Tamala Motown was the catalyst, what came next turned a generation of teenagers with no great expectations, a job maybe, marriage, kids, the usual follow the narrative in the depressing early 1970s from the Midlands to the far North of England into the greatest teenage musical, fashionable revolution that if you missed it then you had never lived in my opinion. The late sixties and early seventies gave way to the Fashion and Music identification of who, what you are, what you stood for with the word discipline not entered into our Dictionary unlike the post war generations, i.e. our Mums and Dads. Mods, Skinheads, Smooth Heads, Crombie Boys and the one we never mention, the Head Bangers, heavy metal music followers for the unconverted. My early introduction to all the teenage cultures was always at a Football Match, you would see the lot, the

Skinhead with his Levi or stay pressed trousers, the famous checked Ben Sherman or Fred Perry Shirt, braces, Harrington and those stand out Doctor Martin boots in Tuxan Red polished better than any Police Sergeants on duty anytime of the day. The Smooth boy, the Mod, the Crombie boys similarly dressed but with a decent hair style long, short, styled to match the style of clothing and personality. So you ask what was this teenage music that prepared you for a nocturnal life of travelling, hitch hiking, bus, coach, train or if you were Lucky a lift with a group of Friends in Dads car usually late evening when everyone else had the good sense to go home after last orders at the pub around 11am. Northern Soul was the name, the raw, stomping, emotional, obscure beat that just grabbed you by the Throat and never let go. Fourteen years of age going on 64 and this Scene, Music, Fashion will never let go. The Story's I could tell would make a book, that by the way I am writing currently. I wanted to tell you about my Favourite Soul tunes, I have so many, each one providing a memory of a person, a venue, a time and place, it's too hard, some are very sad, some are very happy, you see, that's what this Music does to you, it can lift you so high and at the drop of a hat, you hear a soulful sound that just brings all your emotions to a tearful end. We all have many stories, memories about the Northern Soul Scene, mines just another one. I would never want to change how my teenage life was directed by Music and to this very day it remains so. Will our Soul Scene survive the next 10 years? Ask me that in a year or two, I have no time for this World at present. I hate everything about it, Soul Music was founded on a black slave movement that provided the music from the Soul into the Church for singing, dancing and relief from the grind of being a Slave. Freedom was the word, they sang that word loud and clear. I sing that word today some 100 years later. My Soul still fights with them, I now know how it feels to have your Freedoms taken away. My Fight will end when my Soul says so. To the Presidents, Kings, Queens and Politicians, I will never ever surrender my right to choose how I manage my body, my Health. I have no questions to answer. The World that's being created is Evil. So take your proposed World to the Devil, he will accommodate you, not I and many others. God Willing we are the Mighty, My Soul will remain intact just like my Music. Nothing can ever take it away.

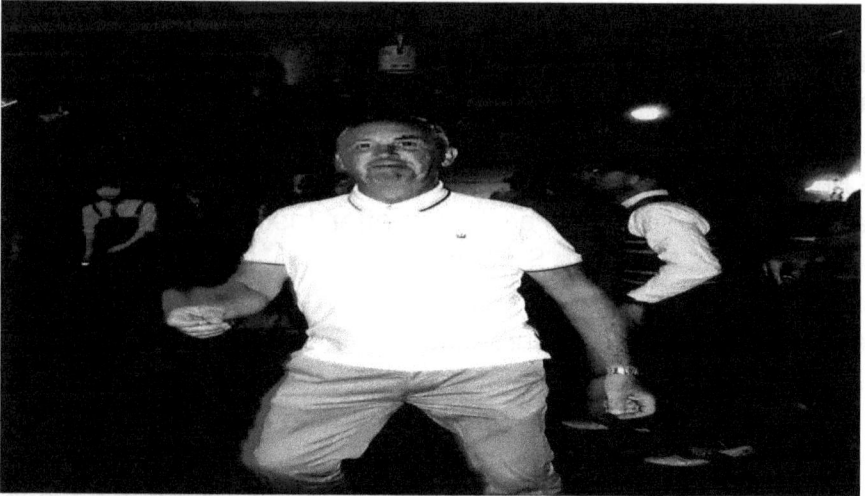

Tony Gallagher out on the floor in Japan © Tony Gallagher

2019, The Jam Jam club, Kobe Japan © Tony Gallagher.

Below: Tony Gallagher In Full Flight © Arw Photography

Wigan Casino, 1973 Dance Floor © Tony Gallagher

Chapter 12

Ronnie Walker by Dennis Locantore

This continues the Ronnie Walker story that is in Book One Chapter three of John Warren "Our Soul Music Journey ". I first met the late Ronnie Walker in the mid-'70s while wanting to get better as a bassist and play music other than rock. Until that time I had played in bands playing some Progressive Rock like Yes, which was the most demanding music outside of jazz within that sphere of influence. The Sound of Philadelphia was making its mark on the world and none of the players in these bands could play with the feel of those avatars or for that matter their predecessor Motown. Ronnie Baker was an influence as was James Jamerson so I needed to play this kind of music. Only Chris Squire of YES was playing anywhere near as demanding bass parts outside of jazz and R&B. So because I wanted to play more demanding bass parts and music, I began scouring the personals for ads for a bass player with people who were new to me. It was while doing this that I saw an ad for a bass player in a band. I spoke to Ronnie and he said he was playing locally at the Wilson Motel's cocktail lounge in my city Camden NJ. That was good as I was not driving and relied on my father to get to and from any auditions. I came there and sat in with the band which didn't have a bass player at the time as I recall. I made enough of an impression with my quick ears and natural grooves that Ronnie gave me my final audition piece for the following week at another local club. That was "Magic's In The Air ". It was originally played on a keyboard in a Moog bassline so it was rather a demanding part which was intended to confound me, first by figuring it out and then playing it on electric bass. I came in the following week and aced the audition with my skill at doing so. And so I began slightly over a year of playing with Ronnie Walker in his band. At first named MON-TAGE and then renamed ECSTACY, the band was working out of the Norman "Jolly" Joyce's agents' office for bookings at nightclubs in the area. And we were getting to play some of the Philadelphia International stuff and R&B covers of the day like the Isley Bros & Barry White. We even used Herbie Hancock's Chameleon for our break tune. The only original that we performed at the time was "Magic's In The Air". I always wondered why we never performed "The Game Is Over " as that record was set to make a big splash with local airplay on the radio. But Capitol records pulled the record from distribution after a threatened lawsuit over the group's name who recorded it as Brown Sugar . The play "Bubbling' Brown Sugar" cost Ronnie what I believe to this day was to be an easy gold record for him and his partner Vincent Montana, Jr. We used to rehearse right in the living room at Ronnie's house at 5th and Lehigh Avenues.

I used to take the train into Philadelphia and the trolley right up 5th street to make rehearsals. Ronnie was being produced by Vince Montana Jr., at this time and doing stellar work on his records and others at the time. Ronnie and I even got to play on Fat Larry's Band "Center City ". It is Ronnie's guitar that initiates the groove in the intro. Through Ronnie, I got to play with the Salsoul Orchestra and did some other recording sessions. We also kept busy with gigs every week locally playing covers of hits in dance and nightclubs in Pennsylvania and New Jersey. The band members were Chuck Dekker and Ralph Bionsco on guitars and Sal LaBruna was our drummer when I started. Band members came and went and finally, we ended up with a keyboard player named Frank Huckins and John Goodheart on drums. We also had a girl singer with us during this time whose name escapes me now named Roberta (can't remember her last name).

Fast forward to the recent past I was honored to be asked and told him I would do it for nothing. He still made sure I could cover my travel costs for the bridge tolls and gas. Over a period of more than a year, we chipped away at the many songs he had written which needed bass lines.

Ronnie also contributed to a couple of songs I had written all the music for but could never finish lyrics to. As unassuming as he always was, after he heard the tracks he offered to "take a stab at them." What an understatement! One was a love ballad/movie theme that I had a title for called "No One More Beautiful" and the other a moderate tempo pop crossover groove which I had copy written as Sweet Dreams in my first collection of music on cassette tape to the Library of Congress. He also sang the wonderful lyrics to both rights over my music tracks without any effects or vocal sweeteners or overdubs. Very tough to do. After Ronnie did the vocals and lyric's Sweet Dreams became Just a Feeling. Hopefully, they will be released soon.

The CD FOR REAL, FOR REAL of all of Ronnie's songs that we labored over together, was just released in 2021 and is doing very well. The very last song he completed without needing a bass track is the mournful "I've Been Here Before" before he passed away unexpectedly from pneumonia. It is unbearably poignant. I started searching for records over 45 years ago & this is a list of what I found back then. I can remember just some of the records I had that my father foolishly forced me to get rid of years ago. Most were from flea markets, some yard sales, church bazaars and thrift stores. All were bought for 50 cents and no more than $1. If this doesn't make you sick nothing will. The list is in alphabetical order by artists names:

A
1) Dilly, Jeffrey Allen on Mala M-
2) Be Proud You're in Love, Gail Anderson on Salvador M-
3) Taking My Mind off Love, Carol Anderson on Whip VG
4) You're Getting Next To Me Baby, Jimmy Armstrong on Brothers Three M-
5) Tough Girl Billy, Arnell on Holly M-
6) The Hardest Part, Curtis Anderson on Brown Bag M-

7) Blow Me a Kiss, Wayne Anthony on Walana (hairline crack played VG+)

8) Too Young for Me, The Ambassadors on Fleet VG-

B

9) Because of My Heart, Frankie Beverly on Rouser VG+

10) I Won't Be Coming Back, J.D. Bryant on Shrine VG

11) She'll Come Running Back, Mel Britt on F.I.P. VG

12) You're the Best, LaRom Baker on the record company M-

13) Tell Me Baby, Karmello Brooks on Milestone VG+

14) I Don't Like It, Tommy Bush on Rika VG

15) Ain't That Just Like a Woman, Douglas Banks, Guyden M-

16) I'm Happy Without You, Ann Byers on Academy M-

17) She Kissed Me, Frankie Beverly on Fairmount M-

18) I Can Feel Him Slipping Away, Tobbi Bowe, Patheway M-

19) Whatever I Am, I'm Yours, Bill Brandon on Moonsong M-

20) You're Gonna Miss A Good Thing, John Bowie,
     Merben VG

21) Thank You Baby, Matt Brown on Jar-Val M

22) I'll Be On My Way, Bob & Fred on Big Mack VG-

23) Crying Over You, Duke Browner on Impact M-

24) The Streets Got My Lady, Bill Brandon on Piedmont VG

25) Ask My Heart, Eddie Billups on Peachtree VG

26) Taking My Time With You, Maureen Bailey on Embee VG

C

27) She's Wanted (In three States), Larry Clinton,
     Dynamo VG-

28) Thinking About the Good Times, Jimmy Church,
      Peachtree VG-

29) I'm Gonna Make You Love Me, The Combinations,
     Kimtone VG-

30) Stop Overlooking Me, The Cairos on Shrine VG

31) Ain't That Right, Brice Coefield on Omen M-

32) They'll Never Know Why, Freddie Chavez on Look M-

33) Workin', Timmy Carr on Kee VG-

34) Contagious Love, Eddie Campbell on Artco VG-

D

35) I'll Never Let You Get Away, Bill Dennis on Shrine VG
36) Lover, The De-Lites on Cuppy M-
37) What A Lucky Guy I Am, Delegates of Soul
    Uplook VG
38) He Broke You Game Wide, Open Frank Dell,
    Valise VG
39) I'm So Sorry, Don & Ron on White Cliffs VG
40) Love Is Serious Business, Alfie Davison,
    Mercury DJ M-
41) Hey Boy, D. C. Blossoms on Shrine VG
42) No Second Chance, The Deadbeats on Strata VG

E

43) Johnny On The Spot, Dennis Edwards,
    International   Soulsville VG

F

44) Seven Day Lover, James Fountain on Peachtree VG-
45) Sweet Lover, Fortson & Scott Pzazz VG
46) I'm Not Strong Enough, The Four Perfections,
    Party Time M-

G

47) Cheatin' Kind, Don Gardner on Sedgrick VG-
48) I Don't Like to Lose, The "Group" featuring Cecil
    Washington on Prophonics VG-
49) Step By Step, Cindy Gibson on Arctic VG+
50) I'm Telling You, Buddy Grubbs on Bell M-

H

51) Not My Girl, Johnny Hampton on Dotty's VG-
52) I'm Comin' Over, Johnny Honeycutt on Triode VG
53) I Still Love You, Chuck Holiday on Gloria VG-
54) Don't Make Me Love You, The Huns Review on Sorro M-

I, J

56) Do You Know What Love Is, Syl Johnson,
    Special Agent yellow lbl M-
57) I Can't Stand the Pain, Ernie Johnson on Artco VG-

K

58) You Just Don't Know, Ty Karim on Romark VG
59) You Got Me Hung Up, King Tutt on Fun City VG+
60) Is Your Love for Me, Kings of Soul on Down to Earth VG-
61) Say Something Nice To Me, Bobby Kline on MB VG-

L

62) Burning Sensation, Robby Lawson on Kyser VG
63) Fascinating Girl, George Lemons on Gold Soul VG
64) You Don't Say Nothing, Tamala Lewis On Marton VG-
65) No One to Love, Pat Lewis on Solid Hit VG

M

66) Baby I Love You, The Moments on Hog VG
67) No Mad Woman, Jock Mitchell on Golden Hit VG-
68) Stubborn Heart, Ernest Mosely on La Cindy VG
69) You Could Have Had a Good Thing, Billy Miranda,
    Queens
70) All of a Sudden, Melvin Moore on Sky Hero VG
71) I Have a Girl, The Magnetics on Ra-Sel VG

N

72) Going to a Happening, Tommy Neal on Palmer VG+

O

73) Just Say You're Wanted, Gwen Owens on Velgo G+

P

74) I'm Gone, Eddie Parker on Awake VG-
75) If I Had one Gold Piece, The Prophets on Shrine VG-

Q

76) I Don't Have to Worry, The Quotations on Di Venus VG

R

77) There's A Girl Somewhere, Bobby Rich on Sambea VG

78) One Way or the Other, Tina Roberts on Security M-

S T

79) There She Goes, Mac Staten and the Nomads
    Prelude VG-

80) When You Lose the One You Love, Buddy SmithZZ
    Brute (hairline crack record discarded) Thought I'd find a
    better shaped one. In my dreams.

81) Connie, The Servicemen on Chartmaker VG

82) Nothing's Too Good for My Baby, The Springers,
    Wale F record barely played through.

83) Do Whatcha Wanna Do b/w You Dropped Your Candy in
    the Sand Paul Sindab on Hype M-**T**

84) Look Around, Two Plus Two on Velgo VG-

85) This Won't Change, Lester Tipton on La Beat G

86) Lonely One, The Tempos on Riley's VG

87) I Was Born To Love, You Timeless Legend,
    Dawn-Lite M-

88) Baby, The Tokays on Brute VG-

89) Sweet Memories, Robert Tanner on Megatone G+

U V W

90) Wash and Wear Love, Lynn Varnado Gator VG+

91) Girls Are Against Me, The Utopias on La Salle G+

92) Ever Again, Bernie Williams on Bell VG

93) My Love Is So Strong, Joseph Webster on Crow VG-

94) Competition, Timmie Williams on Mala VG

95) I Am Nothing, Al Williams on LaBeat VG-

96) Just Your Fool, Eddie Whitehead on Blackjack VG

98) What Price, Nathan Williams on Lime VG

There were others but I can't remember all of the many that they were that I can remember.

Top: Chuck Dekker, Ralph Bionsco, Sal LaBruna & Dennis Locantore © Dennis Locantore.
Bottom: Dennis Locantore © Dennis Locantore

From Pop Idol to Ronnie Walker Either Way I Was On a Winner. By Paul Kidd

Going back to 2013 I was a lead singer in the U.K. band The Casino Allstars, singing and performing Northern Soul numbers at Clubs throughout the Northwest of the U.K. One evening a friend of mine Gary Cope gave me a call and explained he'd been approached by Pete Waterman at a funeral of a Soul Boy who had passed away in Wigan. It was a known fact that Pete Waterman had been a regular at Wigan Casino, the UK's most famous Northern Soul club, so I had no reason not to believe what he was saying. This being that he was trying to contact me with regard to the band doing some work for him etc. You can imagine my excitement as this could open so many doors for the band going forward and how much I looked forward to telling the rest of the band this news at our next weekly rehearsal. Which I did and everyone was stunned as this could be the difference between us taking a massive jump up the stardom ladder. I just had to wait for him to call me as Gary had passed on my number to him. The weeks passed and I heard nothing and rehearsal always started with a low tone as I explained I had heard nothing. A few weeks later I was DJing at a local club and bumped into Gary and explained that I'd heard nothing from him and just presumed he was too busy to get back to us. Gary explained he was introduced to him by another man who knew him personally and would get a message to him to pass on to Peter and if that wasn't possible, he would get his number for me to call him personally. This was the way to go and within a week I had the number 😁. I left it for a few weeks and thought it had all come to a dead-end when Gary called me and said I have his number here and he's asked you to ring him as soon as possible. With great anticipation, I did just that and the phone was answered by a woman who asked: "who is it?". I gave my name and asked if I could speak to Peter as he's expecting my call, "you must have the wrong number, as there is no Peter here" she replied. Oh, I'm so sorry I was given this number to ring Peter Waterman, do you mean "Chris Waterman" she replied. I guess I just think it may be his brother sorting or helping out his heavy schedule of tv works etc. Chris came on the phone and explained he was no relation to Peter and we both laughed at the mix-up. He did however promote big Northern Soul nights with DJs and soul acts etc. He was enquiring if we could perform and back Bunny Sigler and Ronnie Walker on stage at an up-and-coming event at the New Century Soul Club, Manchester for their 10th Anniversary All-nighter on Saturday 30th November 2013. Obviously, I was never going to turn down the chance to perform with these two great soul singers whose records I'd been playing for the most part of 40 + years. So, I agreed and now had to put the news to the band, albeit maybe not the exact news they were looking forward to. It was still a great opportunity to show our quality and work with a couple of legends. 😬

The thing was we were held to secrecy over Ronnie Walker appearing due to the fact Chris had booked him personally as it was his wife's favorite singer. We could however tell the world we were performing and backing Bunny Sigler and all over our site and the U.K. it went. We had to learn five songs of Bunny's Northern hits, also three of Ronnie's, plus do 4 of our own. So, it began four weeks to learn the new numbers, then perform and record them ourselves to be sent to America for approval pre-performance date. Which we did and were ready in time for their arrival the day before the Soul night which was held at   The New Century Soul Manchester All-nighter in Prestwich, Manchester. We had arranged a recording studio spot at Stockport Pear Studio just down the road from where I live in Bredbury. This was just to do a once-over with Bunny and Ronnie on a Friday night a day before the event.

The band had set up down there and had arranged to meet Dave Moore, his wife Bev, Bunny, and Ronnie at my house for a quick introduction and a cup of English tea.

It was a very dark night and they could not see the house number from the street as we were set back. Dave called me from the pub car park 5 houses up and said he was lost, etc. I explained I'm only 400mts away and would meet them in the front as they walked down the road. What a sight that was as Bunny was with his wife which I didn't expect, both with very large fur coats on and Bunny had a flat leather cap on to, following behind was a very tall man in a black Macintosh trench coat, which was Ronnie followed finally by Dave and Bev. The tea and biscuits were laid on the bar and I explained we are just five minutes away from the studio. We would take 30 mins to complete a quick rehearsal then come back for some nice sandwiches and a few drinks. That sounded like a good plan and everyone was happy. Off we went to the studio and I pre-warned the band we were here etc, we flew through the numbers with no problem and then set off back to our house where Tina was waiting with a nice spread of sandwiches and nibbles to get stuck into. We all started chatting and it was all so interesting to hear the tales both of these guys came out with. I will say Ronnie, ever the quiet gentleman needed a bit of prompting but in time I would know that was his way. Two hours passed quickly and there were hugs and handshakes all around as they left our house, and I couldn't wait to meet up again the next evening for the live performance.

On the night our Set

"I Walked Away", "Going to make You Love Me", "I Cried My Life Away"

Ronnie Walkers Set

"You're the One", Why Did You", "Trouble"

Bunny's Sigler Set

"Let The Good Times Roll ","Comparatively Speaking","For Crying Out Loud, "Follow Your Heart", "Will, You Still Love Me Tomorrow "
Girl Don't Make Wait To Long - Finale

On the night we turned up around 8 pm to set up and do a quick soundcheck. This went fine as the PA they used on the night was second to none, it was just a case of hooking up our equipment and mics. Then it was time to leave our outfits in the changing room and off we went to the nearest Indian Curry house which was a five-minute walk from the venue. We all had a nice meal and some had a couple of beers, I myself never drank beer or indeed any alcohol as it affected my singing, or did once so I never did it again. Warm tap water is all I used for the ten years with the band. I did, however, enjoy a couple of beers after the show which was so refreshing but disappeared in a flash if you know what I mean. So, we got back to the venue and around 10.30 pm the place was already buzzing and the Northern Soul music was blasting out of the speaker. The dance floor was full of great dancers and I joined them for a couple of numbers. We then walked into the changing room to find Ronnie sitting by himself, as it was a surprise appearance, he was kept clear of the main changing room which Bunny occupied. I kind of felt sorry for this quiet gentleman and made conversation with him. Once we started, we never stopped and I think that moment in time is where we became the friends we are today with him in heaven and me still down here doing my best. They announced our band and we went out there and did our business. We went down very well, as we finished, I was to announce that Chris Waterman would come to the stage and sing

137

a Ronnie Walker track for his partner as he was her favorite singer. We started the intro and he stopped the band and with the crowd laughing he explained did you really want to hear him sing, which they all shouted back "YES". He said he'd leave that for another day as he had a very nice surprise as Ronnie was here to sing it himself. Ronnie walked out to cheers and the intro started again and through his songs we played and backed him which was fantastic, to say the least. Next up was Bunny and the same again, the audience loved it and we all including Ronnie made our bows and thanked the crowd.

Ronnie on my radio show after a couple of emails and a phone call chat with Ronnie, he became a regular listener to my then twice-weekly Northern Soul show on KFM radio. He even called in the chat room and became friends with so many people I'm sure they were coming in for him and not me haha. The Casino Allstars came to an end after ten years after some band changes musician-wise in the final year didn't work out. I had other irons in the fire business-wise and needed to make a living and spend more time with my wife Tina and youngest daughter Hannah. It was a hard decision but the right one at the time, I was heavily involved in the Manchester Soul festivals and had a very large venue The Festival Hall in Alderley Edge where I promoted some big Northern Soul nights throughout the year. This and my radio shows were enough to give me my Soul Fix. My brother's song, I never talked much about my brother since his passing but found myself talking to Ronnie about him one time, I explained to Ronnie he had had his troubles and split with his wife and children. He was a self-taught musician and a gifted one at that with a unique voice. Unknown to me he had made a C/D album which I managed to obtain; I was taken back with the quality of some of the tracks but one in particular. I sent it to Ronnie and asked his opinion and what he could do with such a song. Ronnie did no more than work on the arrangement and sang the song himself. This action I will never forget and will be forever grateful to the man.

The Authentics

This is how the story goes, I get a call telling me two guys from Disley want to contact me about singing with them and would I call them on this number. I definitely wasn't interested as I'd got used to my newfound freedom and nights out with Tina at the weekend. I did however ring them to explain this as it was the polite thing to do, they explained they had a studio and had been working on numbers of their own and needed a soul singer to do the vocals. They said they'd accommodate anything I wanted and were more than convincing, so I gave them the challenge to learn "point of view" by the Jaybirds, a song I loved but could never manage to obtain a copy of. Within minutes they found it on the web and had the music written down. They were so professional but more than that a very nice couple of guys, I didn't know where any of this was heading but thought I'd jump on for the ride. The next week I headed up there during the day and we recorded my vocals over the soundtrack. The result was very pleasing to me and one to play on my show, the guys were happy and wanted to do some more and a list was put together. They asked me to sing to one soundtrack and I took it away to come up with some vocals. I had to be honest to myself and although it wasn't for me, I knew just the guy who could work his magic on it. That being Ronnie Walker, I spoke with Ronnie and explained about these two pro session musicians Clive and Chris had got me involved with them and had come up with a soundtrack that I knew was for him. I duly sent him the track and within no time "No One Will Ever Know" was born. Ronnie had worked wonders with his writing skills and vocals, as I knew he would.

Clive and Chris knew nothing about it so you can imagine their surprise as I next met up with them and played them the track Ronnie had done. Not only that we had a facetime call and Ronnie met them both. Everything looked like it was going to be more fun from now on as Ronnie was more than interested in working with them both and in return they would help out with anything needed on his latest album he was working on. Within a couple of weeks, we had the track finished with backing singers I included, not only on that song but we had a cover of "Lord What's Happening to Your People" completed too. Things were moving very fast and more top-end quality musicians wanted to get involved in this new venture.

Then disaster struck and out of the blue Ronnie passed away, along with it my hopes of working with him for many years to come both here and in the US.

The Real for Real CD Ronnie's Last Contribution To The Music Scene.

For Real For Real was almost finished and waiting for a few finishing touches before it was to be released, which we the Authentic's were looking forward to helping out with prior to Ronnie's passing. Now I just had to get involved with finishing Ronnie's Cd ready for the soul market as it was gathering dust in Philadelphia. With time to think and work things out regarding which would be the best way to go about production etc.Finally, after a year in the making, working together with studios both here in Stockport U.K. and in Philadelphia, USA. We finally between Ronnie's family and The Authentic's finalized the CD and got it produced for sale both here and in the USA. Now one thing I'd learned from talking with Ronnie was how over the years he had never received his just rewards regarding the royalties or indeed promised payments for many contributions he had made to the soul scene. I guess he was just happy doing what he was good at singing and writing great soul music and not at all bothered about chasing the dollar. However, I wasn't going to let that happen this round and made sure that after the manufacturing costs of this CD which I hope sells out quickly and every single penny/dollar made after manufacturing costs will be going direct to his family. We finally did it between Ronnie's family and The Authentic's. We got it produced for sale both here in the U.K. and the USA.

So go get yourself a copy and enjoy listening to The Man, The Legend that is Ronnie Walker R.I.P

Ronnie Walker by John Warren

I have had the great pleasure to ring Marianne Chesnovsky, several times which I love to do as we are very spiritually aligned Marianne was Ronnie Walker's partner for over 40 years and she bless her, has been very supportive of our book's project & we did a Chapter on Ronnie Walker in Book 1 of John Warren "Our soul Music Journey".

Marianne met Ronnie in 1975 when she was 20 years old in New Jersey she was in the company of Terry & some of her friends who married some of Ronnie's band members who were Chuck Decker. Ralph Biansco, Frank (Clive) Huckins, The age difference was 9 & half years and it was Ron showed interest in Marianne first & she told me he was also more stubborn than her but their love was to last all the decades because they were soul mates & had a love that few rarely find. She also shared that he was a better cook & also a better driver.

I really enjoy having a chat with Marianne and losing Ron has been very hard on her because looking at that smiley face we all saw when Ronnie performed that she saw every day made life very tough when it was no longer there to brighten up her days. The love of his fans and getting to know his fans has also helped pull her through some dark days! Those good lads Paul Kidd & Dave Starr and the radio show has been a blessing which she tunes in to every week and loves going in the live chat with her soul family. They put on a big show playing all Ronnies tunes on the Anniversary of his passing and I set my alarm clock to make the last one they had in January 2021. Being a spiritualist, I do try to help with people who are struggling & to watch out for signs that he is "still around"

One day she informed me that the Grandfather clock that had not chimed for over decades that was close to a photo of Ronnie which she spoke to everyday "chimed" which gave her affirmation that is close by "in spirit " So she talks to Ronnie a lot & I know Ronnie really enjoys that & for couples who are close in doing so is very empowering! Marianne told me that Ronnie taste in music was across the board in many genres & he was a big collector having over 12,000 DVD's which he watched most & he also collected Homer Simpson statues "Good on you Ronnie " & also had a massive woodworking collection because he used to make furniture but sadly a lot got wet in a massive storm and were destroyed. Marianne likes bears so Ronnie loved to buy her bears and other things because Ronnie was a giver. Because of work commitments she has worked for Sears for over 47 years, did not get to see Ronnie perform overseas on his trips to UK, & Spain, which is sad because seeing Ronnie was a moment in time when I fondly recall him singing in New Jersey, where he lights up the stage with that incredible presence he held. She told me most of Ronnies songs were her favorites but one unreleased song "Magic's In The Air" which I sense she will bring out on a C/D in the future is a standout for

142

her. Talking of CD's in March 2020 a new one of Ronnies came out called "For Real For Real " there are 12 tracks and 2 bonus tracks the released ones are one MD records record with the Authentics which Paul Kidd played on "Lord What's Happening " a version of the Kenny Smith mecca classic & the incredible "No One Will Ever Know" just stunning X/O. The other C/D tracks are 1 "You're So Not Here',' 2 "I Just Want To Try", 3 "Love The Way You Touch Me", 4 Love Is Just A Word ',' 5 " So This Is Forever", 6 " Next Time " , 7 I Just Lost A Friend " ,8 "I Knew It", 9 "Why", 10 "I've Been Here Before, (a big favorite of mine) I remember it was the last track he cut on the 27th December in 2018 a few weeks before he sadly passed off pneumonia. 11 "I've Got You To Know ", 12 "Love Is What We Reach For". The CD is an exceptional work that my dear best mate Dennis Locantore played bass on also Joe Mas is on Guitar, Joe Paglia piano on "So This Is Forever " & finally Stephen Ambrosino on Guitar. Ronnie Walker also played guitar and on the keyboards. The graphic design is fabulous and done by Linda Devine. It is a Cd I will treasure and play often.

Ronnie & Marriane had 4 dogs over the years, the first German shepherd, a golden retriever, Akita, Shiba Inu / Australian Cattle Dog mix which is her companion now Ronnie's only with her "In Spirit"! In the future with Dennis Locantore, I would like to release the stunning unreleased X/O track an iconic 6 mins 30 seconds long "No One More Beautiful " which I always felt was as good as you can get, and a possible movie theme and is Oscar award material in my humble opinion which Dennis and Ronnie have registered it together. Finally, Ronnie left a big mark on this planet with all the music he put down from the very first time I heard "You Got To Try Harder " at the Blackpool Mecca to this Iconic Cd that was recently released. I truly wish I got to spend more time in your company.

From Amanda: (Ronnie Walker's Daughter)

Starting back in the late 80's, the Ronnie Walker the music world knows was doing music gigs at weddings and events when he wasn't working his part time jobs. At night he would come home and help put a child to bed, sometimes watching Dr. Who with the infamous Tom Baker as The Doctor until they fell asleep. That child was me; and that was my first introduction to the nerd world, so thank you Dr. Who (and Dad). My Dad has a huge influence in my life; I got the artsy gene from him as I am a photographer, cosplayer (aka I dress up in costume and attend anime conventions), and I stream on Twitch. Growing up, I always remember him working on music and coming up with melodies and lyrics. He would write everything down on notepads or notebooks, he would also make several changes and do several recordings of songs until they were just right. Whenever I hear "Where Do You Go " by No Mercy, I flashback to a time in our kitchen where my dad was listening to his Sony Walkman practicing for gigs. I always loved hearing my dad sing when practicing. I only got to see him sing live once or twice, so being able to hear him practice makes it that more special now. I even asked him if I could tag along on his England and Spain trips to be his "paparazzi", he LOVED his fans overseas so much. I got more involved in his music in the last few years of his life as I had moved back home. I got to tag along to the studio as he worked on "For Real For Real" , and one session he had me take some photos of him in his happy place: the studio. When he would be working on music in the basement of our house, he would have me listen to portions of it to see how it sounded or what I thought of it. He would also ask me for input on what drums to have for backup or double check timing of vocals. I'd like to also thank my dad for the musical ear as it has been super helpful. For the song "I Just Lost a Friend" , he originally had wind blowing in the background in an earlier version. I told him to keep it and have the wind in every song as an easter-egg: he chuckled at me and said "no". I have to say I like the version that was released, but still wish the wind made it in there somewhere.

Ronnie Walker
by Marianne Chesnovsky-Walker

The regular life of Ronnie Walker is like a "B" side of a 45 record; different from the "A" side. The last 4 decades he was a talented vocalist, song writer, & musician as well as a regular hard working husband, father, & grandfather.

Music was always his first love, but he always had other jobs as well. Fortunately, his job at Sears for twenty five years, among others, gave him the flexibility to do both. Ron was a mentor for more than a few young people that he worked with and gave life lessons to those who were interested. Ronnie's influence rubbed off on some who are now responsible adults. I often heard from former co-workers what a huge impact Ronnie's life lessons had in their lives. Makes me so proud that his co-workers looked up to him. That was just who Ronnie was, missing him everyday is an understatement. He built things, fixed things, and was into all kinds of electronics & tools. We always had the latest version of technology. Ronnie was our daughter's best friend, caretaker when she was a baby, & her biggest cheerleader throughout life. Ron brightened my world; so lucky he was my person!

The A side of the record was the entertaining side; constantly singing at clubs & bars in the 70's, working the lounge in Atlantic City casinos in the 80's, and then working many events & fundraisers in the city. Places like the Franklin Institute, The Art Museum, & the Please Touch Museum were just some of these places he got to perform in the 90's. He also got to perform at multiple wedding venues & events.

In early 2000, things changed when the UK welcomed him into their world of Northern Soul. People were so in awe of him & treated him like the true talent he was. Ronnie was invited back time after time and even was invited to Spain until 2017. He was so touched at how they loved his music & the opportunities that were given to him. He met so many friends along the way. In the summer of 2019, after Ronnie passed away, my niece was in London and sprinkled some of his ashes at Kensington Gardens and Abbey Road. Our family felt that he would have approved. We were all so blessed to have known Ronnie Walker. I found a few things Ronnie wrote that tells you who he was:

A never was has been,

Ain't so bad my friend

Seen some of the world

Not as much as I'd like to

But wherever I've been the love I felt, tells me I win

Funny all this time now I get it when it is so late

I want the world to know I was here,

People say that was why we have children

But children die just like I will.

The Music, the music I write, the music I sing goes on forever

Good bad whatever it is mine it is me

It is God's gift to me so that I can be remembered

So I can live forever, I need to do more because this is why I live.

The world may say I'm wrong, but it pleases me to believe this.

Top: Ronnie Walker © Marianne Chesnovsky-Walker
Bottom: Ronnie & Dennis Locantore © M. Walker

BETTER LATE THAN NEVER

Ronnie Walker rises from the depths of obscurity.

BY TIM WHITAKER

RONNIE WALKER, the Philadelphia falsetto soul singer, was 14 the first time he sang for an audience. "There was a jazz musician who lived across the street from me," Walker, now 50, recalls. "He grabbed me by the hand, took me into a bar and had me sing in the middle of the room. I sang 'Bye Bye Blackbird.' They passed the hat around and I made $13."

A year later, Walker signed a record contract—actually, his mother signed it for him—after auditioning for a local producer on the phone. In 1967, when he was 17, he scored a local hit with "Really, Really Love You." He sang the song at Philadelphia record shops and on local TV dance shows.

But not much happened after that. Walker did record some more songs, and wrote a bunch more, but his voice somehow got lost beneath the avalanche of talented soul crooners and blasters emerging out of Philadelphia in the '60s. As time passed, Walker, who still does some party and wedding gigs, became little more than a soul music footnote, unknown to all but truly hardcore Philadelphia soul aficionados.

The story would've ended right there, if not for Europe. A few years back, Walker received a postcard from a couple British

filmmakers working on a soul music documentary. "I wrote back and they came to Philadelphia and had me sing a couple of songs for their cameras," says Walker. "They told me my music was popular there. You could say I was a bit surprised."

It gets better. Local Philadelphia soul music archivist David L. Brown, who helped the filmmakers locate Walker, recently released a CD of Walker's music, titled *Someday*, on his Philly-Archives label (available at www.philly-archives.com). The CD includes Walker's "Really, Really Love You" and 21 other songs rarely heard by anyone.

"All this was the furthest thing from my mind," says Walker, who today works for Sears. "I didn't know anybody was aware I ever sang anything. Better late, I always say, than never." •

ONE-HIT WONDER NOW STORMING EUROPE!

Ronnie Walker By Tim Whitaker © Tim Whitaker

Chapter 13

The Story of Northern Soul in Japan

by Izumi Sawamoto

I was a teenage mod. 24/7, 365 days, thinking only about Mod. Clothes, music, of course, even TV, only 60s. At that time, in Kansai, there were a lot of Mods. Well, was it really Mod? We had so many mistakes, looking back, we didn't know, but it's funny, we developed our original Osaka Mod style. I'm proud to have been a member. We liked 66-67-era Small Faces-style, funky-soul music, Bruce Lee, Osaka Expo and scooters. We were young and didn't have much money so, to get clothes, records and a scooter; the full set was difficult. Most picked 2 from 3. Eventually, some people got the lot and then lost their passion and stopped buying records or they started a family and drifted away from the clubs. But, let's not dwell on those guys.

In the winter of 1995, at a Mod party in Kobe, I met a man, Ryo Kiitaki, one year older, from the same hometown, Kobe. Ryo said "I'm so glad to see such a young guy!", even though he was only a year older! At that time, I didn't really understand what he meant. I thought: He's cool, a trend-setter, like Steve Marriott with his centre-parting and neatly cropped hair. Brilliant! Dancing like James Brown to "Papa's Got A Brand New Bag", unrivaled on heaven and earth, unfortunately, they hardly ever played that kind of song. Six months later, he asked me to DJ. Compared to Osaka, my hometown, Kobe, didn't have a Mod scene. Ryo had established his 60s party, its theme- create your own playground. This was the beginning of our 25-year DJ partnership and the 'Nude Restaurant' scene. At this time, we were still obsessed with Mod.

Before the 7:30 closing time along the Koukashita, we would ascend the dodgy-looking staircase next to a vintage-clothes shop that led up to a bare, empty-space bar. The staff were wearing Pierre Cardin, new-wave mix, and Motomachi avant-garde fashion.

At that time, even in Kobe, Zonne (the venue) stood out as an 'underground' place. This is where we held 'Nude Restaurant' on the last Saturday of every month. In the queue, teenage boys and girls in floral shirts with boot-cut Levi's Sta-Prest, 3-button suits with button-down shirts, A-line mini-dresses, retro-modern style. Pitch-black, nothing to do but dance; Zonne was such a small place. Once a month we lived our secret lives that even our classmates didn't know about. We turned our backs to trendy music. We liked British Beat: The Small Faces, The Who, The Spencer Davis Group- also, b-sides of 2nd-grade funky-soul; James Brown and Dyke and the Blazers copyists. We felt like outsiders, suspicious characters, looking into a secret garden in full bloom. Like Norman Mailer's 'White Negro', we were thinking: "I'm different.". The Zonne crowd wanted to be a minority; the chosen few. Maybe they all had that feeling, coping with their exploding teenage angst by living in a 60s cult.

In Feb 1997, Ryo went to London and met Keb Darge who took him to the 100 Club where he had his first experience of Northern Soul. All ages, male and female, crazy music and dancing. It was a perfect world for him. It felt different from the Japanese Mod scene...age, style, it doesn't matter, just people who truly, simply enjoyed the music and dancing to it. He wanted to bring this culture to Japan and 'Nude Restaurant'. Keb said: "If you want to know or learn about Northern Soul, you have to listen to a lot of songs. Rather than buy a few expensive originals, you should get a lot of bootlegs and study them." So, Ryo followed his advice. He returned with arms full of bootlegs! We'd never heard any of these songs in Japan's 60s scene. Before, there were separate soul categories: Motown, Funky, Mod, Northern. Nowadays, it's mixed. The records sounded familiar but we didn't know them and we couldn't find thom in Japan.

We soon became absorbed by this fascinating sound. Northern Soul had a profound influence on us and our scene. Fashion- we changed to dress 'easy to dance', shoes- from heels to flat dance shoes. Mods- from competitive individuals to becoming a team! In Paris during the May '68 protests, they had a slogan "Sous les pavés, la plage!". Zonne had carpeted the floor but the dancing was wearing it thin and tattered and you could see the concrete paving below. Let's pull up that useless carpet and sprinkle on the baby powder to the bare concrete below!

Japanese Northern Soul Revolution! Wigan-style dancing, bouncing off one another's shoulders, laughing at some dancer's attempt at an unsteady back-drop and unsure spins. It was exactly like in the film 'Northern Soul' when Matt is in the youth club and the others are making fun of him. We were John and Matt, we just wanted to perfect Northern Soul dancing. 'Nude Restaurant' used to do hardcore things. An open-minded stance suits ' The Story of 'Nude Restaurant'. "Everyone who loves the 60s, if you enjoy it with us, all are welcome!" However, we were playing more and more Northern Soul and the older Mods were looking down their noses and mocking us! Many left and as we went deeper we were left with a crowd of 15 who believed in what we were doing and stuck with us.

This was the beginning of Northern Soul in Japan. At that time, no one in Japan knew anything about Northern Soul. There was an older generation of record-collectors and DJs who had Deep Soul. We looked at the fanzines which had articles about Deep Soul records, some of which had Northern Soul on the b-sides. We relied on those fanzines at first. Then,

I saw the Wigan Casino documentary 'This England' from a friend passing it around. The only person who had experience in England was Ryo. He was our textbook. Ryo played Frank Wilson's 'Do I Love You (Indeed I Do.)', he was the first to wear an imported Adidas training shirt with baggy pants in Japan.

In 1998, a Japanese music magazine named 'Studio Voice' published a Northern Soul edition. The veil was lifted, the mist cleared, this mystery culture was revealed to us. We copied everything but the result turned out differently from the UK and ended up in the original Japanese style. Only the passion was there. We were leaning further and further to Northern Soul and away from Mod.

In 1999, Keb came to Japan for his first DJ tour, he toured all around Japan. He played an event in Osaka before Kobe. He played Larry Clinton 'She's Wanted' and we headed for the dance floor. Keb is watching us from the DJ booth and he looks a bit disappointed, shaking his head at us. Next, he came to Kobe to do an event called 'Northern Voice'. At the end of the night, Keb called up Ryo and passed him a few records like Luther Ingram's 'If It's All The Same To You Babe' and told him to play them and Keb went on to the dance floor and showed us how to dance. It was very different to the Wigan Casino documentary. It was mind-blowing, so outstandingly cool! Afterwards, all we talked about amongst ourselves was Keb's dancing! Before Youtube videos, before the 'Northern Soul' movie, the top 80s Northern Soul DJ and dance champion, Keb was the inspiration that spread out of Kobe's 'Nude Restaurant' into Kansai and beyond so that you can see that style in cities throughout Japan. If you say 'Northern Soul', what do you think of? It's not just one style. It's diverse, taste in music, dance style, fashion, and thousands of differences. However, Nude Restaurant is overwhelmingly Kebstyle. Around 2000, buzz-cut, open-shirted, wide-rockabilly-turn-up-jeans, many 'little Keb Darges' flowing and floating, to and fro on the floor.

It is not an exaggeration to say that Keb Darge is the father of Northern Soul in Japan. Also, 'Nude Restaurant' has incorporated Keb's musical evolution from Northern to Deep Funk and Modern Soul to Rockabilly and Garage. Maybe we are more fascinated by Keb than the main Northern Soul scene is in the UK. As I mentioned earlier, after the 'Northern Voice' event in Kobe, Ryo decided to revisit England. Our current 'Nude Restaurant' DJ, ally and great mate, Seiji Iwabuchi, decided to follow Ryo to England. He worked hard at a petrol station, saving money, to study abroad for one year. Unfortunately, once he was in England, he spent all his money on records and had to return after 6 months! Seiji may appear apathetic but when he has to do something, he does it. Seiji also liked Modern Soul and Deep Funk as well as Northern. He bought some top tunes from Keb Darge: 'Soul Power' by Li'l Ray & the Fantastic Four, 'Gettin' Soul' by Aaron Butler & the New Breed and 'Ghost-A-Go-Go' by Richard Rome, etc. Nowadays, Li'l Ray and Richard Rome are not especially rare but at that time there were only 2 known copies in the world. They discovered more so the price has dropped, which is sad but it is a common occurrence in the collector's world. While Seiji was in London, I went to see him. The day I arrived, we went to 100 Club DJ Shifty's house. One of the records I bought was Wade Flemons 'Jeanette" for around £200 but now it's worth over £1,000.

The record collector's world is ruthless, sometimes up, sometimes down. Such is life. Time and record collecting shows no mercy. When we were in London, the 'Capital Soul Club' were the high-fliers, the new young team whose popularity was soaring. I bought 'I Still Love You' by The Seven Souls at the record bar at their event at The Dome. I still cherish that record. We met DJ David Flynn then, and he continues to be a good 'sensei' to us. He often DJs with us at 'Nude Restaurant'. There was a time when Shuhei Yoshioka and Takuya Kitamura, who

153

were a year younger than I, got into Northern Soul and came to 'Nude Restaurant' a lot.

They also went to England to get first-hand experience. When they returned to Japan, they set up 'Osaka Manifesto'.

Finally, I understood what Ryo meant when he said he was glad to see such a young guy! The same year that Keb first came on tour in Japan, 'Kyoto Soul Survivors' started, then lots of Northern Soul parties began to spring up in Kansai. 'Nude Restaurant' was the catalyst. 'Osaka Manifesto' in 2001, Kobe's 'Tore-Up', 'Soul Clinic' and other one-off events. Kansai Northern Soul was basking in the limelight. The birth of a scene in Japan. In Kansai, DJs and dancers were buying records like crazy, tearing off their clothes and dancing shirtless! Keb said Northern Soul was all about enthusiasm. Nowadays, the current situation has changed, the fever has subsided, except for 'Nude Restaurant', every other event has finished.

The Kansai Soul Scene is a little lonely these days. However, in Kansai, the DJs and dancers are still the best. If you want to listen to the highest quality of Northern Soul, you must go to Kansai, you really should! At the dawn of the Zonne-era, we became a little elitist. Nude Restaurant's attitude was almost like 'If you're not going to dance to Northern Soul, don't come in!', because there was no space! A strict, monastic attitude. In fact, we stopped making flyers and relied on word-of-mouth. A secret society striving for purity. After 10 years we had gained a little confidence in our Northern Soul scene. One day we were visited by Kobe's famous Jazz-Kissa master after hours. In Japan's Jazz-Kissa culture they also have a strict, orthodox attitude to Jazz that can be a bit intimidating. However, Jam Jam's Jazz-Kissa master was cool and stylish and his venue had over 100 people capacity. He loves music flexibly and had previously held DJ events. We really wanted to move Nude Restaurant to Jam and so in 2011, we left our long-time favourite place Zonne. Moving to Jam was the spark that released our stored power.

We set the sails and plotted a new course to spread the word throughout Japan. At the same time, Nude Restaurant's number one fan, and ex-organiser of Osaka Manifesto, Shuhei Yoshioka, joined our line-up. He has extraordinary Northern Soul passion and a record collection to match. Also, he loves Nude Restaurant! That's what we needed to go further. The change of venue, the 4 of us and the influence of Social Network sites led to us becoming more well-known and people coming to Nude Restaurant from across Japan and then from around the world.

Over the last 10 years, we have been featured in a Japanese Northern Soul book, we were the Q & A guests for the release of the Northern Soul film in Japan, articles about us have appeared in Kobe's newspaper and Britain's The Independent newspaper and online web-site. We were also invited to DJ at Japan's largest music festival, Fuji Rock. Awareness of Japanese Northern Soul has really grown but sometimes I miss the strength of those early days. The journey to here was so long. Those that had lived in the UK and returned thought it was impossible to establish a Northern Soul scene in Japan. They questioned how we could get the records, they thought it would take over 20 years. Yeah?! Every Northern Soul scene needs very rare records, but first, you need knowledge and a method to lay your hands on them. The first time I saw a British record dealer's sales list it was very different in taste and quality from what I could get in Japan. I rushed to make an international call: "A-ro, this and this and this! Do you have it?" The dealer replied: "Which list are you looking at?". The British record list sold out so quickly! By the time I got it in Japan, all the good stuff was already gone. Nowadays, it is so much easier to trade person-to-person by ebay or Facebook. But in this era, we were using International Postal Money Orders from the Post Office. For my one record order, I wrote a letter or sent a fax to England and it took one month to get the record. Every week, I gazed at the list in my hand with my little knowledge and limited budget and carefully chose my next purchase.

Every day I waited at the front of my house for the postman to come. There is nothing to compare to finally getting the record into my hands!

In the last few years, Japanese old soul collectors started selling their records. A few years ago, 'Afro-Juice Record Shop' in Osaka bought 20,000 records from old collectors: 'I'm Gone' by Eddie Parker, 3 copies of 'That's Why I Love You' by The Professionals, 2 copies of 'She's Gone' by Hamilton Movement, also…The Cairos, Sam Williams, The Masqueraders, etc. For a Northern Soul fan, this was a coveted treasure trove! However, the old guy who runs the shop knew about Northern Soul so he seriously put the price up! My long-time most wanted record- The Professionals, I finally got my hands on it and from a Japanese record shop, I paid in cash, it was a miracle! 20 years ago, I never could imagine that this would happen. The record shop owner is a beloved, eccentric and moody guy. For some reason, he sometimes gives me a record for free!

I was thinking about the roots of a culture and why the excitement about Northern Soul was so powerful in Kansai. There is a strange relationship between Osaka and Tokyo and there is a connection between Osaka and Kobe. As you know, the epicentre of trend-setting in Japan is Tokyo but Osaka has its own style. It's kind of like London and Manchester, isn't it? Also, the distance between Osaka and Kobe is similar to Manchester and Wigan. A counterculture to London is one of the reasons that Northern Soul flourished in the North of England. I think the same is true about Japan. Kansai Northern Soul is a reaction against the Tokyo scene. In Kansai, the people can be a bit weird and stubborn but in a good way. We have a unique character. Their personality is unconsciously against the fashionable, more glamorous Tokyo scene. That feeling comes out on the dance floor in their sweat and screams. Maybe this is the reason, perhaps… But the truth is, the 4 of us, Ryo, myself, Seiji and Shuhei- 'Nude Restaurant' are in Kobe.

There is no other reason. People laughed at us and looked down at our attempts to start Northern Soul in Japan under these difficult circumstances but, 'Nude Restaurant' made these lasting friendships and what's more, we never gave up because we love it from the bottom of our hearts. Keb told us: "You have put the fun back into Northern Soul, I wish you could teach the British crowd how it should be done." Hearing those words, I feel like my trust in our crew was not a mistake.

Since 1994, we have had monthly events. We had to stop for 6 months because of the Great Hanshin Awaji Earthquake in 1995 that affected Kobe very badly and now because of Covid-19 we have not had an event since February 2020. We don't know when we will see the light at the end of the coronavirus tunnel but, when we do, we will gather at our favourite Jazz-Kissa venue, Jam-Jam in Kobe and proudly play our records and keep on dancing.

That's right! Northern Soul exists in Japan! It exists in our lives! Well, is it really Northern Soul? I guess we made a lot of mistakes, but it turned out well, it's Original Kansai Northern Soul and I'm proud to be a member. Keep the faith!

Glossary:

Kansai - a region in the West of Japan that includes the cities of Osaka, Kyoto and Kobe.

Osaka Expo. - was a world's fair held in Osaka in 1970.

Koukashita - shopping arcade under an elevated railway.

Motomachi - is a district of Kobe.

"Sous les pavés, la plage!" - "Under the paving stones, the beach!"

Sensei - a teacher

Jazz-Kissa - cafe / bar serving coffee and alcohol and dedicated to playing jazz records.

Originally written in Japanese by Izumi Sawamoto

Translated into English by Mark and Ema Bristow

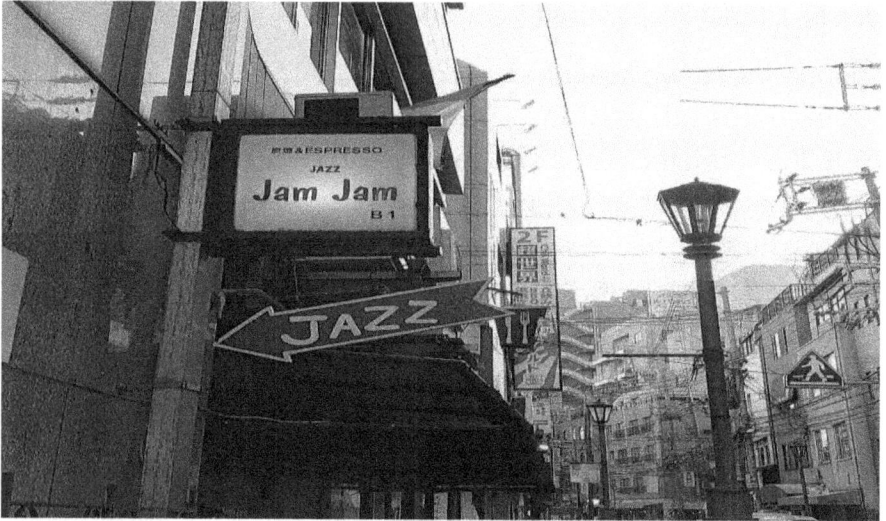

Outside Of Jam © Izumi Sawamoto

Nude Restaurant. Shuhei, Seiji, Me and Ryo © Izumi Sawamoto

Takea Jingi, Izumi Sawamoto & Yusuke Chikusa © Izumi Sawamoto

Keb Darge © Izumi Sawamoto

Nude Restaurant © Izumi Sawamoto

Nude Restaurant and Soul Fans © Izumi Sawamoto

Chapter 14

Mark Speakman Soul Trip Part 2

On the 20th August 2009 I met Johnny 'Redpants' Warren over in Australia. Johnny had a great idea of documenting our stories and memories in order to raise some money to help certain performers who had given us years of pleasure with their fabulous music, but had fallen upon hard times. This will be Johnny's second published book, and I hope you enjoy my little contribution as much as I have in reminiscing and putting pen to paper. The re-telling of my soul escapades from the 1990's to date cannot be rushed, as I have experienced some wonderful moments, both locally and worldwide, which I have documented through my diaries, social media, photos and memorabilia. Back in the 1970's and 1980's it was basically collecting records, attending soul nights, DJing, and seeing the occasional soul artist, however, by the 1990's the scene was most definitely on the up, and with the new millennia came an explosion, which was partly driven by the internet and low travel costs. These days I could write a book on the artists I have met in person, seen performing and conversed with, either in person or on-line during the last twenty years, and write another on my experiences of DJing in the UK and Ireland as well as Australia, Europe and the USA. I have met some fabulous people around the world, fellow record collectors and DJ's, and people who just dig the music. In the last 20 years I have also opened a record shop, closed it and now reopened it, which is a story in itself! So with the publishing date for the second edition of Johnny's book fast approaching, he has been bugging me to get writing, in a nice way of course! It would be impossible for me to do justice to my story within a short chapter, therefore it will be a case of cherry picking a few tasters for you, and hopefully, Johnny will allow me the opportunity to write a further instalment for his 3rd book!

Australia 2008- 2009

My first trip to Australia and attending the Perth National took place back in September 2008, however, this was not the happiest of trips. Upon landing in Perth on a Thursday, I had a phone call to say that my partner, Sue, had passed away back in the UK, news which shattered my life, and subsequently meant that I had to immediately make arrangements to return to the UK. The first flight I could get was the following Tuesday, without incurring astronomical charges for changing the flights, and after a few phone calls back home it was decided that this was the best option as there was nothing I could do by arriving home sooner. This arrangement meant I could attend the National and do my DJ spots, if I felt up to it. I was staying with my best mate from back in the UK, Van Astbury and his wife Lesley, who now lived in Perth. Van hadn't long been diagnosed with Cancer, which had been one of the drivers for my visit. So I attended the National and did my DJ spots, as originally planned, and in attending the event I thereby met some of the nicest people going, who all looked after me during this difficult time. There are far too many people to mention by name, but Denny and Clare Johnson and Pete and Maxine Fowler have a special place in my heart due to the events we have attended together over the years in Australia, Europe and the UK. In March 2009, I came back out to Perth for seven weeks, well it should have been six, but I found out a few days before flying home that Syl Johnson was performing in Perth so I delayed my return by a week to see the man. More to come on this trip as it also included a weekender on the Gold Coast, a five hour plus internal flight from Perth. Other people I would like to mention from my trips down under are Ian and Sandra Astbury (Perth), Allan and Debbie Taylor (Perth), Una Hanlon (Sydney), Mick and Jayne James (Sydney), Vincent Peach and Maureen Leverett (Melbourne) who have kindly made space for me in their homes when I have been over to visit, and I couldn't have done it without these good people.

Prestatyn Soul Weekenders

The Rare Soul weekender at Pontins which takes place in my home town of Prestatyn, North Wales, what a wow! All those artists who have appeared are like a who's who of Northern Soul music, and that's not forgetting the modern soul artists who have also appeared. Where do I start with this one, well it's with a small gripe, as I didn't get asked to DJ, which seeing it was my home town I was a little miffed to say the least, I eventually was asked the following year to do the last spot on the Thursday night double decking with my good buddy Chico (Glyn Parry-Jones) R.I.P , so all is forgiven, as I don't hold grudges, life's too short. For a few years it was the usual last spot on Thursdays with Chico, before eventually a step up into the rare room on Fridays and Saturdays and also spots in the Queen Vic, which was the on-site pub. From the off at Prestatyn, I had a stall selling records with my sidekick Chico (Glynn Parry-Jones), and I could write a book about all the memories and fun we've had sat behind the tables with good company, and when your stall is next to Roger and Jenny Banks (R&B Records) what else would you expect! Those early days at Prestatyn were almost a who's who of UK record dealers, Pat Brady, John Manship, Tim Brown, Simon Hunt, Joe Dunlop, Keith Minshall, Andy Dyson, Mark Dobson (Butch), John Anderson, Dave Welding, Steve Jefferies, Neil Rushton, Damian, Derek Mead and others. The business was always brisk with lots of buyers, but over the years the sales dipped and some of the main dealers stopped coming, but I always took my fair share and I suppose it actually helped my sales in recent years as there were less dealers there. I also believe that as the weekender it became more successful lots of non-record stalls started appearing bringing a commercialized market feel to the main hall, which resulted in many dealers and collectors giving the event a miss. I still enjoy the Prestatyn weekenders and it's still very busy and it is a bonus that it's on my doorstep, hopefully they will be back on in the not too distant future.

Highlights of Prestatyn

I suppose the highlight of the Prestatyn weekenders for me was meeting the Volumes/Magnetics and getting them to sign my sleeve of my "Lady In Green" 45, never in my life would I have dreamt of this happening, but thanks to Ian Cunliffe, I have the photo to prove it! It was the first copy they had ever seen since recording it, so there was no point in asking them if they had any copies tucked away!! How many times have we heard this from artists?? This was a very special moment as The Magnetics was first played in North Wales' by Bob Foster before he sold it to Sam who took it to Wigan, and the rest as they say is Northern Soul history. Other highlights include having breakfast with Lou Pride while doing a deal to stock his CD's in my shop. Sitting and chatting with Jerry Williams' wife Yvonne and their daughter whilst waiting for him to come back from lunch, and then spending the next hour wheeling and dealing with him over stocking his CD's in my shop!! I recall him being a crafty business man, he sold me all his Swamp Dogg CD's. One of the nicest experiences was meeting James Bell in 2005, who introduced himself to me, someone had told him I may be interested in stocking his re-issue of "Amazing Love" b/w "Love Of My Girl", we did the deal and I took 25 copies off him. On Monday morning at breakfast I went over to ask whether he had any copies left over after the weekend, he said he had and I took a further 25 copies off him, he kindly signed and dated every single one of the sleeves for me without me even asking. He told me he was keeping the rest of the press to give out to family members at his next Birthday party. James Bell was a retired plumber, and had a son who lived in Germany whom he was going to visit after Prestatyn. A few years later on his second visit to the Prestatyn weekender he came to my stall to say hello and ask me had I sold all the records, I had a couple left and enquired as to whether he had any more, but he stated that they had now all gone, we had another a nice chat, he was truly a lovely man.

Bobby Eli a man of many talents who has working with some of the biggest names in soul music, Gamble & Huff, The Jacksons, Teddy Pendergrass to name a few, and also pop artists such as Elton John and David Bowie, was another of Prestatyn's highlights, not performing but as Musical Director. Bobby spent a few hours rummaging through Simon Hunt's and my record stock late on a Sunday night, Simon and I were always the last two standing at Prestatyn. Bobby was looking for records with his name on either as a writer, producer or arranger as he didn't own any of his records, Simon and I gave him a helping hand and dug a fair few out between us, which we gave to him for free and thanked him for his contribution to our scene. Bobby went away a happy man, and it was nice to give back a little for what his music had given us.

Hitsville Detroit 2017

One of the many highlights of my soul journey was going to the Detroit a Go in 2017, this event was organised by Neil Rushton and Phil Dick. Myself and Wendy flew out to Detroit roughly 24 hours after I had been DJing at the Algarve Northern Soul weekender run by Chris Dalton and Carol Shepard, mad rush home, swap the suitcases around and off again, lucky the records for DJing in Detroit had been sorted while I was in Portugal. On the afternoon we arrived in Detroit, we unpacked and popped down to the bar for something to eat and drink, of course we bumped into some of the attendees and a few of the artists. On the first night there was a meet and greet in a club in which Melvin Davis was performing, and a few of DJ's were spinning some tunes there as well. Although knackered after all the travelling, we soon got into the spirit of things after having a drink or two with Dave Moore, Pete Fowler, Kev Spittle, Mick Heffernan and Calum Kerr, just to name a few of the gang who were there. Melvin kicked off his spot, and was amazing; seeing one of our Detroit legends performing in his home town club, who would have thought that back in the early days of the 1970's!!

On Saturday night, Kev Spittle dragged me from my seat and introduced me to this little old black lady, saying guess who this is? I just hadn't a clue, "I'm Clara Hardy ", answered the lady and "yes I'm still alive ", we then had a little chat about her recording career, a priceless memory.

Whizzing around old Detroit 60's recording studios, with Kev Spittle, Dave Moore, Pete Fowler and our good ladies, with our guide being Frank Bryant of the Just Brothers of "Carlena" fame was just fabulous. I had always wanted to visit the Motown Studio, so that was another box ticked. The trip to the Motown Studio from the hotel took place on a yellow school bus just like you see in American movies, pulling up at 2648 W. Grand Blvd, was very emotional and almost had my partner Wendy in tears.

The trip to Detroit contained many fabulous moments, but for me meeting John Rhys who wrote Tobi Legends all time Northern Soul classic "Time will pass you by" and getting a photo of him signing my record sleeve after his questions and answers session was tops. I will discuss the record shopping and live acts seen on my trip to Detroit in the next publication. So my stories, I haven't really scratched the surface, looking back on what a life I've experienced, met so many people and visited places I wouldn't have just because of the love of soul music and northern soul in particular.

I look forward to adding a few more in the third edition of Johnny's, Our Soul Music Journey.

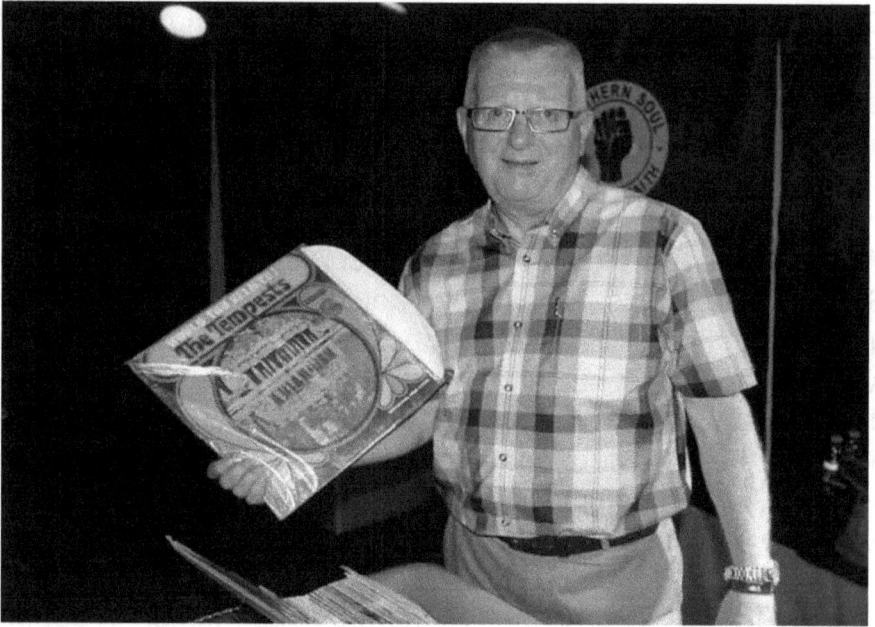

Mark Speakman © Mark Speakman

Chapter 15

Bob Norman – Northern Soul – My Story

My own soul journey started and I didn't even know it had started. I grew up in the south of England in Dorset, in a town called Poole and at an early age, as with most kids at the time, (the early 1970's) I liked the type of music that was played on "Top Of The Pops" by bands such as Slade, Sweet, Gary Glitter and Mungo Jerry. Later I used to listen to songs from the Radio 1 "Top 40 Countdown" on my cassette player. By this time I had moved onto the early disco bands like Stylistics, Chi-lites, George McCrae, Impressions, Miracles, Tavares and The Real Thing.

During my school days I had school mates (those I hung around with at school) and home mates (those I hung around with after school) as I lived in a different area to the school I went to by a few miles. Whilst I was still at school, a mate of mine, Pete Brown, used to DJ at his local Boys' Club in Oakdale, Poole. One day in 1975 I was at his house and he started to play some of his records. The two I can remember were Dana Valery "You Don't Know Where Your Interest Lies" and Frankie Valli "You're Ready Now", both on bootlegs (as I now know) but back then I just thought they were "proper" records. I'd never heard these tunes before and didn't really think about them until a couple of years later when, for some reason, I went to a disco at Lagland Street Boys' Club in my centre of Poole. It was this Saturday night venture that changed my musical path for life.

Lagland Street Boys' Club © Bob Norman

Oakdale Boys' Club © Bob Norman

During that evening, the DJ was playing a mixture of reggae and northern soul and, although I didn't know anything about northern soul, it was just music that caught my attention, mainly after watching an older lad called Butch dancing like I had never seen anyone dance before. He was doing spins, kicks, backdrops and I was mesmerised! There were other people also dancing, but he just grabbed my attention. At the time, I didn't know any of the records they were dancing to that night but when the Righteous Brothers "Rat Race" and Tommy Sands "The Statue" (I found the names later) were played, the dancers would at times during the tunes literally stop like a statue for a second or so before continuing their dancing. After this night I regularly went to the various soul nights in my town, eventually plucking up enough courage to get on the dancefloor after doing what everyone else did, practising alone at home in my bedroom. I went to local soul nights at Oakdale Boys' Club, Lagland Street Boys' Club and Hamworthy Youth Club regularly and if there was soul being played anywhere else locally I was there. Two that spring to mind are Poole Gas Club and The Antelope Pub (I still have the advert / tickets for one of the Antelope nights). So thanks Pete, for playing me those tunes back in your bedroom that day. (Just out of the blue, Pete has just sent me a Facebook friend request Sept 2021). Soon I wanted to have tunes to listen to at home, and this is when I started buying records. Initially I would buy from a local shop / newsagency (Setchfields) that would sell the latest pressings and bootlegs but generally only tunes that I knew and were being played locally, probably bought from the same shop as I was buying from.

In our town there were discos all over the place, playing the radio station hits and a bit of commercial soul music, but because I had records, (just bootlegs then) my mates would get me to take them along so that the DJ could play them for us. Not cool I know, but it gave us a fix. One such place was one of the British Legion Clubs on a Friday night. I'd ride my motorbike there with my record box balanced on the petrol tank, one hand holding the box, the other on the throttle on the handlebars changing gears without using the clutch. Anyway, this was the situation: the DJ would play his own records for a while then the rest of the night he would alternate from my records to punk tunes from another box that the punks had also brought along. We would have to sit there and watch the punks doing the "pogo" or whatever else they did, pushing and bumping into each other, (I never understood what enjoyment they got from all that bollocks) then after about 20 minutes we would get to strut our stuff to our music while they sat and watched, sometimes trying to take the piss out of our dancing. There never was any trouble but it came close a few times. The last time we attended, there was a bad snowstorm so riding home was even more precarious (try riding a motorbike in the snow with one hand on the box of records and the other trying to keep control of the bike). They never had any more nights after this and I never really found out why.

Wigan Casino All Nighters

My first all-nighter involved a 10 hour coach ride to the Casino Club in Wigan. Prior to going I had applied for membership and had to lie about my age, as did probably 70% of everyone else going there for the first time. I waited in anticipation that I would get my membership in time, which it thankfully did. I would have got up on Saturday morning, got my clothes, shoes and towel ready in my bag, then headed off to the "Jolly Miller" pub at lunch time for a few pints, then around 2pm would head outside to board the coach which was full of 16 to 20 year old boys and girls. As I said, it was a long 10 hour trip and as usual in a crowded coach, some were quiet, some were boisterous, some were smoking and others listening to northern soul on their cassette players.

I would have been in the quiet group, being a bit younger. We would travel from Poole through the country roads to Bath, then along the M4, up the M5 then onto the M6 where we would get out at Knutsford and get changed into our all-nighter clothes). Then when we finally arrived outside the Casino in Wigan, those who had already known about the line up outside, the hustle and bustle getting in the door, paying your money then racing up the stairs to get your spot inside. This first time I just followed the people who had been before. Our spot was, looking at the stage, the right hand balcony at the far end overlooking the DJs.

That's where we would set up camp and was where most of the Dorset people would set up camp. I say Dorset but the coach would have soulies from Poole, Bournemouth, Wareham and Swanage. I stayed up all night dancing, watching others dancing, listening to all the new tunes, soaking up the atmosphere, the heat, the humidity, the camaraderie, the synchronised hand clapping to the music, everything. This, no doubt, was one of the best nights of my life so far. At the end of the night or I should say early in the morning, we had to face the long 10 hour trip back to Poole. That used to seem to take forever with most people sleeping some of the way, but I tried and just couldn't get any sleep.

Back then I used to smoke and so I just puffed on fags all the way home and my fingers used to have yellow nicotine stains from all the smoking. So, I would wake up Saturday morning and the next sleep would be Sunday night, then be up for work on Monday morning. Being young that was no problem at all. After I had been a few times, I would take my cassette tape recorder and place it on the inside slope of the balcony where it would sit nicely on a little lip, then I would drop the microphone (that was attached by a wire) over the edge to record a few hours of Richard Searling's and Pat Brady's sets and maybe a few others.

The Jolly Miller Pub

My first all-nighter at the Casino featured Junior Walker & The All Stars live on stage. That would have been March 1978 which was the same month I attended my second allnighter, at the Fleet Centre in Peterborough. All I can remember is we took a coach from Poole to Peterborough and there were at least two rooms and was a dancer there who didn't - couldn't dance on his feet very much, but would do the backdrops, handstands, high kicks, leg spinning and every type of acrobatic stunt imaginable, something I never managed to do.

Oh, and I scored a Peterborough badge too. Tunes from Fleet that I specifically remember are Phil Coulter's instrumental "A Good Thing Going" and The Burning Bush "Keeps On Burning". I went to the Casino again before I attended my first Yate all-nighter in July 1978. That came about as my girlfriend at the time, Lisa, had an uncle and auntie who lived in Yate near Bristol. We had been together for a while, both going to the local nights, but when I found out that her Mum and Dad were going to visit them, we were both keen to join them saying that we wanted to go the local disco there, to which they agreed (I only had a motorbike at this time and couldn't drive a car). Once we arrived, I asked where the "Stars & Stripes" were as we wanted to go to the nightclub. Her parents got a shock when I mentioned that it "went all night", but they reluctantly let us both go to the all-nighter. That night there were other people there from Poole that I knew which made it better for us. Not long after, we both went to the Casino by coach and for the next three years, my all-nighters were varied, randomly going to Wigan, Yate or the local all-nighters in Swanage at the Durlston Court Hotel. After the coaches stopped going to Wigan from Poole, a few of us tried to get there anyway we could, within reason. We got there for a while by a friend's Mum driving us there in her car (I can't remember if she slept in the car or went to a hotel). She would miss some of the motorway by driving through the Cotswolds, as she knew that area really well. I seem to remember that she was from around that way when she was younger. When she had had enough of driving us there and back a few times, we managed to get another one of our mate's sister's boyfriend to drive us. Now this lad loved to drive and drive fast, it was a pleasure for him. I can't remember the car he had, but it was the fastest car on the motorway, so it was his foot flat to the floor and hardly ever travelling under 100 miles per hour. It used to take the coach 10 hours but he did it in 4 and a half hours, overtaking everything. Remember, there were no speed cameras back in those days. Another time, he drove us. We hadn't even got to Bath when, whilst going round a sharp bend, he pulled the gearstick out of its housing and was waving it around in his left hand. That slowed us down, but we got there and back with him changing gears carefully trying not to pull the gear stick out again.

After I got my driver's license, I used to drive to Yate, either with my then current girlfriend Maxine, or with a bunch of lads just before the pubs shut on a Saturday night. The Stars & Stripes in Yate was about 70 miles away through the country roads. I was young and always in a hurry to get everywhere, (not that a 1300L 1973 Mk I Escort was that quick) but how we survived when some of the chances I used to take beggars belief. I once overtook a car just before the brow of a hill, with someone else doing the same thing happening on the other side, also going round right hand country bends in the pitch black on the other side of the road, believing to myself I'd spot the lights of an on-coming truck, car or motorbike, just to cut a few seconds off the trip , how there weren't any fatalities I'll never know. Often we'd get there just as the doors were opening and as there were not many other people in early, the locals would be having a "game of football" for some fun (whilst records were being played) until the place started to fill up.

Yate was where I bought my first expensive record, it cost me around the same as my then weekly wage, 25 pounds for a US west coast Parkway demo of Ben Zine "Village Of Tears". I still have it today and it still hasn't gone up that much compared to some of the other records I have bought, but hey I can't complain! Initially, the Stars & Stripes Club was run by John (Kojak) Harvey I believe, then it shut down for a while. When it reopened, it was run by a local Poole lad called Nick McAvoy and I think it might have run for maybe another 2 to 3 years before finally closing.

Another local gig we attended was the Swanage allnighters and I heard about these nights before the first one had even happened. Being local and easy to reach, we would go into Poole town, generally to the Jolly Miller pub, spend two or three hours there catching up with our friends, some Soulies some not, then around 10 – 10.30 pm we would set off driving the 20 miles to Swanage. I'd try and park as close as I could to the Durlston Court Hotel so, if I needed anything out of my car, it was just outside plus it was hilly, so I didn't have to walk up the hill too far to get in. It was mostly locals who DJ'd and attended although I did hear from someone that a coachload from Wigan had come down for at least one all-nighter. I think it had a bit of a reputation for being a good night as the music was excellent and the atmosphere was great and only less than an hour from home.

Right: The Jolly Miller Pub © Bob Norman
Left: Lisa & I waiting to go to the "Stars & Stripes" Yate © Bob Norman

Back to my time at Wigan and, after the long journey to get there and by the time we would have managed to get in, there would be dancers on the floor from kick off, so we would drop our bags at the usual spot, then either go downstairs to hit the floor or go to the record bar. As I looked through the records, most of them were unknown to me and I had no idea how to distinguish originals from bootlegs.

Swanage Allnighter Flyer © Bob Norman

Swanage Allnighter and dance floor action © Bob Norman

I can't remember what I bought at the record bar, apart from Major Lance "You Don't Want Me No More" for 50 pence on what I later found out was a reissue, but it was cracked, which I didn't notice it at the time as I never took it out of the sleeve. After this episode, I learnt to take the records out of the sleeve and check both sides. If I went straight to the dance floor I would be there for ages. I would dance to anything initially, even though nearly everything was new to me, and I didn't care what tempo, I was just happy to be at the Casino with a thousand other soulies having a great time. Today still, once I'm on the floor I will dance to tunes I don't know, not for hours, but waiting for the next record to be played to see whether I stay or have a rest. As the night wore on, I would venture up to Mr M's, not when it opened but later through the night. To me it was where the older soulies went to dance. I would watch from the balcony but if I went to dance it would be at the back of the room. The dancers at the front would be doing kicks, spins, backdrops, that sort of thing plus they were older, so I thought it best to keep out of their way.

I preferred the main hall though as I always liked to hear tunes from the DJs that I'd never heard before. My favourite DJs were Richard Searling and Pat Brady because they were always putting out new tunes. They would play "new 60s" tunes which was what I liked best but I also liked most of the 70s tunes that they played. I managed to get to the Casino 14 times from March 1978 to September 1981, not a lot in three and a half years but being 260 miles and 6 plus hours by car, 10 hours on a coach and God knows how long on a train (not that I ever took the train), I thought it wasn't too bad.

Most of my times at the Casino I hardly ever "took" anything. On the odd occasion that I did, it would be "blueys" or "dexies", probably only 3 or 4 times bought and swallowed on the coach before we got there, maybe because of peer pressure or I wanted to see if it made for a better night. I don't remember if it was the first or second time I took some, but whichever I ended up chatting to a mate of mine, Paul, on the middle of the main room dancefloor for about 4 hours. We didn't dance at all, just "gas-bagged" the whole time. The other thing I remember was feeling paranoid walking past some lads chatting in the toilets, then standing there having a piss, thinking that they were looking at me and talking about me. Obviously, they weren't, apart from that I was having a good time on the speed.

Wigan Casino balcony at the end of the Era Night © Bob Norman.

My Last Night at Wigan

By this time the coaches from Poole had well and truly stopped, but I still used to subscribe to the music magazine "Black Echoes". I had been buying it for years and this was where I found out that the Casino was going to shut and they were going to acknowledge this by holding a final all-nighter.... "The End Of An Era". I decided I was going and spoke to a few people hoping there might be a coach, but it wasn't going to happen. In the end I drove up with my brother and Mate Andy in my car, which was the only time I actually drove there.

Left: Wigan Casino with the lads © Bob Norman.
Right: Tommy Hunt Live on Stage © Bob Norman

I regularly drove to Yate which I had done the weekend before the "End Of An Era" weekend. We obviously had pre-purchased our tickets which I still have the main part of to this day. I parked just opposite and waited for the crowd to die down a bit before we decided to go in. Being the last all-nighter, it was rammed. I can't remember where we set up that night, but our usual balcony spot was loaded up with a crowd already. Everywhere was full of Soulies.

I don't think I did much dancing that night because the floor was too packed all night. I can remember being in the record bar listening to the tunes and the dancers all clapping in sync, I don't know how many were through the door that night but I'd never seen the place so full, it was just a magnificent night, the people, the DJs, the music, the atmosphere, everything. My bubble burst through. I'm not sure who it was (probably Russ Winstanley), but it was probably three quarters of the way through the night when the music stopped for an announcement.

180

That announcement was saying that this was in fact not the final casino all-nighter, there was another one next Saturday because of the popularity of the present night, or something like that. Well, I felt cheated and I guess quite a few other attendees felt the same, because I said to myself that this is the last night for me and will not be coming back. I still enjoyed the rest of the night and when the three before eight were played, the last one was playing and absolutely everyone was singing and clapping along being the "last ever record" to be coming through the speakers. I remember I had a lump in my throat and a tear in my eye. It was a weird sensation, enjoyment and the sad fact this was my last night in the Casino. I thought that we were the only three from Poole there that night, but it was only in recent years through Facebook that I found out we were not the only ones, there were quite a few from Dorset too, but being so packed I never bumped in to any of them, or don't remember seeing them.

The following weekend, after the Casino had its "final" all-nighter", I drove (again with my brother and Nick McAvoy, who ran Yate) to Birmingham where he had a DJ spot at the Locarno ballroom. I'd never driven in Birmingham before and soon got lost in and around the "Bullring", but somehow we found our way and still got there early. We went in whilst the normal Saturday night disco was in its last hour or so. We met some local girls in the disco and they ended up staying all night for the Northern Soul. I ended up dropping them off at home in the morning and later wondered if they'd ever been to another all-nighter? Getting back to my younger brother Chris, he was once driven to Wigan by a lad nicknamed "Smiler" in his car. I saw a car, it was a 3-wheel Reliant Robin, they left on the Friday afternoon and it would have taken ages to get there. I don't know the top speed of a Reliant Robin but I don't think that they were exactly rapid and I'm pretty sure that they were even worse for road handling. Anyway, they did get there in the end and went to the oldies all-nighter that particular night, and I think they had a chill out day with some soulies Smiler knew on the Saturday.

They then went to the regular Saturday all-nighter as well. I never got to an oldies allnighter, something I regret not trying. The other thing to mention is he was photographed, unbeknownst to him, looking through records in the record bar. That picture I have seen on the internet a few times and have a suspicion it was used in one of the "Northern Noise" magazines. He is the third head from the right in the picture below looking through the records, behind the dark sleeved arm. I think Smiler is behind the first two, in the dark polo. When I first saw the picture, I thought that kid looks like my younger brother and when I looked closer and saw the tattoo on his forearm of the Casino Owl, it was confirmed.

Wigan Casino © Bob Norman

After the Casino, which only lasted two or three more nights from memory, I thought Northern Soul was going to be over. However Yate was still going and I was still getting my weekly Black Echoes paper and there were still adverts for soul nights but not Wigan. After my last night at Yate in May 82, it was a couple of months later I managed to go to the "Top of the World" club in Stafford.

There was a local lad nicknamed "Speedy" (not that he did drugs, but he would dance at a fast pace to most records) he had been to TOTW before and was happy to drive but wanted others to share the fuel cost. This I could understand, so me and my girlfriend (now wife Jacqui and still married) would go with him along with others a few times. One time Harold Melvin was on stage and he sang his popular hits like "The Love I Lost". I was hoping for his Northern hit "Get Out" to come blasting through the speakers but sadly, back then the Northern hits were passed by, but anyway it was a good night. I liked Stafford because I was hearing new tunes again with a different feel to them, still mostly 60s but with a "twist" to them. I think I only took a tape recorder once and recorded one of Pat Brady's sets, with tunes like Leroy Taylor "Oh Linda" and the Twilights "You're The One". I went a few times with the first anniversary being the last. I've just looked at my diary and forgot we also went to the Ric-Tic Revue at the Hinckley Leisure Centre, a good night with the likes of Edwin Starr, Al Kent, Pat Lewis, J J Barnes and Lou Ragland all featuring. Again, Speedy was driving.

Record Collecting

I'm not sure what the first northern soul record I bought was but it wasn't long after I started going to the local Youth Club nights. I saved up my money and bought a "stacker system" with the record player on the top. I would play the few records I had, one of which was "Interplay" by Derek & Ray on UK RCA, probably bought from W H Smith's, and practice my dancing in my bedroom. I would buy initially off a few locals at the local nights, then a while later I would subscribe to John Manship's record sales list. I reckon the first list I received was a list with a number less than 20 and I subscribed for years to those lists. I would also buy the sales tapes to listen to the many records that I never knew. Back in those days the list would, say, come out on a Tuesday and I would receive it on Wednesday, Thursday or Friday.

I'd look through it and if there was something I wanted I would have to ask my Dad if I could use the phone to call and see if it or they were available. What I now regard as "The Good Old Days". Generally though, by the time I got round to calling, what I wanted had usually gone, but "them's the breaks" as they say! I must have bought 50 to 60 sales tapes over the years and this would open up my ears to lots of records I'd never heard played by DJs that I had also never listened to . By now I had a "wants list" but it never crossed my mind to DJ at all. I was always a bit reserved and never wanted to stand out, I was always happy to stay in the background., so I just used to buy records for my own pleasure at home mostly. Back then I would buy and sell records. I'd sell records that I'd had for some time and thought someone else would get the same pleasure from them as I did. Well, that didn't last too long as I immediately regretted not being able to play records that I didn't have any more, so basically no more selling records for me. As I said before, I subscribed to Black Echoes and would generally only read all the articles concerning northern soul and would try to buy recommendations for records from the DJ's columns. Nearly all of them I would be "buying blind" and some I liked when I got to play them, others took a while to grow on me. One such record tipped by Pat Brady was the Four Sights "Love Is A Hurting Game" on Shy Soul. I bought it from Soul Bowl I think for ten pounds, it's grown on me but again I've hardly ever played it out. Another was Willie Parker's "Don't Hurt The One You Love" on M-Pac. I would record such records onto cassettes, which I would then play in my car along with the sales tape cassettes. This would expose me to these new tunes that I would hopefully come to like. I would make these cassette recordings with either 60s records on the whole cassette or 70s on a different cassette and play either in my car. Depending what type of mood I was in, would determine the style of northern I would play, but mostly it was the 60s tapes. I don't remember listening to Radio 1 very often in the car, maybe John Peel late at night or Steve Wright in the afternoon. I basically just lived for the northern soul.

Later on I was offered a record collection in a record box by Nick McAvoy, who was running Yate. I guess I bought this collection after Yate closed for the last time, around 1983, though I would have sworn I bought them in 1979 or 1980, just shows how the memory fades! I paid 175 pounds for 350 records including the DJ box, equating to 50p a record. After I bought it and got them home, I started to go through them, playing both A and B sides of the tunes I didn't know, which was most of them. I would sort out the sounds I liked and those I didn't like. I had no idea of the values back then of the records I now had, as the only references I could go by was from the record lists I would receive to get some sort of price. No price guides back then you see. In this collection was a Matt Lucas "You Better Go-Go" on Karen, The Moments "You Said" on Deep, The Charades "The Keys To My Happiness" on an MGM issue, Dickie Wonder "Nobody Knows" on Golden Triangle, Billy Keene "Wishing And Hoping" on Vault, The Chappells "You're Acting Kind Of Strange" on Bedford, Syng McGowan "That's what I want" on Hope, Bonnie Blanchard "You're The Only One" on CRS and James Fountain "Seven Day Lover" on Peachtree to name a few. On some Saturday afternoons I used to go to a record shop called the Bournemouth Soul Centre, run and owned by a fellow called Keith Clarke (I understand that he now lives in Perth, Western Australia). I used to go there regularly and spend quite a bit of time chatting with him. He was a few years older than me but had come down from up north and used to be into the northern soul scene once, but was by this time more into the jazz funk scene. The records I bought there that I remember were The Casanova Two "We Got To Keep On" on an Early Birds demo, Eternal Flame "Happiness In My Heart" on "Viva" and The King Davis House Rockers "Baby You Satisfy Me" on a Verve issue. I have probably only played the Casanova Two out once or twice. Later on a lad called Pete Widdison moved down to Dorset (he had DJ'd at Stafford), and I bumped into him at a local record fair in the Poole Arts Centre. He had some northern records for sale, something I was hoping to find but didn't really expect to. A bit later, he opened a record shop

185

in Parkstone, between Poole and Bournemouth., I can't remember what records I bought from Pete apart from the Fantastics "Me And You" on Sound Stage 7 for 10 quid. It was a tune I knew from Stafford, and a record I like but have only played it out a few times. I would also pop into a few second-hand shops never to find anything, apart from once, where I stumbled across a handful of records with the larger hole in the middle (American imports) at 10p each so I bought them blind as 10p wasn't much. In this bunch was a Los Canarios "Get On Your Knees" on Calla, Friendly People "I Ain't Got Nothin' But The Blues" on an HPM demo and Joe Matthews "Ain't Nothing You Can Do" on a Kool Kat bootleg demo, plus a few others that I can't remember. My last all-nighter in the UK was the Stafford 1st Anniversary in 1983. I think I got engaged not long after that and by all accounts northern soul venues were getting few and far between although I still got record sales lists and would still buy the occasional record.

We bought a house in 1986, got married in 1987 and emigrated to Adelaide, South Australia, in 1988. At that time, I had around 800 records in my collection, both originals and bootlegs. We sold nearly everything we had, the new washing machine, lawnmower, all our electrical goods as they wouldn't work in Australia I was told, so all we shipped over was our double bed (a wedding present), our clothes, my work tools and my 800 records. That's right, I couldn't bear to part with them! Not long after we had arrived, I was in Adelaide and happened to pop into a record store and couldn't believe that I found a copy of the Buckinghams "Don't You Care" on Australian CBS. I didn't expect any northern soul records at all to be found on an Australian release. For years I would still get my records out at home, sometimes at the weekends and sometimes on a week night and have a dance on my own with the kids looking on thinking "my Dad's a nutter" dancing to his records, but I didn't care. I was hoping that my music would rub off on them, but my son calls it "old fogey's music" although he does like the Valentines "Breakaway" and Court Davis "Try To Think (What You're

Doing) plus one more that I can't think of at the moment. All through my time in Australia I was receiving record lists from John Manship, Soul Bowl, and a few other people in the UK. This happened until I eventually got a computer and then after a bit of a time trying to work out how to use the bloody thing, I would search for northern soul music and record selling sites. It was a case of just mucking about until I got the hang of it, my kids would show me things and a couple of days later I'd forgotten all how to do it. In my work I quite met a few "poms" and especially if they had a northern accent, I would always ask them the same question, ie: "if they knew, or had heard of northern soul". The replies I got back were generally "No, never heard of it", "My mates back in England were into it", "Yeah I know it but not my thing", or "I used to go to such and such a club a long time ago." As far as I was concerned, I was the only person in Australia who liked northern soul! I did find out that Sydney had held soul nights. I got this from reading the football paper "British Soccer Weekly". I cut the ad out of the paper (the Wigan casino night owl) and kept it in my wallet for years, but I had two young children by now and flights were expensive to travel anywhere around Australia back in the early 1990s. If my memory is correct it was around AU $400 (approximately £210 or US$290 return so, being the only breadwinner, it was completely out of the question to go to Sydney for a soul night.

In 1993 I think it was, we had here in Adelaide the "Legends of Motown" tour at the entertainment centre. That day I had been to the Adelaide formula 1 grand prix, and they had an afterparty concert featuring Tina Turner. I managed to see most of her performance, but had to leave early to make it to the Legends of Motown concert, which consisted of the Four Tops, the Temptations and the Commodores. This was my first proper concert in Australia. Me and Jacqui went in, found our seats and sat down waiting for it all to start. After a while, the place filled up and the first group came out (I can't remember which group) and started singing. It wasn't long before me, Jacqui and quite a few others got up from our seats, went down to the front and started dancing. I think that the people who'd bought seats in the front rows were a bit pissed off with us dancing in front of them as they wanted to be able to sit down and enjoy the performance with an uninterrupted view. The miserable shits should have got up and danced as well! I think I was looking to see if anyone else was dancing in a northern soul dance style, but I didn't really spot anybody. If I had, I would have definitely gone up and spoke to them. Anyway, it was a great night and then it was all over, back to playing my records to myself for a few years. Because I was still getting lists and also had some questions I needed answers for about records, I thought I would have a chat with John Manship. We ended up talking about finding records in Australia that were wanted in the UK. I then started to search out the Adelaide record shops and when I could find the time, I would sift through the 7" boxes, also looking for Motown and soul records for myself. However, after chatting with John I started looking for Johnnie O'Keefe records in the local record shops and at the local record fairs. I found quite a few of these together with some Marcia Hines LPs on Wizard containing the sought after track "You Gotta Let Go". My best friend had a phone call to a bloke who had owned a record stall called Orange Box Records in an Adelaide suburb called Norwood. It had been a long time since he had his shop, but he still had what was left of his stock at home. I went to his house but he wouldn't let me look through any of his records, so I had to give him a list of records I was looking for. I hadn't prepared a list so I could only write down what I knew from talking to John, that's all I had to go with. Anyway, he went off with the list and I sat there with a cup of tea, waiting. When he came back he had in his hands a copy of a 7" Marcia Hines "You Gotta Let Go" on Wizard, Gene McDaniels "Walk With A Winner" on Liberty, Cheryl Gray "You Don't Love Me Anymore" on HMV and Dee Warwick "We're Doing Fine" on NZ Mercury. I asked him if he had any doubles, so he went away again and came back with another Marcia Hines 7" and a Gene McDaniels. If I knew then what I know now about Australian Soul records, my list would have been a lot bigger.

I never went back there but I think Barry Simpson did some time later. It still makes me wonder what other records he had and what I left behind because I had no knowledge of what other records had been released here. I kept all the single tunes and one of each of the doubles. With what was left and what I had found elsewhere I boxed them up and posted them to John, for which I received a credit.

Holiday's Back To The UK

My first trip back was in December 1992. We'd been here 4½ years, had 2 kids, a 3 year old and an 18 month old at the time and my wife was homesick and booked our journey back after teeing it up with my boss whilst I was working away in Melbourne. I didn't want to go back home on holiday at that point in time, (I'd got over my homesickness, maybe I never had it, and was still on my big adventure). Anyway, we went back, all staying at my Mum and Dad's house. We'd only been home for an hour or so and Greg, my best man, knocked on the door, said hello to everyone, met our kids and then said to me, "Do you fancy going to the Working Men's Club for a couple of drinks?" I couldn't say no, could I, even after the near day and a half of flying with next to no sleep. Having a few beers and catching up with some people who didn't know I'd gone did the trick. I got to bed late that evening and it put me straight back into UK time with no jet lag. After we'd been there a couple of weeks, my wife Jacqui, (who was going to kiss the ground at Heathrow airport when we arrived) did a 180 degree turnaround and was hoping the time would go quicker so she could get back to Oz. On the other hand, I had caught up with my mates again and was carrying on like I'd never left and could have stayed on longer. With us going back in the winter, it never occurred to me to see if there were any Northern events happening. For one, I had no transport, we also had two young kids and it would have been all too hard.

We generally manage to go back to the UK approximately every five years or so. On our second trip back in 1998 one of my mates gave me a Manifesto magazine to read. I noticed in one of the adverts that there was a Northern Soul event happening at Winsford in Cheshire so I decided to hire a car and go to the all-nighter. We found our way there before GPS, and I wanted to have a couple of pints in a local pub but we were too late, so we paid our money and went straight into the venue. I hadn't been to a soul event in nearly 15 years so I thought to myself, we were going to be the oldest people in there, me 36 and Jacqui 30. Well, I was in for a surprise as the age group was around the same as us, maybe a little older. There were some couples that had brought their young kids along as well, it was like a time warp but everyone older. I was in my element, well chuffed, we met a few people there that night and chatting to them they couldn't believe we had come all the way from Australia and gone there. My other recollection of the night was trying to get a discount on some CDs from Keith Minshull by saying I've come all the way from Australia and can I get a better price. He replied "I don't care if you've come all the way from Mars, that's the price", I can't remember if I bought them or not but I had a great night all the same. When we left in the morning to drive back to the south coast, driving down the M6 Jacqui had gone to sleep. I was travelling in the middle lane doing the standard 70 miles per hour and started getting more and more tired myself. The next services were 7 or 8 miles away and I don't know how I did it but I missed them and now was really struggling to stay awake. I woke Jacqui up, opened the windows and vents to try to keep awake until we reached the next services which were 30 odd miles away. I really struggled but we made it and I decided to park in the furthest corner of the car park, away from everyone and get some privacy. We dropped the seats right back and went to sleep. Not sure how long we went to sleep for but I was woken up by something bouncing off the windscreen. When I wound the seat up I saw that we weren't alone any more but there were lots of other cars parked in this far corner, a long way away from the cafes, shops and petrol station and a million kids having a kick around with a football. Why do people do that? We just wanted to be left in peace!

It was on this trip back that we decided to all go on a trip to Scotland (me, Jacqui, the kids and my Mum and Dad) as we'd never been there before. So, we hired a car and on the way up there I thought it would be a good idea if I stopped off for a while at John Manship's house where I could redeem my credit. In the end, after spending an hour or so with John while the others in the car were getting a bit pissed off waiting for me, I ended up walking out with a load of CDs and one record, which I can't remember the title of now. At this point, as far as I knew, I was still the only soulie in South Australia, so CDs represented the best value for money. When we returned to Australia, I would still look through the second hand record shops searching for tunes to send back to England. On one such day I visited a record shop called "Big Star Records" in Rundle Street, Adelaide. I don't know why, but they had a notice board in the window and I ended up looking in the window that afternoon, maybe I was looking to see if they were advertising any record fairs coming up, as I would go to all these fairs around Adelaide whenever possible. Anyway, whilst looking I spotted a poster advertising a Northern Soul event coming up at the Duke of York pub in Currie Street in the City. Well, I was so excited I was no longer the only bloke in South Australia that liked Northern Soul! I went inside, asked for a pen and paper and jotted down some details, the contact number was for Mark Howlett. When I got home, I gave Mark a call and spent a while chatting about how I thought I was the only soulie here and that I had records which I played at home to myself. He said that if I wanted I could bring some tunes along to play the next night. I said that'll be great and I couldn't wait. I was so stoked that I was no longer in the wilderness and had found other soulies. However, before the night arrived, I had to go away for work, (working in the Cooper Basin Desert at a gas processing facility) so I ended up not being able to make it. I was gutted, but I had to go to work. I called Mark to let him know but I said my wife and I would make the next one.

When we did get to go to our first Northern night in years, (my last one was at Winsford) I was looking forward to meeting my fellow local soulies. By the time we had driven to the City, found a place to park and went in, it had already started. We went inside and I was in heaven, 12 long lonely years in Oz of being a lonesome soulie were over. Northern was blasting through the speakers, it was magic. I was chatting, I was dancing, I was drinking and I played some tunes, this was my first ever DJ spot and I loved it! Other people danced to my records, it was brilliant. I met a lot of people that night: Mark Howlett, Pete and Miriam Feven, Stuart and Sue, Wayne and Alison, Mick and Sue, Todd and Monique, plus others. Apart from Mark who went back to England, I still see most of the others at soul events. After Mark returned home, Pete and Miriam solely took over the Duke of York nights and each time we went more and more people would come out of the woodwork and the attendances grew. I was really enjoying playing my records and getting to know more soulies. After we had been going for several months. I think Pete mentioned that there was going to be a Northern Soul weekend in Sydney, later on in the year, the Australian National Northern Soul Weekender. I was eager to go so I made plans and booked the tickets, flights and accommodation. A hotel in Surry Hills was where most of the Adelaide group were staying so I thought it best to stick with people who we knew. In my quest to save money, I booked a room only, thinking that there would be loads of places nearby to get food from as this was Sydney. I had only been in Sydney twice before, once when we emigrated and spent 4 nights there and once when I went away to work in Wollongong (I passed through it to and from the airport). Anyway, all that I could find locally to eat was a corner shop that had some pies in the small oven on the desk, so it was lamb and mint pies for my breakfast a couple of times. Note to oneself: book breakfast with the room in the future unless I know what is close by. So the Sydney National (my first Nash) was in the year 2000. There was a "meet and greet" on Friday night at the Sydney Globe Hotel. The Saturday all-nighter was at the Marrickville bowling club 9 pm to 6 am, then the Sunday was an all dayer at the Paddington Green Hotel 2 pm till close. The Marrickville Bowling Club had, for me, the best Australian atmosphere I have come across, (reminded me of the Casino, for the atmosphere) although it was nothing like the Casino inside. It was a single story building with a low roof, but with everyone on the floor singing and clapping in time, the heat, the humidity, the tunes, it was magic to me. I never DJ'd at this first National, nor my second in Melbourne a year later, Pete Feven gave me a couple of spots in Adelaide at my 3rd National, but actually the 5th in the series.

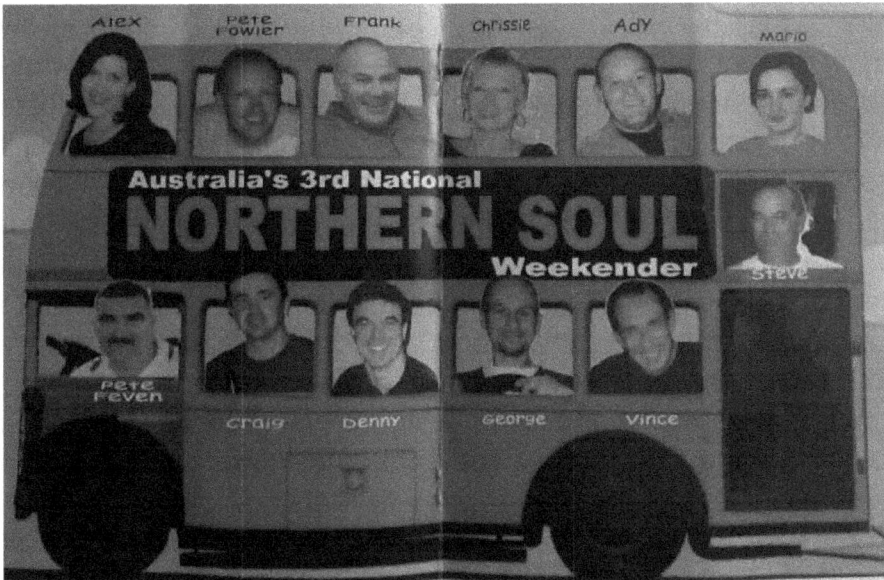

Australian 3rd National Weekender © Bob Norman

The first one was held in Adelaide in 1998 where the soulies in Perth, Pete Fowler and Kev McCord, had been in touch with Craig Bayliss and Vince Peach in Melbourne and the "Sydney Soul Sisters" (Maria, Chrissie and Alex). They decided to compromise with each other and hold the inaugural event on neutral ground, which was Adelaide. The second year it was decided Perth be the host, then Sydney the following year. Melbourne was (at that time) the only city left, so they organized the 2001 Weekender.

It was therefore Adelaide who took responsibility for the 2002 "Nash" courtesy of Peter and Miriam and returned to Perth in 2003. Finally Brisbane jumped on board in 2004 and so this was the format thereon, clockwise round the country. I missed the first two Nationals as I had not found out about it yet and when I found out the first one was in Adelaide just over a year earlier I was gutted I missed it, after all it was my home town now. Each year I have been going to the Nationals I meet new people, mostly expats now living here or in New Zealand and in recent years, travelers attending from the UK such as Roy Burton, Duncan and Sue McAllister, Mark Speakman and Chimene & Neil, who I met at the Sydney National in 2005. I don't know how we started talking but we were at the bar ordering some drinks and I would have probably said something like "Hello, is this your first National, as I haven't seen you before"?, and as it turned out, Chimene is from my hometown so we had a good old chat about Poole and asked if we knew the same people or went to the local soul nights in the area. Mark Speakman I first met at the Perth National in 2008, he had come over to Perth to catch up with his longtime friend Van Astbury, a soulie and resident of Perth. Sadly, Van passed away a few years ago now. I miss having my yearly chats with Van and Leslie. Mark has been to lots of the Aussie Nationals and always brings some tunes to sell and DJs here. Listen to Mark's spots as he plays some rare tunes that don't get played out here in Oz. Duncan and Sue McAllister I met at the Gold Coast Nash in 2009 after which they came to Adelaide to catch up with some friends of theirs, but whilst here they popped round to my house for an evening. I can't quite remember if I did a barbecue for them, I can remember playing records that evening. They have returned for several Weekender's saying "This will be our last", but they make it back for one more. I've had some great times with our Duncan for sure, always seeing the funny side of things and having a laugh.

Then we came to meet Roy Burton (RIP), I met Roy at the Gold Coast weekender, he had come over with his mate Mike Ritson who publishes the "Manifesto" magazine. I remember me and Roy walking back to our hotels along the Esplanade in Surfers Paradise at around 7am, half cut and wobbling up the road, chit chatting all the way. Roy has been to the Australian Nationals a lot over the subsequent years, and I like having a few beers and conversation with him. He also does a write up for Manifesto entitled "Soul in the Southern Hemisphere ". When I get the chance, along with a few fellow expats, I would send him stuff like upcoming events, playlists, etc., for inclusion in the magazine.

I have been in Australia longer than I lived in England, coming up for 33 years in fact. Before Covid, I would try to get back around every 5 years, each time when travelling back, stopping at different countries to experience different parts of the world. I've been to Africa, Asia and North America, with South America on my list of places to visit next, if we're allowed to travel. On my next holiday back to the UK in 2006, I went to a soul night at the Southampton Social Club with my brother-in-law, courtesy of a ride from Tim Smithers. I also did a DJ spot for Tim at the Bournemouth Railway Club

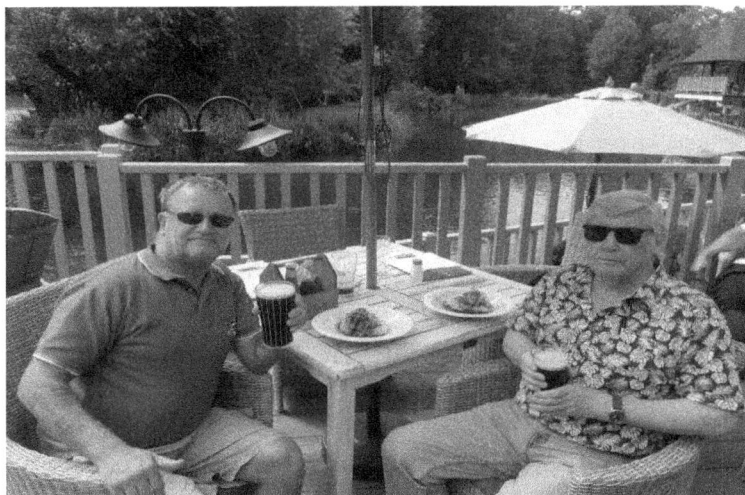

Bob Norman & Roy Burton © Bob Norman.

Roy passed away recently in 2021, and will be sorely missed by all of the soul family in Australia. He was such a big help promoting the Australian scene in his Manifesto articles.

To date, this was my most satisfying time as a DJ, and I got paid (I didn't want the money but Tim said I had to take it). Anything I put on the decks had the whole floor full. I didn't know if many people there that night would have remembered me from my younger days or not, I know I certainly remembered quite a few faces. It was also great to see Chimene and Neil who I had met in Sydney and had travelled down from Shrewsbury for the night. During my 2011 trip back, I also did another DJ spot for Tim but not at the Railway Club venue as this was out of action, so it was now at a hotel on the Westcliff side of Bournemouth. That night my mate Roy Burton came down to see me DJ and have a few beers. He had planned to leave before it finished to travel back home but ended up staying till the end deciding he was going to spend the night at a local Hotel. I don't know what was on but everywhere he tried was booked out. We even tried hotels on the way back to my Mum and Dad's house but nothing, so poor Roy had to spend the night on the sofa in the lounge before catching the train home in the morning. Whilst on this trip back, I attended the Kings Hall in Stoke for the first time. I really liked it, the floor was crammed most of the night in the main room. I was dancing to records I had not heard before, trying to listen to the DJ as he might announce what he had played, because I wanted some of these records in my collection. For me I like to hear tunes I've never heard before and dance to them, some are not my "cup of tea" and yet others like I've just mentioned, I just want to hear them more. Some people don't think the same way, they are stuck only with what they know and, as I've said to lots of people, every record you've ever heard in your life, you would have had to hear it for the first time once, so why stop at the "top 500" tunes. There's heaps of other tunes out there that are just as good if not better than the top 500. My tastes have changed over the years with the introduction of latin, R&B, gospel soul, crossover, although the new style of funkier soul is going to take a while. On my next trip back to the UK in 2016 I went to quite a few nights in our local area but also made the journey to Stoke and the Kings Hall again. This time I was a bit disappointed with the music. I don't think there were many tunes I didn't know but I managed to get to dance to (in the rare room), courtesy of Soul Sam, Arthur Willis "The Hurting Is Over", a tune I came across on YouTube a few years earlier and one I really wanted to own. I'd never heard anyone play it before and was very surprised to actually hear it let alone dance to it. I've only danced to it one more time, when Mick Heffernan played it at the Perth Australian National in 2018. I didn't stay all night at the Kings Hall, as I promised my wife we'd leave at around 3am, but just as it nearing 3, Ted Massey was DJing and playing the records that really appeal to me so I managed to stay for half his set before I had to leave to keep the wife happy. I doubt whether I'll make it to another all-nighter there, but who knows, maybe I'll try somewhere else if I manage to get back to the UK in the future. Whilst on this trip, I arranged to catch up with Roy Burton and have a few beers with him and a good old chat this time where he lives. He met me off the train and we went to one of his local pubs for lunch and a few beers before I headed off back to Poole. Before we returned to Australia, my brother said to me that he had no use for and didn't want his records anymore so did I want them? I told him yeah, what do you want for them? "Nothing you can have 'em" was his reply. He was more into the modern side of Northern Soul so when I looked through the two boxes, approximately 200 records, there were many that I didn't know, some I knew the artist and title, but not what the tune actually was. There were the odd ones that I did know as I either remembered them or I had a copy myself. One such record was Roscoe & Friends "Broadway Sissy" on TEC which I thought was worth around 200 pounds so I mentioned that they were worth some money but he just wanted to get rid of them. He said he wasn't going to listen to them anymore, so I boxed them up and sent them to Australia with the other stuff we couldn't carry in our suitcases.

Since I have found other soulies in Australia, I have been to every Australian National from Sydney in 2000 to the last one in 2019 on the Gold Coast in Queensland, plus quite a few various "mini weekenders" that have been arranged by different states, usually the capital cities. The Gold Coast crew used to put on a great mini weekender at Billy's Beach Bar which was organised by my mate Baz Symes (who is also from Poole and now lives in Adelaide) until the complex was knocked down for redevelopment.

I've also been to the Coffs Harbour mini weekenders, organised by Mark Webb on the coast in New South Wales, somewhere midway between Sydney and Brisbane. These are great Weekender's, if anyone can manage to attend, they won't be disappointed. The 2020 "Nash" was supposed to be in Sydney but Covid-19 put paid to that, and the rearranged 2021 one has gone the same way. Since I have been attending our Nationals, I have met loads of great people from around this big country. I have often worked away in the different cities and I get the chance to socialise with some of these great friends and attend their local soul nights and occasionally do a guest DJ spot. So for me now, I have lots of soul friends in Australia that I now class as my "big family". One such time I was working in Brisbane, I was there for a couple of months. I had a get together with Steve and Elaine Griffin at a local restaurant on the South Bank, which is always nice to see a friendly face. I would also spend some time with Steve Byatt and Chrissy Flisk stopping the night with them quite a few times whilst I was there. I also caught up with Gary and his mate Mark who was also from Adelaide and we already knew each other. That day we went to the Gabba cricket ground to watch a game of Aussie rules AFL. I have no idea who the opponents were, we just spent the whole day on the lash and I was pissing myself laughing at these two best of mates taking the mick out of each other all day. I had to work the next day and I was dog tired, but the day out was excellent. I've also worked in Melbourne a few times, and I always make sure to listen to "Soultime" with Vince Peach on the local

PBS 106.5 radio station. On one of my earlier work trips there, I was picked up by Keith and Vera Sutcliffe. She was a good soul, our Vera, gone but not forgotten. Anyway, we went round Vince's house for a while and if my memory serves me correct, we all went to the Cherry Bar where Vince did his usual DJ spot. On another working trip (9 months in Melbourne) I wasn't too far away from Keith and would catch up quite often, talking shit, drinking beers, playing records, then crashing on his couch in the early hours of the morning. Also on this trip I would drive to Mark and Ann's once a month on a Saturday and spend the evening at the Melbourne Soul Club nights put on by Steve Bardsley and another fella who I can't remember.

At the end of the night, we would, (including Mick and Gail Smith), go back to Mark and Ann's and sit around the table having a cup of tea and a chat before "hitting the sack" for the night. On some Sundays I would try to catch up with Vince at a bar called the "Aviary" where he would be doing an afternoon session. I think I made his life a bit easier sometimes, as he was able to pop outside for a leisurely smoke and didn't have to rush back as I would start the next record for him. Always a good time.

Back to the Nationals, apart from the Adelaide ones, I would usually have my flights and accommodation booked nearly a year ahead. The packing was usually done a couple of nights before and the record sorting usually takes me a couple of weeks including the final refinements once I know the actual DJ roster, taking out what the DJs before me might have in their collection. Then it's a case of getting up early on the day of the flight to go to the airport where there would be other travelling Adelaide soulies, so I end up having a chat and a beer while waiting for the flight to somewhere around this big country. After the flight arrives at the destination, it's either an Uber or a taxi to the accommodation, dump the bags and records in the room then head off to the pub for more beers and a catch up with the local and interstate people I haven't seen in twelve months.

I normally have all good intentions of only having a few drinks, but I am always chatting and seem to be there a lot longer than I anticipated, meaning more beer than I planned, usually resulting in being "half cut" walking back to the room to get ready for the first night. But hey, I love it. It's slightly different when Adelaide hosts Nash. We have hosted it five times to date, the first three were organized by other people, mainly Pete and Miriam, Todd and a collection of others. I personally have been involved with the last two here, 2012 and 2017, so it makes it difficult to have a drink with visitors when we have to be helping and making sure things run as smoothly as possible. However, it doesn't always go to plan; in 2012 at the Dom Polski Polish club they ran out of beer on the Saturday night. As much as they tried to keep up they just couldn't, so Paul Davy and his mate Rob Messer from the UK went out and bought several cartons of beer that we ended up selling at our own makeshift bar. They were pre-warned about what demand to expect but they thought they had it under control, and us Brits we do like to drink. The same thing happened in 2017 at the German club where the arrogant manager devised a stupid queuing system for the bar so there was always a huge crowd waiting for a drink which annoyed everyone and again the idiot didn't have enough bar staff. Again he was pre-warned but didn't listen, he thought he knew better. We were drinking way more beer than they served at the Big German festival "The Schutzenfest", which I thought was saying something.

Getting back to the Adelaide soul nights at the Duke of York, these were held for a few years, until the owners either sold the pub or wanted to go in a different direction. After this, Todd Cavender, a local Australian lad, took over the running in the mid 2000's with the new venue being the Enigma Bar in Hindley Street in the city. Hindley Street is the main entertainment street in Adelaide with lots of colourful characters walking around, the young girls wearing not too much even in the depth of winter, the drunks, the strip clubs, the fights, you know the stuff. I think this put a lot of people off going there and the attendance numbers were down over time, so it wasn't viable for the owners to keep letting us use it. So, a short time after it was canned and a few of us agreed to try and get something happening again. This was when Tom Moore suggested a small pub called The Hictorian in a quiet part of the city he used to go to after work with some colleagues for a few drinks. A quiet pub in a quiet part of the city, excellent. This was our first venue for "Adelaide Soul City "as we called ourselves. We first hired the downstairs of the pub but after a few nights, the manager gave us a discount on the hire, because he was so happy with the bar takings. We outgrew downstairs and then went upstairs to a bigger room, which meant carrying all the DJ gear (turntables, lights, mixer, speakers etc.) upstairs to set up for the night, and all back down again at the end of the night, when people were going home or off to one of the night clubs. We were going great there, then the owners sold the pub and the new ones wanted to turn it into an eating venue. We therefore had to find yet another venue, which ended up being a small club/cocktail bar called "Cushdy" on Hindley Street again, about 300 meters form the Enigma Bar where we were a few years earlier. We used Cushdy for some time, I can't quite remember how long it was (2 or 3 years) until the numbers dropped off, again probably due to the location and trying to find somewhere to park. It wasn't viable for them to let us keep going, so we were on the hunt again for another Northern Soul venue.

This time we ended up hiring another upstairs venue (more humping and carrying) at the German club in a quiet part of the city with plenty of parking. We had a small partitioned off area at the back separated from the main dance hall by a heavy curtain. It was generally quiet on a Saturday night there, so they didn't mind us using it, as it made them a bit of money from the hire fee plus the healthier than normal bar takings. The friendly bar staff were always glad to see us as they were busy for once. After a short while we had outgrown that smaller area and the committee agreed to let us use the main room for our nights at no extra cost. One thing we had to be mindful of was the time we had to stop the music at 1am sharp. On many nights Otto, the club president, would be looking at his watch and as soon as it was 1am, he would immediately switch all the lights on, so that was the signal to end the night. I didn't mind as I'd generally been up from the early hours going to work that day. We had some great nights there and for some time we were regularly getting over 120 people in. Our music policy was and still is "something for everyone", Tamla Motown, classic and rare Northern Soul and a sprinkling of modern thrown in. Well, all good things came to an end and that happened when the committee decided they wanted to make it a live music venue. The next venue we hired was the Irish Club in the centre of the city, this time ground level so no more climbing stairs with heavy gear. We were there for some time then we decided to go back to the German Club but the upstairs hall was no longer available to us. The German Club was a massive place with separate rooms on three different levels. We hired several of them during the next year until it finally came to a stop to make way for redevelopment.

We still have our soul nights, now back at the Irish Club under the same "Soul in the City" banner. They always used to run once a month, generally at the end of the month, apart from February and March when we don't have any nights as Adelaide hosts the "Fringe", an arts and entertainment festival. In more recent times we began running them once every three months, as there are now other events happening to the south and north of the city. So we thought there wasn't enough room to hold multiple monthly events. Finding Northern Soul here in Adelaide and starting to DJ was when my record collecting took off in earnest. I had been buying occasional 45s from John Manship or occasionally Soul Bowl and I remember talking to John Anderson over the phone asking about records from his lists and waiting for his reply after he had had a long drag of his cigarette. But when I started to search for records on eBay, well holy crap, there were always all sorts of awesome records popping up. I have missed out on a few, and as a beginner for example I bid too low on a Lillie Bryant "Meet Me Halfway" on a Tay-Ster demo. I came second on that attempt with my bid at around $300 thinking I would get it cheap with only a couple of othor biddors in the race and the fact that the seller made no mention of Northern Soul. I now know that I should have gone a lot higher, but them's the breaks as they say. I also came second on Bill Bush "I'm Waiting" on Ronn by 76 cents! It went for $1100 or something and the winner beat me by a fraction. Back in the day, you sort of knew other people's eBay ID and I lost to a local lad here in Australia. I now have a copy that I bought for a lot less than the price I bid and missed out on the other one, I might add. Some of my bigger ticket records I have won on eBay include the Executive Four "I Got A Good Thing Going" on Lu Mar, William Powell "Heartache Souvenirs" on Power House, Parliaments "This Is My Rainy Day" on Cabell, New Wanderers "Ain't Gonna Do You No Harm b/w "Let Me Render My Service" on Ready, Eric Mercury "Lonely Girl" on Sac, Lonnie Russ "Say Girl" on a Kerwood yellow issue, Joey Delorenzo "Wake Up To The Sunshine Girl" on Mi-Val, Yvonne Vernee "Just Like You Did Me" on Sonbert, Vondells "Hey Girl You've Changed" on Airtown, Nomads "Something's Burning" on Mo-Groove, Johnny Hampton "Not My Girl" on Dotty's, Dynamic Three "You Said Yeah" on Del Val, De-Lites "Lover" on Cuppy, Paris "Sleepless Nights" on Doc and Parisians "Twinkle Little Star on Demon Hot to name a few. If I knew then what I know now, I would have bought another Parisians at the same time as I was in talks to buy one from a UK seller directly but one came up on Ebay and I happened to win it. I should have got the two as the price they have been selling for in recent times is way more than I would have paid for a pair of them. The day I won the Nomads was at the Sydney Nash in 2010, it was a Saturday afternoon at the pub. I was looking through a record box that someone had brought over from England. I came across Bobby Kline's "Say Something Nice To Me" and it was in great condition so I thought I'd go to the ATM to withdraw some cash. On the way I checked my eBay account and lo and behold I'd won the Nomads for a reasonable price, so I got the cash out for the Bobby Kline and went back. When I got back, the record was in someone else's hands as they agreed on a price and so it was gone. At the time I did feel some sort of relief as I was going to spend a lot on the Nomads buying both on the same day was gonna hurt. Now, of course, I regret not holding the record until I got back. Apart from Stewart Ames "Angelina Oh Angelina" on J&S and some new previously unreleased tunes, I haven't been buying much lately because the prices have shot up and our dollar has dropped a long way from where it once was, I never set out to collect all the records I have, it just ended up being an addiction. I used to spend any available hour I had on the computer or my mobile phone looking for records to buy, staying up at night and not getting enough sleep, but I would do it the next day and the day after and so on. I think Covid has put a stop to it in the end. But do I regret it not a bit! However, I'm now at that point in my life when I do think about retiring, so my head is thinking I should sell up but my heart keeps arguing "keep hold of them a bit longer". I do like to occasionally have a play and dance to them at home, plus playing some of them out to other people to enjoy or have a dance too.

Well I think I have covered more than enough, I've been writing bits and pieces of this for nearly a year now to help out my friend Johnny "Redpants" Warren. Hopefully someone might get some pleasure from my participation in Book Two and any profit's raised will help artists that are still around who have given us so much pleasure from their hard work over the years to give us this thing called "NORTHERN SOUL" – a way of life

Keep the faith and many thanks to Bob Norman

.

Tommy Hunt Live on Stage © Bob Norman

Gold Coast National 2019 Bob Norman, Jacqui Norman & John Warren © Bob Norman

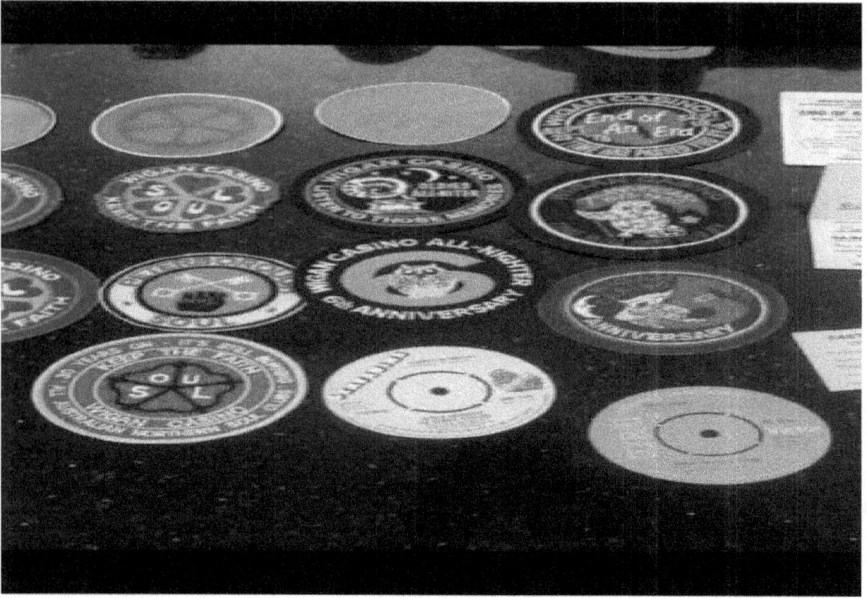

My Badges © Bob Norman

Bob Norman & Jacqui Norman © Bob Norman

Chapter 16

My soul story, by Netti Page

I have always enjoyed music and my personal journey started when I was about 13. Much to the dismay of my father ("turn that shit down"), my mother bought me a small radio with a built-in tape recorder, something like a mini "Boom Box", but without the battery option. We were living in rural Bavaria at the time, where music culture mostly consisted of traditional "umpa style" dancing whenever someone got married, in the local pub. Luckily there was an alternative Radio Station and I soon started creating cassette mix tapes to share with friends. Soon a portable turntable with a built in speaker followed, starting my life-long obsession with collecting music on vinyl.

There was one live Band I enjoyed called ZAPINZA, who played mostly 60s covers. I had a huge crush on their organist and would do anything to see them. I would break out through the window and climb down the balcony pillar in the middle of the night, in subzero temperatures, then cycled 20km through the snow to the venue. I have also always loved dancing but in that scene one was not to dance without a partner. Constantly tapping my feet restlessly, I was soon looking for alternatives. A slightly older friend of mine had a car and she invited me to join her to a Discotheque called XANADU. There I was no longer at the mercy of a dance partner to be able to groove. I was still significantly under age but with the help of make-up I got in. Following this success we checked out other clubs in the area and I never got turned down. The music played was mostly 70s soul and disco, as well as "Schlager ", German sung popu-lar hits, which much later, in the German Scooter Scene in the 90s, became a big thing.

At the age of 18 I left school and moved to a slightly bigger town in South Bavaria called Bad Reichenhall, to train as a nurse. The town was famous for its healing climate and most inhabitants were elderly. There was one night club about 10km out of town but we are now in the early eighties and 80s pop was huge there. Soft Cell's version of Gloria Jones' "Tainted Love" got me curious about the original but it took another 30 years before I finally owned the original of this record. My DJ career started when the Nursing School juniors were asked to organise the Senior's leaving party. I had upgraded my portable turntable to a different model, which had a set of speakers and started playing my collection of 45s to everyone's amusement.

The thrill of entertaining at that party left me craving for more. I therefore asked at my local Bar, which was run by a lady owner and she had DJs play music there regularly. I tried my luck and asked: "Are you looking for another DJ?" and was told "no, who are you asking for?". I said "me" and she quickly changed her mind. "Of course" she said, but you will only get paid in cock-tails. "Deal", I said. On arrival each night when I was playing I got presented with the owners' huge book of cocktails to choose from, leading to many happy hangovers. Despite not getting paid I managed to save enough money for the odd new record. Once I had completed my nursing training I bought a "proper" stereo with my first pay cheque.

Buying records in rural Bavaria was almost impossible, so I travelled to Munich regularly, where they had a few good record stores. My collection grew but so did my craving for alternative music and I soon discovered a very different night club called "LiBella", in Kirchweidach, where only alternative music was played. It was quite a drive away, in the middle of nowhere but I now had a car and nothing could stop me. Even though quite a range of music was played at the LiBella, for me was the "Twisted Wheel" of rural Bavaria. People would travel there from afar and get together for a great celebration of alternative music. We danced to Punk, Ska, Mod, Psychobilly, Goth and

Hiphop. DJs would mix things up, about 5-6 songs each genre, to keep punters of all types of tastes happy. Similar to the "Twisted Wheel", the venue had to change location after the small, sticky, dripping with sweat on a full night. The only difference to UK soul stories was that there was NO public transport to get there. I had to drive 1 ½ hours each way, picking up a number of my friends on the way. The only condition was not to fall asleep in my car on the way back, which, needless to say, failed every time. It is a miracle I only fell asleep while driving home once. I crashed into a side barrier and the noise woke me, narrowly escaping a concrete wall. After 3 years (1982-1985) of wicked nights at the LiBella, the concrete building was deemed to be torn down to make way for a Supermarket. We protested but to no avail. A new building was found in Altenmarkt an der Alz, which was much nicer and quite roomy but we all felt that it was never quite the same. I continued to go there, nevertheless, even long after I had moved away to the middle of Germany. Perhaps one of my enjoyable memories of the LiBella was their annual boat cruise on the lake "Chiemsee". I met two of my closest friends there during my first trip, Simone Hofmeister and Thomas Schuebel. On one occasion my car broke down on the day of the boat trip, so I decided to hitch hike the 300 km with my then partner Michael. The two of us were standing on the road for hours, without success. Desperate, I decided to get changed into a short skirt and asked Michael to hide in the bushes. Within seconds a car pulled over. Michael jumped out and we managed to both get a lift, arriving at the peer seconds before the boat was leaving. How lucky was that! And the best of it all, LiBella is still going strong in 2021. They have a Facebook and a Wikipedia page!

I had been into alternative music for most of my life but it wasn't until I met my (now ex-) husband Goetz Neugebauer, that I got introduced properly to northern Soul. Goetz had been a "scooter boy" since he was a teenager and northern Soul is huge in the scooter scene in Germany. I had always wanted to ride bikes and with Goetz' encouragement (and while 3 months pregnant with our daughter Dorothea) I got my bike license. Goetz got me an old PX200 Vespa and I was "in"! I still remember my first Allnighter as if it was yesterday. Immediate upon hearing my first proper Northern Soul record I was in heaven. I couldn't believe how happy the music made me and I was immediately hooked. I wanted more and started looking for events playing this sound within the 500km radius (a day's ride) of my home in (luckily very centrally located) Ludwigshafen/Rhein.

For our wedding I insisted we hire a party boat in good old Li-Bella tradition, so we shipped up and down the river Neckar, dancing to tunes by DJ Pepe.

There were occasional weekenders in "proper" venues but the bulk of the events were "Scooter Runs", usually organised by a local scooter club in the middle of a field, with a party tent with rough wooden floor, a mobile alcohol vendor and portaloos, if you were lucky. Northern Soul would be played non-stop Friday afternoon until Sunday lunch time. Everyone would turn up on their scooters, pitch their tent Friday afternoon and leave to ride home Sunday. Usually there would only be a flyer with instructions to the local swimming pool, for people who could be bothered getting cleaned up half way through the weekend. There were scooter runs throughout spring, summer and autumn almost every weekend. Not many girls would go, as camping rough was a put off, so the ones that did got treated like queens. I absolutely loved it and don't think I ever paid for a single drink. I was too busy having a good time to think about DJing and it wasn't until I moved to New Zealand with Goetz and Dorothea in 1997, that my DJ skills got used again.

My first long-distance scooter journey in Germany was from Ludigshafen/Rhein all the way to the annual "Eurovespa" event, which was held in San Remo/Italy that year. Our convoy consisted of three visiting New Zealand Scooterists in a car, Goetz on a Vespa with sidecar and me on my PX 200. Half an hour into the 16 hour journey it started pouring down with rain and it soon became apparent that my rain protection "Onesee" was not up to the task. Things were escalated further by my rookie mistake of fitting a "Onesee" into my boots, not over them. Soon I found myself dripping wet from top to toe. Attempts to dry my riding leathers under the hand dryer during breaks proved ineffective and embarrassing, as I stood there, in the female toilet, in my underwear. I realised I could do nothing else but to accept my fate. I was grateful the journey took place in summer and the closer we got to Italy, the warmer the weather got. Once it was time to cross the Alps on those small windy 180 degree steep uphill corners the rain stopped and my focus went entirely towards not falling off or crashing into oncoming traffic. We stopped somewhere halfway to the top and the next day was a breeze with sunshine and absolutely breathtaking views.

The "Eurovespa" was a huge annual event, attracting thousands of Scooterists from all over the world. Most attendees were catered for my "mainstream" entertainment, such as Brass Bands and Cover Bands playing contemporary hits. However, there was also a small nightclub that played mostly French and Italian Mod sounds and some Northern Soul. I was in my element immediately and danced all night long. For the ones that haven't been, Scooterist in Italy are allowed to cut traffic jams by riding on the median. There are as many female as male riders, so I was by no means "special". However, one day I took the Goetz' Vespa with a side-car to the event, transporting our two male New Zealand friends in the back and in the side car. A Japanese Scooter Magazine photographer thought that this was worth shooting and so we got featured on the other side of the world. I don't have a copy of that photo but there is one with Goetz riding, me on the back and our scooter friend from New Zealand, Michael, in the side car.

Upon arrival in New Zealand I purchased a second hand set of DJ turntables and a mixer, to try and earn a little bit of extra money. I got the odd "corporate gig", which I could only describe as "I was young and needed the money", playing mostly chart hits. However, I mostly ended up playing with local alternative Bands, usually for free drinks (this culture seems a worldwide one). Northern Soul was not known by most New Zealanders, unless they were British Expats or Scooter Boys, and the development of the small yet hearty scene in New Zealand has been covered by my chapter in book one. My role as "warm up" DJ for local Bands in the late 90s and early 2000s allowed me to introduce this music to the wider public in the Auckland underground music scene. I would play a good portion of Northern but also 60s Garage, Motown, Ska, Mod and 60s RnB, as well as a few disco staples. This always worked well when warming up for Bands and mostly also at parties. I can recall only one occasion, when after a successful start with Soul and Motown I was asked if I had any "Trance" music. Needless to say, I apologised, packed up and left. Both, our home at 37 Formby Ave, Pt. Chevalier, Auckland and Goetz' scooter shop "Scooter Emotion" also were regular party venues. We often hosted overseas Bands brought to New Zealand by Auckland event manager John Baker. Northern Soul as the complimentary music played to get the crowd going. And then there was the Ambassador Bar, 5 minutes walk from my house in Pt. Chevalier. With turntables and a mixer ready to go, I spent most weekends spinning my Soul records there, usually either to compliment live bands or with other DJs. The Bar's owner and very gifted artist Peter Roche would serve Absinth, which regularly set the Bar alight when serving this drink. Lucky the Bar was made out of marble.

After a couple of years of living in New Zealand I went back to Germany for a visit. I borrowed a scooter off a friend of mine and set out to attend as many of my beloved "Scooter Runs" as possible. Luckily this subculture had largely remained unchanged and I enjoyed several fun weekends with very little sleep and lots of dancing. I also attended one formal Vespa

Club of Germany event, which traditionally had a Cover Band playing contemporary hits, similar to the "Euro Vespa". The event wasn't big enough to warrant an alternative dance venue, so half the attendees were bored Scooter boys and girls. But then something really bizarre happened. Someone in the German scooter Northern Soul scene had worked out that "German Schlagers", traditionally considered way too cheesy to dance to by anyone under the age of 60, had a similar rhythm to Northern Soul. Most Cover Bands would still know how to play "Schlager" and so did the one hired for that event. One of the scooter boys got up and requested a "Schlager" set and immediately the party got completely out of control. Everyone got up to dance. Someone in their 50's swapped clothes with a lady in her 70's and both were partners dancing wildly. There were steel cap booted topless scooter boys doing back drops next to old couples performing something reminiscent of an American Coloured couple's 40s jive dance clip. Shoes were thrown into corners, skirts were lifted and swung above heads. It was the craziest thing I had ever seen. If any readers of this article would like to know more about "Schlager", it is only a google search away. I only have one 45 in this genre, Marianne Mendt's "wie a Glock", which is actually Austrian, not German, but a good example. I had been looking for a copy of this record, which is considered rare and therefore hard to find. I got lucky during another visit to Germany over ten years later, at a Flea Market in Berlin, where a seller didn't know the history of the records. He made fun of me for picking it and almost begged me to take it off him for one Euro. To understand the attitude the reader needs to know that among the Berlin "in-crowd", anything Bavarian or Austrian is considered extremely uncool. I politely thanked the seller and walked away, excited about my find. One of my Australian Soulie friends, Bernhard Schmitz, an Austrian expat, who lives in Sydney, shared my excitement. I was fortunately able to play the record when I was invited to play a set during his regular radio soul show. During a different journey back to Germany I celebrated my love for Northern Soul by going to a proper UK Weekender, Cleethorpes 1999. All my German Scooter Friends went with their cars and I hitched a ride. We stayed in one of the caravans, which was shaking precariously every time someone moved and had the most narrow bed I have ever slept in. But it was worth every minute. I even met fellow UK expat Chrissie on the dancefloor, not realising she had moved from Sydney back to the UK!

Unfortunately, back in New Zealand, my marriage with Goetz ended but this did not change my love for Northern Soul. I continued my quest to promote this music by DJing at as many events as possible. One of the common issues all DJs face is "requests", which exponentially increase, the more one plays rare, unknown sounds. The internet is full of suggested comments on how to deal with this situation but I usually stick to a friendly apology to avoid an escalating scenario. On one occasion I was playing in a Warehouse kitted out as a beach Tiki Bar, with a giant temple made out of rather wobbly ply. The DJ booth was at the top of the structure, with a small peeking window above a set of fake temple steps, made out of paper mache. The party was in full swing, when one customer decided it was request time. Unfortunately, instead of climbing up the ladder to the side of the structure to talk to me, he climbed up the temple front, making the whole structure wobble dangerously. The record skipped off the turntable and the construction started to swing back and forth. Luckily security came to my aid and a major disaster was avoided. For weeks after that I had nightmares about large Tikis, my gear and my entire collection of records collapsing on top of me. Other common hazards can be wooden floors, especially in older buildings and particularly when located above floor level. I recall a Christmas Party on the first floor of an old villa. I had tried to be as prepared as possible, by positioning a number of chairs in front of the DJ booth, but without success. Alcohol levels of attendees did not help and so this lady kept jumping up and down in front of the turntables, shouting "don't make the record jump" to me and thereby making the record jump. This went on for the duration of the song, despite me shouting back: "no, YOU make the record jump", while waving my hands to try and make her take a few steps back. Luckily my next choice was not appreciated and the lady walked away, mumbling something disapproving that I was glad not to understand.

Other rather unusual gigs involved playing for the first ever New Zealand show of Kitty, Daisy and Lewis, a UK Band. My then partner Kris and I played before and in between the Bands at the Monte Cristo Room in Auckland. However, after the Bands had finished, the party was moved to a different room, but we were not! A camera was installed to film us playing, with a screen visible to punters, but we had no idea about the crowd response. Did they like the song? Did we empty the dance floor? Our first ever "blind gig"! We continued playing records until people had left for the night, taking turns at walking over to the dance floor room next door. Having a camera pointed at ones' self when playing records is never easy. For a while Kris and I had a radio show at Radio Ponsonby, Auckland. The show was called "Soul Deep" on a Sunday afternoon and featured 60s Soul, Northern Soul and early 70s Funk. It was initially started by Manchester Expat Soulie Chrissie and her friend Tanja, who kindly "gifted" it to us. The show was aired from an upstairs room at the Chapel Bar in Ponsonby Rd, which was later moved to Ponsonby Central. Each show was recorded with a sound and visual feed, so no scratching in rude places or picking your nose while on air!! Unfortunately, Radio Ponsonby did not survive and I was left with the occasional guest spot at the much more established Auckland student radio 95 Bfm. I know many stories of UK DJs going for digging trips to the US regularly since the beginning of Northern Soul and even though I can always be found in record stores when going anywhere, I only did a proper "digging trip" once, with Kris, for 2 whole weeks. We hired a car, starting in Memphis and making our way to New Orleans via Little Rock (great but also quite scary digging there), Austin/Texas and Dallas/Texas.

There was a two day record fair in Austin Texas, where I was one of two girls digging! No queue at the toilets and great deals for me.

Our regular Northern Soul nights in New Zealand are covered in my chapter in book one, but it is worth mentioning that since this was written the scene has grown even further. Our new venue is now the Pt. Chevalier RSA Auckland, which has an enormous sprung wooden dance floor. Staff at the RSA are very welcoming and we now have up to 150 attendees of all ages throughout the night. We also have a number of new DJ, including "DJ Special Brew" Gary McLeod, "DJ Soul Finger" Adrian Ritchards, DJ Elboy Elliott Winthrop (Fingerpop), DJ Dave Best (Richard Edeson), and young upcoming female DJ Baby David (Jessamine Edison).

Excitingly and not covered in book one is the Northern Soul scene developing on New Zealands' South Island, promoted mostly by fellow Soulies Stuart Shaw, Ian Partner and Liz Clingan. Liz started their website, "Northern Soul in Canterbury" in 2016, after moving to Christchurch from Nelson, which slowly gained momentum with 49 members. Ian and Liz were keen to push the movement and in April 2021 Liz started the "Canterbury Soul NZ Club", which also incorporated Motown sounds. This move quickly increased the membership to 108 at the time this article was written, with ever growing interest. Liz, Ian and Stuart have been putting a number of events on in Christchurch and are planning several in the future. Also on the South Island there is also a regular night in Queenstown, organised by DJ (Chris) Langston, called the Nitty Gritty, which features Northern Soul, 50s, 60s, R&B and Funk. We are fortunate to have Chris play a set at our next Soul Night at the Pt. Chevalier RSA.

I am grateful for Johnny Warren's support for the contemporary Wellington Soul Band "Jamie and the Numbers" (Simon Bayliss on guitar), who have published Northern Soul covers on 45 recently. Starting with an absolutely stunning version of The

Precisions' "If This Is The Love", followed by Melba Moore's " Magic Touch" and "You Don't love Me" by Epitome of Sound. Their fascinating story will be covered by Simon Bayliss in a separate chapter in this book. I am confident that in New Zealand "The Only Way is Up" and that "it will never be over" for us. KTF.

New Zealand Flyer 2011 for their first ever weekender © Netti Page

Netti first px 200 © Netti Page

Top Left. Dr. Explosion at Scooter Emotion has top left to right: Jorge Munos-Cobo, John Baker, Alvaro Coalla, middle row left to right Netti Page, "DJ Skinny" Michael Simons, bottom left to right Amanda Reed, Felix Dominguez © Netti Page.

Wedding boat soul party © Netti Page

Ambassador Flyer © Netti Page

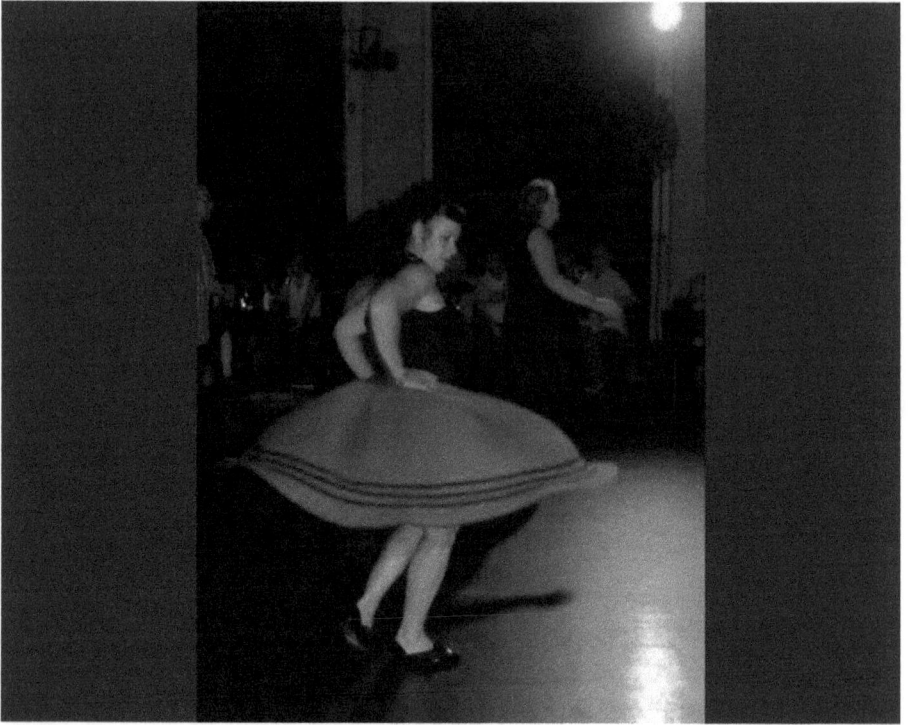

Netti Page In The Zone © Netti Page

Chapter 17

Simon Bayliss Soul On The Dole From The West Midlands To Wellington

Out of the grimy concrete laden husk of 70's Birmingham emerged hundreds if not thousands of soul loving casuals, revivalist mods, suede heads into a scene that could for all intents and purposes originally be classified as mod but probably identified on a generic level as an RnB/soul scene it certainly like much of the country carried the old Mod philosophy of clean living in tough circumstances (see Pete Meadon ex Who manager). The city itself was and is a rough tough hard working-class environment and used to have a broad spread-out cross-section of diverse youth culture who were not without their differences and many confrontational moments. That cross section or collective if you will of soul music loving Brummies would find their common ground whether you were inspired by a young smooth soul girls like Jackie Graham singing and playing with a band called Ferrari along with Dee Harris (later of New Romantic band Fashion) or whether just up the road you were watching Dexys Midnight Runners and the intensity of one of their live soul revue, your tastes or rather thirst for exciting soul music if you were a Brummie could generally be quenched by the city's amazing diverse musical talent.

I have to say especially from a cultural perspective I still feel blessed to have grown up where I did , yes I was skint and there were no jobs especially in the 70's and the 80's blah blah blah but one night you could go to the Star Club (the City's Communist Social Club and a music venue) and for 50p watch bands like indie darlings The Nightingales (and one of John Peels fave bands) and then the next night you could go out on the piss in Moseley (UB40's manor) and then walk up the road to ACAFESS a Jazz Reggae social club run by the roughest hardest Jamaican crew you could ever meet but experience some of the best live music and DJ's ever, it was an incredible place but the only downside was you could only get Red Stripe Lager there mind you the curried goat used to go down well. Then on a quiet night I'd be down my local The Camp pub in Kings Norton with my mates rubbing shoulders with the likes of big Jimmy Paterson from Dexys and occasionally Kevin Rowland would be in there drinking, so bizarrely Birmingham as a place to grow up was culturally very rich and inspiring for me. It was the late 70's and Thatcher's Britain although young was in full swing and slowly succumbing to the iron bitch ladies deconstruction of the working classes in the Midlands (as in fairness it also was with the rest of the Country) every other kid on either a YOP/YTS scheme, the dole or probably a chronically underpaid job and you may well ask where was my place in this grim inner city concrete backdrop, well the oldest son of Harry and Viv... 2 siblings (older sis younger bruv) I grew up on the south side of the city in the shadow of the Longbridge Car Factory. Blues territory for those football fans among you and as an interesting side note went to school with quite a few of the Zulu's who were the Birmingham City FC crew as it were ,or the football gang for all you Saturdays Kids novices and if there was such a thing as a PC football street gang they were known as the Zulus because of their multi-cultural or racial hardcore membership.

One thing that can be said about multicultural allegiances within the context of youth subculture is that chances are you're going to get a much more interesting and diverse set of musical influences and I think this was certainly true of many of the football clubs and cross over youth subcultures whether that be casuals, mods, suede heads, skins etc. So anyway as a 13 year old teenager diving into the revolutionary punk scene I had been quickly influenced of the likes of The Jam and was also drawn to 60's bands like The Who and The Kinks which looking back seems like a natural progression from Punk to Mod and of course with the rich influence of soul and RnB music in those genres and on those bands in particular my tastes grew and diversified I'm happy to say into a very eclectic mix, but one which I identified as being mod in its ownership if that makes sense. If you think about it is perfect for those inner-city kids trying to live that Pete Meaden mod Philosophy - clean living in tough times.

The Mod scene in Brum started off in a very cool elitist vibe, you could only get decent 60's influenced garb from the Rag Market by St Martins Church in the centre of town or if you had some money places like Route 66 in Oasis Market in Dale End another part of the city centre or even a bit later on Paradise Garage up by Lewis's for a short while it was a great scene, seeing bands like The Merton Parkas at the Underground (Digbeth Civic Hall) or bands like The Mods and The Lambrettas at The Golden Eagle (a bikers pub on Hill Street which is sadly now a car park) great bands great times. It was around 1979 and The Jam had already climbed the heady heights of stardom and were at that point a regular act appearing at the Birmingham Odeon but they were the royalty of late 70's modernism. Sadly as the mod scene started to proliferate it almost imploded under its own expectation of tribalistic tendencies, for example Quinton Mods were having punch ups with Northfield Mods to be honest this kind of confrontation between factions of our own youth subculture became rife all over the city consequently those of us that were around in late 78 to see the birth of this awesome revivalist scene with fresh new wave bands and the wonderful array of music that had been before started to drift away from the scene hugely disappointed in how things had started to go it was a cool eclectic modernist scene that was exciting and addictive and turned into a bit of an unpleasant night out to be honest. I reckon those of us early mods had drifted out of the scene by 1982 at the latest, for me the love of the music especially The Jam and the incredibly sharp clothes kept me connected to it. I just never mixed with many people in the scene after that time.

Along this journey I had taken up playing guitar and bass and writing songs and although many bands I played in were never really mod or typically soul influenced I carried those influences into pretty much everything I did or played on or even wrote for that matter.

Birmingham's great music scene probably doesn't really gets full credit for the amazing bands it's spawned over the years, I mean around this time you had the likes of The Beat, Dexy's, UB40 and a little later on bands like Swans Way and modsters Ocean Colour Scene and of course there were the older bands such as ELO, Moody Blues, Black Sabbath, Spencer Davis Group, The Move, The Applejacks, The Rockin Berries etc etc etc. and that really is to name just a few and at some point you would have gigged or been in the pub with some of these guys & yeah I've been in bands with members of Dexys jammed with guy's from Ocean Colour Scene shared rehearsal rooms with Napalm death and PWEI truly a diverse music scene if ever there was one. Looking back I realise how incestuous our brummie music scene was I mean I remember being in the car with a band mate of mine Micky Billingham from Dexy's going up to Handsworth to Dave Wakelings Dad's (of The Beat) house to borrow his Rickenbacker guitar so we could rehearse in town with a bunch of other geezahs....or when I used to play session bass for The Rockin Berries who's drummer (Simon) I used to go to school with and who used to play for Racey and who's manager was the ex-drummer of Wizzard & playing football with lad's from Ned's Atomic Dustbin or Adam from The Stereophonics just normal stuff but with people that were in bands having or who had had hits.

Although my musical journey had its specific Punk/Mod origins I'm happy to say it was diverse in its output and eclectic in its influences and so I believe I got the best of both worlds if that makes sense.......now to fast forward a few years and not dwell too much on the many awesome bands I played in that were signed and any records that I made (that weren't hits) and of

224

course the people I met in the music business that have become lifelong friends. I'd been 10 years out of Nursing School and me and my beautiful wife Tricia were picking up our 1st brand new purchased car from the Vauxhall dealership in Selly Oak in Birmingham something we were really happy about as we had never been able to afford a new car before but on that day 11th of September 2001 in the showroom there was a TV where of course we witnessed one of the most profoundly sad and devastating terrorist attacks in living history , if I were to say it took the shine off the day that would be a colossal understatement.

To introduce another shortcut to this tale Tricia and I like every family & couple talked deeply and thoughtfully about the rhetoric of what was about to happen to the world politically and from that day onwards and with a very young family (2 girls and a boy) we felt we had choices to make. One thing I can say about me and Tricia is we never made rash decisions and it was within a few months and after much deliberation that we decided we were going to emigrate to the beautiful country of New Zealand and attempt to give our kids what we thought would be a more peaceful and safer childhood we couldn't have been more prophetic could we after numerous more terrorist attacks and a global pandemic that still threatens the worlds safety here we are in a country where we can go anywhere, hug anybody, go to concerts, football matches I mean after a 3 month bit of collective effort we really did kick the virus in the arse and will again with the current outbreak.

After being offered Theatre Nurse jobs in Hamilton, Palmerston North and Auckland I opted for a job at Wellington Hospital , it wasn't an easy start I came across a few bullies and arseholes and it was tough navigating my way around them but after 12 months found my feet and settled in nicely, it's at Wellington Hospital I met Mo (Maureen) a keen singer songwriter who I hit it off with straight away, we started doing a bit of recording together and jammed occasionally in fact one nightshift when it

225

was quiet I brought my bass amp into work set it up and Mo, myself and the Anaesthetic Consultant all had a little jam session in an empty operating theatre fuckin hilarious talk about fun. Mo collared me one afternoon and suggested I bring my bass round to her house and meet her husband and have a jam with his band who at that time rehearsed in their living room. I needed to quench my thirst for playing with a decent drummer and so I thought I'd give it a go And so this is where I met the Lerwill brothers Craig on drums (or P as he's nicknamed by Geoff and Mark) Mark on guitar (or Hog as he's nicknamed by Craig and Geoff) and Geoff (or Hippy as he is named by Mark and Craig) & before I even start to start to describe them as people the fact that they have developed nicknames for each other and their parents who they don't even call Mom and Dad is bizarre but funny to say the least.

Anyway I hit it off straight away with these cool dudes musically and on a personal level, in a weird kind of way every Sunday practice became my musical fix and we'd sit down after practice and talk shit and solve the world's problems with our blokey chit chat. After settling down in NZ and a few years later still playing with the Lerwill brothers we were about to meet someone that would really shake us up as a band.....

It was mid 2019 I'd gone to The Sports Bar in Wellington which was also a music venue, me and the wife were there to watch our daughter Ellie sing in a variety show featuring a whole bunch of singers (probably around 30 in total). I stuck with it and sat through some great talent, some average talent and some to be kind not so great talent just to wait to see my daughter Ellie sing, anyway it was towards the end of the show Ellie came on and sung her heart out and man she was great really how proud I was I mean it was the first time she'd sung in front of an audience, she was stunning and had a soulfulness and style all of her own incredible, however not to shoot off into too many tangents I will come back to that fact but for now I'll continue my story about the night in question....

So I made it to almost the end of the show phew and it comes to the last singer of the night a girl called Jamie who strolled confidently onto the stage and in a very assured manner and in a very articulate manner announced she was going to sing her version of a gospel song called "Wade In The Water" well of course my ears pricked up I'm always keen to hear someone's interpretation of a northern soul classic whatever it is. Anyways my patience was rewarded 10-fold because what I heard gave me goosebumps....this girl delivered a pitch perfect soul driven 3 minutes of pure delight.....my jaw was on the floor, my ears were in ecstasy and my heart was swooning with delight . After the show I thought I need to speak to this girl and try my best not to appear sycophantic or creepy in any way or at least less than I normally do when meeting a talent of this magnitude. As luck would have it after the gig people were kind of chilling, hanging out and reflecting on the night and of course she was there across the bar with her hubby also relaxing chatting to her mates and as luck would have it after I'd subtly mentioned to a couple of people how impressed I was with Jamie the guy who was running the show (David) encouraged me to talk to her, he told me she was friendly and easy to talk to so. I did my best to stay as nonchalant as possible and try to be cool but my gush-ing response to her incredible talent got the better of me and I ended up telling her how awesome I thought she was blah blah blah....lol. In our first ever conversation I did actually end up asking her if she fancied recording an old soul tune of her choice with me and my band, I'm happy to say after a day or two deliberation and to my surprise she agreed to come and do some recording. Obviously, I must have been cool enough not to frighten her away with creepiness after all....lol....but briefly going back to my daughter after her success in starting to sing as a hobby she ended up recording some songs. She did in-credible versions of some 70s and 80s alternative songs and a couple of originals and you could only possibly imagine how good they were with a whole new urban, soulful style that I'd not heard since Amy Whinehouse. To be fair she didn't sound like Amy per se just reflected that beautiful soulful quality with what sounded like an English twist, weird but amazing. A week or two after recording it I sent a copy of her version of "Town Called Malice" to Any Crofts one of Paul Weller's team/band (the connection being Weller is the original writer) Andy replied within minutes and asked me for the original multitracks. I emailed them over to him and he set about playing on it and producing the track, Paul Weller even encouraged us to release it and Andy featured it on his Radio Show wow what a turnaround within a couple of months of doing her first show.

She recorded more songs and got more interest in the music industry with offers of top-class music management from an Australian Company who are made up of predominantly two women who have worked for multiple labels Polydor, Acid Jazz etc etc and have had experience being Tour managers for the likes of Kanye West to The Style Council so no mugs really and record deals with US labels and the added offer of working with Adele's writers and so and so forth a true whirlwind of incredible opportunity for an incredible natural talent but at that moment in that time it wasn't to be. She had no real desire to become famous or extend her singing to a bigger or wider audience, and she wanted none of it no record deal no management nothing not interested at all urrgh I played in bands all my life since the age of 13 desperately seeking out opportunities like this and this girl my beautiful eldest daughter falls into this amazing situation without much effort and says thanks anyway but no. So as a parent I was profoundly gutted and disappointed beyond belief but you know as musician and writer with my hand firmly on my heart I could only admire her integrity in saying no to something she had no real passion to pursue, I should have known really this is a girl that when we took her as a child for her booster injections she hid under the Drs desk and wouldn't come out also a girl who as an 9 year old we told her to stop eating all of the sweet prunes and dried apricots but she instead sneaking back to the fruit bowl and persisted on filling her face with the lovely sweet fruit then consequently complained when she spent half the night on the toilet.

She definitely knows what she wants and doesn't want, that girl has always been a bit of a feisty one.

So anyway, back to Jamie we'd made our connection and had a bit of discussion over tea and biscuits about influences and direction and how we wanted to present ourselves, I mean we knew we weren't a full-on working band as such but we wanted to be seen as musicians in a group together and not just a random one off recording project. I pretty much suggested we aim to pick an old Northern Soul tune as that had been the genre that had inspired me to speak to Jamie in the first place, to be totally honest it had been a bit of a vision of mine to do a new age Dexys meets The Jam meets energetic new age soul band thing for a while, I'd just never had the chance to give it a proper go maybe this was that opportunity.

I sent 4 or 5 tracks (mp3's). I can't remember the names of all the songs but I do recollect The Flirtations "Nothing But A Heartache" being on the list and The Precisions "If This Is Love". I'm very happy to say Jamie picked the brilliant track "If This Love" to record, as soon as we knew what we were going to lay down in the studio me and the Lerwil brothers set about learning the guts of the song, guitarist Mark is not just a gifted guitarist and songwriter he is pretty much our musical director and he transposed and tweaked things whilst the rest of us in the band Geof, Craig (P) and myself set about learning our parts whilst I at the same time farmed out the brass arrangement to a guy called Chris Selley who was involved in Jamie's talent show entourage, he went about scoring and arranging the dots for his brass cohorts (Andy and Damian) for the recording session so all things considered everything fell into place quite nicely. I was in luck in that I managed to snaffle some studio time with the brilliant producer/engineer Lee Prebble on the 12th and 13th of March 2019 at his legendary studio The Surgery which is a very well sought after recording facility in my Kiwi hometown of Wellington NZ, it wasn't the cheapest studio by far but trust me when I say you pay for what you get and for his amazing talent and instinctive musical ear generally what he offers is priceless & 18 months -2 years on and in my humble opinion Lee has now become an extra member of the band and he is so worth his weight in gold. So I took a bit of a risk… personally paying for the recording and the mastering. I thought if this turns out ok I might as well pay for this to be pressed as a 7" single and see what we can do with it. I set out aligning all these ideas into one thing our own label Deltaphonic Records of which I did all the basic label designs for on my night shifts at the hospital using the most rudimentary version of photoshop, I then got all these designs polished up (in layman's terms done properly) by a family friend called Anne another extremely talented individual especially with photoshop. I lined up a good pressing plant Zenith Records in Victoria Australia the head honcho there is a guy called Paul who I've become very friendly with and who also loves his soul music so win, the only pressing plant in NZ is in Auckland and is currently a bit too pricey for my Nurse wage meagre budget . Mike Gibson does the mastering for us (Munki Productions) he used to own a recording studio in the old secret service building in Wellington another talented dude we have a great respect and a good relationship with so in effect we by chance or rather without knowing it set up a really great family of people for our new labels recording production line.

So, for a moderate amount of outlay I'd created our very own record label, the name was random I'd wanted something that was culturally connected to NZ and that sounded retro, I dried up for ideas for a cultural connection I looked at some Maori names or Pasifika based words but nothing kinda sounded right I eventually picked Deltaphonic simply because it sounded retro and it might have or rather infer a soul vibe to it.

We were doing cover versions of other people's tunes so I had to learn quickly about licensing and what I could or couldn't do and track ownership, sync licensing, video licensing etc etc. APRA were a big help and they set all the legal agreements up for me so I didn't get myself into any trouble with lawyers and publishers to be quite brutally honest I couldn't have done it without them and they were lovely people to deal with too, a great credit to NZ music industry they've been a huge part of this projects existence and I continue to be grateful for their guidance. I'd also befriended a videographer geeza a friend of a friend called Jeremy another amazingly talented dude who shared similar celluloid interests as me and had as weird and crazy ideas as myself so he was great and we clicked straight away as this session might have ended up being a one off I decided to document the recording, I thought I'll make this look as indie as possible so I asked Jeremy if he would be able to put together a pastiche of images from my Samsung phone in black and white to look live and a bit grainy, in essence some-thing that would give us a basic and decent music video. To say he obliged would be an understatement, his final edit was fan-tastic and not only gave us an indie feel but looked really cool yet another talented and cool person added to our team. I have to give him a massive big ups coz during the Covid lockdown and general pandemic turmoil of 2021 he became gravely ill and had a monumental battle to claw his way back from illness, at this point in time he's looking like he's gonna be ok so respect Jeremy and as the Mods say keep on keeping on dude. One logistical downside in the filming of the 1st single was I didn't get enough footage of Craig the drummer who can be seen mostly playing the tambourine in our music video the reason is I was actually playing myself when he was playing so I failed to get heaps of those drumming moments but hey he still looks cool and the drums on the track are impeccable.

So March 12th comes along Jamie, Simon, Mark Craig, Geoff and Lee are all in the studio, Lee has a very relaxed way of working with people well us anyway and it may take a while to line everything up with mic's, click tracks and headphone fold-back but when we get started our work process & dynamic is really smooth and professional he really does have a way of bringing the best out of us. We pretty much lay the basics of the track down live drums, bass, keyboards and rhythm guitar all together with a couple of hours for a few bits and bobs of over dubs. As a bunch of musicians, we have generally hung out and worked together quite a bit and know each other inside out, we are pretty slick in the studio when it comes down to recording sessions. Needless to say, when we came to do the vocals the track in itself was already sounding pretty groovy and tight but when Jamie stepped up to the mic and sang those first lines we were just like in wow mode it was incredible. She brought her personality to the track and added an extra dimension of soul to this already excellent song we'd recorded and brought a life to the song which was so powerful. Call me idealistic but I'd like to think we captured a bit of **kiwi soul magic** and were about to show it to the world.

I decided to only get just 300 singles pressed mostly down to the fact that I was skint to be honest but I thought to make these look a bit more collectable and indie I'll buy a kids stamp kit and number every single 1 - 300 shouldn't take me too long (famous last words...lol) this idea turned out to be a moment of genius because by making such a well performed and recorded song even more collectable especially among the Northern Soul community we in theory would sell out of every single in a really short space of time and we most certainly did. I sent out 30 or 40 promos to DJ's, Radio Stations and other record labels and got some wonderful reviews and feedback. We even had the UK publishers of the track contact us and ask if they could press the track for release in the UK/Europe. Along with some great Radio support and DJ's from all over the world. We got to the point where we just said "like ok let's do another track" and kept going, it kind of escalated and grew organically, we mix cover versions of old skool Northern Soul tunes with our catchy well written originals effortlessly and people loved it. We don't gig heaps in fact sometimes I feel we are more of a recording pro- ject especially as you could count the gigs we've done on one hand. So we repeated the process with a 2nd single "Magic Touch" which turned out fantastically but the video for this fell by the wayside we had an Indian girl doing an animated film but her life was profoundly affected by the Covid pandemic and so it never happened in the end & to be fair she had done about 1min 15 secs of the video before we abandoned it. Also and probably just as much of a problem there are two publishers for that song who couldn't make their minds up on how much to charge me for a video license I won't say who but one of the publishers was great to deal with and the other was not anyway consequently no video.....rolls eyes. I think although the track sounds great we lost a bit of kudos on that track and if you go on some of the soul vinyl selling websites this is the single that holds the least value. I mean it's still changing hands for 30 pounds+ but we have other singles which are going for 125 quid a time, so whether we attribute that to having no video or loss of commercial momentum I'm not sure.....

Anyway it was around this time that a fella contacted me from Australia a certain Mr Johnny "Red Pants" Warren, he purchased a few singles from us and was very complimentary of our product generally we kind of hit it off straight away although his drive and passion for music was at times unbelievable I found myself drawn to his energy and his friendly vibe, it didn't take long for us to become friends and we now probably speak once or twice a week whether it be about what we are doing as a band or even new potential projects. I think if ever this label thing we have going grows big enough to turn into a more viable business he'd make an amazing label MD.

Johnny has been a great influence because of his advice and knowledge in fact it was his introduction to Robert Paladino writer and producer of one of the most famous Northern Soul songs of all time "You Don't Love Me" by The Epitome Of Sound that influenced us to record "You Don't Love Me" and as we got on great terms with Robert we asked him to do a voice over at the end of the vinyl single to dedicate the record to Eugene Thomas the original singer of The Epitome of Sound who had sadly died of covid the year before. It ended up being a touching and very poignant tribute from one friend to another and in my humble opinion you can hear the affection and love for his friend in Robs voice. We also went on and sampled original drummer Mike Paladino's drumming and placed it into the mix of the track. I'm actually really proud to say we play on the same track as NYC very own The Epitome of Sound. How cool is that?

As my chapter in this starts to wind down I get the feeling that in many ways this is just the beginning of a whole new world and direction with this soul band Jamie and The Numbers, the band that we started by accident. Since we recorded the 3rd single we were picked up by a really happening soul label in the UK called Superfly Funk and Soul Records run by Pete Brady and Will Foot out of Northern Ireland. They are great guys, great DJ's, progressive in their thinking, have original ideas and also share a vision with us on how we can go forward with our music.

Ironically it was within a couple of weeks of agreeing terms on doing an album with Superfly we had another big soul label want to do an album with us but without looking at the deal on paper we already knew we'd made the right decision with Will and Pete and so that's where I'll leave it for now I'm sure there's some other interesting detail I've probably forgotten but maybe I'll save all of that for book 3 of this particular soul journey, certainly there will be more to say when the 3rd single gets released and when Superfly release the debut Jamie and The Numbers album until then Keep Right On people. x

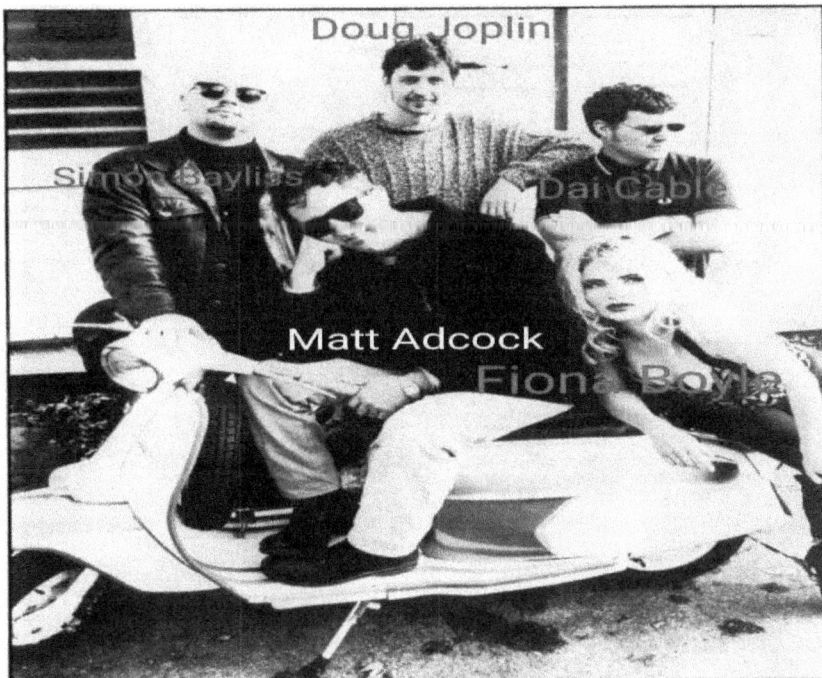

An early Simon Bayliss Group. Doug Toplin, Simon Bayliss, Dai Cable, Matt Adcock © Simon Bayliss

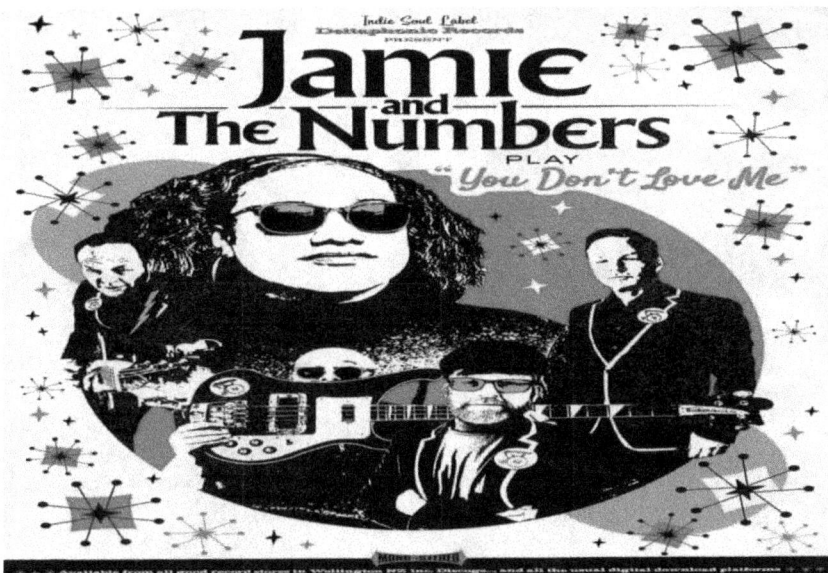

The cover of the new 45 that was released October 1 2021 to remember Eugene Thomas who his gone never forgotten © Simon Bayliss

Top: Simon Bayliss © Simon Bayliss.
Bottom: The Numbers deep in thought with Simon Bayliss © Simon Bayliss

Chapter 18

Barry Simpson - The Man In the Suitcase

Bags packed for an Allnighter

On a cold, March Saturday morning in 1999, I walked out of work, eased into the comfort of my car, snapped on the seatbelt, and drove home. A face like a smacked arse, every day was the same. Sue-Ellen was such a misery. Maybe she would re-think having pulled the wage's a big mistake, anyhow it's not my problem for the next 3 days.

Barry's Audi with LI Soul number plates © Barry Simpson

The weekend is on. I loved my car. A battleship grey Audi A4, so comfortable and cosy once the heater was on, like one of those old woolen blankets. You know the ones, the ones your Nan always had over her legs in winter, and that's what it felt like and the weather, its normal bloody cold. A cool number plate too, L1 5OUL. Saturdays began with a soak in a freshly drawn warm bath, good god how I hate avocado. To this day white is the way to go. Even the tiles matched, breakfast, coffee and a bacon sandwich had become the standard. Two unread Manifesto magazines are ready to read on the bath table. I grabbed the first, took a bite of the bread bun, settled down in the hot soapy water and began reading. Manifesto was not a story book but a magazine full of articles by the likes of John Vincent and Mr Potato Head, interviews about Northern Soul, with the David Leedham`s red-eye special in the centre spread in which Kay and I often featured and a cracking gig guide from which I'd plan the weekend. The Arts centre in the town first up, then a few of the lads and I will be heading to Stoke. Allniter here we come!

Badge and flyers from Adelaide 1998 © Barry Simpson

Flicking through, an article in the April edition number 22 about a Northern Soul weekender in Adelaide caught my eye. They had a Saturday event at the Boltz Café in Rundle St and an all-dayer at the Crown & Anchor Hotel in Grenfell St. $10 for a weekend of soul.

I read through it and thought how cool that would be, popping over to Australia for a weekender. I noted the name in the bottom corner, Mark Howlett from Adelaide, he had one of those email address thingies - mmm. I remembered sending my first email to Adrian at our head office in Leeds. We were on the phone when I pressed send and then heard the "ping" as he received it. My my, we were easily pleased back then. April 1999, plenty of time to organise a trip to Adelaide. It would take me almost 20 years to pull together the CD (from a catch-up with Tom Orr at Rawtenstall station around 2002) to badges and tickets from Maria Orlovic. Fancy an allnighter in OZ Baz I sure do.

Now if you remember 1999, you will recall the world was changing. Computers, P.C`s, were becoming outdated as quickly as they sold, 250 became 300 the next week, 350, 400 mhz. When should you buy? Not yet anyhow I had decided, not just yet. I put together an email and took it to my brother-in laws place to send to Mark, often referred to in the annals of Australian weekenders as "some bloke", who promptly replied and I collected it 2 weeks later. He put me in touch with another couple of soulies around Australia, explaining that the Adelaide weekender had supposed to have been a one off. They would grow to be held in a different Australian city each year around this time. What the organisers had done was put the Cities names in a hat on talc bottles and drawn the next one out, Perth, and the event would build to become an annual circuit, the starting order would be Adelaide, Perth, Sydney, Melbourne. Then Brisbane joined the party a second time round in 2004 and the circle was complete.

Here is a collection of my soul stories including the Australian nationals. The first five of which I would travel to from the UK then. Eventually, packing a bit more than a suitcase, 47 record boxes, a container and moving here. But my soul journey began many years before.

The years have melded into a jumble of days and months which I have tried to unravel and form a running story, sometimes jumping forward and back in time, a story that I have had to rethink since a message I received from my older sister took it all back one whole year to the summer of 1969.

Before all the bag packing began

Just before secondary school first year, 11 years old with a blonde feathered haircut, Ben Sherman round my knees, that's me, one of eight brothers and sisters. I often joke about growing up with two older sisters being difficult, it was the hand-me-down clothes you see…Winters were so cold the ice was on the inside of the windows, bread and jam for tea some nights and second hand Christmas presents. The Sunday matinee was the family highlight or thunderbirds, crowded round the television and a roaring fire.

The summer of 1969, Kings Hall Carlisle

One Saturday, I have no idea how it came about, but with probably around two shillings (a florin) in my pocket I went to the Kings Hall in Carlisle with one of my five sisters, 14 year old Julie, and her boyfriend Terry. They taught me to dance, step and clap my hands to the music. I don't remember the Kings Hall being anything flash. Toilets and cloakrooms up the narrow staircase, a bit of a stage and a huge mural of the King Crimson album cover behind the small stage with a couple of record players on a table beside it. There was a sort of tuck shop at the other end and chairs lined the walls.

Soul boys Barry and Wilky © Barry Simpson

The music was across the board, very broad as I recall, but Do-
ris Troy "I'll Do Anything" and Tammi Lynn "I'm Gonna Run
Away From You" were songs I definitely remember as well were
T Rex "Ride A White Swan", Don Fardon "Indian Reservation",
Max Romeo "Wet Dream", St Cecelia "Leap Up And Down",
Rod Stewart "Maggie May", Barbra Lewis "Someday We're
Gonna Love Again". There was no alcohol, it was Coca Cola,
coffee, mars bars and polo mints, that was about it. The music
included "Northern Soul " before it was ever called "Northern
Soul ". 16 was the age limit but I got in, only being stopped once
about my age and I still recall Tom asking me if I was 16, me
saying yes, him telling me to stand by the door with my mate
Anthony Wilkinson, then probably Johnny Hardcastle, with his
German Shepherd, telling us to get in. A tanner (sixpence) to
enter a noisy paradise. Anthony and I would go there almost
every Saturday, Anthony`s Aunty Viv made sure he had the

coolest clothes, my how he did look smart in his Crombie. Me, my jeans or borrowed Levi's and a purple jumper with the sleeves rolled up so as to hide the holes in the elbows. I also had a cool second hand, green jacket, bought from Jackson the tailors which I frequently wore. Popular records with skinheads around the time were "Get Down And Get With It" by Slade and "Resurrection Shuffle" by Ashton, Gardner & Dyke, these providing the required breaks for the acrobats. It was now I would see for the first time backdrops and splits. The lads would stand in two lines facing each other stamping their feet then one would jump into the middle and do these marvelous acrobatics. I remember one time it happened and everyone crowded round to watch the lads leap about, the bouncers came running over pushing everyone out of the way to stop the "fight" ! But then stopped and watched too. In their Levi or Falmer jeans, skull caps, Doc Martin boots and football scarves tied to their wrists, lads like Tony Grier or Crocket would entertain the cheering crowd. Another fashion accessory of the time were automatic umbrellas and black driving gloves on one hand, although I'm not sure if the umbrellas were allowed into the dance hall.

I was "on my way" ....

During 1969 and later, days of bread strikes, dustbin strikes, and the coal miners strikes creating power cuts, saw the Kings Hall close some nights. I remember one such Saturday we were directed to another venue across town on the west walls of the city. My first ever visit to what would become one of Carlisle's iconic venues, the Twisted Wheel. A large hall, St Cuthbert's, on the ground level was a sort of coffee bar with toasted sandwiches and a television but the action was down a few sets of stairs into a massive hall, orange plastic chairs laid around the walls and a DJ stand on the right, powered by batteries. I now had a part time job delivering newspapers, this allowed me to go out more.

242

Thursday, Friday, Saturday, and Mondays were the best. Back then smoking in the venues was normal and a florin (two shillings) in the ciggy machine, by Clarkes the newsagents in St Annes, would get you a 10 pack of "Numbers" (Players Number 6 cigarettes) which Wilky and I always shared.

Top: Kings Hall, Carlisle © Barry Simpson
Bottom: Pink Panther © Barry Simpson

By late 1970 the Saturdays at Kings Hall occasionally made way for the west walls venue which became the "Pink Panther" for a few years and I just remember having the best of times. A perfect mix of Glam Rock, Pop and Soul, with Tom Foster doing the lion's share at the Kings Hall seemed to keep me in another place.

Our hero DJ Feds, Dominic Hetherington and Jim Woodford covering the occasional breaks and later Dougie were among the Panther regular DJ`s. Feds had started DJing earlier at the famous Carlisle club, the Cosmo with John Nicholson around 1970, later alternating between the Wheel (as the Pink Panther would later become known) and Flop's , another famous Carlisle club. Going so often, Wilky and I got to know the doormen and, very often we could be ushered through a crowd or even let in free by Rueben or Dave. Sounding cool on a Monday morning in the classroom, chatting about the weekend's events, being the young soul rebels, but actually not knowing this yet. I remember a friend telling me to enter the school pop quiz and, after some prefect had asked me who sang a version of "Pretty Woman", I answered "The Newbeats'. I never heard back... probably thought I knew too much already as a first year. But to be honest I never gave it a second thought. The only reason I knew was someone had mentioned it at the Kings on Saturday. My outfit often included my faithful green jacket which around 1972 would often be updated. On occasions I'd go into town and buy coloured trim from Woolworths or the local market and stitch it around the edges, changing it now and again from black to white, bright green or red and change the buttons to those silver blazer buttons and back to green, maybe it was the resourceful boy scout in me, but never mind, I thought I looked great just like the big boys. By this time I was a Friday and Saturday regular at the Pink Panther record shop spending lots of my hard earned pennies on records which were around 32p each or 50p for a back catalogue. Number one in my collection is Dandy Livingston "Suzanne Beware Of The Devil" so, already I was looking outside of the mainstream.

Dave would often keep a selection for me to listen to, God only knows what gems I may have turned down. I would look through the back-catalogue list in a clocking-in card holder on the left of the counter. He would often play them for me loud throughout the shop or if it was busy through one of those old orange bulbus listening booths. My older sister gave me around 20 records which I still have today and I still play them today at gigs.

Tunes like "Double Barrel" by Dave and Ansel Collins, "Young Gifted And Black" by Bob and Marcia along with Aretha Franklin to name just a few. I was a vinyl junkie going through the early stages of being born. These precious early discs were stored in the very appropriately sized Schweppes crates, ideal for the job at hand for a short while anyway. Here I got to see Edwin Starr and a new band called Sweet Sensation just before their smash "sad sweet dreamer" hit the charts. By late 1974 I was working part-time at the local Tesco, then later full time. I worked the twilight shift with a guy called Peter Burns, it was always a treat, his humour was top class and with Chantal, who later married and created a lovely family. The Winthronics music centre was switched on and Major Lance "Investigate" would belt through the store. One day we received a delivery of orange plastic skateboards for a special promotion. Well you have to try them out eh! We gave them a damn good try out, sometimes stacking them on top of each other. One at a time, two`s up and three`s up, but we always cleaned them before we put them back on sale. That was until one night we forgot. A call to the deli counter the next morning to explain how 6 skateboards had made their way from the home and wear department to the Quosh stand at the other end of the store, led to a right rollocking.

I`m not sure it stopped us though! It was pot shots at the sparrows flying around the hanging PG Tips sign and skittles with a new product called Pot Noodles or Pringles and great music banging out of the Winthronics record player all drowned the misery of late nights and 60 hour weeks.

Those early days in retail were fun as I recall, but as it grew so did the pressures. Hours were long, very long, but the pay and benefits were fantastic later on.

Shirt with all my patches © Barry Simpson

Bottom: Barry Simpson DJ with Didi © Barry Simpson

It was the local youth club for a year or so, catching up with old school friends David and Lynne Troughton, her friend Sue and David Leadbetter at Belah Youth club. I kept the poster drawn by Lyne and still have it to this day. We had some great times. Popping into the local for a quick pint of Tartan, at 19p a pint, afterward, snow ball fights, the Silver Jubilee disco, late nights and the cracker incident whereby, I'd got drunk on cheap beer, fell over our settee and crashed my suede shoes into a plate of buttered cream crackers not funny now, funny at the time, but hilarious after cheap beer. Then there was the night of the house rewiring. Leady and Didi had convinced themselves that one of the wires was paler than the other, reckoning it was brown and the other black, of course they were both black it's a circuit dipstick. It reminds me of an old joke Simon Evans told me about the electrician's invoice, "$1 to cut the wire, $1000 to know which wire to cut" happy days.

Bags packed for the first ever allniter, Wigan Casino.

During this period, 1976, I met up with Brian Talbot and Gary Crozier. Over the time we talked about a place called Wigan Casino that had dances all night, playing great music and didn't serve beer. Gary had been a few times and Brian`s sister went weekly. So, we made plans to go one Saturday, a week after the 3rd anniversary. It wasn't so much planned for the date but more around the arrival of my membership card. I managed to acquire this in time having bought the Blues and Soul music magazine after that a weekly order was placed for box 22. I feel certain that if I checked my record room I would find the exact Blues and Soul magazine with the cut out coupon. I kept everything and diarised most. We took the train down around 10.00 and arrived sometime after midnight. I recall being nervous about getting in as I was not 18 until November and it did stipulate on the member application that one had to be 18. I didn't fancy the long wait for a train home in the cold Wigan night. I don't recall too much about that first visit except walking around the balcony and looking through record boxes in the record bar. A cloakroom up a narrow flight of stairs was where we left our coats and soaked up the atmosphere.

I mostly just stood around watching and wondering how, and if, I could have a dance. I did find a spot and had a go, but soon gave up & watched the others. The place was sweaty with dirty streaks running down the walls, the toilets inches deep in water, people lying asleep and terrible coffee for sale. I don't recall it being absolutely fantastic, no ecstatic clapping recalled at this stage, but good enough to "most likely pay another visit". We returned on the train, most likely went straight to bed, up for tea and relived the night, then ready for work on Monday. As a memento, I bought a 3rd anniversary screen printed badge and later stitched it on my shirt, and a copy of "Long after tonight is all over" by Jimmy Radcliffe on Stateside, which I still have in my collection. I did indeed go again and again. I met up with another Carlisle lad, Danny Spiers with whom, over the years, I would swap stories, information and buy and sell records. Danny would in turn introduce me to Ivan Ward, George Rouse and Steve McCubbin. Over the next couple of years our crew grew and grew to fill a coach, soulies in duffle coats and Polyveldt shoes were coming out of the woodwork, so much so that sometimes we filled two coaches. For me, the dress code included baggies from Jackson the tailors, my brown bag and yellow shirt adorned with the badges. The coaches would pick us up at the Wimpy Bar around 8pm, sometimes also stopping at London Road and Penrith, then a stop at Forton services for a break would see us there outside the Casino around 11.30, queuing for an hour or so. I often read about the heat when you opened the doors into the main hall, yes it was like that, the thunderous clapping did occur and Sticky carpets too. I have a fond memory of being totally in the zone when "Looking For You" by Garnet Mimms came on and stuffing the coke bottle into my trouser pocket, hearing Danny Spiers play Bobby Paris "I Walked Away", ploughing through record boxes for next week's spot. On one occasion I bought Teddy Vann, ``Theme From A Coloured Man" and Brian Hyland "Joker Went Wild '', maybe 10 pounds and 25 for Teddy. As I left the bar a guy stopped me and asked if I was selling so I, showing them off, said yes (but not really) and put a 20 pound price on the Brian Hyland which was big at the time. He promptly produced 20 quid, I handed it over, and walked back in to see Rob Sharp and bought another, I still have the invoice in my record room. We stopped at Forton on the way home many times, for a wash and change, breakfast and a game of pool. I was always as usual, on the hunt for keepsakes, nicked a red pool ball which, once again I still have, it is on display in my record room.

The Carlisle crew also included Gary Crozier, Debbie Norman (Uttley), Paul Brady, Paul Bell, Stanks, Steggs, Sandra McNamara and Anne Graham, Gill Coleman, Christine Sores, Cally and Sue, Neil Rogerson, Chris Hetherington, Kev Sowerby, Chris Blythe, Andrew Lindsey, Ashy, George Rouse and Elaine, Craig Smethurst, Dot Bailey, Wally Wieghtman and

Wendy O`neil, Carol Hall, Mally Tinkler, Brian "Tally" Talbot, Gary Wild, Alan Bailey, Kev Blackburn, Sheila Bowden and Alison Bailey, Cynthia, Ivor Taylor, Tally, Mark Harrison and Linda Birrell, Begsy and Pandy, Tiny, Kevin Blackburn, Tom Jones, Pauline and David Munn, Julie Norman and Katrina, Ian "Maggie" Maghill and Jackie, Greg McGeorge, Paul Brady and Christine and so many more. We were making our own history, but we didn't know it yet.

Top: Carlisle Soul crew at Wigan Casino. © Barry Simpson.
Bottom: Carlisle crew out on the floor. Wigan Casino © Barry Simpson

During this time soul nights began around Carlisle with Ivan Ward, Danny Spiers, Steve McCubbin and I often DJing. We had many great nights at the Melody Club where, in 1979, Brian Rae would DJ at my 21st and Pip McDonnel, his roadie & friend also present. Both of which are still great friends today, catching up whenever we are in the UK. My birthday cake was probably one of the first Northern Soul types of cakes. The Thursday night trundle up the steep staircase provided us with our soul fix with the recent tunes bought at the Casino or from dealers such as John Manship, John Anderson's Soul Bowl and Rob Sharp that week. I particularly remember Roy Hamilton "Crackin Up" was £4 from Soul Bowl (I still have the postal order counterfoil) and Frankie and Johnny "I'll Hold You" was £4 too. I also recall a John Manship soul pack 100 for £10, from which, in later years, would prove a great investment as many regularly sell for £50 to £100 these days and a copy of the Sinceres which was valued at £200 around 2004. I was John's customer number 80 and continued to buy over the years up to the time of writing. I lost many a tune because the manager was in the office around 9.00 and I couldn't nick in and use the phone. I'd been in the office a few times, having been asked to do tannoy sales "because you DJ". That ended abruptly after announcing to the customers that the hairdryer we had on special would "give you a nice blow job for £9.99 oops! We had occasional soul nights around the city at the Kings Hall where Ivan Steve started the Tempo club and Sunday sessions at the Enterprise. They also organised an allnighter at the iconic Carlisle Cosmo with Brian Rae, Soul Sam and Rod Luker. Later an all-dayer was organised with Richard Searling DJing and reporting the 750 attendees had made it one of the best he had attended, this according to the Rambler in the Black Echoes magazine. These were great days, out almost every night meeting up with friends at dances most nights, yes the 70's, good times and we had our summer of love too, 1976. Hot and sticky, with soaring temperatures and droughts but great summer walks into town. Work was taking me around the country as a trainee manager, but here in Carlisle we could play football on the roof and if the ball went over the edge we just called below to look out. ELF 'AND' SAFETY would have had a field day. Some days were so hot your chair got stuck in the roof bitumen. Later, around 1978, it was discovered that our crew member Debbie Utley (Little Debbie Norman), during an afternoon cup of tea with her aunt, was a cousin of Mike Walker, the casino manager and she should say hello when she next attended. From these early meetings Mike was persuaded to organise a few allniters at the Carlisle Market Hall. The only problem would be the light in the morning through the huge 100 yrs old massive skylights and I do recall curtains being discussed. They never eventuated. The Allniters, 4 in total, ran from 1979/80 with the original casino decks in situ and I was privileged to DJ with them alongside Richard Searling, Dave Evison, Alan Rhodes, Brian Rae and Keith Minshul after receiving a letter from Mike confirming it. We even had our names in the Black Echo about it. A good job I kept all of this info, diaries and cuttings, you never know who may call you a liar eh! Coz unfortunately some do! One guy here in Australia told me "You didn't DJ at the Casino coz I went every week and I never saw you". Hey, you just have to laugh don't you!

DJ offer from Mike Walker of Wigan Casino © Barry Simpson

Right: Barry Simpson DJ's at Wigan Casino © Barry Simpson

Prior to the letter arriving, a girlfriend of mine, Sandra, gave me a slip of paper from an old Kays catalogue with Mikes Walker's phone number on it which asked me to call. Not a strange thing I hear you say, but I held on to this, amongst all my other pieces of memorabilia, and later put them on display in my music room. On this piece of paper was an address of a block of units in Perth, Western Australia. I had no idea why it was there, when or why I had written it, nor who it belonged to. Some 35 years later and living in Western Australia, I was teaching OHS to a class of students. Whilst collecting their licences for identification I noticed that one of the student's addresses was familiar. Sure enough when I got home and checked, he lived at the address I found on the paper FROM 35 YRS AGO. NOW THAT IS WEIRD! During promotion for these Carlisle allniters events the newspaper ran articles on the Carlisle scene, one proclaiming "the dead city gets some soul". On one occasion Danny and I were asked along to the Cosmo so a TV crew could film us dancing and it was broadcast on border TV. We danced to Bobby Paris' "I Walked Away" and Teddy Vann's "Coloured Man". While the Carlisle allniters were taking place, Mike asked Danny and I if we would like to DJ at the Casino and, after around a millisecond of thought, we said yes. Once a fortnight alternating with each other or weekly if a spot was needed. The record buying just got serious. On my first spot I remember playing Jay Traynor but forgot to drop the needle on the record, after a second or two the crowd did that slow hand clap until I placed the needle and off they went. I still remember the feeling and it's probably what keeps me going. The thunderous clapping was definitely there when I put a recent purchase by the Stemmons Express "Woman Love Thief" on the decks. From my "casino diary" I noted DJ spots almost weekly in 79 in both the main hall and in Mr M`s. Particular note is made of the Edwin Starr concert when I DJ`d in M`s because at that time I really wasn't into live shows. The Elgins were also performing one night and got to see the last of their set after my M`s spot. Once, I noted, double decking with Gal. Other memories include catching up with Kev Joss in 2000, not having seen him since the 70's. He once said I was one of his favourite DJs at the time (in a Soul Cargo article he wrote). He also arranged a deal around a copy of Rita and the Tiaras " Gone With The Wind", which went down in some sleazy petrol station one dark and rainy night. There was a couple sitting watching us exchange packages and money. I often wonder what their thoughts had been that night. I remember Ivan Ward, Steve McCubbin and Ken Harkness coming to my house to sell some records and a record box which I still have to this day. They had been record hunting in the USA and found an English Darrell Banks on London demo and an Evie Sands. I bought a record called "You're Gone" by Celeste Hardie for a tenner, Ivan said it had belonged to the now legendary DJ Ian Levine. I also bought Vessie Simmons ``I'm Gonna Make It With You" for £3 and Black and Ward" Long Time" £3. The oak wooden record box was £10. Later, 40 years later, I would catch up with Ken via Facebook, he had moved to Melbourne in Australia, sadly he died before we could catch up. At the Casino TV cameras were invited to come and film for a program "This England" but many of the Carlisle crew didn't go on those occasions, it was cool not to go. But in later years the show would become a great visual record of a fabulous time. In hindsight I wish I had gone. I also had the pleasure of meeting Sam and Kitty from Emmerdale there, had a drink and got their autographs, again which I still have. She wore dark thigh length boots. Not sure why I remember that now!

Bags Packed For Work

Whilst travelling the country with work in Wolverhampton, during the later Wigan Casino days I would visit the Tartan room at the Queen Victoria hotel and the Locarno for a soul fix, A cricket club in Lytham, a night in Bury and a couple of nights in Basildon was the farthest south at the time. Sadly, none of my new workmates had heard of or liked Northern Soul and the travel dried up. I do recall catching up with a guy in Walsall at a pub called the Black Swan, or its local name "Mucky Duck", and buying a copy of Gloria Jones 'Tainted Love' and 'Wow 'by Andre Gagnon from him. I recall I was going to pinch a pool ball as a memento but it wouldn't fit in my pocket, they were so big. In 1978 I bought a Lambretta Jet 200 from Gary Etheridge and hung out with the scooter crowd. The whole scooter scene was kicking off again and a few of the guys were buying new ones and I joined them in 1980 with a new Lambretta Jet 200 from Horner's in Manchester. I named it the Canadian Sunset, a scene I painted on the side panels, added a back rest and wheel rack and crash bars, and changed the backlight, or rather my friend Stephen Humphries, a scooter enthusiast, did. The music influences came from Aswad and the hugely popular Exodus album by Bob Marley along with Madness and the Jam and, of course, northern Soul. We met in the Prince of Wales Pub in Denton Holme Carlisle and had many scooter runs out. Scarborough scooter weekend was a big event for the Carlisle scooter club, the "Borderers' ' (I designed the club badge) with around 20 attending. Rudies night club hit the spot over the weekend. The gathering saw a few chopper style Lambrettas and some great paint jobs with a trip to Arthur Francis on the way home for some parts, George Rouse picking up a new exhaust. I had some great times out with the lads, we got pulled up a few times after a few greabo (Greaser motorcycle riders) skirmishes in Penrith and Blackpool but were fortunately let free without charges. A quiet life in the main. Andy Francis the Lambretta Dealer, builder and enthusiast from Carlisle, rebuilt the engine, added a Dellorto carb and sprayed it metallic maroon after a seizure got me stuck at Mungrisdale lane end in the Lake District, for my sins. Once, my mate Craig Smethurst and I went to Wigan Casino on our scooters and stopped at his Nan's on the way back for a break. During the home journey I was tired and squinting due to the rain and I'm sure I fell asleep and woke up a split second later behind a truck. Another break was called for. But having added a Vespa to the fold and working away they went the distance. My Dad sold them to some young kids for 200 quid, "coz you never used `em and they blocked the coal bunker". My scootering days were over.

Carlisle Scooter Crew © Barry Simpson

Bags packed for Canada

I had been to Canada in 1980 and a trip to Sam the Record Man in Toronto yielded only albums, which at 37 cents each seemed a good deal, shipping back and selling them over time. My biggest profits came from 3 Elvis Costello albums "live at the El Mocambo" for $3. I sold one for 10 quid, auctioned one to £17 in the Record Collector and kept the last for myself. On my return I found that "Time Won't Let Me" had been boot-legged and lost a bit of money on it, buying The Velours cover up Peter Jarret "Run, Run, Run, Baby Run" as a consolation but it didn't go mental. The Casino was going downhill musically, and visits dropped off by winter of 1980. I never went to the last night. It was during a trip to Corfu in 1981 that I read the news of the Casino closing definitely, later burning down it was never going to re-open now. Time to move on……..

In Carlisle the Twisted Wheel and the Pagoda rang out to a new sound, new romance and a new wave of bands like Tears for Fears, Duran and Japan, Boy George and Culture Club to name a few sprang into the charts and the 80s sound continued to fill the clubs around the country and Bacup, where I had now moved to from Warrington, with Horace's the place to be. This didn't stop all the northern Soul, with very occasional visits to the Parr Hall when I lived in Warrington for a couple of years. Once in a while catching up with Brian Rae again, who lived round the corner in Sankey. The daily 40 mile journey to Raw-tenstall had taken its toll and I moved there in 84. The Royal Hotel in Waterfoot on a Friday and Saturday providing what little Northern I could get to hear.

Bags packed for the North East

From 1987 to around 1990 the career and family consumed much of my time in Washington and the soul fire dimmed within to an ember until a charity "dress police" parade in 1994.

Lots of us had dressed up, or rather dressed down, at work to raise money for charity over the weekend. On Saturday, while I was on a day off, I loaned some fancy dress to a mate (I see you giggling now), my old Wigan shirt covered in badges and some baggies. That day he was approached by a guy and asked, "You into northern Soul mate"? he said no... "but my mate is..." the fire was re-ignited. He left details of a soul night in Springwell near Gateshead. He was Kev Hughes and, together, for the next few years we did soul nights and allniters every weekend and all recorded on calendars and in diaries. I also DJ'd at some local events and met many more new friends like Gazza White, Karen and Jeff Greenhaff, Steve "bully" Davison originally from Carlisle. People ask me how I remember everything, diaries I say, diaries, and every year. One Saturday we did a soul night in Newcastle, a soul night in Carlisle and an all-nighter in Blackburn, Tony's. We also visited Carlisle, Penrith, King Georges in Blackburn, the Carlton in Morecambe, Kings Hall in Stoke. Now, around 1998, very happily single again, It was here in the Springwell Village centre, Gateshead I met another great group of soulies, Horse, Tracy, Dikka, Brenda, Mickey, Chris, Hillary, Dekka, the famous John Powney, Matty Turner and a cracking lad called Duncan McAllister, a great collector, DJ and soul enthusiast who along with his fabulous wife would visit us in Australia later. A tune I remember from those days is Howard Guyton "I Watched You Slowly Slip Away" which Matty had played. I just had to have it and just like that I was collecting again. Other soul nights were in the Arts Centre, Blackfriars and Station Hotel, where I met some great people like Karen and Jeff, Gazza white and Tomma. A record I bought around this time for about 75 quid was Bettye Swann ``Kiss My love Goodbye". One night I picked Matty up in my Audi to go to the Arts Centre. I saw a space to park and Matty was like "no way are you getting in there mate"... "watch me" says I. He was a tad impressed I think by the "f@@k me, how did ye dithat". These Geordie guys made me feel so welcome and asked me to join them at the Cleethorpes weekender.

Bags packed for Cleethorpes

Cleethorpes was another experience. Usually a weekend in June or July. We crammed into a Chalet on the Friday and it was party time till Monday with the obligatory fancy dress and dive in the swimming pool on the Sunday. I heard such great music I hadn't heard before and met some fab people like Roger "honk-honk" Banks and his wife Jenny, Pete and Viv Coulson, Ted and Karen White, Leon, Tony and Amanda and of course I bought records. I met up with Andy Rix again, having previously met at the Newton Aycliffe soul nights and asked if I could see his Shrine records which he duly did and allowed me to hold them, even JD Bryant. But such a great guy as he was, he showed as much interest in my Motown pink series. The stories of how he acquired the Shrine records, the cost of phone calls, asking the listener to turn over the JD Bryant and read out the title again and the record that arrived in the envelope are ones I will treasure. "We can get a man on the moon, surely we can fix a shattered record", probably ``The Prophets ``One Gold Piece". Over the next couple of years, based in Washington, I travelled the country with my job as a trainer from Canterbury to Aberdeen and DJing at the likes of Bretby, Winsford, Preston Grasshoppers, the Carlton and the Kings Arms in Morecambe, the Cumbrian Hotel, Pine Grove Hotel and the Crown and Mitre in Carlisle and local events in Newcastle like The Arts centre, the Station Hotel and Black friars.

During this period was the Swon's event in Blackburn with a showing of the complete movie in an auditorium. A highlight then was meeting Bobby Paris in 1999 at the Swon's event. The promoters showed the complete 24 hrs of Strange World of Northern Soul, an outstanding video recollection of northern Soul by the one and only, Mr Ian Levine in the auditorium. After a chat I asked Bobby Paris if he would autograph my "I Walked Away" record for me. "Are you sure? " he asked, on the record"? Yes I replied, it ain't going nowhere".

I remember Bobby filling up with tears, saying "I wrote that song during a very sad part of my life". Later I would acquire 6 different versions on acetate, a demo, an issue, test press and a first draft of the lyrics via his ex-wife and Johnny Redpants, lovin it!

At the time I was chasing a huge lot of Motown memorabilia. I won it and one favourite piece is my Berry Gordy Telegram about JFK's assassination, inviting everyone to pay tribute to him. It proves he was in Los Angeles that weekend and not Detroit at a meeting. Another is a Christmas list in Berry's own hand from 1961 with all the till receipts, signed by Berry or Raynoma Gordy. It shows a sweater for Barrett Strong, a watch for Mary Wells, a cigarette lighter for Marvin Gay and a car for the Miracles.

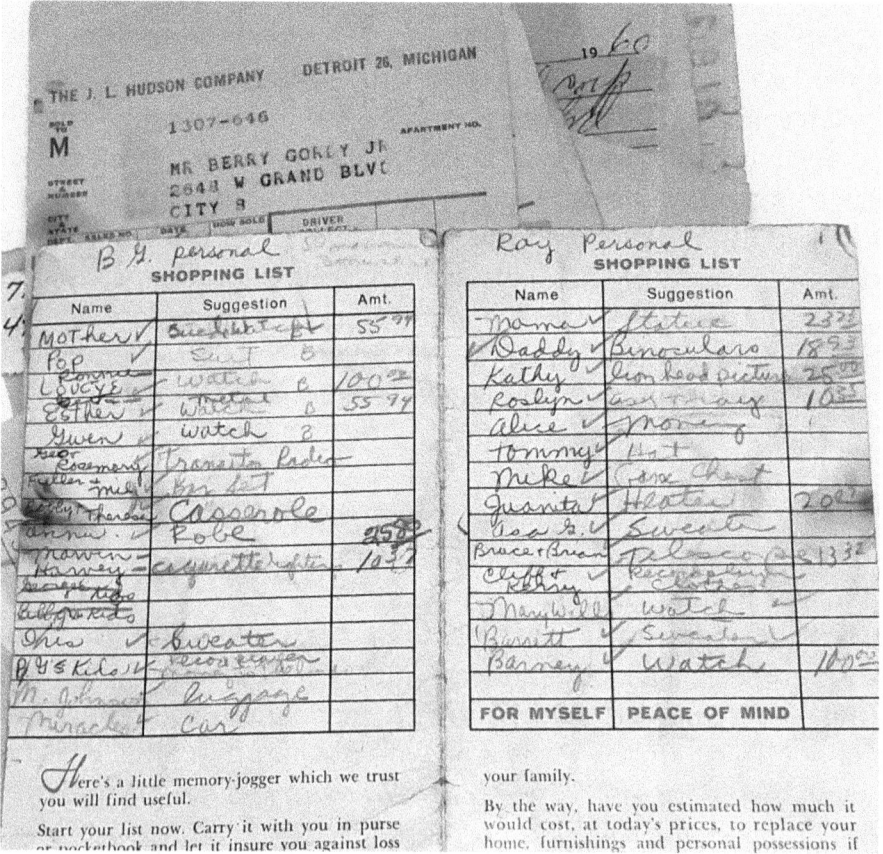

Motown Xmas List © Barry Simpson

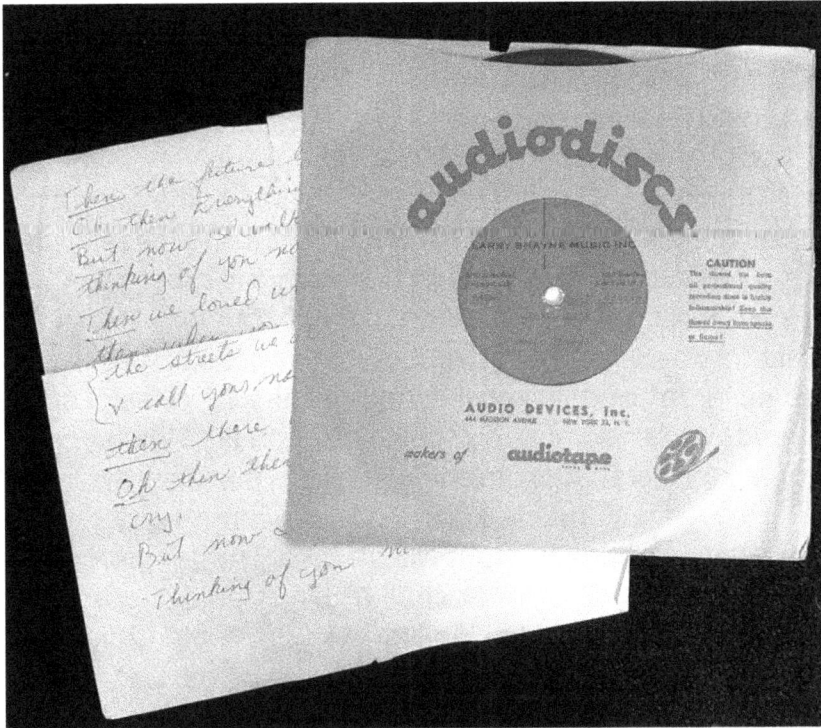

Bobby Paris acetate © Barry Simpson

In Blackburn I met Ady Croasdale again, who after mentioning I was going to Australia for a soul weekend, introduced me to Mike Ritson, the new owner of Manifesto magazine. We chatted and discovered his cousin Loraine Ritson was a friend of my sisters, he was also from Carlisle and his sister was moving to Perth Australia soon. His Dad was the famous Geordie comedian Bobby Thompson. On one meeting in later years, Mike revealed that when his father had died he had travelled to the north east for the funeral and the station was so packed with fans, he had felt like royalty. We caught up whenever he was over in Australia for the nationals. Locally, in Newcastle, we had soul nights at the Bowes Incline and a few at Cassidys too (after my return from Australia in 1999), in February and May of 2000. Kev and I continued our UK travels seeing the Dells at Trentham Gardens among the highlights all these recorded on Dave Evison's Calendar.

Bags packed for Perth Australia

Perth in 1999 was my first trip to Australia for a soul weekender. At the Airport I found my baggage was overweight, so I phoned Duncan McCallister for help. He came to the airport and we discussed putting items in his boot, contacting his relative in London if I didn't get aboard there or paying the difference. I got on, passed through to Bali and on to Perth, but I had to send a separate bag back having bought more things. Here, in Perth, I met some great people on the back of the Manifesto article mentioned at the beginning, with Roy Burton R.I.P bringing my copy of Mike Ritson and Stuart Russell's book "The In Crowd" for me. Roy, affectionately known as "squadron leader" sadly passed away in early 2021 but will be fondly remembered as a big fan of Northern Soul in Australia. Sitting enjoying a pint at the Moon and Sixpence, an English style pub in the City, I overheard some guys talking about soul and introduced myself. Vince Peach, Brian and Janet Sharkey, Brian Cunningham, Tom, Phill, were from Melbourne and we sat and chatted for a long time before getting ready for the event.

A meet and greet was organised at a pub in Leederville and a Saturday event at the massive Embassy ballroom after a BBQ on the South Perth Foreshore with Sunday at an Irish club in Subiaco. Here I met John Smoljo (who later, would post about local events on the Yahoo NSIO (Northern Soul in Oz) site (set up by Steve Bardsley), he also liked the Bobby Paris so I gave him one of my 3 embroidered t-shirts, he had the red and I kept the white and blue ones. I met so many others from around the country whom I would get to know over the coming years. Sadly John Smoljo passed away far too young in 2009.

Top: Guys at the moon and sixpence © Barry Simpson
Bottom: Perth Allnighter © Barry Simpson

Among the local DJs, such as Robbie Burns, were many who took the long journey across Australia. Pete Feven from Adelaide, Craig Bayliss and Vince Peach from Melbourne, Maria Orlovic, Alex White, Ady Pountain & Pete Morgan from Sydney.

Pete, I remember, played "Love You Just Can't Walk Away" by Dean Courtney during his spot after me. It was immediately added to my wants list. Being the only non-ex-pat, I always tried to bring something a bit special over and there was a bit of competition on who would bring what. Which only increased as time went on, the willie waving became noticeable from around 2005 when labels and W/D would appear after the record titles on playlists the DJ's would put up on Steve Bardsley's Yahoo Northern Soul In Oz site.

Desperate for food on the Sunday, I visited Chicken Treat, a local fast-food store and promptly fell asleep leaning against the window. I was probably not a pretty sight from the other side and woke up an hour or so later returning to the event not that refreshed. Up on to the stage walked a guy with dreadlocks and a plastic suitcase from which he produced some albums. The DJ was a guy called General Justice. My immediate thoughts were omg what was going to get played. But my goodness, I remember a tremendous set of great sixties soul music such as Sam and Dave banging through the speakers. I'm not sure if we spoke at the time but certainly have since and discussed this great time I witnessed. Well done sir!

Some tunes from the event included: Willie Hutch, "Love Runs Out" The Inspirations, "Your Wish Is My command" Dean Courtney, "Love You Just Can't Walk Away", Christine Cooper, "Heartaches Away My Boy" Don Thomas, "Come On Train" Maxine Brown, "Torture"

Maxine Brown was a Sydney choice, she is a favourite of Maria Orlovic whom I would later bump into at Cleethorpes when Maxine had an appearance with Dennis Coffey and the first appearance of the incredible Dean Parrish. It was discovered that he had changed his name, having been originally called Phillipe Anastasi as reported in "Stomping ground" by Rambler (a columnist for Black Echoes) back in 1978.

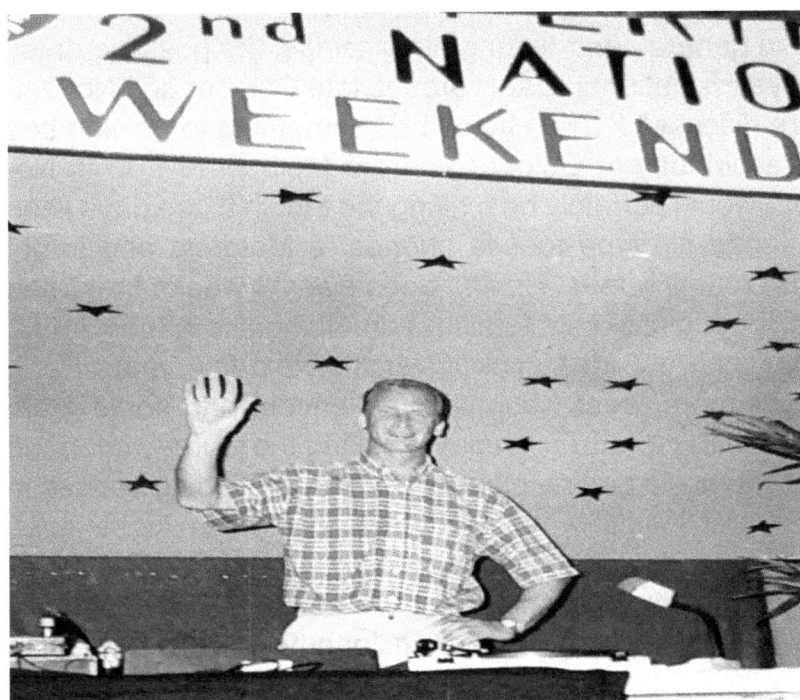

Top: Barry Simpson & General Justice © Barry Simpson.
Bottom: Barry Simpson DJ Perth © Barry Simpson

265

The whole show was fantastic I have to say. In January 2020, I had been in discussions with Dean Parrish about him coming to Australia. Backing by the MOD SQUAD were in initial discussions. But of course, as we all know, Covid happened and then Dean sadly passed away early in 2021. Not before leaving us with a catalogue of classic northern soul records.

My set from 1999 included: Lorraine Chandler, "what can I do" James Fountain, "Seven Day Lover" Francis Nero, "Keep on loving me" Stanley Mitchell, "Get it baby", Earl Jackson, "Soul Self Satisfaction The Ambassadors, "Too Much of a Good Thing" The weekend came to a finish with the draw. Sydney was picked out of the box by Adelaide's Miriam Feven for 2000 and it was all over red rover. Well not quite ! In the Moon and Sixpence on the Monday afternoon I joined a few soulies, Chrissie Finneron, Pete Morgan, Tim Jones, Hilary Webster, Tom Orr, Brian Cunningham, Lee Garnett, Janet and Brian Sharkey, Kev Cunningham and myself chatting over the weekend, soul and life in general, and among other things, the possible dates for next year's national. Dates around late October and November were discussed. The choice had something to do with Lee Garnett's birthday in October and the Melbourne Cup in November. I would certainly be making the trip. In those days I had one of those flip type mobile phones, a Motorola and forgot about the roaming fees. Having been away 4 weeks I returned to have a couple of bills totaling something like £800. Something to watch out for I think. Over the next few years Perth would see more great National Weekenders and some great memories with more English guys making the journey later and some great music getting played. It isn't easy finding venues in Australia and if you want a different one each night, even harder. That said, some great venues have been sourced over the years by the "Committee". One being Rosie O'Grady's where I first met my long-term friend Johnny Warren. There was also The Talk of the Town in 2003, Gilkisons Dance studio and a Polish club with Fridays or Sunday at an Irish club and many times it was a struggle to get ready on time, once still finishing off setting up when a guy was DJing. On one of these events I, again, caught up with Duncan McCallister and Ginger Taylor who spun the classic JD Bryant for me. Here is a small cross section of tunes at these events over the years. All available on the top quality well produced CD`s. Fortson and Scott, "Sweet lover" The Incredibles, "Miss Treatment" Carl Hall, "Let me Down Slowly" The Valentines, "Breakaway" Percy Wiggins, "It Didn't Take Much" The Entertainers, "Love In My Heart" Lou Rawls, "See You When I get There" The Perigents, "Love On A Rampage" The Sapphires, "Slow Fizz" Albert Washington, "I'm The Man", Holly St James, "That's Not Love" being my rare play early on along with Jackie Day "Naughty Boy" and the Cautions all first plays in Australia. Interestingly another I played was the Ivories on a rare Despanza number. This record is more famous for different texts, so much so that the number was almost in-consequential, probably due to rarity. In those days 470 was a rare number and I had not seen it catalogued until the Tom Kline book highlighted it in the 90's. Next was the long flight home, Christmas, a new job, Easter, Christmas conference then Sydney here I come.

Bags packed for Sydney

It was here before I knew it. October smacked me in the chops good and proper. Love was in the air, the night before I was due to fly to Australia. I had been asked out on a blind date and driven from Carlisle to Newcastle for a night out with friends and met the amazing Kay, the future Mrs Simpson. All through the holiday we kept in touch and met up on my return.

Sydney 2000, organised by Maria, Alex and Chrissie, the Sydney Soul Sisters. Their photo is one of my favourite Aussie soul pics of all time. The main promotional material displays a shot of Tommy Hunt mimicking pushing a double decker bus.

They produced a commemorative booklet which contained a spread about Australian releases by Frank Driscoll who has a fantastic collection of Australian soul.

Barry & Kay Simpson © Barry Simpson

The Sydney Soul Sisters Chrissie, Maria & Alex © Barry Simpson

George Coumbis, another Aussie soulie had been organising soul allniters for many years before in Sydney, well before the current circuit and has a great collection to boot.

Sydney's early soul history

Here is a brief account of George's recollections around the beginnings of soul in Sydney. The Soul Scene in Australia essentially began in Sydney in 1979-1980 in a little pub in Pitt Street, smack bang in the Sydney central business district when the Mod (Revival) Scene was reaching its height in Australia. These were heady times when Australia's premier Mod Band called "The Sets" would attract upwards of 750 punters to gigs. Hundreds of scooters all in a row outside the roughest and toughest Sydney pubs was a sight to behold. George, being a tad under age, managed to bluff his way on to the record decks and played a set full of classic Motown and Stax sounds. The response was overwhelming, the place went wild and the Aussie Soul Scene was off and running. It was at Sydney record Fairs that George discovered the wealth of rare soul sounds that had been released throughout the 60s and 70s on attractive and colourful Australian Record labels like Festival, Stateside and W & G as well as locally released issues of US labels like Chess and Atlantic, also with their own distinctive and unique Aussie created label designs. As there was literally no one else searching for these sounds at the time , it was like taking candy from a baby for George as Aussie Rock N Roll record dealers were only too glad to off load sounds like Little Carl Carlton's Competition Ain't Nothing on Oz CBS, Clara Ward's Right Direction on Oz Verve , Jessica James and the Outlaws "We'll Be Making Out" on Oz Stateside, The "Fabulous" Jackie Day EP on W & G, The Shirelles' "Last Minute Miracle" on Oz Scepter and a host of others, all at around 50 cents or a dollar each! Let's not forget Tony Middleton's "To the ends of the Earth" on Polydor. Then at one Record Fair in early 1982 George came across one particular stall holder named David Milton, who would not only go on to become a crucial figure for the Aussie Soul Scene but would also become a club owner and promoter of Dance Music in Sydney throughout the 80s and 90s. Dave Milton had migrated to Australia from the UK with his wife and babies in early 1982 having enjoyed a long association on the

UK soul scene. He had been a regular punter at Manchester's Twisted Wheel from 1964, the Blackpool Mecca and The Torch when the Wheel closed. Over time Dave relented and allowed George a Tuesday night one off to play his type of soul music. Tuesday was usually a dead night of the week, and which if it bombed wouldn't have mattered at all from a financial point of view. Imagine Dave's surprise when in 1983 the first night of "The Groovesville Soul Club" came and the place was packed to the rafters. He couldn't believe that he would ever see a dance floor in Australia filled with people dancing to "Seven Days Too Long" and Gloria Jones' "Tainted Love". Within a space of months , the night had become so popular that Dave gradually promoted George's night in importance from Tuesdays to Wednesdays then Thursdays and by 1985 Friday nights (when the club was renamed "The Freezer".

George had also adopted the DJ alias of DJ "Agent Double O Soul" and the notoriety of the soul scene in Sydney was such that George was interviewed by National Australian Style Magazine "Stiletto", the Australian equivalent of the UK's Face Magazine. However, the licensing laws would soon change (to 24 hour around the clock trading in areas such as Kings Cross) and with that change, it was only natural that George thought: "What about All-nighters?". Well, yes... but until now George had promoted and run the nights solely by himself with only the valuable cooperation and assistance of Dave Milton. But All-nighters would be a major undertaking, and if nothing else George needed another DJ, at the very least to relieve him on the night so he could attend to other things like tickets at the door etc. Hardcore Northern Soul DJs and collectors weren't exactly crawling all over Australia in the late 1980's , But one day out of the blue George got a strange inter-state call at work from what sounded like a Scouser, living in Melbourne who had heard about the success of the Groovesville Soul nights in Sydney and had somehow got a hold of George's number. The person down the line was of course Vince Peach and after an exchange of their personal favourite Northern Soul sounds, and what turned out to be a very expensive telephone call, it was agreed that Vince would come up to Sydney to be the special guest DJ at Australia's first ever full scale Northern Soul and Motown All-nighter. So on Saturday 14 December 1991 on a burning hot summer Sydney night Australia's first ever All-nighter took place at St Elmo's Night Club in Sussex Street Sydney. Over 350 soul fans voted with their feet and a legend was born! Some of those who were there on the night and who were to become stalwarts of the Australian Soul Scene and still there included Dave Worsley and Ann Cox, Alex White, Maria Orlovic, Steve Byatt, James Grygell, Alan Curley, Andy and Fiona Nevin (who had been regulars at Wigan Casino). George and Vince alone handled DJing duties for the whole 11 hours !!! Max too, it must be said, was an integral part of the Sydney and scene, by now Vince had also been inspired to promote the first Melbourne Northern Soul all-nighter at Inflation Nightclub and reciprocated by having George down there as special guest DJ along with Frank Driscoll manning the decks! The next major development was at another Record Fair in Sydney in 1994 where George once again came across a stallholder who was unusually selling a rather large quantity of original soul records. After the usual introductory banter between George and the stallholder took place, the man introduced himself as Ady and said he was into Northern Soul. George hesitated for a moment and then asked, "You're not Ady Pountain, are you?" The answer was yes and it was indeed the same Ady Pountain. Ady had established a reputation as one of the pioneering DJs at the Top of the World All-nighters at Stafford, a leading UK Rare Soul all-nighter along with the 100 Club in London. Ady had recently moved to Australia on a semi-permanent working assignment and like Dave Milton and other expats from the UK before him never expected any sort of soul scene to exist in Australian, and certainly not one created and driven by Aussies!

The Friday meet n greet was supposed to be a few drinks in the pub, the Globe Hotel, but some record spinning took off and a fantastic start to the weekend began with an impromptu soul night. It set the scene for Friday nights to come and the meet n greets were relegated to Thursdays. Saturday afternoon a few gathered near the city in a bar with many wearing the applicable soccer shirt from the UK leagues, Carlisle was mine but Huddersfield, Rochdale, Chelsea, Manchester City and United were worn with pride. Over the weekend Frank and I organised a catch-up and did a bit of record searching with Frank finding a Billy Soul "Big Balls of Fire" in a shop, we had only been talking about it recently and it seemed like such a coincidence. Wow, I'd forgotten about Max or "Max the doorman" as he became affectionately known. He could be found around the Sydney scene and Aussie Nationals in the early days. Another well-known Sydney sider in those early days was Mat (Mathew Macdonald), most will remember him as the smart guy in fabulous suits and smoking lovely cigars. At each event he wore a different suit. The Red one was my favourite, always a pleasure to catch up with the smartest electrician on the block.

The Saturday all-niter was in Marrickville Bowling club. It was fantastic and goes down as among the best in Soul Australia. I met Nancy Yahiro here with her then partner Gabrielle who had come over from the USA for the national event and we spoke a little that night. Currently residing in Darlington in the UK, Nancy has plans to move to Spain. My spot was Sunday afternoon in the Paddington Green Hotel around 3.00. But on seeing the records I had brought, Frank Driscoll and Pete Morgan offered to share their Saturday spots with me, a gesture I have never forgotten, never will and have tried to, on the occasions I thought it necessary, to also share my spot with others. I remember chatting to Alex White at the time and I'm sure she had just bought a Chuck Cockerham and Anne Sexton on IMPEL. We sat by the bowling green discussing records. It was the weekend of the Gay Mardi Gras and to see the sights we saw was an absolute eye opener, guys in pink pinafore dresses and white heels, some BIG guys in thongs and chain mail vests. To each his own but a great weekend.

They didn't produce a T-shirt at this event so I "found" a bowling club T-shirt that would do. At the Saturday afternoon get-togethers we would sometimes see Paul Cridge selling the badges and T-shirts and Pill like stress balls as usual, which I collected as a social history project. The weekenders had sets from The Soul Sisters and great guys like Ady, Peter, Bernhard, Rob, George and the star camera footballer, my good friend, Keefy doing the opening set at the one in 2005. Keefy had gone into some sort of high kick, backdrop and put my camera into orbit….. no harm done but a laugh we continue to this day.

Over the years a number of different people have helped organise the Sydney Nationals which gives everyone an experience. Some of those in the Sydney scene included, obviously, the Soul Sisters but also Una Hanlan, originally from Glasgow, Scotland and a Casino regular. Una has been active on the Sydney soul scene for a number of years, our paths first crossing in 2005 and future nationals, but more so at the "big thing weekender" in 2010. Una does lots of work around the indigenous and homeless communities in Sydney at the Wayside Chapel which I visited around 2017. Bernhard Schmitz, another of the national organisers, is our local anthropologist, posting many fabulous pictures of the indigenous wildlife for our pleasure and has connections in the record industry with Record Shack. Bernhard is into a more modern feel and works with Sabina, his wife and another organiser, Paul Freeman on the Eastside Radio show. The National that year focused on a modern room and I have to say it was a more acceptable modern to my banging Northern ears, with Dallas Hyde on the Sunday producing some masterpieces. These guys are responsible for the amazing 2015 venue, Bondi Surf club national and what an outstanding venue that turned out to be. I recall standing at a bar in Mojacar a couple of years ago and a guy walking around who looked like Paul, it actually was Paul. Over on business and saw the advert for a soul weekender. Small world. I met Steve Byatt, a great laid back scooterist, a long time ago at the Nationals and it's always a pleasure to catch up.

His involvement in the 2005 Nationals saw a second double CD with a cross section of great soul. The CD and the badge depicted the Opera House image as did the 2010 and a CD for the 2015 nearly never happened but, relenting to many requests, a CD was produced minus a jewel case but containing many great tracks. A lot of work goes into producing these great mementos of our music. Favourites of mine from that CD are Bileo and the Herbie Goins track. In Sydney, soul events have been held at The Bar Broadway, St Elmos, The Globe, Soul Biscuits (ran by Keith Miller, with Steve Bardsley who flew in from Melbourne each month to DJ), to name but a few and a radio slot on the "Fire on the wire" on East side radio. Bernhard and Paul also present the Sounds of soul also on East side radio in recent times. Maria moved to the UK, married Arthur Fenn and continues to DJ around the UK with everyone else still ensconced in the scene here, Alex moving to Melbourne and Chrissie moving to New Zealand, catching up with another stalwart of the aussie scene, Netti Page, whom I first met in 2000 and on the dancefloor at every national since. OMG, as I type this I go back to a time, around 2015 when Duncan McAllister and Sue were here in Sydney. Duncan has a problem with Garlic and needs to be careful. Unbeknown to him his food contained Garlic so off he went poorly for a good few hours. Around 3.00 am after the National Weekender here in Sydney we were making our way back to our hotel when Duncan got his second wind and suggested we go for a night cap. We ended up in a bar, relatively busy for 3.00 am, and sat down for a drink. The bar was closing and we were asked if we wanted to continue. We had to go through into a different area so they could close up. This we did and ended up with a couple joining us, brother and sister apparently. The drink and chatter flowed on into the morning. As the time passed the girl was talking to Sue and offered her a book as a gift. Just then another female customer and a security guard approached and asked for her book back, OMG, this girl who we had never met had stolen someone's book and given it to Sue as a gift. We left......I suppose you had to be there.

The music was always great and here is a selection from over the years Shirley Wahls "That's How Long". A Melbourne selection and a great double sider that always reminds me of Pete Feven The Jackie Beavers Show, "We Are Not Too Young To Fall In Love", Ronnie Dyson, "Fever" , Ronda Davis, "Can You Remember", Jerry Gainey, "You Don't Love Me", Bill Harris, "Am I Hot Am I Cold" (a top Sydney spin back in 2005 and still sought after), Jeanette" Marshall Donovan and Broomfield, "Since I Found My Baby", Lena and the Deltanettes, "Turn Around Baby", Barbara Hall, "You Brought It On Yourself", Bileo "You Can Win", Bernie Williams, "Ever Again" on the rare Bell issue being one of my rare plays and again a first in Australia.

After that first weekend in 2000, I flew up to Cairns and had a few days holiday, renting a car and would later drive to Brisbane. The hotel was an absolute disgrace, so much so, I moved out the next day. I had been walking along the esplanade and spotted some adventure things to do, went in and booked a white-water rafting trip and a bungee jump. Whilst there the tour operator offered some choices of accommodation for me as I drove south and showed me around the attached backpackers lodging. Being a bit prudish I opted for the single room as opposed to the dormitory, got to watch the records, and a corner room with a great sea view. That night, or should I say early morning, I was woken by knocking on my window. What the heck, I'm on the first floor. While drawing the curtains, I found two young girls standing on the veranda. They must have climbed up the pipe. They explained that they had forgotten the door pass code and couldn't get in. I let them through to a dorm. How naïve was I, they could have been axe murderers…….., me, a handsome Englishman alone, in a foreign land, imagine the headlines, "Englishman lets mad axewomen into a backpackers lodge and carnage takes place". Anyhow all was good, the lodge was fine and recommendable as was the Bungy Jumping, well it was only 300 ft. It was here I met two lads from Liverpool, who became friends for the next 20 yrs and attended

Kay and I`s wedding, Paul and Ferret. One night in a local bar someone gave us some tickets to an all night club so off we went, up for anything these days. What we weren't told was that it was a '" Gentlemen's Club". We didn't hang around long but I do remember a dog rough chick asking us for $20 to take her skimpy bikini off. Paul offered her $20 to keep them on..... needless to say we were asked to leave! The next day we packed up and headed for Airlie Beach for a night then down to Hervey Bay. I have to say, this trip was an eye opener for me, a "prudie English manager" type. In Airlie beach the accommodation was a dormitory with which I now felt a tad more comfortable. That is until I came back around 2.00 am to find young girls straddled across the beds in the hot night air covered in a loose sheet. It was a mixed dorm I later found out, but I kept my clothes on and wrapped up so tight in the blanket and pushed so far into the wall you would have needed to chisel me out! Paul, Ferret and I parted company and I headed for Hervey Bay. In for a penny they say. "Yes the mixed dorm will do" well it was late! Up early the next morning and off to the shower room for a shave and get an early tour in. Whilst shaving I could hear the shower behind me switch off and out strolled a girl letting it all swing, put on some make-up and proceed to tell me she had an interview that morning. I quickly packed up and left what I thought was the lady's area. I asked the room service where the Gents were and having pointed to them, she advised "or you can use the mixed shower room if you wish" pointing to where I had just left. A few days camping with Koala camping tours in Fraser Island followed with me declaring "boys in this tent, girls in that one" but that only lasted one night once it was discovered half were travelling boyfriend and girlfriend so it all seemed pretty decent after that. The journey South continued through the night. Through a storm and floods I saw a truck pulled over with its hazards flashing and I remember thinking "Don't stop, you could wake up with an ass as big as the Lincoln Tunnel ", recalling a Madonna line from an 80's wrestling movie. Then down to Brisbane and a catchup with Hammy, whom I had met at the Aussie national Weekenders. Here, at the local rugby club, I tasted the magnificent Morton Bay bugs, definitely worth a try. I also caught up with Kev Core who "cleaned" my rare copy of Joey DeLorenzo, a recent purchase (and one of only 5 known at the time) from my old friend George Hunt. The deal was organised in such a hurry I had to borrow the £1,200 from a mate before driving over to Carlisle to pick it up, handing over the said amount to my good friend Horse the next day. Kenny Burrell had played it earlier, around `99 at the Ritz in Manchester and Ginger Taylor had one too. I would later swap this with Dave Flynn in Japan and turn down a copy of Candi Staton `Upper Hand" in the deal and regret it a little even now.

Then it was off to the airport and a flight back to the UK for Christmas, Easter, Christmas conference, then off to Melbourne.

Bags packed for Melbourne

Melbourne was next, I shared rooms at the Seville apartments in the city again with some of the Melbourne crew and arrived early to catch up. Over the week, on a visit with Brian Sharkey to Frank's to collect the CDs, I saw Tom Orr with a hair dryer trying to dry them off & an impromptu BBQ with the all-important snags. Frank has a great collection which I was privileged to peruse. This was the first time I had seen a drive through garage on a house and thought "what a great idea".

The Friday was at the Cherry Bar, AC/DC Lane. I know the guys were stressed about the event and the dollars they had put into it but it was a fantastic success. What a belting night it was. You could see the joy in the lads' faces as the realisation of an epic weekend hit them as they stood at the door. The music was just right and the venue was amazing. If you have never been to the Cherry Bar then all I can say is poor you. Vince Peach, from Huyton in the UK, had been DJing here with Pierre Baroni, who sadly passed away in 2021, for around 20 years, Pierre was a great Soul DJ and his 3PBS radio show had a big following.

Vince also does a weekly radio show, Soul Time for 38 yrs and has become the longest running radio show in the world. Vince has also interviewed some of the soul scene's greatest names. Saturday afternoon was spent touring the bars of the main drag, but I've never been one who could hold my liquor. The Saturday allniter was in the HI-FI bar, a venue the guys would use a second time. The dance floor was on a "bit of a hill" and this was Melbourne, smoking was still allowed, and on the dancefloor too, which didn't go down well with the well turned out soulies. There was a sort of observation area at the top of the stairs and the whole venue filled up pretty quick. At 1am the Turntable Terra, as my good friend Steve Bardsley would name me, hit the decks for an hour of soul and this goes down as one of my favourite spots. That Sunday morning when a crowd of us hit the bars to chill, I fell asleep around 11.30 am and was asked to leave under the vagrancy laws.

The Turntable Terra (Barry Simpson) © Steve Bardsley

The Sunday was upstairs in the Planet Café in Fitzroy, another cool venue and out of the window I saw George Coumbis climb out of a limousine and up the stairs to join us again for the last night. Ralph Tee had made the trip and played a spot, a bit modern for me, a lot modern for me. After that it was back to

Vince`s with a thick head, top bunk over Glenn Polk Smith and that mercy dash to the loo calling on Hughie as I ran and pebble dashing the porcelain. OMG I hope Vince can laugh at it like I do. Collecting the memorabilia continued with Vince giving me one of his Twisted Wheel memberships (framed and in the record room). Melbourne would break the mould twice on badges through the years, once with a rectangular badge, but in 2009, no separate badge. Here I got the CD of the artwork from Keith Sutcliffe and got 10 made, 3 left the country, I have 4, and 3 to people around OZ. Keith and Vera Sutcliffe, Mike and Margaret Wood and Justin Roche were among many of the people who helped in the organisation of these great events, Melbourne held some of the best Weekender's. Another memory I have was a Weekender with the Saturday held at Doveton soccer club and Brian Sharkey taking a sign off the clubhouse window and handing it to me "no boots allowed" it read.We all had a good laugh at its significance.

Some tunes from the Melbourne years include: From the "out on the floor" compilation which Tom was feverishly trying to try Phil Flowers, "Where Did I Go Wrong" , Mamie Lee, "I Can Feel Him Slipping Away" a Melbourne choice but massive all over Australia , Margie Joseph, "I Can't Move No Mountains", Ivories, "Please Stay" Paris, "Sleepless Nights", Chris Clarke, "Something`s Wrong", Betty O`Brien, "She'll Be Gone", Barbara Dane, "I'll Be On My Way" A current play in the UK at the time chosen by NSW but I'm sure a favourite of Kev Core from Queensland too. My contribution included the seriously rare Joey DeLorenzo "Wake Up To The Sunshine" Monday, which saw a trip to the Mornington Peninsula where I would spend the rest of the week with a great couple, Brian and Janet Sharkey. Brian and I stayed up all evening and night, through till the next morning. We played every record in my box, around 115, the B sides, and started all over again, Beer, cigarettes and black black coffee, bed the next day and do it all again. What a great time we had.

Janet sadly had to go to work but supplied the white pack cigarettes from work with Phillip Morris, plenty of beer and great music. Then it was time for the journey back home, arriving back, only to find the airport had sent my baggage to another country. It would catch-up later that week.

At one of these Melbourne events I remember talking to some bloke about a record, I think it was Tommy Navarro "I Cried My Life Away" and the price, which I felt was a bit expensive. "You just redefined expensive" he said and walked away and left me standing at the top of the stairs thinking WTF. Anyhow, it was in reference to the appearance of the rare Don Gardner "Cheatin Kind" arriving on these shores in a number of pieces. Checkout "The broken record, John Manship" on YouTube. It was actually my wife, Kay, who began to open the box having seen it damaged. The FedEx driver had just handed her a squashed clear plastic bag.

The Cracked Don Gardner © Barry Simpson

Kay`s dad immediately said take some photos first which she did, and videos. I can still remember exactly where I was, sitting at the traffic lights on my way home, when the call came in. "The record has arrived," Kay told me, " but it's broken," she said calmly. I knew she wasn't joking, never where records are concerned. But John sorted it out true to professional form and a refund was given. There are some miserable people who will think ha ha, but hey ….. I'm not. In retrospect it was the best thing to happen because in those days it was around $24,000 AUD. You could probably get one for not too much more, maybe $25,000, as a few more have surfaced so it doesn't hurt me to talk about it because it all ended well. Like it says in the video too, I found a piece in our dog, little Frankie`s coat, rest his soul. Another record story was the sale of Al Williams from Frank and the "crapping ourselves 100`s times' ' while Frank waited for the arrival of the AUD $4K in cash via the postman and me, the lovely white demo. It was probably the longest 3 months between us ever. All's well that ends well. The 2011 national was held in a huge warehouse type place, out of town it felt like after a train ride and what a great night it was, completed with a drive home on a double decker London bus, a master stroke of an ending by the Melbourne organisers. What a great night, some of us got dropped off in the middle of nowhere but it was easy to get a cab and no problem getting back to the hotel. Sunday night was at the Platform Bar. Another cracking venue, Melbourne is so full of these great places. It was an old railway arch with a stage at one end and a bar along the side. It quickly filled up and was hot, very hot with many outside in the beer garden early on. My set included some great classics such as Larry Clinton, "She's Wanted" on the rare Red issue, Frankie Beverley, "Because Of My Heart" on the rare Rouser label But the Melbourne CD had some gems too…Richard Stoute, "What Bag I'm In", Billy Prophet, "What Can I Do", The Nomads, "Something`s Bad" On leaving the Platform Bar on Sunday I got a cab to a Kebab store in Lygon St. While standing in the queue to collect my Kebab I realised I didn't have my record box with me. In absolute panic I ran out, picked up a cab and headed back to the Bar which of course was closed. An hour later when I got back to my hotel, I had convinced myself that at least they were all paid for, fuck it, bugga, bugga, bugga, What now... but like ET, I phoned home as I sat in the chair and explained my predicament to Kay and spied the record box under the table , WHAT! OMG I must have been so drunk I didn't realise I'd been back to the hotel, dropped off my records and went for a Kebab.

It would appear now that when you are drunk you can still fold your clothes up neatly, make a coffee, clean your teeth, but also return home with said record box before going for a Kebab. That was one sweet tasting Kebab I can assure you. Melbourne, alcohol and Barry don't mix well. Actually, Barry and alcohol don't mix, period!

The backstory to the red issue of Larry Clinton

The story goes something like this. One day a thrift store owner was, apparently, struggling for cash. The vet bills for his pet cat had gone mental as it had swallowed something like a pen top and needed surgery. If you have and love your pet you will understand the pain. With income low, apparently he took to the streets, visiting thrift shops, looking for bargains to sell in his own store. Whilst in one he came across some records.

At home doing some research he discovered the rarity of one on a red label by Larry Clinton. He cleaned off some of the green paint, put it on the decks, pressed play and placed the needle on the record, began treading the floorboards and said a prayer... "please don't jump, please don't jump, please....". His prayers were answered and the surge of joy he felt was enormous he told me. The rest is history, home, Christmas, Easter, Christmas conference and then off to Adelaide.

Bags packed for Adelaide

Kay joined me on this trip in 2002. We stayed with Pete and Miriam Feven, Adelaide's soul family, Andy and Mike, even at that early age could teach us something about soul. Pete, a Rochdale lad and Miriam and Mike had stayed with us in the UK and we took Mike to a hockey match while they went to a Weekender. One of the players gave him a signed hockey stick. On another jaunt we ended up at Newcastle United's ground and had a quick show around by a groundsman and we stood on the half-way line and looked at the height of the stands. One could get air-sick climbing up there.

Pete Feven and & soul crew in Enigma Bar © Barry Simpson

The Friday in Adelaide was in the Duke of York. This was the location of the Adelaide soul nights for around 4 years after the first National and became the venue for the meet and greet in the afternoon and here I met a great guy for the first time and we often recall this first meeting, Alan Dyer. I also recall asking the barman for a shandy and a glass of white wine. He returned with two glasses of white wine. I asked where the shandy was, he replied "sorry mate I fowt you said a shardny" (Chardonnay) in a deep aussie accent. We still laugh at that today. Pete had just received a 12 inch single and it was quite a talking point around the event. People had their thoughts on who it might be, but Mr Soul went down a scream when Andy played it at the Enigma bar on the Sunday.

The Enigma Bar became the monthly venue for Adelaide for quite some time. Then the smoking laws changed and trying to keep a metre away from the bar, have a dance and buy a drink really demanded some planning in those days. The Enigma Bar was the location of the infamous camel in the ute scene. It may have been Saturday, but it may have been Sunday, to be honest at these events one day is five. Anyhow, everyone is crammed into the Enigma bar downstairs. The huge sliding doors were open, and people spilled out onto the street, drinking and generally being merry. Then a ute drives by with two camels in the back, I look at Howard, Howard looks at me, "did you just see what I think I saw". But by the time we realised it, they had gone and no-one else had seen it, or at least admitted to it in case of drunken ridicule. An often shared giggle, Saturday night was in the Dom Polski. What a great venue. Pete and Miriam had gone early to put bowls of nuts on the table and get set up. You certainly got a feel for how big the place was going to be when you walked up the huge stairwell. I think Vince had his hair cut short by this time from a mop of black bushy hair to a sort of crew cut. What a great weekend that was.

The Dom Polski would serve the soul scene well over the years, a shame the bar wouldn't. But it's all down in folklore now for the next two events they would run out of beer. But in 2012 the committee did a master stroke, used a van and bought cases and cases of wine and beer to sell to the thirsty crowd, well done. It all added to the memories After a week touring the wineries it was home again. 2002 proved to be a canny year, the best year. I married my amazing Kay.

We organised the whole wedding in Bali on our return. In three weeks it was all sorted. A northern Soul wedding, all the Geordies and the Carlisle crew were there. Horse doing the famous streak. DO I LOVE YOU playing throughout the wedding march. Here we are 20 years later!

Barry & Kay Simpson's wedding © Barry Simpson

Over the next 15 years the scene across Australia would grow and in Adelaide, the home of the first National saw its 5th national in 2017. The first had been held in the Boltz café, next 3 at the Dom Polski with a fantastic Friday night event at the Kaos café going down a storm. Organisers changed but had included, as well as Pete and Miriam, Tom and Angela Moore, Todd Cavender, Alan and Elaine Dyer, Paul and Sian Davy, Simon and Tracy Evans, Bob and Jackie Norman, of course Mark Howlett from way back in 1998. Mentioning Elaine Dyer reminds me of when we moved to Perth from Adelaide. Kay and I had moved into a rental until our house purchase was complete. One day we were sitting in our back garden and could hear an English accent. Kay said "I'm sure the Dyers have a relative here, get your address book out". Sure enough we had moved in 2 doors away from Elaine`s sister Carol.

Weird stuff always happens. Another memory of the Adelaide girls meeting the winner of Australia's got talent, OMG we had a laugh on that for years. The Punk rocker. At one National, sadly for poor Val Smith, she was carted off to hospital with a broken ankle, the floor was highly polished and no talc was needed, in fact sand would have been better.

John and Val Smith are again long-time friends from the soul family we create. The story of how Jackie broke her ankle sends shivers down my spine to this day. Some of the great records from the year's CDs included some great sleeve notes by John Phillips from Brisbane, who along with his wife Carol, would help Kev and Veronica with the last Brisbane National in 2019. Here are some of the great tunes played over the years from the Adelaide nationals. The song that, back then, said Adelaide, was the Bobby Womack track "Home Is Where The Heart Is", Guitar Ray, "Your Gonna Wreck My Life" this always reminds me of Adey Harley from (Sydney), Gladys knight, "No One Could Love You More". Pete Feven from Adelaide spin. Carl Spencer, "Cover Girl", Charles Sheffield, "Voodoo Working" , The Twans, "I Can't See Him Again" (always reminds me of Bob Normanfrom Adelade). Nu-Rons, "All Of My Life", Arin Demain, "Silent Treatment", Mr Soul, "Soul On Wax" My contributions being Joe Jama, "My life" and Jimmy Burns, "I Really Love You" first time spin's in Oz.

In 2012 I had just purchased the original Motown master tape file copy of Frank Wilsons "Do I love You" and had got it copied to vinyl. I often play it in memory of soulies no longer with us including another Carlisle lad, Ian Parker, who had sadly passed away earlier that year. Christmas, Easter, Christmas conference and November for the next Australian National weekender.

Master tape of Frank Wilson "Do I Love You" © Barry Simpson

Bags packed and off to Brisbane

This year, 2004, Brisbane joined the roster after discussions that allowed the Perth crew to include the weekender in their holidays, an extended stay if you will. After all, they were flying the breadth of Europe. Here we caught up with another Geordie, Neil Hammond (Hammy) and his good lady Karen. I also met many other soulies such as, Hilary Webster, Steve and Elaine Griffin, Kev and Veronica Core, Jeff Gordon and Leanne White who had helped to organise the National in 2004. They produced a double CD with the help of Barry Symes, he and Ainsley really focused on modern soul which Hammy enjoyed more too and a second room was born. I was invited to write the sleeve notes for the CD which I did with pleasure. It featured a big modern soul catalogue as well as a belting northern one too, entitled "We Got Togetherness" and aimed at showcasing some great modern soul and bringing together the two "genres" at one event.

Not a first, but they certainly made a bigger thing about it and the first "Modern only" room was born. Although not full, these were early days. With other modern soul DJ's like Dallas Hyde, Rob Goodburn, Bernard, Paul, George, Alex and John Coney it would certainly blossom.

Here in Brisbane, the Alliance Tavern was the original and regular soul venue and used for record sales during the weekender. There had been a soul night at Jamesons in Adelaide St way back in 2001, which closed shortly after and the regular nights moved over the road to St Paul`s Tavern in Spring Hill. This was used as the Friday venue for the national event, Saturday was Milton`s Polish Club, the Sunday the Hamilton Hotel.

The Alliance Tavern Brisbane © Barry Simpson

Brisbane Soul Crew © Barry Simpson

The Polish Club was the "Night of the Pies". OMG, the pies here were fearsome and I reckon I had 6 at least. During my DJ spot I included the mega rarity Larry Clinton 'She's Wanted" on a Dynamo white demo, the first in Australia. More copies would make their way here as copies became much easier to find. I sold this on when the incredibly rarer red issue landed on my doorstep a few years later. A note to add is that the tickets were made along the lines of the Wigan Casino memberships and for those who kept them you will see what I mean, four blocks of print and folded. Outside of the nationals, soul weekenders were held at Billy's Beach bar for a few years with Roy Burton from Manifesto declaring it to be the best weekender venue in the world. Roy would promote soul in Australia for many years through the Manifesto magazine. The 2009 Nash was held on the Gold Coast with Barry Symes, Kev and Veronica Core, Ainsley and Lynda White being the organising committee. The Thursday night meet and greet was in a club in Orchid Avenue and there was Karaoke which absolutely went down a treat.

The main event, Saturday allniter, was at The Croatian Club, in Carrara which is a fair way from town and a free coach was organised to carry the crowds there. As it was between a grave-yard, crematorium & a football field with no houses nearby we could be as loud as we wanted. The Sunday all-dayer was back at Surfers Rowers Club with an extra night on the Monday at Billy's for those staying over. Tunes from the weekender, from my notes, included Mamie Galore, "I Can Feel Him Slipping Away", Jo Ann Garret, "A Whole New Plan, The Delicates, "Stop Shoving Me Around", The Cleptomaniacs, "All I Do", Jazheim, "Just In Case", Billy Davis, "Stanky Get Funky", Lester Tipton, "This Won't Change" and the Australian only Marcia Hines, "You Gotta Let Go My contribution over the years was the re-cently acquired Don Varner, ``Tear Stained Face" and Cecil Washington, "I Don't Like To lose" and Rita & the Tiaras, " Gone With The Wind". I will be forever thankful to Kev, John, Johnny Redpant's Warren, Gary and Steve for their support during the Nationals. Once again though we must not forget their wives who absolutely put in their 100% too. You see some really strange things when you go to these weekenders. In 2014, whilst in the hotel, I recall seeing a really nosy neighbour oppo-site. Every time I opened my curtains he was there. The first time it happened I threw open the curtains wearing only my jocks and saw him standing staring. I ran inside and shut the curtains. I kept them shut all weekend. Now and again I would take a sneaky look, hiding behind the curtain. He wasn't there. Then I would try and surprise him and throw the curtains open... he was there. I screamed at him to bugger off the dirty old man and drew the curtains again and kept them closed all weekend. There are some weird people around! On Monday morning, packed and ready to leave, I thought I'd give him what for. I flung open the curtains and saw him, "get lost you dirty pervert" I screamed. He too had screamed; he had the same striped top as me... OMG... It had all been my reflection on the mirrored building opposite, I PMSL to this day.

Then there was the taxi story… Here, you have to understand I have a Cumbrian/Geordie accent and people very often call me Murray or Beau when I speak over the phone, how I'll never know. My very old friend David Troughton and his wife Sue had come over to Australia for a holiday with a northern Weekender on the list. Anyhow, I had booked a taxi for us and duly waited in the foyer. A taxi pulled up and I asked if it was for Barry Simpson, he said no and carried on waiting. Soon he left. Others who had joined the queue after me all got their cabs and left. I called the taxi company who told me my taxi had been and waited a while then left but they would send another. Sure enough, here comes the taxi, the same guy that I first spoke to and we got in, half an hour later by this time. Out of interest I asked who the taxi was for when he first came, someone called Beau, I grinned to myself. Only for a second as the pain from the hip kicked in. Crutches were the order of the doctor for the next 3 months. I had just had the hip replaced a few weeks prior. The daily injections weren't a good feeling either, but all's well that ends well.

Bags and container packed for Australia

In 2004 Kay and I emigrated to Australia, bringing my 47 boxes of records in various sizes (some of which I later sold), settling first in Adelaide, renting a house up from the beach for 2 years before moving to Perth in 2006. I wasn't the guy who chucked his records in a skip and pulled them out later, or gave them away, or sold them, they were always there. In Adelaide Pete and Miriam Feven ran soul nights at the Enigma Bar in Hindley St after the Duke of York events ended and I did the occasional DJ spot there in between Kay and I flying to Melbourne and Perth and Sydney for weekenders and soul nights. Steve Bardsley's Northern Soul in Oz, Yahoo site and his "Northern Soul Nightshift" website had attracted many more people to the scene, many returning after a long absence. It was a great way of finding out about the scene, people and records.

I Have to say I thoroughly enjoyed life in Adelaide, the long beach walks, coffee crawls and the pace of life, but work got me to Perth in 2006.

Steve Bardsley, Pete and Miriam Feven, Kay and Barry Simpson. Pie and Peas in Adelaide after a soul night © Steve Bardsley (2002)

Christmas, Easter and a Christmas conference in Sydney, this year would definitely be different. From the start of my trips I collected everything I could regarding the Nationals just for times like this, a bit of social history, usually 6 or 7 CD`s, T shirts, badges, tickets and flyers to give away to friends and promote the Australian scene, but also some entry hand stampers, pens, mugs, stickers and other merchandise. Some went to the States and sand to Arabs comes to mind, last but not least, many of the banners. As I said earlier, Sydney almost didn't produce a CD in 2015, in the end they did and a 45 recording of The Falcons ``Good, Good Feeling" which I have the test press for the museum. Perth also did a couple of 45s, one being the classic Big Daddy Rogers ``I'm A Big Man" and the other was a white label Tower of Power B/W the Soul Communicators with labels reversed. It is interesting to note whilst the black fist was a normal "symbol" of northern soul, only one CD out of 21 carried the image which had been included on its badge. On the badges, it appeared for the first 6 nationals and only 2 more after those. For the 22nd National, Brisbane kicked us into the future with a surfboard shaped USB featuring around 200 tracks. Back in 2004 the Brisbane CD had a big poster style insert that carried the track listing. I have to say these CDs were very well done.

Bags Packed for Chicago

In 2009 I made the trip to Chicago for a soul event at The Ambassador Hotel, at which I also had a couple of DJ spots. Here I caught up with my old friend Johnny Redpant's Warren who in turn introduced me to Tim Schloe and Dave Cuban with whom we spent some of the tour. We had the pleasure of seeing Jimmy Burns and Lou Pride, among a host of others singing live, meeting Bobby Hutton, looking very resplendent in his cape and Ruby Andrews, who pointing at my copy of the TIME magazine hoped "this mother fucker`s gonna change America". Standing at the bar after a show, buying Jimmy Burns a beer and chatting, he told me about a time in the 60`s when he wasn't allowed through the front entrance of the Ambassador Hotel, how times had changed and how happy he was to be there tonight. He had just sung his heart out to us with a great rendition of "I Really Love You". What a truly smart gentleman he was in his trilby hat and smart shirt and was very happy to autograph items for me.

Lou pride was another great performance too, with the thunderous "I'm Com'un Home In The Morn'un" bringing the house down. This was such a fantastic event for the artists as well as the fans. Included in the tour was a great trip to the Motown museum on West Grand Boulevard. On the journey there we picked up a gentleman who introduced himself as MEL BRITT and it was worth the trip just to see his face when everyone sang the words to ' 'She'll Come Running Back" at the Detroit Smoke n Grill.

The passion of collecting and Barry Simpson 9,562 miles to add another "gem " to his collection © Barry Simpson

Motown museum © Barry Simpson

At the Motown Museum John and I moved up through the door and up the stairs. After introducing ourselves to a lovely lady at the top "I'm Barry and this is my friend John". Hi was the reply, "I'm Francis Nero, welcome to the Motown Museum". Stunned, and gathering ourselves together, we made our way to the auditorium for a sort of meet and greet, then we were treated to a question and answer session by Dennis Coffey and a tour of the studios including the Snake pit. I have to say I was disappointed at the quality of the displays. For such an important part of American musical history it should have been mind-blowing, maybe I just expected too much being an avid Motown collector and fan. As mentioned earlier we had lunch at the Detroit Smoke and Grill and, among others, met Laura Lee, the Capitols and the Vandella`s sang an acapella version of "Cool Jerk" and Billy Wilson. John and I sat down for lunch and noticed that Francis Nero was sitting alone so we invited her to sit with us, she said she didn't think she was allowed to but she did and we had a great chat.

Francis told us she was half Navajo, a diabetic, the first lady of the SOUL label and happily signed just about everything we had from the till receipts to lottery tickets to a Motown t-shirt from the souvenir shop. I also did an interview with Mel Britt who told me he had been in the MISTS. I asked him if he really wanted her to come running back, he just smiled. But to see his face when everyone sang the song was priceless. Another experience was when John and I went outside to take some photographs and on return we met a guy trying to get in. I asked, "My name is Barry can I help you", "possibly, yes" came the reply, "I'm Carl Carlton, I've come to meet some English guys...........What a great day we had. On another day some guys went into Chicago record hunting and I found myself in, probably the most junky junk shop ever and stuck upstairs on a shaky wooden mezzanine I found a couple of albums, one by the Dovells and one by Jr Walker which I still have. Then it was all over.

Bags packed and back to Australia

In Perth there were a few different soul scenes going on. A regular Woodvale Motown night run by the fabulous Robbie Burns and more Northern/disco edged one in the city at an Irish club. In Fremantle there was a club called the FLY BY NIGHT, generally a live band venue that had Motown events, at which I would DJ monthly for a number of years from July 2006. Kay and I started the TIME TUNNEL and promoted MOTOWN @ SOUL events beginning at the FLY BY NIGHT now in its 10th year at time of print.

I recall one guy saying to me that our events would be like an amateur night because of our "crappy equipment", yet we only ever have used the best and I would definitely consider we have succeeded. Believe me, as all promoters know, it is a team game and the wives do just as much work. Kay carries equipment, lugs the speakers around, records the CD`s and prints all the sleeves as well as running the door. Our first event in 2012 had 250 in and it was a great night, but these events weren't cheap to run and on many occasions we were out of pocket. When we were in a position to, we paid our DJ`s, generally at our anniversaries If we were going to do ok, and still do for their hard work and the investment in their records. I don't mind people having their jealous digs at me, but when it affects my wife as it seriously did, then that's just not on. This is why we kept away from certain groups of people on the Aussie soul scene and still do. I recall at one event a DJ asked if they could put their own flyers out, I said sadly not as we cannot promote another venue. She told me she had already put about six out so she would try and collect them. Alas she missed one which was found by another promoter who then came onto stage, screwed it up and threw it in my face saying "one rule for one eh". One *"lady"* leant quietly against the bar at one event and tore our flyer up in front of me. The reality is none of it mattered a jot, because our success achieved on our own proved everything.

Our hard work paid off and the second anniversary had 389 attending, peaking at 441 on the third anniversary. I remember looking down at the crowded dance floor and seeing all the empty seats as everyone was now on the dance floor and I thought "job done". During one November we were given a free event with advertising, sadly it fell on the same weekend as a Perth national and didn't go down well with the promoting committee the email said. But we had a different audience and their event wouldn't affect ours. Visiting DJ, and total soul aficionado, Duncan McCallister and Margaret "Soul Munga" Wood did a spot for us and, all in all, the night was a success for the FLY and the Fringe event in general. These were great years for the Time Tunnel with regular monthly attendances of around 200, also running Perth's first regular Modern and Disco nights until the FLY lost their lease and we had to move. I spent a few days helping John and the crew dismantle the venue and the historical things we found were just amazing. The hall had been a military Drill hall back in the early part of the last century and had officers' names on doors, hook holes on the wall with names like "gun oil" above. A lot of the items found under the floorboards are on display as is the history of the place with photos. One could almost smell the atmosphere.

Bags packed for Europe

Over the next few years, Kay and I had MOTOWN events around Perth, weddings, birthdays and our own soul events too. I also made the trip to the Hitsville Weekenders in Spain a few times and Benidorm. The Benidorm trip was hard and painful and I definitely was not myself, travelling with crutches due to the pain of an arthritic hip, the pills and the injections. It was hard work indeed and had me at the end of my tether I can tell you. One morning Duncan, with whom I shared a room, told me he had lost his Friday tablet. He went on to explain he needed it for his inhaler.

We searched the room high and low, laying all our drugs across the table and checking, warfarin, pain killers (I was up to 80 a week by then) Tramadol and Clexyne. No luck. We stripped the beds, stood them on their sides. Checked in the wardrobes with no luck at all. Then I had a brainwave......"Duncan today is Saturday. Might you have taken it yesterday, Friday". We cracked up. We had such a great time here and in Germany! Over a 4-week break in Europe, Ginger Taylor invited me to do a spot and Brighouse in the UK. What a great night that was, except for the 2 hour traffic diversion. Travelling back up North where we did a massive charity event on Silloth Green, run by Dennis Peacock, with DJ spots at all these events. The Silloth event was a huge success raising lots of money for the Fairydust charity. It was a great sunny day and I caught up with lots of old friends from Carlisle and my sister from Ennerdale. If you are ever in Ennerdale, stop off at the Shepherds Arms Hotel for the night, a warm bed, great food, beer and a great fire.

Bags packed for Melton Mowbray

Then it was down to Melton for the wedding of John Manship, from whom I have been buying records since the mid 70's at Baldocks Lane, (I was customer number 80 according to the number after your name on his lists), and the gorgeous Theresa Price. We did some work on the wedding speech while Kay helped set-up the Hall. This was a great opportunity to catch up with old friends again and buy some records, collecting a rare 78 of "MONEY" Barrett Strong. These late 60's 78rpm records were made to order for jukeboxes in the southern states that still played 78s and ordered especially for them and as such, are pretty rare items. The wedding was held at the fabulous Harlaxton Manor. I was up early that morning, I had to make Kay's wedding Fascinator & my buttonhole, I did come in handy. Nice to see Soul Sam live again soon filling the floor after the wedding dance which kept going into the early morning.

John had produced a book, a price guide that was so heavy at over 2 kg and included DJ`s from around the world and their collections, of which I was proud to be included and display some of my rare collection. I imported around 40 to Australia for the guys and as usual they proved to be a great source of information. The previous Price Guide also included an introduction written by me, telling a brief history about my soul life, again around 40 were imported and sold around Australia. I was proud to have been quoted as having one of the world's top Motown collections. That said, I know certain people who would tear those pages out…. Only to be reminded of it each time they opened the book and with this, I am very satisfied.

Bags Packed For Germany

Then it was over and on to the next phase, Kay flew back to Perth and I flew to Germany for, yet another soul weekender run by Marc Forrest. Marc has been on the scene for many years and his name would often crop up and even outbid me on John Manship`s auctions. This was such a great event, HIP CITY SOUL CLUB and their 29th anniversary, the Friday was at "Das Hotel" in a cellar, like an old basement with a few rooms and a bar. From the front it looked like an old English Terrace house but once inside and down the staircase, OMG. You need to visit just to go to this venue. What an incredible space. If this was what the old Twisted Wheel or Cats was like, then no wonder people got hooked. The atmosphere was incredible. The Saturday event was at Privatclub, Skalitzer Str. Here, I happened to bump into Ash Pederick from Perth Australia too, who had made the trip down from Denmark and shared a few stories and a drink, enjoying the great music. Another catchup with Ady Pierce, the Silver Fox. It had been so long, like 20 years since I had seen Ady.

Once I bought a Don Ray in 1999 and forgot to sign the cheque, "no panic, it's not as if you are going to leave the country" .I was actually at London airport about to fly to Australia for a month. During our stay for the weekender, Duncan and I had a few days free, so the obligatory tour of Berlin was done with the same great sights taken in. This was one of the hottest summers on record. We slept with windows and doors wide open almost the whole weekend. It was a struggle to keep cool but the steins of beer helped lots.

One morning we needed food badly to enable us to take our medicines so we headed for a café and ordered some soup……….. obviously not speaking German. Let me tell you tripe watery soup, after a night on the beer is no good!

DJ group in Germany © Barry Simpson

Bags packed & back to Perth Australia

Over the coming years we did regular monthly events with the FLY team at another venue in Fremantle, this proved very hard work. It had no car park, a lot of negativity, lots, most from the usual certain quarters, a long walk in the rain and no alcohol licence. But we made a success of it all the same and once a licence was given all went well but numbers weren't the same as the old venue due to its size, location and costs but we stuck with it because many of the customers were now, by and large our friends who wanted to go out and have a great time at our events. There were other people trying other Motown events nearby which were going to be the next big thing and had different people playing records, but they were not as successful and as we stayed true to the FLY for many years this would pay off for us later. When we began the gigs in Warnbro Bowling Club, I asked Phil Herriot to DJ as I felt he could play what we needed, he did and continues to do so. Kay and I have always got on extremely well with and been loyal to our venues and their teams, the events went from strength to strength and I'm sure this is one of the reasons for our success. Then SOMETHING FANTASTIC HAPPENED!

Time Tunnel, Fremantle Social © Barry Simpson

Dance floor action at the Fly © Barry Simpson

I got a call from the FREO SOCIAL, "would you like to run an event there? " said Benita. Robert, a barman from the FLY, had told the guys at the Freo Social about us and they were very keen to have us on board. The Freo Social is the old FLY BY NIGHT venue and the council had spent millions of dollars renovating it, and what a great job they have done. After months of planning and promoting the night was upon us. What a night. 350 attending, a fabulous setup, light show and music, the floor was busy all night. We got lots of great feedback from people and an email from the FREO asking us if we would like more events. WE WERE BACK WHERE IT ALL BEGAN. The numbers would increase at the next event to 400 but the Covid 19 restrictions hit Perth and numbers were capped. Each following show was a sell-out. By the time of printing we will have had our 9th anniversary in August, with 70 tickets already sold by May with no promotion such is the demand for these great events at which we try to provide a professional show, it was not just "a few decks thrown on a table and stick the disco on" as someone spitefully had said. I retired 3 years ago but calls for specialised training have kept me busy 6 days a week and sometimes 7 which was hard as our Church is very important to us.

Covid prevented fly in workers from eastern states and a growth in the local economy has led to this. I train in high risk work such as Forklift, Dump truck, OHS to diploma level, working at heights and First Aid among others. I love "busy" and think I've done quite a lot but always with the support of my great lady, Kay, to whom I owe so much. Who knows what more needs doing? I will keep on doing it if it feels good. As you have read, my story is a long one that dives back and forth in time and I hope you have found it entertaining. I have tried to include lots of little titbits of memories in the hope that they trigger off yours and take you back to those great early youthful days where it all began. As they say KEEP ON KEEPIN' ON!

Barry Simpson's Record Room, West Australia © Barry Simpson

Chapter 19

Jayne Hulme - All Aboard the TransGlobal Express

"Get the trans-global express moving....!"

My Soul Journey is somewhat different to the ones I have read before, I was born in 1969, I missed the beginnings of the scene. I didn't attend the big venues or small venues at the time, I could only listen later to the stories told and photographs from the time and obviously listen to the music.. one aspect that will never change! The music that led us all to begin our Soul Journeys, no matter where we were in the world, we had one thing in common, the love of what was Northern Soul. I hope you enjoy my humble beginnings as a late arrival and my journey that started with one song in 1982! My Trans Global Express Soul journey began, when, at the tender age of 12 , 1982. I was in my bedroom as per normal after school, listening to the radio...the usual dance hit tunes of the time.. The odd ones caught my ear, Boomtown Rats, Dexys Midnight Runners, Come on Eileen, Stranglers, but something was missing, then I heard it , The Tube 1982,"Trans Global Express The Jam", now this really caught my ear! Not the lyrics, as they are quite difficult to hear in this Weller Classic, but the backing tune, the beat, everything about it!

At 12 years old, in Barnsley, South Yorkshire, I had been vaguely aware of a Mod Revival (as I learnt later) that was quite a large movement in Barnsley & surrounding areas, but being only 12, I hadn't really been able to explore this. Yes, I saw the odd scooter and the odd Parka, but didn't know what it was about, so as always in these situations, I asked my dad! Who explained to me they were Mods, not his cup of tea, as dad had been a Rocker, slicked back hair, (Eddie Cochran style) white shirt, bootlace tie etc... nonetheless, I needed to know more !

I have always been an avid reader and my search began. Fortunately, I had an early morning paper round, and my reading materials were free! It's strange when I think back to starting my paper round at Allots shop, Monk Bretton at 5am, having the responsibility at such a young age for sorting, marking, folding and then bagging an hours' worth of papers and magazines, something that is alien to most 12 yr old's today! Nonetheless, this gave me the opportunity to scan the papers and music magazines for any information about this "Mod Revival" and more importantly to me, Paul Weller! Yes, I was hooked on Paul Weller....at a time when all my peers were madly in love with Wham, Duran Duran, Spandau Ballet etc, I was different and I knew I was. I still remember the conversations in the girls' cloakrooms at school,

"Who's Paul Weller?"

"God, he's ugly!"

"How can you fancy him ??"

And many more derogatory comments, but it wasn't about the looks (even though I did and still do fancy him) it was more than that! It was what he represented and what he had brought to my ears...! So, the summer of 1982 continues, I'm sourcing magazines, newspapers, TV pages for music shows, I couldn't get enough to fulfill my craving for this new "scene/movement" I had discovered. I'm sourcing the clothes, the shoes, the look of what a Modette should look like and wear, on my £6 a week paper round, I didn't get very far.... Being Only 12, I was obviously too young to really be going off places, alone, as no one else shared my interest, and mum made sure that I remained "a normal girl" regarding clothes etc. as possible, and probably while she still could buy my clothes and dress me as a girl!! The music was generally easy to source, I had my parents old 45s, not many MOD tunes, but 50s & 60s groups, with the beat I generally craved, even the odd early one by Cliff Richard & the Drifters (mums favourites) and dads, Eddie Cochrane, Rolling Stones, Swinging Blue Jeans, The Animals. I knew what I liked, and I couldn't get enough of the music... modern music didn't interest me, apart from the so-called Mod Revivalist bands, The Jam, the Chords, Secret Affair, The Specials, Selector.. Hence, my quest for everything Mod began, in earnest. On my small earnings from my paper round! My 13th birthday approached, I was now allowed to attend Rebecca's Under 18's disco, Barnsley Boys Club, Beckett St Youth Club, and 65's Club disco in Barnsley. As a newly qualified teenager, off I went to the clubs, not knowing what to expect!!!! Monday Night, the week after my 13th birthday, 1983, I attended Rebecca's U18 disco, for the first time… It was absolutely packed !! Quite a small dance floor and the hits of the time being played by the DJ, yes, I knew them and yes I danced to them. Then halfway through the night, a tune started up, the intro caught my ear instantly, but almost everyone left the dance floor, except two young lads, dressed in Boating jackets, Ben Sherman's, two-tone trousers and so called Jam Shoes! I watched, transfixed...I hadn't seen this type of dancing before, I'd never heard this tune before, but within 30 seconds, I joined them on the dance floor to this tune that had me in a world of my own ! The tune.... Interplay, Derek and Ray! I had to have this record!

The following day was Barnsley's Second Hand Market, quite a few record stalls to be searched.. Finally, there it was Interplay Derek & Ray A side, B side Mike McDonald, God Knows ! 50p, I didn't haggle, I was so pleased to find it. The stall holder said " That seems a strange purchase for a young girl ?" So, I told him where I had heard it etc and he said, have you heard these ? And presented "There's A Ghost In My House" and "Under My Thumb " He said you can have all three for a quid ! I bought them… Coincidentally, I'd received a small Panasonic Radio, tape player and a pop out turntable unit for my birthday (which I still own and it still works) I now had my first Vinyl, to go with all my parents 60's vinyl! I was so happy ! The following week it was the under 65s Club at Wilthorpe, Barnsley..Yes, I had a good dance, then once again a track started and my ears pricked again. Not many danced to it, but a small group were doing a dance I'd not seen before, the dance and tune was the Flasher, Mistura ! Once again, 30 secs later I was doing the dance !

In Barnsley, in the 80's we were lucky, we had a youth club event every night of the week, and you could travel anywhere in South Yorkshire for 2pence !! Now, together with my partner in crime, Lisa, a neighbour, who was 2 years older than me, we made use of the 2 pence travel around the county, especially seeking out these young Mods & Modettes around the local villages. We were drawn to each other, No issues, no conflict, no suspicions of these strangers entering their territory, all that mattered was the scene we were beginning to explore, we all had one goal to find and share whatever we could about the Mod scene ! The revivalist Mod scene seemed to concentrate in certain areas of Barnsley, Cudworth, Wombwell, Wath, Brampton, Great Houghton to mention a few. Lisa and I travelled on the bus to seek these like minded people out and once again were welcomed with open arms. A must for me was acquiring a fishtail Parka, however, I was having some issues convincing mum that this was a necessity. Nonetheless, I persisted and eventually received £30 to buy some ladies Jam shoes from Rebina Shoes, Sheffield..a well-known shoe shop that sold alternative shoes for Mods, Rockers, Punks and anything retro, it was an amazing place to be and meet like minded people. Unfortunately, we didn't get that far, so we popped off at the Army & Navy store near Hillsborough, Sheffield, as my eye was drawn to a Fishtail Parka, displayed in the shop window ! Ten minutes later, I emerged with my prized possession..and extra...A small, wool lined ,with hood American 1951 Fishtail Parka and a size 4 pair of black Monkey Boots..price £30 ! A parka I still possess and wear today! On arrival at home, in said Parka, I quickly explained to mum that they didn't have the shoes, so I bought the parka and monkey boots for the same price. I believed I had got a bargain, mum didn't see it that way !! Fully dressed up with my Parka, my Fred Perry's, Ski pants, Ben Sherman's, I now felt that I fully belonged to the scene. At school, we had a bit of a uniform, grey, black or navy, my uniform consisted of a white Ben |Sherman, Black Ski Pants, Black V Neck Jumper, Boating Jacket, Parka and yes, my ladies jam shoes or monkey boots. I was different, no one dressed like me and I loved it and didn't care, I had found my passion and no one could do anything to stop me. However, the music quest continued !

We spent nights hanging round bus stops, pub doorways, youth clubs, cemeteries and occasionally, especially at Grimethorpe, a group of us huddled together on the hot plate in Grimethorpe Colliery car park (where Brassed Off was filmed) to keep warm, listening to new tunes someone had found on a battery operated cassette player ! 1983 soon became 1984, Lisa and I were finding more and more like minded people, but none in our village Monk Bretton, Barnsley. We had to travel!! The Yorkshire Traction 306/307 and 226 buses became our favourite routes, as I mentioned earlier anywhere in South Yorkshire for 2p !! We arranged to meet our fellow "Mods & Modettes" on the bus, always sitting at the back, playing our latest finds on our tape recorders, most of the music being socalled Mod tunes, The Who, The Kinks, Small Faces, The Jam, The Chords and the odd Motown tune, not much in the way of what was called Northern Soul. Yorkshire traction came to the rescue again in April, 1984, when us non scooter owners found out we could get the bus to Morecambe Scooter Rally in April 1984. Off we set, a beautiful bus journey that took forever, however, the sight when we arrived was more than we could have hoped for. Despite the weather being horrendous, we saw scooters as far as the eye could see, we were finally taking part in our own Quadrophenia!! We were only there for the day, but that memory will last forever, my first scooter patch and badge purchased, I was happy as pig in muck.. then I saw R Dean Taylor There's a Ghost in my House for sale, a fiver!!

I paid 35p for mine, I was beaming...especially now when that was a fiver in 1984, it's going for less than that now, so I won't be making my fortune any time soon ! A great time was had by all and we reluctantly set off back home...on the bus !! As we entered the borders of South Yorkshire, we noticed, for the first time, lots of men in groups and lots of police in groups around the entrances of the collieries that we had in South Yorkshire, Barnsley area. Now, we knew that there was something happening in the area as most of our dads weren't going to work and most mums had started working more hours, but this was the first time we had seen these pickets and police. My dad was the Fitter at North Gawber Colliery, Barnsley and had initially stayed working as they had to ensure the collieries were kept safe, a hard task that had to be kept clandestine, due to fellow miners attitudes to men working during the strike, but dads job was essential. This is the reason why Dad had not discussed the strike, as he didn't want us talking about what was going off. The first time I realised something wasn't right, was when we were entitled to free school meals ! Fantastic, I thought, you get to go in first on free school meals. However, this excitement was soon quashed when I arrived at the dining hall to find out virtually ALL the school kids were on free meals..!! Moving on through 1984, most of MOD group friends now had another common denominator, nearly all our dads were on strike !So, we tended to focus on our 2p bus journey to the Rotherham side of Barnsley, Brampton, Wath, Wombwell and Darfield. We met up regularly, outside the colliery areas and watched the entertainment, shall we say, between the pickets and the police. One particular night, we had settled down, on the benches opposite, Houghton Main Colliery (now destroyed) with our mates, a few on scooters to watch the "entertainment" There were a few pickets there, but nothing prepared us for what was about to happen ! Within 30 minutes of being there, a black van pulled up in front of us and out jumped 6 burly policemen, all wearing white shirts, we knew they weren't South Yorkshire Police, as they wore blue shirts, and they started verbally abusing the lads in groups, taunting them, asking if the pickets were our parents!

Some of the lads answered back and received a clip around the ear! We did report what had happened, but nothing ever happened as you can imagine! The miners strike continued through 1984 and we continued spending most of our time in Brampton and surrounding areas, mainly due to the great Miners Welfare Clubs who allowed us underage youths in.

It was here at Brampton Miners welfare club, that we heard about a South Yorkshire Mod group "The Gents" that were appearing in the clubs in the area, they were at the club the following week. From what I remember, we all piled into the club, sat ourselves in one big area, all in our Parkas, we were bloody boiling, but we didn't take them off. The Gents came on stage and started with their version of Shout! I was in awe. More Mod and Soul tunes were played and we danced, with our parkas on, till we were dripping with sweat. It was amazing. What made it more amazing that older scooterists had also turned up and I finally got to see the original "Italian Stallion" custom scooter, ridden by Martyn Scully, Barnsley Vikings SC, who had been in Quadrophenia, a film I had heard so much about, but had yet to see. For me, this was the icing on the cake! We attended every Welfare and Working Men's club that we could, to watch The Gents. If we couldn't get in, we sat at the back doors listening and waiting for the band to come out, this made some very miserable and hard times easier. We had our music and a common bond, with friendships that are still strong today! Unfortunately, my travelling days around South Yorkshire in 1984 came to an abrupt end, when my left knee collapsed during a rounders match at school! Subsequent visit to Barnsley A&E dumbfounded the medical staff there, my Knee cap had basically decided to fall out, their answer at the time; stick me in a plaster cast from hip to toe! The plaster casts were changed every 8 weeks, and every time when they removed it, it was a crying shame, as each cast was brightly coloured with group names, Tamla Motown logos, Ska, Mod badges and union jacks. The final cast I had was cut and removed from the back of my leg, so I could save it. It took pride and place in the corner of my

310

bedroom, until my younger brother decided to try it one day and damaged it! For nine months my adventures around South Yorkshire were curtailed, somewhat, but that didn't stop me venturing locally, where we finally came across older lads and lasses who had Northern Soul Records!! Yes, I loved the Mod and Ska sound, but once again, the Northern Soul sound had me hooked instantly. One lad, Andy, I forget his full name had just bought "Out On The Floor" and he brought it to my house once, with a few other mates and he danced, as I would say, properly to Northern Soul spins and backdrops included! I had never seen this before and once again I was transfixed. My contribution to these regular nights at each other's houses was my song's Interplay, GIMH, Under My Thumb, Judy In Disguise and yes, recently acquired The Snake!!

When I look back now, I look at the knee injury as part of my Soul Journey, it led me, a 13/14 yr old in Barnsley to finally start exploring and enjoying new tunes. Yes, I started my soul journey late, with the Mod Revival in the early 80's, courtesy of Paul Weller, The Jam and Trans Global Express and I have to confess that it wasn't until I was in my 20s that I found out the backing tune to Trans Global Express was "So is the Sun, The World Column" Subliminally, Paul Weller had started my soul journey! I came to the scene via the Mod/Scooter revival, which obviously had its roots in RnB, a genre that is still my preference today, as you will find out later in subsequent Soul Journey books. I often wonder why, when my peers were hooked on the new romantic scene, I completely rebuffed this, I was different, I knew I was different. I dressed differently, I listened to different music, I didn't hang around with the usual crowds! The fact that quite a small group of like minded teenagers found each other in such a short period of time, no mobile phones, no internet, just 2p bus rides around South Yorkshire (Thanks Yorkshire Traction) is probably unimaginable today! What's more unimaginable, to us youngsters, us late arrivals, is the stories of those that were there at the time the Northern Soul Scene started.

311

Even less communication opportunities than we had in the '80s, but they found each other.

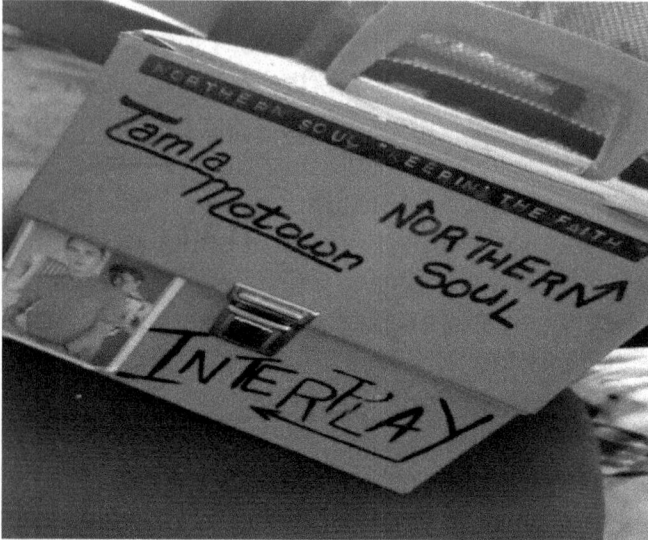
Jayne Hulme's record box © Jayne Hulme

Morecambe Run Scooter badge 1984 © Jayne Hulme

The stories I have read over the years and more recently from our soul music journey Book one, only emphasises the connection that people of all colours, class and creeds have come together through Northern Soul music, that has literally become our soul and we search out and find these souls everyday of our lives.

My soul journey continues in the next books, a journey that took me back to where I belonged and opened up avenues for me that I never thought possible for a lass from Barnsley. A story and life choice that will never end, until the end. Here ends the first journey aboard my Soul Trans Global Express!

Jayne Hulme © Jayne Hulme

Jayne Hulme on the dance floor © Jayne Hulme

Scooter Rally © Jayne Hulme

Chapter 20

The Impact of Northern Soul Music

By Robert Paladino (The Epitome of Sound)

From 1960 through to 1964, our group, The Brooks Four, went from singing 20's/30's/40's classic standard songs, i.e., "The Great American Songbook", in 4 part harmony, to writing, performing, & recording "doo-wop", with releases on three record labels, and a re-issue on a fourth label. This was a very special and a joyous time for me! Full of learning the ins and outs of being in the studio, appreciating and collaborating with many fine artists, musicians and arrangers, which I still regard as a wonderful musical segment of my life. However, like evolution in our own lives, things change, and although some are welcome changes, some are not quite what we expected, and a bit disappointing. Our Vocal Quartet broke up on Easter Sunday, 1965, and I was overwhelmed with dismay and confusion, and soon developed a lack of self-confidence over it. Six years had passed after my father died at age 46, and I was still very vulnerable to loss and suffering, and trying to cope. To me, a very meaningful relationship had ended! We had come extremely close to "making it in the business" as that term was often used by artists, musicians, producers and songwriters. One such almost or should 'a made it story, occurred in 1961. Our vocal group had a repertoire of approximately 34 four part harmony songs, and we felt we were ready to work venues, hotel lounges, dinner/restaurant gigs, and even resorts or cruise ships, and therefore we journeyed into New York City to seek out a good, reliable booking agent. We went to the Mecca of Managers, Publishers, and of course Booking Agents, The Brill Building, located at 1619 Broadway! We began knocking on doors of Booking Agents and Artist Management Reps., like so many others did before us and after us as well.

As quickly as the doors opened, they shut, with the paraphrased response, we are not talking with anyone today, come back in a week or two, or you can leave your promo tape with me, and your contact info, and someone will get back to you. Well, we were prepared to sing live, and didn't have tapes with us to leave. After knocking on quite a few doors, and doing the same on other floors, we decided that we should just go and visit the famous NYC Radio Station, WNEW, 1130 on your dial. WNEW Radio, was the home of William B. Williams, who dubbed Frank Sinatra, "The Chairman Of The Board", and many other great DJ's, like Bob Landers, Martin Block, the host of the famous "Make Believe Ballroom", Gene Klavan and his sidekick, Dee Finch, Dick Shepard, Steve Allen, and so many others.

In those days being young adolescents, we walked everywhere when we were in NYC. We walked to the Radio Station, which was located at 565 5th Avenue, & 46th Street. When we arrived there, we were greeted by someone at the desk, I believe it was a young lady, and she asked what we were here for. We answered along these lines, we are a jazz vocal group from New Jersey, and WNEW is our favorite station, and if possible we would like to talk to someone about our career. She said, let me contact our Public Relations Director, Dick O'Shaunessy, and see if he is available. In a few minutes Mr. O'Shaughnessy greeted us, made us feel relaxed and comfortable by asking us about our group, etc., and then he said, let me hear you sing something? We sang a Four Freshman song, "If I Knew Then", which by the way was one of the most played vocal groups of that era, and especially played on WNEW. After we sang, He just smiled at us, and then he said, "Let me see if the Capitol Records A&R Man is still in the building". We were soon introduced to Roy, a sharply dressed man from Capital Records. Mr. O'Shaughnessy said, fellows, sing the song you did for me for Roy, and we did. Roy asked if we could sing another song, but up tempo, and we sang "Day In, Day Out " for him. Roy said that he would like to record us doing an EP Demo of 4 songs, 3 of our choosing, and a Classical Melody that he had written lyrics to, called "Oh, So Little Time". He said if you want to bring in your own musicians that would be fine, and left us with a demo of the song's backing track, along with his lyrics, and said to learn it, and when we were ready, to give him a call, and sing it to him over the telephone. In the interim, he asked who of us was to be his main contact for the group. I was elected, and gave Roy my home phone number. The following week, we called Roy from my house, and along with his backing track, we sang "Oh, So Little Time". He really liked the arrangement Bob DiLeo did, and our harmony and sound, and he asked if we had selected the other 3 songs to record, and if we were getting the musicians to back us up. I said, we did select the songs, and we also had a 4 piece group, piano, bass, guitar and drums. My brother Mike, future drummer with The Megatons/The Epitome of Sound, would be on drums. Roy said we would record at Nola Studio in NYC, and that he would call me with a confirmed date and time. I got the call, and we arrived at Nola Studio approximately 45 minutes before our scheduled time. We were in the outer lobby area, and we were told to sign in on the ledger of artists. I once again was designated by the guys to sign in. I was amazed to see the signature of the artist recording before us, as it was the famous singing star, Nat King Cole! I thought it was a good omen for us, and pointed out to the boys and the musicians. Roy arrived and we introduced him to our musicians, and he put us all at ease, and relaxed. We went into the studio, and recorded all four songs together with the musicians in a matter of an hour, with just 1 take, or 2 at most, for protection purposes. We heard the playbacks, Roy gave us a demo and we went home, feeling like we did a good job, and the musicians were also very happy and excited about what we accomplished that night. About a week later, I got a call from Roy. He said that he played the demo for Judy Garland, at a private party she hosted, and that she loved our group! He then said, I want to manage your guys, and that he would prepare a contract for us to review with our parents, and he would be present to answer any questions or concerns our parents, or legal advisor may have, and after the signing, we can start on building our career together. I was so happy, and immediately called the guys, and they were excited and thrilled about it too. Then, I made a big mistake! A game changing, and life altering mistake! A mistake of colossal proportions, or as I would later describe as, the Mother ``F"ing dumbest mistake I have ever made. I told a friend of ours who lived two blocks from me, all the details of what was happening with Roy, from Capitol Records in NYC. It just so happens, although I didn't know it at the time, that my friends' uncle also worked for Capitol Records in NYC, and he was either Godfather to Tony Bennett's' Son ', or vice versa. Nevertheless, he told his uncle everything I told him. About 2 days later, I got another call from Roy, and he asked if I told someone about our plans? I said, yes, that I just told a friend of mine. He said Bob, your friends' uncle, told me that he knew about our plans, and because they were both slated for bigger and better things at Capitol Records, it was a sort of a promotional competition between them, and therefore he had to bow out of his management contract offer to our group. The reason was because it would put his chances for advancement in jeopardy, as it would be deemed a possible conflict of interest. He said that he was very sorry, but he could no longer be our Manager, as that risk would be too great for him to take. Again he said he was very sorry, and asked me to please explain it to the group.

Needless to say, I was heart- broken, blamed myself for opening my mouth to the wrong person, and to this day I regard that as the downward turning point in our career. And if I needed reinforcement to my negative feelings, in 1969, I wrote a song called "Sunday Girl", recorded it at Venture Sound in Bound Brook, N.J., and went into New York City to try and shop it around. I eventually went to the Capitol Records facility to try and reconnect with Roy, as he was an A&R man. I was told that Roy had been promoted and was now working at Capitol Records as a Vice President, on Madison Ave. I went there cold, and found his office.

His Secretary asked how she could help me? I explained that I was a friend of Roy's, gave her my name and that I was in the City, from N.J., but stopped in to see him without an appointment. She said, ok, let me tell him you are here, and see if he is available to see you. I thanked her, and within a few minutes, his Secretary said, I will show you to the conference room, and Roy will be right with you. So, he remembered me, and was kind enough to see me. When we met, he was so nice and asked about the group, etc. I told him that we broke up in 1965, and that I was doing music projects independently. I then congratulated him on his promotion to V.P. He said he was Vice President of Artists Relations, and that he only handled 2 artists, The Beatles, and The Beach boys! I was genuinely happy for Roy, but the mistake I made four years earlier, felt like a 50 pound bag of salt had just been poured over the wound that never really healed. Although, it convinced me even more that because of this missed opportunity, we "shoulda" made it in the music business!

Around 2017, I tried to track down Roy, even though it was many years since we last talked. In the 70's while playing at the Jersey Shore, I somehow and somewhere, lost the jazz demo we recorded for him at Nola Studios in NYC. I hoped that if we could connect again, perhaps he could make me a CD of the demo, so that I could share it with the other guys in the group, and with my family. While I was searching for Roy's whereabouts, I contacted Nola Studios, and unfortunately, they did not keep protection tapes going back that far in time. Well, I did locate Roy via email, and I sent him a message, trying to explain after all the years, who I was, the ep recording we did for him, and what I was hoping he could provide me with. Roy had to be in his 80's, when he responded to my email. His sad and very strange response to me was that he Did Not remember me, our group, or his own song, "Oh so little Time? I was blown away, and I kept inserting little bits and pieces of information to help him remember, but it was to no avail! He said he was living in LA, and involved with a local theater group, as he had done

319

some acting, and written screenplays for TV after his Record Executive career ended. I was shocked and taken back with his not being able to remember our connection with him. He did, however, acknowledge knowing and working with my friend's uncle, but not the competitive incident between them at Capitol Records, when he was going to manage our group. I thanked him for our little chat, but just shook my head, and chalked it up to time, as time does change things for certain people.

Again, I'm taking the liberty of telling my story by moving around in time. Prior to the breakup of our group, I began playing Bass, and then subsequently continued writing and recording independently, and also performing with combos, which became not only my musical transitional path, but also part of my coping therapy.

By the time mid-1966 arrived, I found myself in a complete "Time Out" from music! I was now employed in a day job with A Medical Equipment Supplier, as a Quality Control Inspector. I still played for occasional weddings, private parties, and New Year's Eve celebrations, but in reality I was virtually a part time musician and a singer, for hire. An associate of mine in the QC Department, Barry, was an R&B and a Motown lover of the music. He convinced me that He and I should run dances in the local Elks Hall, and charge admission. Barry thought that we could make some extra money on top of it all. My brother Mike and our dear friend Joe DeJohn, were already playing with soul music group The Megatons, throughout New Jersey and New York, with great popularity. Four White Musicians, and a Black lead singer was an exception, and not the rule in those days, as mixed race groups were few and far between. We decided to have our first Dance Nite on a Sunday, which was an off day for The Megatons. Barry arranged for the hall, the tickets, and the advertising, and The Megatons agreed to perform. Money in terms of payment for the Megatons was not discussed, as they realized that they would be paid in accordance with the net ticket receipts.

Well, that night was a full house, but most were admitted without tickets, and Barry and I for the sake of total accountability, broke out even. And, The Megatons performed that night for gratis, and were straight up guys about it, considering the circumstances.

Of course, those who have read about The Epitome of Sound, (formerly The Megatons), know that in 1967 I composed two songs, "You Don't Love Me" & "Where Were You", especially for the soul music group, The Megatons, featuring lead vocalist, Eugene Thomas. We recorded those tracks at Venture Sound, a two track studio in my home town of Bound Brook, New Jersey. It has been documented many times over, that I wrote, produced, and played my grandfather's 1927 acoustic guitar with only 3 strings, on both sides. All of this is in fact the truth, although I have seen references made on occasion, that the late, great arranger and eventual musical director for Gladys Knight, Tony Camillo, then co-owner of the studio, produced it? Let me once again qualify this erroneous mis-quote. Tony Camillo, had no producer influence in the project, however, after we laid down the rhythm tack, he asked me if he could add strings, baritone and tenor saxes to the track? Since he was bringing in the musicians to do other recordings, his fee would offer me a reduced pricing. I agreed, paid him his fee, and he took the arrangement the Megatons & I had done as the backing track, and added his musical enhancements, which turned out to be the icing on the proverbial cake! When the Sandbag vinyl label was being prepared, I gave Tony credit as the arranger, and used my shortened and former stage name Robert Pala, as Producer. The reason for shortening my name was because I had received a call from the graphic artist working on the label, who said he couldn't fit my full name, on the limited registration space he had to use for the Producer credit. After several years of hindsight thinking, I suppose, I could have just used my first name initial "R", and my last name, Paladino and it could have fit, but maybe not? Allow me to yet again step back and continue in the chronological course of events, to when I took the demo to New York City, (NYC), in an effort to find an interested record label. I knocked on doors, which I was accustomed to in my vocal group days, and through trial and error, found only a couple of interested labels, who wanted me to leave the demo with them. I didn't want to do that, because I was in the City, and just had the one copy, and also, it didn't sound like the most logical way to work out a deal at the time. I guess I was concerned that it would be copied, and some underhanded things could happen. Call it creative demo paranoia, or maybe just a bit of street smartness, but that was the way I chose to have it go down. In any event, on my next excursion into NYC, Eugene Thomas and I decided to go together, and once again, we had 0 leads. As we were in the elevator, leaving the Brill Building, the elevator stopped at a floor, and a young black man entered. He immediately spotted the manila envelope containing the demo, which I protectively held under my arm. He asked, "What do you have there", pointing to the demo? Thinking quickly on how I would answer, I remembered Nick Massi, from The Four Seasons, telling me that when He and Tommy DeVito were producing artists under their Vito-Mass Production Co., that whenever he wanted to get into see a Record Company Exec., unannounced, he would tell the secretary, to tell them that he was one of the Four Seasons, and they were thinking of changing labels, or he would say who he was, and that he had a hit record, they should immediately hear. So, my response to this man was to borrow Nicks' line, "I have a hit record here"! He said, I'm Alvin Cash, and I have an office in the Building, and I would like to hear your demo? " We both knew who he was, a big time soul music recording artist, who recorded among others, the hit record "Twine Time", and so we both said in unison, "sure"! We went into his office, and he put You Don't Love Me on the turntable. He listened to the first part of the record going into the hook, "I'm Gonna cry, Cause I know you Don't love me" part, he stopped the playback. He took out $500 from his pocket, and gestured to me personally, "I'll give you this right now, but I am gonna want to record it with another lead singer"! I thanked him, and said, No Sir, we are going to go with what we have, as is!

He gave me his phone number in Chicago, should I ever change my mind. Nothing else was ever said between Eugene & I, other than Alvin Cash listened to our track, and liked it. A few weeks after our NYC experiences, I received a phone call from Mike Symanski, who introduced himself by saying that he hoard rocordings of a couple of my original tunes that I recorded with a guitar player and drummer at a studio in Harrison, New Jersey.

These were songs that I had written, and were very roughly recorded demos, which I never went back to finish, or even get an acetate demo, (today, I regret not getting a copy)! Mike explained that he and his financial partner, Johnathan Meyers, have a new Record Label, Sandbag Records, out of 1650 Broadway, NYC. He asked me if I had any other original songs that I have recorded? I filled him in on the two new soul music tracks, and we made an arrangement for him and his partner to come to Bound Brook, N.J., to hear the demo. Mike & Johnathan came, they listened, and they made me an offer! If we could reach an agreement, our record would be the first release on Sandbag Records. We discussed the details over pizza at the Brook Park Inn, which was a local restaurant run by the mom and dad of a former classmate of mine, Mary Anne Pulsinelli . My mom and dad would take me and my brother Mike there, when we were kids, so it was a place full of fond memories and very good Italian food. Just an added bit of trivia, eventually the bar would have one of the first color TV's in town, and I and my buddies would go there to watch the newly aired Batman TV Shows, featuring Adam West as Batman, Burt Ward as Robin, and a host of celebrities, playing the character parts, Burgess Meredith, as the Penguin, Caesar Romero, as The Joker, Julie Newmar, as Cat woman, and Frank Gorshin, as the Riddler.

I told the guys that I had a deal with Mike and Johnathan from Sandbag Records, NYC, explaining to them what I had been offered, and that in return, the Sandbag execs would do their best to push the record and the group! They had agreed to set up promotional pictures to be taken in NYC, purchase group clothing, arrange for Record Hops with known Top 40 NYC Radio DJs, and get them spots on TV, performing with big name recording artists. So, in May of 1967, I signed a Producer Contract with Sandbag Records, for my productions, "You Don't Love Me" and "Where Were You". The group selected a new name, "The Brandywines", which was used in the Management Contract, they individually signed with Mike & Johnathan. However, prior to the pressing of the record, Bob Ligatino, the bass player's wife, Linda, suggested that they rename the group, The Epitome of Sound, which was agreed to by all. The Epitome of Sound was printed on the record label, but the contracts were never amended to make the group name change, although their individual names and signatures appeared. History dealt the final outcome to Sandbag Records, the two partners, and to The Epitome of Sound, and Myself. Propriety Indiscretion at Sandbag Records reared its ugly wrath on what had become a chart hit @ Number 11 in Cleveland, Ohio, mainly from the groups' exposure on the "Upbeat TV Show". Johnathan Meyers announced to me by phone that effective immediately, he was dissolving Sandbag Records!

The Epitome of Sound was no more, having just 1 record release in 1967. The group dispersed and went their separate ways, as was explained in Chapter 1 of Book 1, "Our Soul Music Journey", by Johnny Warren. Sometimes, dreams take longer than expected to happen in one way or another, and can materialize when most unexpected. I believe that is what is known as fate! After a three year stint, playing with Nick Addeo & Company, I have now been working at AT&T since 1976. It wasn't until the early 90's when our department first issued us personal computers. The Internet was in its infancy, and some of us were not experienced enough to get the full benefits from the evolving Information Age. I for one was not just computer illiterate, but I would admit to it by jokingly saying that I was computer infantile!

It was in 1995, when I began to receive Songwriter Airplay Reports from The American Society of Composers, Authors & Publishers, and (ASCAP). I would see reference to International Airplay, but no reference to song title or group name. There was no online account access then, so I had to call and speak to someone at ASCAP, or write a letter directly I had been a registered ASCAP Songwriter and Publisher Member since 1962, but never received royalties of any substance. Then, I received a Tax Reporting Form from ASCAP, which said that I had received a certain amount of royalties for the year 1995. I did not in fact receive these royalties specified. I contacted ASCAP by letter stating my facts and enclosed a copy of their Tax Form. My guess is that by immediately responding to ASCAP, and under their 3 yr. retroactive policy, they were able to correct the error and/or recoup the songwriter royalties and direct it back to me. We also never received Publisher Royalties, and not until sometime later, I realized that although I and my brother Mike, and another friend, had been registered as Publisher, (Lynnette Music) with ASCAP, since 1962, and listed on both sides of the record, our royalties for YDLM/WWY were being received by someone else? In time I would gather enough information and understand that Publisher monies due to me were being received by others, in other countries, and without my permission. I have since resolved the publishing issue, establishing Pala One Publishing, and transferring registration of YDLM/WWY with US, ASCAP and acknowledged by International Songwriter & Publisher Societies. Bootlegging or illegal duplication and sales of recordings has turned out to be a big problem for US Artists, Record Labels, active and inactive, Writers, Producers and Publishers, and I've been told by trusted people in the Northern Soul Community, that certain people involved, have made a great deal of money with my records and from so many others! A couple of years ago, I caught a bootlegger duo offering my record (Black & White DJ Copy) on eBay, as I spotted a flaw. I contacted them and told them to desist or I will take the necessary steps to discredit them. They responded to me with an apology and a license request. I agreed, authorized the license, and shared the money with the EOS members. Let me just say, that this form of extortion and fraud of personal intellectual property in itself unchallenged, is what I would classify as sheer robbery by those who have zero creative talent, and their actions are indicative of what leeches are known for! Enough said about this.

Facebook and YouTube have been great resources and media sites for me and others to learn more about the Northern Soul (NS) phenomenon, it's history and culture that has lasted decades and continues to grow worldwide today! I have met many Northern Soul fans from various countries, and many have become and remain friends, as well as their families and mine have become part of each other's lives, as we share our thoughts and feelings, not only about music, but things in general. The same thing has happened with Radio and Event DJ's and Venue Planners. Beside liking and supporting our recordings, they are wonderful people and conveyors of Northern Soul, R&B & Soul Music. Without these dedicated people, there would be a limited NS Scene today! In my Chapter One of Book One, I have mentioned many of these stalwarts by name, thanking them for their support.

Northern Soul Music and its supporters have probably unknowingly, created numerous "musical life preservers" for certain Artists, Songwriters, Record Producers, Publishers, Radio & Event DJ's & Planners. They have created occupations, resurrected artist careers, inspired young performers, enticed new fans, and made some record collectors richer or poorer, depending on market timing. Their passion and love of the music and their expression displayed on the dance floor, within this community is unquestionably full of passion and love! All in all, the music still has a ways to go to reach its deserved ultimate level of recognition and acceptance for the unique music form and dance it truly is.

Movies and documentaries have been made, but I feel that the true story needs to go beyond just a "back in the day" retrospective, because if that was the extent of the NS Movement, it would have ended there. It continues, and has touched generations who lived through those early days, but as equally important, they continue to support and perpetrate the music genre, and have handed it off to many others who have been introduced into the culture.

So what exactly has been the impact of Northern Soul Music upon me? Firstly, Northern Soul Music was the conduit which has allowed me and Epitome of Sound group members, Joe DeJohn, Mike Paladino, and Eugene Thomas to reconnect with each other after 43 years of separation. Soul Trip USA in Orlando, Florida in 2011 was the venue that facilitated the reconnection, as we were both invited there by KeV Roberts, after I located and connected with Eugene, thru his niece, and the rest became history, so to speak. Eugene was able to travel to the UK, and perform at the famous Blackpool Tower, and meet his many fans in person. I know how overjoyed and proud he was to have done that. He also did several interviews and guested on various DJ hosts, NS Music Radio Shows in the UK. I also had the pleasure of doing remote Radio Interviews and wrote about The Epitome of Sound and Myself.

I was honored to be asked by the authors, Richard Searling, and Johnny Redpants Warren, to write book chapters for Richards' "Setting The Record Straight" and Johnny Redpants Warrens', "Our Soul Music Journey", published by Soul Man Jan, the late, Jan Lisewski. Eugene wrote his chapter for the book, but before the book was released, he sadly passed away. After Joe DeJohn's and Mike Paladino's Chapter 2, I added "A Fond Farewell" to Eugene, in his memory, and to his fans. Eugene and I got a chance to go back into the studio, a home studio as it were, to try and recapture the magic from 1967. An impossible task, due to many 21st Century new recording technologies. We did however record a 2 sided demo, an original that I wrote, and one that Eugene wrote. Both tracks had live piano, bass, and guitar, with added electronic drums, horns, and strings. They were in fact demos that needed enhancements, and with my track, still remains an active work in progress. Eugene went on to write two more songs, "I'm Through With You" and "Lovely Lady". He worked with a co-producer, close to where he lived in Ridgewood, NJ, to record and release on vinyl on their joint record label, Sweetbeets. Both tracks were well received upon release, and became successful. They can be listened to on YouTube, by searching for the recordings of Eugene Thomas, as well as his live performances. In 2018, I wrote and produced "Cause My Lover's Gone and Ethan's Theme", released on 7" vinyl on Redpants Records, and performed by UK Soul Singer, Johnny Boy Pryers. Johnny is a great young talent who is destined to become a big success! Because of Covid, we have talked about doing other projects together, and I look forward to doing that in the very near future.

Simon Bayliss, bass player with New Zealand group, Jamie and The Numbers, contacted me and said he would like to cover "You Don't Love Me', and make it a tribute to Eugene Thomas. After listening to Jamie and The Numbers, I agreed to have them record my song. Jamie has a very soulful, distinctive R&B voice, and the musicians in the group are top notch. Simon asked my brother Mike and I to add to the track, and Mike recorded added percussion, as I was able to do a video and vocal intro, and at the end of the recording and video, I spoke words of tribute to Eugene Thomas! For it was his great soul voice that gave You Don't Love Me, and The Epitome of Sound a second chance to be heard by many!

Robert Paladino, Eugene Thomas & Michael Paladino
© **Robert Paladino**

THE EPITOME OF SOUND
Sandbag Record, Inc.

The Epitome of Sound © **Robert Paladino**

Robert Paladino, Christine Burroughs, Steve Bardsley
Orlando Soul trip USA © Robert Paladino

This is what the Impact of Northern Soul Music has meant to me, Eugene, and Mike and Joe of the Epitome of Sound. Another day, another listener, another like after hearing our music! We are Grateful, Much Appreciative, and so very thankful for being embraced by all the Northern Soul Music Lovers, World Wide!

Chapter 21

Pat Gwinn, It's The Story That Never Ends

From birth we've all been entertainers. Constantly smiling, doing cute things to garnish the attention of our parents, grandparents, friends and even our pets. As we matured, we were able to refine our entertaining attributes to captivate the imagination and hopefully the heart of the one we aspire to become our life long partner. To think that we are any different from an on-stage performer is hard to imagine. When the microphone goes on – you're on! When you speak to someone – you're on! Think back to your days in school. Remember speaking before the class? You were being taught a life skill that would follow you through every day of your existence and let's face it, you use that skill more than you ever needed algebra.

Since an early age, I was fortunate to know what I wanted to do in life as an occupation. It has been said that if you love what you do, you feel as though you have never worked a day in your life. I fell in love with the idea that someone could speak into a microphone and people all over the world could hear you. As a child I wondered how one band would play a song on the radio and another band set up and be ready to go live so quickly. Well, that was before I knew the station actually had records. I thought the man on the radio was, well, sort of a god, so to speak, admired by many. As I grew up, I came to understand the importance for which radio was intended. Radio was to be more than a jukebox playing song after song.

The mission of the station was to support the community it was licensed to serve. Information, news and given the ability to warn the communities of possible danger with Emergency Broadcasts, etc.

Over my 40 plus years in broadcasting I have been fortunate to interview so many entertainers. I have been saddened to report some of the world's harshest events. Amazing entertainers such as Wink Martindale, General Johnson, Lenny Williams and dozens more... to news events such as the space shuttle Challenger exploding after liftoff, the twin towers falling in New York City on 9/11, to the drowning of two boys whose mom drove them into a small lake. The one constant remains: music has a healing power that we can all relate to and escape our trials and tribulations.

Sometimes the things we can't change, end up changing us. The pandemic locked down the world for nearly 2 years. Bringing about many changes of how we embraced life, work and our own mental well-being. Music has the healing power to take us away. Uniting generations with lyrics and melodies you literally recall where you were when you first heard the song. Brings those rush of emotions that take us back to a prom, a wedding, a special someone. In the decade of the 50s, the evolution of rock n roll challenged parents to accept a new norm. The 60s brought about music being used as a platform for change that carried on into the 70s.

The stories behind the music have always intrigued me. From Wink Martindale sharing the story of Elvis Presley's first song airing (That's Alright Mama) and the commotion it caused at the radio station that evening that started a lifetime friendship with Martindale and Presley... to Cuba Gooding, Sr. claiming the Main Ingredient disliked the song they eventually became most famous for singing – Everybody Plays The Fool. The song was intended to be presented as a country song. RCA presented the song to country artist Charley Pride who rejected the song. The Main Ingredient needed a couple of more songs for an album before going on tour. Cuba said they reluctantly recorded the song, and wouldn't you know it? The song the group disliked turned out to be one of the group's signature songs. A great story from Fred Thomas, and confirmed wholeheartedly by

LeRoy Harper, Jr., whenever you heard The Godfather of Soul, James Brown, say "I Got YOU" during a song, it wasn't a reference to the mere song but instead, it was placing a musician on notice! Thomas and Harper said band members were monetarily penalized for missing a note in the song, a payroll deduction! Talk about perfectionists! Harper said rehearsals were pure jam sessions with James Brown and "attention to detail and watch da Boss" at all times.

James Brown, LeRoy Harper, Jr (saxophonist) © Leroy Harper Junior

Jim Stodemire of The Entertainers:

"For musicians, one of the obstacles to creating good recordings for the people is getting it to them. "Pat Gwinn At The Beach" is the ultimate way for us to reach the ears of our friends and fans and present our music to people all over the world, many who may have never even heard of us. I think that is just one of the advantages of having someone like Pat Gwinn in our corner - presenting our music to people who may end up making Carolina beach and soul music their favorite genre. "Thank you" to Pat Gwinn and his staff for all they do for us and Carolina beach music!"

Dianne Pope, The Tams

"Pat Gwinn is one of the best radio personalities in Carolina Beach Music. Pat never forgets the artists who made the hits. He tries to give everyone in the Beach Music industry a chance to shine. The Tams will always be grateful to all that Pat does for us. We love and respect him for being one of the greatest to ever do this Carolina Beach Music and Pat goes all over the world. Thank you so much! Dianne Pope and the Tams.

As the originator of a website which has evolved into a Facebook blog entitled "I'll Go Where The Music Takes Me Music Reviews". I have been directly involved with efforts to expand market interest in Beach Music through working in multiple organizations such as The Association of Beach and Shag Club Dee Jays, The Beach Music Association International and other organization since 1990. This involvement has expanded my knowledge of the music and it's artists. Additionally, it has resulted in my direct exposure to traditional and internet radio that focus on Beach Music. However, no one media source either traditional or internet have combined both formats to convey Beach Music to the world except "Pat Gwinn At The Beach". PGATB has reached out to not just the local Carolina Beach Market but through the intergration of traditional and internet radio PGATB touches every part of the world. This unique approach allows those who have no or limited internet resources to not only hear this style of music but to learn of the artists and musical history. In Short PGATB is the complete package bringing Beach Music to the world.

Michael Roberts
"I'll Go Where The Music Takes Me Music Reviews"

Drawn as "Where It All Began". © Rev. Frank Lybrand

Imagine begging your agent or producer to allow you to record a song. It happened in Atlanta when The Tams begged Bill Lowery for permission to record one the group's biggest hits. Charles Pope detailed the story of Joe Pope and the group going to Lowery to ask to record "Be Young, Be Foolish, Be Happy." Lowery refused. The song had been recorded by two other acts and "had no legs". Joe insisted. The group added a bit more energy and a doo wop sound that made it different. As you know it became one of The Tams biggest hits. The Tams got their start singing on the street corners of Atlanta. The members of the group all were poor, growing up in the ghettos. Joe Pope took care of the group making money as a pool shark so to speak before the group got a real footing. The uniforms came about by accident. The Tams bought matching sweaters and the tam-o-shanter (the hat worn) is where the name for the group came about.

The Tams © Pat Gwinn

In the late 50s and 60s, "soul music" was heard in the south by way of "Charlie's Place", a club at the end of Carver Street in Myrtle Beach, South Carolina. Atlantic Beach was also another mecca for soul music or black music. Billy Scott told me of the days of performing in the "Chitlin Circuit", which was the term for the southern route of safe, acceptable venues traveled by black performers during Jim Crow days. "I would go perform in these clubs on the Chitlin Circuit. I was thrilled to perform my music. If I had money to get something to eat and a place to sleep, I would be happy". That start to the business for Billy Scott was the theme for so many artists. On the Friday we first started our syndicated show, Pat Gwinn At The Beach, Billy drove from Augusta, Georgia to our studio in Abbeville, SC to be our first guest.

Billy described those days and about his favorite defining song, (I Got The) Fever. "I got a phone call from Roy Smith. He was a songwriter that thought the song was a perfect fit. Roy was so excited that we went over and Roy started on the piano and started singing "I Love You, I Love You, Yes I Do".

336

I was immediately hooked. I couldn't wait to get to the studio to record it. As it turned out, it was my one and only gold record!" Billy said.

Billy Scott © Pat Gwinn

Thankfully times changed. The era of Jim Crow ended. Both black and white men and women could go to clubs together. The music was alive. Music became a unifying source to heal the past of the country. A world of emotions and expressions were exploding. New & exciting genres of music were forming.

Just what is beach music?

The term "beach music" came about when white kids came to the beach to hear black music and would refer to it as "beach music" … music they heard while they were on vacation at the beach. Other definitions have been presented.

General Johnson, former Showmen and Chairmen of the Board leader, defined it as: "Music you can dance to… it got to the place if you couldn't shag to it, it wasn't beach music. I'd love to see someone shag to "Higher and Higher" (Jackie Wilson), they'd break their ankles!" laughing as he said. Johnson warned artists to adapt shows to the audience but not allow the audience to dictate what they perform. "The future of beach music lies in the artists. You've got to please the college kids, that's tomorrow's crowd. You can't be selfish as an artist. If the work you do is to satisfy you, you may as well perform in your basement."

Jackie Gore, a founding member of The Embers, described beach music.

"We formed The Embers in 1959. We were the only white band playing on the college scene. We were the inspiration for many groups. Beach music originated on the coast of North and South Carolina. We opened The Embers Club in 1968 down on Atlantic Beach in North Carolina. We filled that place up every time we Played there all during the summer and then when the college kids would go home, they would say 'where is that beach music we would hear down on the beach' and that is where the term beach music came from – was people hearing The Embers play in 1968 to 1972, the four years we had that club. That's where the term 'beach music' came from regardless of what anyone else tells you. I was there!" Jackie Gore. In 1969, Jackie Gore penned what has been the anthem of Carolina Beach Music. Jackie said, "I wanted to write something for the young people. I knew most of their parents, a lot of the young people were following us around so I decided I'd write a song for the young people. I sat down at my kitchen table and started singing, ``I Love Beach Music, always have and I always will.." I started adding song titles like Under The Boardwalk, Sixty Minute Man… and that's how it fell into place. As it turns out, everyone seems to like it."

Writing this chapter in "OUR SOUL MUSIC JOURNEYS" has been a joy, finishing it on the other hand has been somewhat of a challenge personally. The month of October 2021 was a mixture of trials, joys, sorrows & celebrations. As I looked at my schedules for a typical Monday, I noticed at any time during that day we were on a radio station somewhere from 6 in the morning until 10 at night. Celebrating the music & the stories behind the music is an opportunity of pleasure, but it is work. The artists who put their heart & soul into recording & performing have become an extended family of sorts. Northern & Southern Soul, Motown, Carolina Beach Music... showcasing them to the masses of listeners that, too, become extended family.

Jackie Gore © Pat Gwinn

BEACH MUSIC HALL OF FAME

FEVER by Little Willie John

This boogie ballad, written by Otis Blackwell and Eddie Cooley, became one of the sexiest beach music songs ever. Released in 1956, it smothered the Southern jukeboxes, the very same year Bardot made one of history's sexiest movies. Crooned by the creamy pipes of Little Willie John, the torchy tune had no trouble hitting #1 R&B.

Ten years later, small in stature but huge in voice, he stabbed an ex-con to death and became a con himself, convicted of manslaughter. Now, all but forgotten around the world, his rich voice lives on at the beach. Like Stevie Wonder's mama told her young son, "If you're gonna call yourself Little Stevie Wonder, you better be as good as Little Willie John." The one-word classic we honor, is none other than FEVER.

Lifelong Fan - STEVE BAILEY

FLAMINGO by Earl Bostic

Written by Ted Grouya and Ed Anderson, this jazzy groove was a minor hit for Herb Jeffries and Duke Ellington. But in 1951, it was the magical alto sax of Earl Bostic that jetted this tune to #1 R&B and dropped a million quarters into the Myrtle Beach jukeboxes. One of the great instrumental rhythms...danced and romanced to by foxtrotters, swingers, shaggers and jitterbugs. Flamingo...by the sax maestro Earl Bostic.

Lifelong Fans - FLAMINGO GRILL

GOOD ROCKIN' TONIGHT by Wynonie Harris

Good Rockin' Tonight was a nightlife tribute written on a brown paper bag by Roy Brown and offered to slick Wynonie Harris who turned it down. So Roy Brown sang it over the phone to a record exec and recorded it himself in 1947. Only after the song flooded the jukeboxes in the Big Easy did Wynonie cover it. But without the creamy pipes of Roy Brown and his Mighty Mighty Men band, Wynonie knew he had to win the audience. So he rocked it harder, added some clapping, some hoy hoys and up the chart beanstalk it went. Good Rockin' even caught Elvis' ear. He dug the song so much he covered it on his second Sun Records release.

Lifelong Fans - ATLANTIC ENTERTAINMENT - CHARLES STAFFORD

HONKY TONK by Bill Doggett

So what artist had the #1 R&B song for 1956? Was it the romantic groove of Still of the Night or the sexy vibe of Fever? Was it Little Richard, Chuck Berry or the Platters? No - it was a Philadelphia-born organ player named Bill Doggett who created this Everest of boogie instrumentals. The song features Billy Butler on guitar, Shep Shepard on sax and Bill Doggett on the Hammond organ. It became a huge crossover hit and dominated white and black jukeboxes and became Bill Doggett's signature piece. This monster instrumental groove, which put a penny in a million loafers, was called Honky Tonk part 1 and part 2.

Lifelong Fans - CAGNEY'S OLD PLACE

IN THE STILL OF THE NIGHT by The Five Satins

While on guard duty, Fred Parris put his rifle in his lap, picked up a pen, snooped the title and a smidge of the melody of a Cole Porter classic and wrote one of the most romantic doo-wop ballads in history. With only four of the Five Satins, the B-side song was recorded in the basement of a church and released in 1956. Maybe it didn't soar at the time, but the song did chart R&B and pop and is now a monster fav at oldie shows and in the young hearts of slow-dancing baby boomers. The song we honor is...In the Still of the Night by the Five Satins.

Lifelong Fan - JIMMY G

"A Musical History Worth Remembering!"

Our family of affiliates are just that! A family. It is more than asking a station to air your programs but to know it is a good fit for the needs of the station… to know the impact a heritage festival in Lineville, Alabama can have a positive impact on the community and the station…

to celebrate successes when a station begins to recover from a massive flood from trail of destruction of Hurricane Ida in New Jersey… to walk through a studio gutted by fire… a facility you had been standing in hours before. Sadly, October showed us just how quickly things can change.

The outpouring of support to radio stations in need is so appreciated. How wonderful it was when radio station operators in the same town, reached out with offers of equipment to assist with a rebuild. An amazing 18 hours later the signal was restored. It's a fresh restart and a startling reminder of how we should take nothing for granted. Boom! Just like that the roller coaster changes course and you wrap up your month with a beautiful new Granddaughter, Lydia Winter Gwinn born on October 30. That final weekend of October offered us all to experience every emotion imaginable.

Laughter. Joy. Hope.

It's The Story That Never Ends

Pat Gwinn

Chapter 22

Paul Stuart Davies - Gloria Jones

Gloria Jones – an Introduction Gloria Richetta Jones is a singer with a hugely impressive history in the music industry, despite never quite reaching the height of fame that she so richly deserved. She is best known as the original singer of 'Tainted Love', a song taken to number 1 by Soft Cell in 1981 and that has since been covered and sampled in big hits by Marylin Manson, Rihanna and The Pussycat Dolls. When I stayed with Gloria at her home in Sierra Leone in 2020, she told me that although the song is credited solely to her then-producer, Ed Cobb, Gloria actually co-wrote the song with him. Like many young artists wanting to go places in the music industry, she didn't argue when her name was left off the composer credits, just happy to be a signed recording artist. This omission has cost Gloria a fortune in-the-future royalties considering the success that the song has had over the years in its many forms. Gloria is also remembered for her work with UK Glam Rock band T Rex, in which she played clavinet and provided backing vocals for her then-partner, Marc Bolan. During her time at Motown records in the early seventies, Gloria co-wrote with Pam Sawyer (under the pseudonym LaVerne Ware) songs for artists including Marvin Gaye, Diana Ross and Gladys Knight (the huge hit 'If I Were Your Woman'). Whilst at Motown, she also recorded the wonderful album 'Share My Love' (1973), but it failed to chart due to poor promotion from the label. Other albums recorded by Gloria include 'Come Go With Me' (1966), 'Vixen' (1976), 'Windstorm' (1978), and 'Reunited' (1982). Gloria Jones now lives in Sierra Leone where she set up the Marc Bolan School of Music, providing free music education to children living in poverty. She is always looking for help to raise funds for the project and has given her life to this cause. A truly remarkable lady!

Gloria Jones © Paul Stuart Davies

Gloria Jones & Paul Stuart Davies in Sierra Leone 2020
© Paul Stuart Davies

Paul Stuart Davies - Kim Weston

Kim Weston – an Introduction Agatha Nathalia Weston, like many stars, opted for an alternative stage name. As Kim Weston she signed to Motown records in 1961 where she recorded several albums worth of exquisite material, without the label ever putting out a solo album. She did however score minor chart hits with 'Love Me All The Way', 'Helpless' and her biggest solo hit 'Take Me In Your Arms (Rock Me A Little While)' (no. 50 in 1965). Her biggest success was when the label paired her with Marvin Gaye for the duet album 'Take Two' which spawned the forever classic single 'It Takes Two' in 1966.

Having married Motown's A&R man, William 'Mickey' Stevenson, Kim left the label when her husband felt that they were both unappreciated and Kim spent the next few years releasing albums on several labels including 'For the First Time' (MGM, 1966), 'This Is America' (MGM, 1968), 'Big Brass Four Poster' (People, 1970), and 'Kim Kim Kim' (Volt, 1970). Throughout the late seventies and early eighties, Kim turned her attention to helping others, running her successful Festival of the Performing Arts in Detroit, educating the next generation of performers.

Kim often visits the UK to perform to her fans on the Northern Soul scene, where her most loved songs include 'Helpless', 'A Thrill A Moment' and 'I'm Still Loving You'. Like Gloria Jones, Kim has often been named 'Queen of Northern Soul'. After moving to Israel for some years, Kim now resides back in her hometown of Detroit. She is looking forward to her next Gig!

Kim Weston © Paul Stuart Davies

Chapter 23

People and the Places by Steve Bardsley

It was my pleasure to write Chapter 7 of the first book in the "Our Soul Journeys", this Chapter in Book 2 covers some of the amazing soul artists I have had the pleasure of meeting and I share some of their stories with our readers. I have had the pleasure of being entertained by many great soul artists over some 50 years and have had the opportunity to personally meet and chat with many of them. I have enjoyed listening to some of their great stories, many of which have not been told, so hopefully readers will enjoy hearing them as much as I did.

I tell some of their stories, some of which are untold, writing the list of some of the names associated with soul music I have had the pleasure and privilege to meet, brings back so many great memories and reminds me what an amazing phenomena soul music really is, in particular Northern Soul. For me, meeting with and talking to soul artists in person enhances the experience of owning their records, it makes them more significant than 7 inch discs of plastic. Listening to the stories, the passion for the music and hearing about how it was and what was happening when the records were being produced and recorded, mainly in the 1960's is just remarkable. I hope readers of this book will enjoy these memories.

What I do always find amazing is how so many artists advise they did not know until many years later how people in the UK had listened to their records and they did not know how much they were appreciated there. Frequently in the U.S. the records the artists released more often than not went mostly unheard, often released only in their own local area, many remaining unsold and so fading into obscurity.

For me, owning a record with an artist, writer or producer's name on it, after having had the pleasure to meet them in person, to meet the ones who actually made the music is such a privilege and gives a different meaning to the record. For me playing a record after meeting those actually involved in creating it, is always so much more satisfying. It's also an experience which is becoming less likely to be possible in the future, as many of the incredible record producers and artists from 1960s' have sadly now already and/or are getting closer to passing away, as I guess we all are now.

One of the sad things though and an often recurring theme is how most of the 'Northern Soul' artists were never paid for many of the records they made and some artists after record the records went back to work at the local car wash, as waiters or to other low paid jobs, many sadly never became aware how in the in the late 1960's and the 1970's the songs they had recorded and which they though had disappeared into oblivion had become revered on the U.K. 'Northern' scene.

THE TWISTED WHEEL

The Twisted Wheel in Manchester is perhaps the most famous soul club of all. "The Wheel" was a pioneering club and its owners the Abadi brothers loved soul music and so brought artists over from the USA to perform there. The Twisted Wheel Club is why we have the term "Northern Soul". I first set foot in the Whitworth Street "Twisted Wheel" as a wide-eyed teenager when barely 16 years of age, I went to see Edwin Starr. Yes, I said 16 years of age, there is a misapprehension you had to be 18 years old to get into the Wheel, which was not true, as anyone who actually went there will tell you. This is because the "Twisted Wheel" did not have a liquor licence, in those days they were not permitted if a venue wanted to stay open more than 2 hours after midnight. As alcohol was not served there was no requirement for patrons to be over 18 years of age.

347

The many kids inside the Wheel under 18 years of age were therefore not breaking any licensing or other laws, other than perhaps taking pills. Back in those days drugs were very much frowned upon by the authorities and the penalties for possessing them were draconian, even a first time offender caught with nothing more than slimming pills could face a 6 month jail sentence. As there was no alcohol served on the premises and the Wheel was frequently an "all-nighter" the pills were used by many. Although I never got into them, I was soon to find the Pills were a big part of the all-nighter scene. It was though my passion for seeing soul artists perform that took me to Twisted Wheel in the late 1960's and early 1970's. The Club was then located at No 6 Whitworth Street. Let's face it, as a soul fan when artists like Edwin Starr and Junior Walker were in your neighbourhood, you would have been crazy not to want to go and see them. At the Wheel I was fortunate enough to see artists including, Edwin Starr, Junior Walker, Jimmy Ruffin, Bob and Earl, Inez and Charlie Foxx, Jamo Thomas, Arthur Conley, Fontella Bass, Johnny Johnston and the Bandwagon, Ben E. King, The Shirelles and Alvin Cash and the Crawlers, who were totally amazing. I suspect the famous Northern Soul 'back drop' dance move became popular on the Northern Soul scene after first being seen at the Twisted Wheel, this when performed by Alvin and the Crawlers as they performed "Twine Time," and after which everyone was so impressed they wanted to dance like them. It's occasions like this which are very impressive on a teenager and which have stayed with me forever. For me it's what makes watching and meeting live artists so special, everyone was different in their own way. It was also great how so many of the artists performing enjoyed meeting and talking with their audience.

I was not what you would call one of the "regulars" at the Twisted Wheel. I went frequently, but not religiously every week as some did, there were other soul clubs I also liked. I went to the Wheel mainly to see the live acts and so picked my visits depending on who was performing.

For me it was fascinating to watch the performers, whose names I usually had only seen in print, OR on records, flyers and posters. I was also fully aware I was not one of the seasoned old boys in the Wheel. Although a lot is spoken about the camaraderie on the soul scene and it is true you sometimes made new friends, the reality is this was 1969/70 in the North of England. These were dangerous and violent times, local gangs protected their turf, drugs were sometimes involved, there was not much money about and if you had any someone else wanted it, you had to be alert. Soul clubs did not always provide the friendly environment portrayed in some of the modern day books and films which reminisce about the Northern Soul scene.

The truth is you sometimes only had to look at someone the wrong way or for slightly too long and you could be in trouble. Some people on the scene were out looking for trouble, to steal your pills or money, not nice, but that's the reality. I was lucky though, my first time inside the Wheel brought a few surprises, none bigger than meeting Bill from Droylsden in there. Bill was one of the older 'Scooter Boys' I had got to know as a kid and who I first heard talking about The Twisted Wheel. I had always got on particularly well with Bill, as like me, he was a Manchester City supporter and I sometimes saw him at Maine Road in the 'Kippax'. I had only been inside the Wheel for a few minutes when I was spotted by Bill, he grabbed hold of me and said something like "Steve, what the 'farck' are you doing in here, come with me!" Bill then gave my friend and I a whirlwind tour of the club. Bill's "tour" of the Twisted Wheel was more like a who's who of the people in there. As he walked us through the club Bill said to us quietly so no one else could hear, things like; "don't hang around here near the arches, its where the 'Scousers' are, so watch your pockets, don't go anywhere near that guy there, he will be after your money and pills if you have any. See that guy over there, he will try to sell you pills, don't buy them they are no good. Be careful of those guys over there, they will turn you over the first chance they get. See that guy there, he will try to sell you records, don't give him any money as you will never see them." The information from Bill just kept coming; "If you go on the dance floor stay away from that guy, he is one of the best dancers in here and likes his space. Don't talk to those two over there, they are most likely undercover cops. Keep away from that bloke over there, he is as bent as a nine bob note, be careful chatting up girls here, they may be spoken for and their boyfriends will have you."

My friend and I were almost dizzy trying to absorb all what Bill was throwing at us, Bill went on; "See that guy over there, well that's Ivor and he owns the joint, never flash your money in here, always watch your pockets, don't hang around the bogs too long and be careful, this is a great club but you need to be wide awake! Last but not least, don't tell anyone I just told you any of this. OK Steve, you and your mate are on your own, have fun". Bill disappeared into the crowd and we didn't see him again that night, but thanks to him we were no longer rookies, we had been given the heads up and so watched our step at all times. We were now aware of where not to go, who to stay away from, what not to do and what not to say. We heeded Bill's advice and never got into any trouble, not all newcomers to the Wheel were so lucky though.

I remember when the much expected bad news came announcing the last night at the Whitworth Street Wheel would be in January 1971. It would be an 'all-nighter' and the regular visitor and the much worshipped Edwin Starr would perform. This though wasn't as many people believe actually the last night at the Wheel, it opened again just one more time the following week, the first week in February of 1971. It was not however an 'all-nighter' and stayed open only until midnight. However; contrary to common belief, the very last night at Whitworth Street "Twisted Wheel" was not the 'all-nighter', at which Edwin Starr performed. 'The Wheel' in fact did open its doors one more time the following week, not as an all-nighter, instead closing the doors for the very last time at midnight.

Anyone who did get to see Edwin perform at that last all-nighter though did get to see something very special, whether it was the last night or not.

EDWIN STARR

Although the closure of the Whitworth Street 'Twisted Wheel' was massively disappointing, it wasn't as is often portrayed the end of the soul scene in Manchester, in fact, it was the start of a new one. The 1960's and 70's soul scene is often referred to as an 'underground' scene and remembered only for soul clubs such as the 'Twisted Wheel', the 'Blackpool Mecca', the '(Golden) Torch', the 'Catacombs', and then the legendary 'Wigan Casino'. The reality is there were lots of other clubs in the U.K. playing soul music, many with live artists. The term 'Northern Soul' wasn't used either, it was supposedly first introduced by the 'Blues and Soul' magazine columnist Dave Godin in 1969. I believe the notion Dave Godin was first to come up with the term 'Northern Soul' is an unlikely one, as I first recall seeing the term 'Northern Soul' around 1968, in the Manchester Evening News newspaper, in an article about Edwin Starr performing at the 'Twisted Wheel'. In the newspaper article Edwin referred to the 'Twisted Wheel' as 'the hub of Northern Soul'. I therefore believe it was Edwin Starr who first came up with the term 'Northern Soul' and this in Manchester, rather than it being Dave Godin in London. I was one of the lucky ones to see Edwin Starr perform at the 'Twisted Wheel' and was quite surprised when I first met him, as he was a little shorter in height than I somehow expected him to be. Although perhaps short in height, Edwin was a big character and performer, with a big generous personality and an unmistakable shout out style of singing.

Edwin was an amazing performer and it was so obvious he loved it. Edwin was such a nice guy too, he was always willing to stay behind after a performance and chat with his fans, nothing was too much trouble, he really appreciated his British fans, that's why he left the U.S.A. to live in England where he was

351

more appreciated by lovers of soul music. Edwin was a regular performer at the 'Twisted Wheel' and the last live performer to play at a 'Twisted Wheel all-nighter'. After moving over to England Edwin convinced J.J. to join him, he put J.J. in touch with the people at the UK Contempo record label, Edwin did a lot for the UK soul scene. I asked Edwin why he decided to use the name Edwin Starr, this instead of his real name Charles Hatcher. Edwin explained Don Briggs the manager of the Bill Doggett Combo signed him as a member of the group saying it would make him a star. Edwin liked the sound of this saying he would become a Star, Mr Star. From then on he used the name Starr instead of Hatcher. He used Edwin as his new first name because this was actually his real middle name. Edwin Starr was born and soon he really would become a Star as Don Briggs had promised, albeit without being part of the Bill Doggett Combo. Edwin went on to record "Agent Double O Soul" (1965), Back Street (1966), Headline News (1966) and "S.O.S" (1966) all on the Ric-Tic label.

At the request of Ed Wingate Edwin became a virtual member of the group "The Holidays" with J.J. Barnes and Steve Mancha. J.J. recorded "Please Let Me in" (1965) and "Real Humdinger" (1966) on the Ric-Tic label, whilst Steve Mancha recorded "Friday Night" (1966) and "I Don't Want To Lose You" (1966) on the Groovesville label. The 45 RPM record "I'll Love You Forever" was then released on Ed Wingate's Golden World label as being by "The Holidays", the thing was, this was not "The Holidays" featuring Steve Mancha, J.J Barnes or Edwin Starr, Edwin's voice was actually dubbed onto the record later. Wingate released the track as being by "The Holidays" because he didn't want it to clash with Edwin's "Stop Her On Sight" which had just been released on Ric-Tic (1966). The four young artists who actually recorded "I'll Love You Forever" never did receive the credit for it. Many still today believe this record by the Holidays features Barnes, Mancha and Starr, the reality is only Edwin Starr's voice is on the record and he wasn't in the recording studio when it was made, it was dubbed on later.

Edwin and J.J. were both given contracts with Motown when Ed Wingate sold Ric Tic/Golden World to Berry Gordy in 1967. Berry Gordy was upset many of his Motown session musicians were earning extra cash by moonlighting at Wingate's recording studios, the Golden World studios had better recording equipment than did Motown, so Gordy bought it. At Motown Edwin did better than J.J. Barnes, who wasn't given much vocal work, the story goes, Marvin Gaye believed J.J's voice was too similar to his own. Marvin was a family member having married Berry Gordy's Sister, so was always going to record the tracks of his choice. It didn't take J.J. long to work it out and he moved to the Groovesville record label. J.J. had the last laugh, recording "Baby Please Come Back Home" on Groovesville, a record he was working on with Stevie Wonder whilst at Motown.

When Stevie found out J.J. was leaving as he wouldn't have a future at Motown, he gave him the song as a parting gift, never taking credit for it, the record became J.J. 's first hit at Groovesville. Meanwhile Edwin recorded "I Want My Baby Back" (1967), "Way Over There" (1968) and "Twenty Five Miles" (1968) all on the Gordy label. In 1970 Edwin recorded the song he is most remembered for "WAR", a cover of the original by the Temptations. In 1970 Norman Whitfield produced the Temptations LP "Psychedelic Shack", which features "War" as track 2 on side 2. Motown decided not to release "War" as a single on the Temptations believing a protest type song wasn't right for them. Whitfield wanted to put it out on a single though, so he asked Edwin if he would like to record it. Edwin hadn't recorded anything for around 6 months and wanted to get back in the studio, he sensed the song suited his shout it out style, stipulating he be allowed to record the song with the feeling and intensity he believed was right for it. Whitfield agreed, the single was released and "War" shot to No1 on the Billboard Hot 100 chart, it sold 3 million copies, won a Gold disc and would see Edwin nominated for a Grammy award for best R&B Male Vocal Performance (1971).

War is the song Edwin is forever remembered for and one of the most popular and everlasting protest songs ever made. "War" though is my least favourite song by Edwin and I once asked him if he enjoyed performing it live. Edwin replied with his famous mischievous grin he would keep banging it out so long as it kept being asked for, which he did until he died of a heart attack in 2003.

Edwin's headstone reads "In loving memory of Charles Edwin Hatcher, our agent 00 Soul, Edwin Starr, 1942-2003, keep the faith, always loved, never forgotten".

IN
LOVING
MEMORY OF
CHARLES EDWIN HATCHER
OUR AGENT 00 SOUL
EDWIN STARR
1942 - 2003
"KEEP THE FAITH"

ALWAYS LOVED, NEVER FORGOTTEN

Edwin Starr's grave © Steve Bardsley

J.J. BARNES

Every Northern Soul fan knows of J.J. (James Jay) Barnes and his Northern Soul classics "Our Love Is In The Pocket" and "Please Let Me In," both big favourites of mine

I first met J.J in England in the 1970's. As already mentioned J.J. actually came to live in England for a couple of years after his good friend Edwin Starr convinced him to come over and join him. It was Edwin who put J.J. in touch with the U.K. Contempo label which released many of his records, including another favourite of mine "Sweet Sherry," in 1974 which has a very credible version of "These Chains Of Love" on the flip side. Talking with J.J. is like talking to an encyclopedia of soul music, the first time he performed as a paid artist was in 1961 supporting Aretha Franklin and the Miracles, he was young, inexperienced and felt out of his depth doing so, but he was though also quite ambitious.

Around the same time J.J. released his first ever record, the 45 RPM single "My Love Came Tumbling Down" on the Kable label, which went nowhere. J.J recorded not only as a solo artist but also in one of the many line ups of the Holidays, which include the Four Holidays, the Holidays, and the Fabulous Holidays. J.J.'s stint was with Steve Mancha, Jimmy Holland and Eddie Anderson, who did not actually perform live but just recorded together, some of their tracks would later become big on the 'Northern Soul' scene such as "I'll Love You Forever" and "Makin' Up Time" (1966) on the Golden World and Polydor labels, and "Never Alone", "Loves Creeping Up On Me," "I Keep Holding On", "I Know She Cares" (1967/68) on the Revilot label.

J.J surprised me saying Jimmy Ruffin was actually one of the original members of the Holidays which was something I never knew and would ever have guessed.

Steve Bardsley and the signed records © Steve Bardsley

J.J. brought quite a few records to England with him and took a great deal of interest in a record I asked him to sign for me, an original 1965 release of "Please Let Me In" on the Ric Tic label. Just like Major Lance, J.J. was intrigued as to how a record collector in England had somehow got his hands on a record hardly anyone had wanted to buy in the U.S.A. and this on the American Ric Tic label release.

In those days there were import restrictions, taxes and duties on records brought into the U.K. so they were far harder to get than they are today. J.J was not aware any of his Ric Tic recordings had actually ended up in England.

If any of J.J.'s records were actually released in the U.K. it was usually on the orange Polydor label. J.J. was therefore delighted to sign the Ric Tic label for me. When I explained to J.J. I had bought the record from a second hand store in Manchester, he was more perplexed than ever. I still have the record today and will always keep it. You could sometimes buy imported records in England, some independent record shops brought them in, others were advertised in magazines such as 'Black Music', 'Blues and Soul', 'New Musical Express' etc., and there were imported record lists going around the clubs. 'Blues and Soul' magazine used to print the U.S. top 100 singles to whet everyone's appetites, but soul records were not imported in commercial quantities due to import restrictions. J.J. did tell me to be careful when buying records from the U.S. by "James Barnes" as some were not by him, this because there were a couple of other "James Barnes" floating around at the time who also had released records in the U.S.A. I believe one of them may have actually been Jock Mitchell.

J.J. told me of his initial excitement when he was signed to Motown in 1967 and how after many years of not really making it big, he believed his chance had finally come. Contrary to common belief, J.J. did actually record tracks for Motown, but was disappointed they were never released. J.J. did write songs for other Motown artists, some were released including "Show Me The Way" by Martha and the Vandellas. A problem for J.J at Motown was Marvin Gaye, who was not too pleased that Edwin Starr and J.J. Barnes had both been given contracts with Motown, this when Ed Wingate sold Ric Tic/Golden World Records to Berry Gordy in 1967, the same year Berry also bought the Inferno label. J.J was disappointed to hear on the grapevine how Marvin Gaye had told Gordy that if J.J. did not go then he would, Marvin believed there wasn't room for them both. Obviously J.J. was disappointed, he had no intention of competing with anyone at Motown, let alone Marvin Gaye who he greatly admired. Once J.J. heard about the ultimatum given to Berry Gordy, he knew he was doomed.

357

Marvin was part of the Gordy family having married Berry's sister Anna. J.J knew the marriage was a turbulent one and Berry would not want to displease Marvin in any way, he realised Marvin would get the tracks which suited them both. The story goes Berry Gordy wanted to give J.J. a chance and told him if he sang in a way that was different to Marvin there may be a place for him as an artist with Motown, however if not he could only ever expect to be a writer. J.J. didn't want to change his style, took the hint and moved over to the Groovesville label after having spent just a year at Motown. The irony is J.J believed Marvin was a better singer than he was and also that their styles were not all that similar, but he knew there was no point in trying to compete with family, it was time to move on from Motown, or he would only ever be a writer and not the recording artist he wanted to be.

Motown was a family business, something which continued way into future generations and which saw Berry Gordy's daughter Hazel marry Jermaine Jackson of the Jackson 5. Like working in most family businesses. J.J. knew there was always going to be favouritism and so he moved on, a decision he would not regret. After moving on J.J. always retained a healthy respect for Motown and their artists, when asked who he thought was the best singer he had known his answer was without any hesitation was David Ruffin. J.J. explained how at Motown frequently when a new song was written and no one was really sure how to sing it, they would ask David, after which everyone just tried to sing it like he had. J.J. did say the best all round artist he ever knew was Stevie Wonder, an amazing talent who had it all, an amazing voice, creative songwriting ability, was an accomplished composer. Stevie could play many instruments, including the piano, synthesizer, drums, guitar, and harmonica and was always there to help anyone he could.

J.J. also said Daryl Banks had an amazing vocal range and a unique style of his own which he greatly admired. J.J.'s move from Motown to Groovesville turned out to be most opportune, it wasn't long after leaving he released his most successful single "Baby Please Come Back Home" which reached No. 9 on the U.S. Billboard R&B chart, and which would later become and remain massive on the U.K. 'Northern Soul' scene. J.J. had the last laugh on Berry Gordy with "Baby Please Come Back Home", he was actually working on it with the help of Stevie Wonder whilst still at Motown. When Stevie found out about the ultimatum given to J.J. by Berry Gordy and because of it he would be leaving Motown, he gave the song to J.J. Stevie took no credit for it and let J.J take it with him to Groovesville, this as sort of parting gift, something for which J.J. will always be grateful to Stevie. Somewhat ironically, J.J did finally get to see some of his records released by Motown on the UK Tamla Motown label in the early 1970's, including "Real Humdinger," which was produced by Al Kent and released on Tamla Motown mainly for the 'Northern Soul' scene in England where J.J. had become so popular, this despite the lack of success back home in the U.S. This release is a good one, it's really an E.P. single with "Please Let Me In" and "I Ain't Gonna Do It " on the flip side.

After recording a couple of records on the Casino Classics label in 1979 J.J. then worked with the UK Northern Soul legend Ian Levine in the 1980's and released several records on Ian's "Motor City" label, including a new version of his Revilot classic "Our Love Is In The Pocket" and also a version Frank Wilson's "Do I love you" on the Inferno label. In 2000 J.J. recorded "Talk Of The Grapevine " written by Ian Levine for the Achievement label. "Talk Of The Grapevine" is what some refer to as a tailor made 'Northern Soul' record, it's brilliant all the same. I used to play this record at 'Soul Biscuits' in Sydney when I was a resident DJ there and it always filled the dance floor. I was however to learn the hard way that J.J Barnes is perhaps one of the most 'bootlegged' artists out there and so I always remind record buyers to be careful when buying J.J. 's Northern Soul records as there are a lot of bootlegs about.

I would recommend any soul lover definitely give J.J. 's later releases a try, in particular "Talk Of The Grapevine", along with his unreleased Motown tracks published much later on the "Cellarful of Motown" CD compilation. J.J. keeps on keepin' on and performed live on stage in the U.S.A. to adoring 'Northern' Soul fans in late 2017 at the 'Detroit a Go' event. YouTube clips of J.J. performing live at "Motown a Go" in 2019 aged 76 can be found on the Internet, all showing what a great singer and performer he still is, as well as being a really nice guy too.

MAJOR LANCE

It was some 48 years ago when I first met Major Lance in Rafter's nightclub, which was located on Oxford Street, Manchester, where he performed in early 1973, not long after the famous night at the Torch in Stoke on Trent of December 1972, where the Major recorded the album "Major Lance Live at the Torch". I went to see the Major that night too, but didn't get in as the place was totally rammed by the time we arrived. The live album was released in 1973 on Contempo and I still have the actual one I bought way back then. I recall the Major was booked to return to the UK in the summer of 1973 and perform a series of concerts for the International Soul Club, but the tour was cancelled, I believe due to the Major's poor health at the time, so although I didn't get to see the Major perform at the Torch, I was luckier than those who didn't get to see him perform at all. Outside of having met performers at the Twisted Wheel, this was one of the first occasions I met and talked with an artist I admired so much and whose name was on a record I owned. It was a magical experience for a teenage soul lover.

At the time I thought this was the first occasion Major Lance had been to England, but he told me he had first visited the UK almost ten years earlier in 1964 and performed at the Twisted Wheel (this would have been the Brazennose Twisted Wheel and so before my time).

I had taken along one of my Major Lance 45's on the OKeh label on the night just in case I was able to meet the Major after the performance, but really never expecting to. The record was "You Don't Want Me No More", which became a big Ian Levine spin at the Blackpool Mecca. After his performance at Rafters the Major stayed on to talk with his fans and was delighted to sign my record, he was interested to know how, as the record had actually never been released in the U.K I had a copy. I told him I also had almost every single he had ever released on the OKeh label and also others on Dakar and Volt too and that my favourite record was one his newer releases "I Wanna Make Up Before We Break Up" and we discussed how this is a very different style to "You Don't Want Me No More."

Just like a lot of the American soul artists I would meet, the "Major" found it hard to understand why he was more popular in England than he was in his home country the U.S. We spoke about the OKeh record label and the Major told me his record "Monkey Time" virtually saved OKeh as a recording company when it became their first hit record in almost ten years. Of course thanks to the Major there were also many more on OKeh to follow. The Major signed my "You Don't Want Me No More" and at my request he signed the actual OKeh label, not the record sleeve. I still have this record today and it will go with me to my grave.

More than 30 years later I was still playing the very same record here in Australia, often at the 'Melbourne Soul Club' and 'Soul Biscuits'. I recall a member of the self-appointed 'Soul Police' in Perth WA coming up to check if the record was an original after I had played it on the Friday night of the 2003 Australian National in Perth. Inspecting the record this guy quickly realised it was the real thing, but on seeing the handwriting on the label he with great delight told me the record was 'severely devalued' because of the label writing. I told him I didn't think it was and in fact it was worth more because of it.

The self-appointed member of the Soul Police laughed and asked why. I explained the writing on the label was actually Major Lance's signature as he had personally signed the record for me in Manchester in 1973. The look on the face of the 'Soul Police DJ' who would have been about 8 years old in 1973 was priceless. Not surprisingly this DJ or none of the other Soul Police ever asked to inspect any of my records again. As already mentioned, I didn't get to see the Major perform at the Torch, because although we travelled from Manchester to Stoke-on-Trent to see him, we didn't get in, as we arrived too late. The place was packed and there were dozens outside who also did not get in. Although almost every soul fan over 60 years of age you meet today tells you they were at the Major Lance concert at the Torch, if it's true the place must have held 50,000 people, the reality is though they could not have squeezed more than 1,600 in there on that night.

The Major Lance concert at the 'Torch' was the first time Ian Levine got to DJ there, but although myself and the guys I went with didn't get to see Ian DJ, or watch Major Lance, we did listen to the Major and the somewhat ordinary band accompanying him, to do this we climbed onto the roof of the 'Torch' via the rear of the building. It used to be an old Cinema and we were above where 'The Major' and the band were performing. It's a good job the roof did not cave in under the weight of us, as we would have ruined the live recording made on the night. I believe you can hear us stamping our feet on the roof, well I guess that's just my wishful thinking. These were exciting times for a teenage soul fan in the UK. In 1980 living in Australia, I was shocked to hear the Major was serving a four year jail sentence in the USA after being busted for drugs, "Um Um Um." After getting out of jail the Major relaunched his career but in 1987 was struck down with a heart attack, he fortunately recovered. I got to meet the Major again on a visit to the USA in 1990, where in Atlanta, Georgia the Major told me he now had 10 kids. The "Major" didn't really recognise me though, he was almost totally blind having been struck down with glaucoma.

Full credit to the Major though, he was still out there giving it his best, thankfully he did not know that in just 4 years-time he would suffer another heart attack and die at just 55 years of age. RIP Major Lance.

JIMMY RUFFIN

I was lucky enough to meet Jimmy Ruffin before and after he performed at the Whitworth Street, Twisted Wheel in 1970, I think he performed there about four times that year. At the October 1970 gig I was fortunate enough to get his autograph on one of the flyers sent out to Twisted Wheel members, this was a good day as I recall Manchester City had earlier beaten Ipswich Town at Maine Road 2-0 and I had the program autographed after the game by both of the goal scorers, Colin Bell and Francis Lee. I still have the program from that day and the Twisted Wheel flyer too, which I had framed along with my Twisted Wheel membership cards from 1969/70 and 1970/71.

The frame also includes an original 45RPM Tamla Motown record "I've Passed This Way Before", which is a special record for me as it was one of the first records I ever bought in 1966 and was the last record I bought in England before emigrating to Australia when it was re-released in 1975. What a priceless souvenir this is, it holds so many memories, it hangs proudly next to the bar which houses my record decks, amplifier and record collection.

I had always thought Jimmy Lee Ruffin was younger Brother of Motown singer David Ruffin, but Jimmy told me he was actually born five years before David. I was shocked to hear this and then even more so when Jimmy told me it was he who had first been asked to join the Motown group the Temptations, but he refused so he could concentrate on his solo career.

It was only then his younger Brother David Ruffin was considered as a member of the Temptations. Somewhat expectedly Jimmy was always asked to sing his 1966 hit "What becomes of the broken hearted, it became a major part of his rendition in any performance. I was surprised to learn the song was not actually written for him, it was actually written by William Weatherspoon, Paul Riser and James Dean for the Spinners (the Detroit Spinners), but Jimmy heard it and knew he had to get it for himself, which he did. The record was produced by Weatherspoon and Mickey Stevenson.

The backing band on the record is the Funk Brothers and it was originally recorded for the Motown "SOUL" label, but had many releases including on the Tamla Motown UK, Australian and New Zealand labels. The rest is history, the record was a hit all over the World, the biggest of Jimmy's career reaching number 7 on the Billboard Hot 100 and number 6 on the Billboard R&B charts. It went around a second time too, being re-released in the mid 1970's introducing Jimmy to a whole new and younger audience at around the time Jimmy's brilliant "Tell me what you want" 45 RPM single was released in 1974 on the Polydor and Chess labels, Motown then capitalised on Jimmy's UK popularity re-releasing "I've passed this way before on a Tamla Motown single. I was surprised to learn what a big influence Jimmy had been at Motown, perhaps because a lot of limelight went onto his younger Brother David Ruffin as a member of the massively successful Motown group the Temptations. It was Jimmy who actually first recorded the Eddie Holland and Norman Whitfield composure "Beauty Is Only Skin Deep" on a single, although the Temptations made it famous in 1966, it was actually first recorded as an album track by the Miracles in April 1964 with Smokey Robinson as lead, it was also recorded by Jimmy Ruffin in 1966 but not released, the Temptations released their version in August 1966.

Jimmy's version was eventually released by Motown, in 1979 on a somewhat weird Motown compilation LP released of all places in Venezuela, it was called "Motown Superstars Sing Motown Superstars", which included amongst other things first time releases of "Reach Out I'll Be There", not by the Four Tops but Thelma Houston, "The Tracks Of My Tears" not by Smokey Robinson but by Martha Reeves and the Vandellas, "For Once In My Life" not by Stevie Wonder but Diana Ross and "Love Hangover" not by Diana Ross but Junior Walker and the All Stars. The album was also released again in 1983 on UK Tamla Motown and US Motown labels. Jimmy moved to England in the early 1980s where he was far more popular than he ever was in the US and later recorded for Ian Levine's Motorcity label, including the single "Wake Me Up When It's Over" in 1988 on the Mare label, a track written by Levine and Trench. Ian has remixed this track several times and recently released it as a limited edition 45 RPM single on the Detroit City label, which as a bonus has the excellent "One In A Million" on the flip. This single is a marvelous tribute to Jimmy Ruffin and the tracks are possibly some of the last he ever recorded. RIP Jimmy Ruffin who passed away at the age of 78 in 2014.

ARCHIE BELL AND THE DRELLS

Every Soul lover knows Archie Bell and the Drells, usually for "Here I Go Again" or "My Balloons Going Up", yet in the U.S.A. Archie is best known for his 1968 No 1 hit record "Tighten Up", which has a massive following even today and somewhat re-markably even has its own dance. In fact, in the U.S.A. Archie is actually known as "Mr. Tighten Up". The amazing Gamble and Huff production "Here I Go Again" was first released on the U.S. red and black Atlantic label in 1969, and wasn't a hit in the U.S.A., most likely because it was released as the B side of "A World Without Music".

For most Soulies' it's the 1972 UK Atlantic re-release on the blue and orange label that is most remembered. It was a chart hit in the UK and so is perhaps more of a youth club track than 'Northern Soul', but is a dance floor filler wherever it's played today, and still is one of my favourite all time tracks. What a thrill to meet Archie in the U.S.A. at the 2006 'Soul Trip USA' reunion in New Jersey. Archie Bell and the Drells performed live on stage and were excellent.

I was fortunate enough to spend time chatting with Archie after the performance and then later during the event, I told him my favourite record of his was "Here I Go Again", Archie signed page 37 of my Kev Roberts "Northern Soul Top 500" book and also gave me a picture of himself back in the day, which he made special by writing "To Steve from Archie Bell, here I go again" on it, a nice touch from the great man. Archie told me he was amazed how British 'soulies' picked up "Here I Go Again" when he thought it had been a flop. Archie told me how he first started singing when just 10 years of age and how he was in-fluenced by Jackie Wilson and Sam Cooke. Archie's career was looking promising but it took a backward step when he was drafted into the U.S. Army and sent to Vietnam in 1967. He came home on leave in December and rushed to the studio and added some vocals to an instrumental made by the TSU Tor-nadoes which became "Tighten Up". The record was a huge U.S. hit in 1968 and "Mr. Tighten Up" was born.

Archie told me that because he was serving in the Army in 1968 some of the tracks on the "Tighten Up" Album were credited to, but not actually performed by him. Archie advised he believes the vocals on "1000 Wonders" may have actually been sung by a James Taylor (not the horse with no name James Taylor) and when you listen to the track it is quite apparent it's not actually Archie singing. Archie advised he thinks "You're Mine," also credited to him, was in fact most likely by the TSU Tornadoes vocalist Cal Thomas, Archie was not in the recording studio at that time, he was in the army, so can't be sure who it was.

In 1969 Archie was discharged from the Army and from then sang on everything attributed to him, including "There's Gonna Be A Showdown " and the tracks on the album of the same name, this at the same time Archie's brother, Lee, joined the Drells. After this success there was a lean spell. Archie and the Drells needed to eat, so they went 'disco' in 1976 and hit the jackpot recording the massive disco hit "The Soul City Walk". Archie and the Drells went their own separate ways in 1979 but got back together in 1987 recording the Ian Levine production "Look Back Over Your Shoulder" released in the same year on Ian Levine's Nightmare label and in 1988 on the Achievement label, and it was also released once again in 1999. It's a 'Northern Soul tailor-made' of which the intro always reminds me of the O'Jays "I Dig Your Act" and was a record which helped Archie make a few dollars when needed. This year Archie will turn 77 years young, he still enjoys performing, mainly country and western music.

ARCHIE BELL
"Mr. Tighten Up Himself"

CREATION PRODUCTIONS
P.O. BOX 12614 WINSTON-SALEM, NC 27117
(336) 788-3818

C.P. PRODUCTIONS
P.O. BOX 24334 HOUSTON, TEXAS 77229
Graves.bell944@aol.com
(713) 455-3844 (281) 458-5231

GRAHAM ENTERPRISES
233 CHAPEL AVE. NASHVILLE, TN 37206
PHONE/FAX: (615) 227-8491

Archie Bell signed promo © Steve Bardsley

PAUL LEWIS

It was amazing to meet legendary soul artists like Edwin Starr, J.J. Barnes, Archie Bell and Major Lance, Ray Charles, Wilson Pickett etc, also meeting lesser known artists has been just as enjoyable, in particular those artists you find you have a connection to the past with. I met Paul Lewis at one of Kev Robert's 'Soultrip USA' reunions in Orlando USA in 2011. Paul who was there with Timmy Thomas. On hearing I was from Manchester Paul told me he played saxophone with a band in a Manchester club way back in 1975, the band was KC and the Sunshine Band.

I told Paul I was actually there at that performance and it was at the Watersplash Club in Salford. Paul was amazed, as he had never before met anyone in the U.S. who had actually seen KC and the Sunshine Band perform at the 'Watersplash Club' in Salford, he was delighted to finally meet someone who had. It was almost unbelievable how KC and the Sunshine Band came from Miami, Florida U.S.A to the 'Watersplash Club' in Salford. The 'Watersplash' is a rarely mentioned and little known Manchester club, it played a lot of black music, hosted live acts and a lot of black kids lived in the area and so went there. It was a real club rather than a 'glitzy' disco. KC and the Sunshine Band were not really yet recognised as a 'disco' band in 1975, that would come later, in fact they were not KC and the Sunshine Band then, their name was KC and the Sunshine Junkanoo Band, an inter-racial R&B group from Miami, Florida, founded by Harry Wayne Casey (hence KC). In 1975 the band was then known for just three songs, "Blow Your Whistle" (1973), "Sound Your Funky Horn" (1974) and "Queen Of Clubs" (1974), none of which could really be referred to as the "disco." But, KC and the Sunshine Band would soon become famous, sell 100 million records worldwide and become the first group to have four number one chart topping records in a single year (1975) since the Beatles.

I mentioned to Paul the KC and the Sunshine Band gig was my *last* live concert in England before I emigrated to Australia. Paul told me that was pretty amazing as it was his *first* concert at which he had ever performed outside of the U.S. Paul explained he was then only 16 years of age, it was the first time he had been out of the U.S.A. and he was as nervous as hell about it. Therefore, Paul's first concert in England was coincidentally my last there. It was really great chatting to Paul and he told me some things I never knew and would never have guessed. For example; how it was George McCrae and not Harry Wayne Casey that sang the shrieking high vocals on the 1974 KC and the Sunshine Band recording "Queen Of Clubs" for which George has never been credited.

Paul is a now a music executive, still performs as a singer and is the founder of OSG (the Old Skool Gang) a group which performs hits of Smokey Robinson and the Miracles, the Temptations, The O'Jays, Harold Melvin and the Blue Notes, Al Green and more. It's a small and very connected world when it comes to soul music and it was great chatting to Paul about his trip to Manchester and his performance with KC and the Sunshine Band at the 'Watersplash Club' in Salford, way back in 1975, it's something I will always remember very fondly.

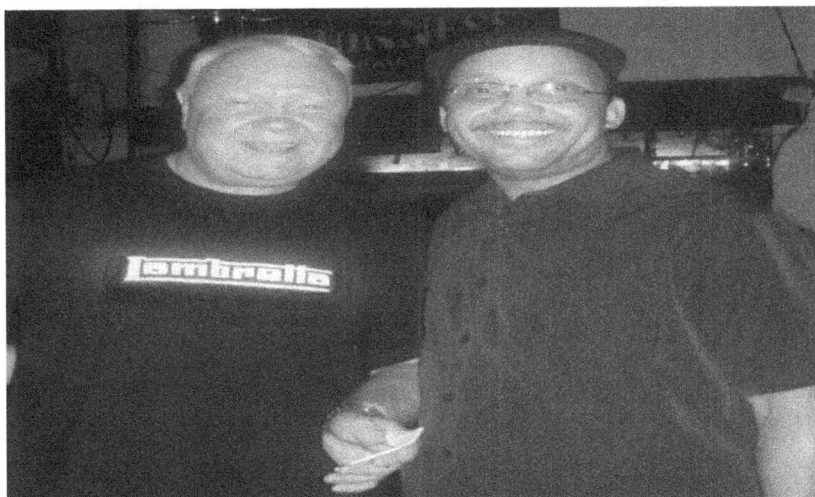

Steve Bardsley and Paul Lewis © Steve Bardsley

TIMMY THOMAS

Timmy Thomas might not be what you would called a Northern Soul artist, he is though without doubt one of the greatest and most talented soul artists, performer, musician, keyboard player, producer and songwriter ever known, most famous of course for his hit and ever enduring song "Why Can't We Live Together" which was recorded in 1972. I met Timmy at Churchill's nightclub in Miami Florida U.S.A at one of the Kev Roberts Northern Soul reunions. The gig at Churchill's had been arranged by Jan Lisewski, a good friend of Timmy's and the editor of Book 1 in the "Our Soul Music Journeys" series of books.

Steve Bardsley and Timmy Thomas © Steve Bardsley

Jan Lisewski unfortunately passed away shortly after editing and creating much of the artwork for Book 1 in this series, some of which he and I together worked on, he will be greatly missed. R.I.P Jan. As a good friend of mine Jan introduced me to Timmy Thomas in Miami and so I was able to spend a little more time chatting to him than most would. I asked Timmy to sign a copy of the flyer for Soultrip 2011, which I was using to collect the autographs of all the artists I had met there. Timmy signed it with pleasure. Then to my surprise Timmy pulled out of his bag an A4 sized promotional photograph of himself, signed it and gave it to me as a gift, it is signed *"To my friend and Soul Brother Steve, let the World live together, Timmy Thomas"*. It's something I will always Treasure.

I mentioned to Timmy I had the record "What's Bothering Me", released in 1970 on the Climax label and asked if it was one of his. Timmy was surprised, saying yes it was by him and I was the only person he ever met who had it. I explained it was quite popular on the Northern Scene and sells for about £40, he was pleased to hear this, as he wasn't aware of its popularity. Timmy laughed saying he would take a look around his studio for any of the records that didn't sell. Timmy explained if you listen to the words on the song it's actually a precursor to "Why Can't We Live Together", as although the sound is different, the message is similar. I asked Timmy what he was doing nowadays and he said he was still heavily involved in the music industry, as a writer, producer and musician and he was also a University Lecturer nowadays, lecturing as one might have guessed, in music. It really was a privilege to meet such a great man, after chatting with him I soon realised he has always believed in the "Why Can't We Live Together" mantra, it is far more than just a song to him, he really would like to see people of all races live together in harmony. It's hard to believe Timmy wrote, produced, sang and played the Lowrey organ on "Why Can't We Live Together" almost 50 years ago, this when not many were prepared to listen. Yet the song still sounds great today, ironically it's perhaps more appropriate today than it ever was.

TERRIBLE TOM

I was delighted to meet Terrible Tom in Las Vegas at Kev Robert's 'Soultrip USA' in 2018, this 44 years after first hearing his record "We Were Made For Each Other" recorded on the Maverick label and played at the 'Mecca'. At the Soultrip I mistakenly attempted to enter the private area reserved for performers at the rear of the Tropicana Hotel function room, not realising it was for VIP's only.

Terrible Tom and Steve Bardsley © Steve Bardsley

A lady stopped me on the way in to the VIP area explaining I couldn't go in there. I apologised and explained I had come all the way from Australia and just wanted to meet Terrible Tom as one of his records had been a personal favourite of mine for over forty years. The lady said she would go see Terrible Tom (Tom Bowden) and ask if he might agree to meet me and if he did I could come into the VIP area. A few minutes later she came back and said "follow me, Tom would be delighted to meet you". I was fortunate enough to have the opportunity to talk with Tom privately for about half an hour, which turned out to be far more fascinating than I ever expected.

Tom was of course delighted that I liked his record and asked me exactly what I liked about "We Were Made For Each Other" as it wasn't a hit when released. Tom explained he is one of the soul artists who never realised his record was popular on the UK Northern Soul scene and was only made aware of this by Kev Roberts, this many years later.

Tom told me his real name is Tom Bowden and he began singing when just 9 years of age, when he also supported his family shining shoes on the Street. Tom said with a big smile he once received a big tip after shining the shoes of the President of the United States of America (Harry Truman). Tom progressed from being a child street performer to working with many all-time great soul artists, including Aretha Franklin, Ray Charles, B.B. King, Bobby Blue Bland, Count Bassie, Etta James, Shorty Long, the Temptations, the Four Tops, Marvin Gaye, Wilson Pickett, Jackie Wilson, Sam & Dave, to name just a few. Tom even stood in for Dave Prater (of Sam and Dave fame), it was therefore Sam & Tom on stage. Tom was once a fearsome boxer, the nickname "Terrible Tom" not coming through from his time fighting in the boxing ring, but out on the streets of California. As Tom was still a very handy boxer he became the bodyguard and driver for some famous celebrities including Stevie Wonder. Tom still carries the scars from being shot on the streets and stabbed in a race riot when he was in prison.

Tom told me he has in his time been a bit of a rascal, mentioning a few things I won't repeat here. Tom's on the right track now and although almost 80 years old, is doing good for others. Tom is a pillar of the community, he started a program to help recently released prisoners transition back to normal life, something he had difficulty with and so wants to help make sure others don't end up in the same difficult situation. Tom explained he still performs today, mainly Blues music which he loves. Tom is still overwhelmed regarding the popularity of his record and how it was a favourite on the U.K. 'Northern Soul' scene.

I explained this was because it was played by a UK DJ named Ian Levine. Records like "We Were Made For Each Other" illustrate the amazing contribution Ian made to the scene, without him playing it, the record would have been lost to the world. It was a privilege to meet Tom and so kind of him to spare his time, this after it looked like I had tried to gate crash the VIP room at the Tropicana Hotel in Las Vegas.

THE DEL-LARKS

Signed Del-Larks promo © Steve Bardsley

In 2006 I was lucky enough to meet Sam Campbell and Ron Taylor, members of the original Del-Larks when they performed for 400 visiting UK Northern Soul Fans what was going to be for the very last time, their monster Northern Soul song "Job Opening (Part 1)" in East Brunswick, New Jersey USA.

I was fortunate enough to be there and witness the amazing performance and later was able to chat with Sammy Campbell who told me he actually wrote "Job Opening". Sammy was kind enough to sign a few things for me and spare his time to talk about his soul career, which incredibly began when he attended Lovelace Watkins church in the 1950's and after which the Del-Larks were formed. Ron told me the Del-Larks were not much more than a cover band until they entered a New Jersey talent show in 1957.

The talent competition was tough with performers including the Nonchalants, the Admirations and the Parliaments. The Del-Larks however won the competition, after which they were approached by an unknown little old Hungarian lady who was well connected in the music industry, she took them to New York to meet Ahmet Ertegun and Jerry Wexler of Atlantic Records, where they did an impromptu audition and got their big break being asked to cut a record for Atlantic. Things didn't work out as planned though, the well- connected little old lady wanted a 50/50 split of all payments made to the group, which understandably they didn't agree with. Suddenly their record was transferred to Atlantic's subsidiary label ``East West" and there was no further mention of a recording contract. The relationship with Atlantic was over almost as quickly as it had begun and the big break for the Del-Larks was gone. They were back on the road performing.

I asked Ron how the Del-Larks Northern Soul classic on the Queen City label came about, he explained he and Sammy were doing it tough, feeling down and hoping for a job opening, they wrote a song about the way they were feeling. The record was released on the Queen City label, but they only had enough money to press 500 records, so like a lot of records popular on the Northern Soul scene, this one wasn't widely released, so didn't get much exposure and didn't make it.

The Del-Larks joined up with a band called "New Testament" and recorded for the Scepter label with not much success, they worked hard performing around New York City and Brooklyn and were booked to tour Jamaica but it fell through, as did other planned tours, after a couple years the group disbanded.

In April of 2006 Sam and Ron reunited once again as the Del-Larks to perform "Job Opening" for Kev Robert's Soul Trip USA, this was going to be the very last time the song was performed. The great news is after this successful SoulTrip performance in front of UK Northern Soul fans, the Del-Larks decided to get back together again and so thanks to Northern Soul they are still performing today, including "Job Opening!

DEAN COURTNEY

In 2018 I again travelled to the USA, this time for the Soul Trip reunion in Las Vegas where I caught up with many old friends, including Kev and Sam Roberts and my friend of over 50 years Barry Pearson.

As young teenagers living in Droylsden, Manchester, Barry and I used to listen to records together in Barry's house, mainly the Temptations, Motown and Northern Soul. We both loved Dean Courtney and so it was amazing for us to both meet him all these years later now we are both in our 60's. Who would have believed our passion and love of soul music would have lasted so long. Dean's "I'll Always Need You" on the RCA Victor label from 1966 is of course legendary Northern Soul stuff, written by Leon Huff and Len Barry, yes the Len Barry of 1-2-3 fame (his real name is Leonard Warren Borisoff) and he recorded "I'll Always Love You" first in 1966 for his album "It's that time of year".

Dean Courtney signed promo © Steve Bardsley

It's the Dean Courtney version of "I'll Always Need You" though which Northern Soul fans remember, this as they race to the dance floor on hearing the storming intro and the lyrics *"Castle in the sand is built by hand, don't need no bricks to make it stand"*. Well if you can't dance to this one you must be dead already. I always used to play Dean's slower "You just can't walk away" on the MGM label as the ender at Soul Biscuits at the Bar Cleveland in Sydney, which as it came to an end was often then met with the chants "one more, one more" and it was easy to know which "one more" they wanted. What an absolute pleasure it was to meet Dean personally in Las Vegas, a nicer and more modest man it would be hard to meet. Dean was of course disappointed he didn't have much success with RCA and felt they didn't promote him or his records well enough and that's why he moved over to MGM.

I was surprised when he told me the females singing "I'll Always Need You" with him on the record are Cissy Houston and Dee Dee Warwick. Dean was kind enough to sign a few things for me at the Soul Trip, including a T Shirt with his image on it, which he actually signed *"Best wishes to Johnny"*, as I had it signed for the author of this book Johnny Warren, this so as to cheer him up a little, as he was supposed to come with us to Las Vegas for the Soul Trip, but then couldn't make it due to some quite serious ill health issues at the time, which he fortunately has now overcome.

FREDDIE CHAVEZ

Every Northern Soul fan knows the Freddie Chavez Northern Soul classic song "They'll' Never Know Why" on the Look label, which was actually the B side of "Baby I'm Sorry". I met Freddie in Las Vegas where he performed "They'll Never Know Why", Freddie's voice is still as good today as it ever was, he really is a great performer. Freddie is such a nice guy and he took the time to talk with me and told me some amazing things.

Steve Bardsley and Freddie Chavez © Steve Bardsley

Freddie performed at concerts with the Platters, Mitch Ryder & the Detroit Wheels, he is from Albuquerque, New Mexico and founded "Thee Chekkers", in which he sang & played keyboard, the band was produced by John Wagner of Delta Records, who owned one of the best recording studios in town and is where they recorded "Please Don't Go / Lack of Love" on Look 5007. Freddie told me although "They'll' Never Know Why" had plenty of airplay on local radio stations around Nashville, it didn't sell when first released in 1968.

The record was released again on the Look label in 1977 due to its popularity on the UK Northern Soul scene, but the release wasn't an official one. It was released again in 2013 on the Soul 7 label, a subsidiary of Jazzman records and there have been a couple of other "unofficial" releases on "Look" alike labels. A genuine original of this Nashville beauty on either the white DJ or light blue Look 5010 label can sell for over £1,000 or more, so potential purchasers need to be wary of what they might be actually buying, originals rarely come up. Freddie formed the Freddie Chavez Foundation in 1974, a 6 piece band which is still active today, playing soul, pop and Spanish music.

Freddie told me about a little known CD of his which features songs he wrote and recorded in the late 60's through to the mid 70's, most of which he had forgotten about as they were never released (other than "Lack Of Love" and "They'll Never Know Why") both which he had to re-record for the CD due to record label conflicts. All the other 8 tracks on the CD are original re-cordings from the 70's that were shelved until recently when their Producer John Wagner reminded Freddie about the songs. He and Freddie then decided to polish up the tracks and release them on this CD, which is called "Time And Time Again". You can listen to clips from the CD and hear more about the amazing Freddie Chavez story in the YouTube video which can be found at the following link:

https://www.newmexicosound.com/product/time-and-time-again-fredie-chavez/4

LOU RAGLAND

As already said, I went to Las Vegas for the 2018 Soul Trip and this is where I met Northern Soul legend Lou Ragland. It was such a shock when I heard Lou had passed away less than 2 years after we had been chatting in Vegas.

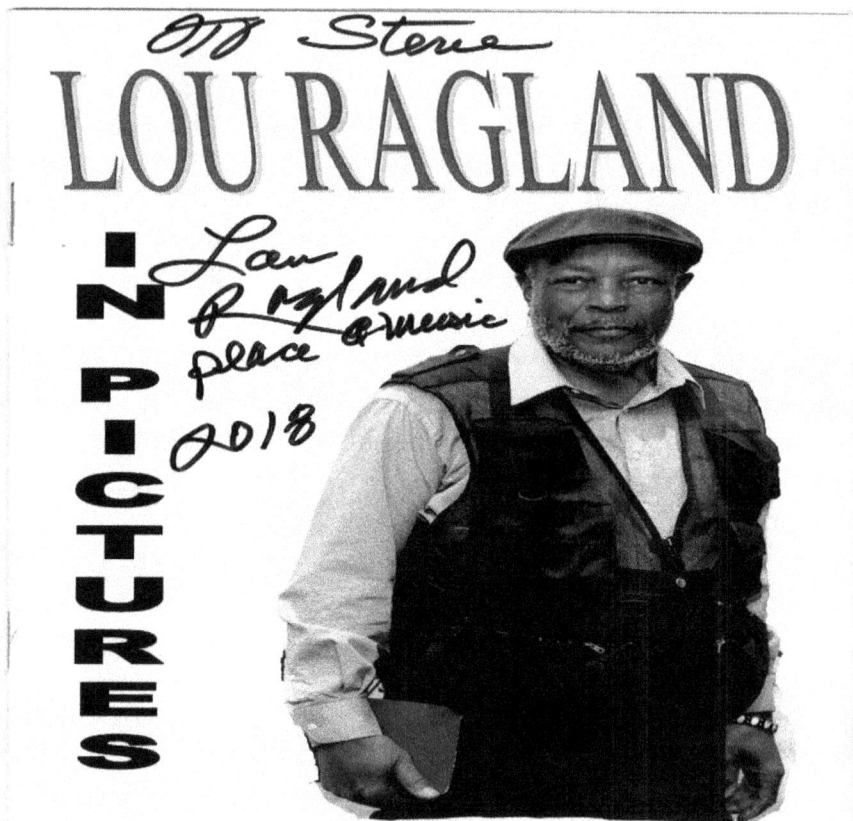

Lou Ragland Signed promo © Steve Bardsley

Lou released the Northern Soul classic and one of my favourite all-time records "I Travel Alone" in 1967 on Amy records. I found Lou to be a very modest man, he did tell me how he was not only a singer, but also a writer, studio engineer, record producer and played the Saxophone, the Tuba the Clarinet and Keyboard and of course he had a great voice.

Lou was born in Cleveland, Ohio and during his career sang with the Dominoes and the Ink Spots. Lou fell in love with Doo Wop after first hearing Frankie Lymon and the Teenagers when he was just 13 years old, after which he formed his own high school band "The Monclairs". This information intrigued me, until Lou adviood tho band was definitely not the Montclairs, we all know as being famous for the Northern Soul classic "Hung Up On Your Love. Lou would turn professional as a backing singer for the soul singer Kim Tolliver, who at the time was an extremely popular performer in Cleveland.

In 1963 Lou formed the band "Lou Ragland & the Bandmasters" releasing "Never Let Me Go". I was surprised to find Lou was a close friend of Edwin Starr and it was Edwin (RIP) who introduced Lou to Bell Records, their subsidiary label Amy releasing Lou's Northern classic "I Travel Alone" in 1967; which at the time did very little in the USA, just like so many other Northern soul classics.

 Lou recorded with the band Volcanic Eruption releasing "I've Got Something Going For Me" on the Way Out label in 1970 (re-released in 2006) and then formed a band called Hot Chocolate. I was again intrigued until Lou advised this wasn't the Hot Chocolate famous for "You Sexy Thing" and "Everyone's A Winner" with Errol Brown upfront. Lou became Vice President of the Cleveland record label, Saru Records Inc, a label recording some tracks which would later be picked up by the Northern Soul scene, including "Just To Be With You" by Bobby Dukes (later released on Calla). He would later be involved with the "Great Lakes" and "Casino" record labels.

When Edwin Starr toured the UK with the "Ric Tic Revue," in the 1980's he asked his old friend Lou to come over to England and be part of the tour and Lou took up the invite. Lou told me this was the first time he had ever left the USA and he really enjoyed his time in the UK and was surprised how he and his record "I Travel Alone" were so much appreciated in the UK on the Northern Soul scene and this is why he always looks forward to meeting and performing for Northern soul fans who visit the USA. RIP Lou Ragland, another who has joined the all too many artists up there in Soul Heaven.

DEAN PARRISH

I was saddened to hear Dean Parrish passed away aged 78 in June 2021 (RIP). I got to know Dean quite well, meeting him several times and he was kind enough to record sound bites for the intro and the ender to the weekly Soul radio program "The Soul Scene" which I co-produced and presented in 2008 for Radio 3RPP here in Melbourne, Australia. Dean not only recorded the messages, but he paid the postage to send the CD's from the USA to Melbourne, Australia. I had a great deal of difficulty convincing the management of Radio 3RPP to allow me to use Dean's messages at the beginning and the end of the radio show, as they included parts of his Northern Soul classic from 1967, "I'm On My Way". We wanted to use the sound bites with Dean's voice as the ender for the radio show with him saying *"Hi this is Dean Parrish here, for another week that's the end of the Soul Scene, from Brian and Steve the Heart and Soul team, it's time for them to be on their way"* this was immediately followed by his record "I'm On My Way" to end the radio show.

Community Radio Stations operate differently than public broadcasting stations (PBS). Whereas a PBS is usually funded by subscribers to individual radio programs, a Community Radio station such as "3RPP" is commercially funded, mainly by advertisers. This means they have to do everything just right, the radio station with the help of the radio program Presenters have to find businesses willing to pay to advertise during a radio program. If a Community Radio program is unable to find and/or keep advertisers it doesn't last long. Community Radio Stations are also understandably want to ensure copyright is not breached, their radio program Presenters are responsible for ensuring copyright is not beached and for playing sponsors advertisements at precise times within their programs, this so the advertisers can tune or check the tapes and ensure the advertisements they paid for are actually delivered 'on air' and at the specified times.

If Community Radio Station DJ's don't play the advertisements at precisely the right time, they risk losing that advertiser and the funding that goes with it. If a Presenter breaches any copyright laws the show is terminated. This means there is a lot at stake producing and presenting a Community Radio program, which gains partial funding from advertisements, mistakes are just not tolerated to the extent they might be on a PBS. There were a few mistakes in my first show, but I soon got the hang of presenting live radio and was able to deliver a program which attracted advertising income and make it viable for "3RPP," and so was given a regular weekly 2 hour program.

I came up with the idea of having Dean Parrish do the intro and ender for the radio show and asked Dean to make the sound bites. The station management were concerned about copyright, wanting assurance the sound bites had been recorded by Dean and I had permission to use them. I explained the sound bites were the permission, or why would Dean have recorded them, included the name of the radio show and the presenters and sent them from New York to Australia? This was still not enough for the radio station management and before the sound bites could be used they insisted I obtain a letter from Dean confirming I had permission to use them. Once again Dean kindly obliged, he sent the required letter by Airmail, when it arrived the radio station management advised I could still not use the sound bites. When I asked why, they advised because the letter is not signed by Dean Parrish, but by some guy named Phil Anastasi. I explained this is Dean's real name and his recording name is Dean Parrish. This was not good enough and I again had to contact Dean and ask for another letter, this time one signed with the signature "Dean Parrish".

Dean again obliged by sending another letter. After another couple of weeks waiting and presenting the second letter to the radio station management I received their stamp of approval. I was then able to use the sound bites at the beginning and end of the Soul Scene radio show. I still have the letters and the CD with the sound bites which Dean sent over in 2008 and treasure them greatly.

Dean was not only a great artist but also a very nice guy. His Northern Soul classic from 1967 on the Laurie label "I'm on my way" was one of the "three before eight" played at Wigan Casino, truly legendary Northern Soul stuff, of course it was not his only record popular on the Northern Soul scene, there were others including "Determination", "Tell Her", "Skate" and "Bricks, Broken Bottles And Sticks". Dean has appeared alongside Mitch Ryder and the Detroit Wheels, the Capitols and although Dean never recorded for Motown but mainly with Laurie, Musicor, Boom and ABC, he did perform as part of the Motown Revue.

Not long after recording "I'm On My Way" Dean decided to start acting instead of singing and reverted back to his original name Philip Anastasi, appearing in minor TV roles and movies. Dean was a guitar player as well as a singer and in 1972 returned to music playing guitar as a session musician for Jimmy Hendrix. Like many American artists on the Northern Soul scene, Dean was never aware any of his records gained popularity in the UK, this until 30 years later when Russ Winstanley, one of the original Wigan Casino DJs asked him to perform in the UK. Phil Anastasi again became Dean Parrish.

RIP Dean Parish you made a massive difference and for this you will always be remembered fondly.

WELDON McDOUGAL III

I first met Weldon when I arrived at the Hilton Newark Hotel in New Jersey in 2006, the Hotel was certainly not a Hilton, but it was conveniently located about an hour's bus ride from New York City. Weldon was at the reception desk with Kev Robert's, Kev handed over our wristbands and introduced me to Weldon, who I must confess I had never heard of, but will now never forget. Weldon may not be well known as a soul artist, but he is a very accomplished singer, a prolific songwriter and an amazing record producer. Weldon could talk the leg off a chair and is willing to spend any amount of time reminiscing about his past and his achievements, which I might add were many. Weldon was the founder of many soul Groups, including the Larks, the Victors and he is also one of the best story tellers and leg pullers you could ever hope to meet.

In New Jersey with Weldon McDougal III © Steve Bardsley

Weldon assisted many black artists to gain recognition in both soul and pop music, he played a major role helping to create the "Philly Sound", he worked alongside Gamble and Huff, Bunny Sigler. Weldon once worked for Motown as a promotions man and was a founder member and co-owner of the Harthon record label, Dynodynamic Productions and the co-producer of Larry Clinton's Northern Soul classic on the Dynamo label "She's Wanted". Later that week Weldon would sign the sleeve of my copy of "She's Wanted" at the Clef Club in Philadelphia, where we got to meet him again and also watch some great live acts perform, including the Tymes and an impromptu, totally unexpected and absolutely marvellous Acapella version of "Me And Mrs Jones" by Billy Paul, who just happened to be at the Clef Club at the time. On seeing hundreds of British soul fans pouring into the club Billy asked if he could perform for us, he did Acapella because he didn't have any backing musicians or tapes with him, it was however a truly amazing, moving and unforgettable performance.

**Clinton, Larry
She's wanted

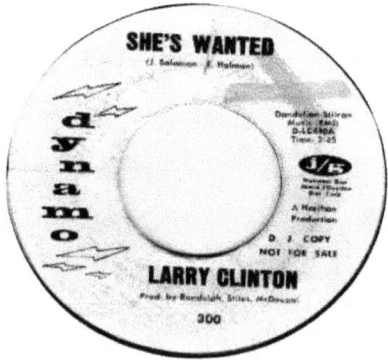

Larry Clinton record signed by Weldon McDougal © Steve Bardsley

The Clef Club is famous in Philadelphia and is over the road from the Philadelphia International studios where many great soul records have been recorded. We arrived at the Clef Club in one of, three coach loads of British Soul fans, who had come to see the live performances arranged by Kev Roberts. I am not sure what happened but they were not expecting so many of us. The bar man told me "we were expecting a few British soul fans today", he also advised they would not have enough food or drink for the hundreds that had arrived. I quickly ordered four beers and two Hoagies (long bread roll type sandwiches) for Elizabeth and I. Billy Paul was at the bar getting himself a Hoagie and was quite surprised watching all the English soul fans pour into the club. There were not enough seats and some of the soul fans started to complain, some even left the Club to tour Philadelphia, oh boy did they miss out! Kev Roberts quickly arranged for more chairs to be put on the dance floor in front of the stage, this meant we very luckily ended up with one of the best seats in the house on the second row of the dance floor and just inches away from the performers.

It really was an amazing afternoon and one of the highlights of the 2006 Soul Trip. Anyway, back to Weldon McDougal, who was also staying at the Hilton Newark Hotel and so would be seen around the place quite a lot, he was always getting up to mischief. If you were at the bar with Weldon he would ask what you wanted to drink, he would then order for you and one for himself and then disappear leaving you to pay the bill. I think he must have got everyone at least once! You also never wanted to let Weldon know your Hotel room number, if you did then expect him to have booked a few Hoagies or drinks for himself using it, he was a real rascal but a hell of a nice guy. Weldon passed away in late 2010 leaving a remarkable legacy to the world of Soul. It was a privilege to meet and know such a great man. RIP Weldon.

JAY PROCTOR

Jay Proctor was lead singer of Jay and the Techniques, famous for "Apple Peaches Pumpkin Pie " (1966). This was the song I heard entering Rowntrees Sounds in Manchester for the first time in the early 1970's. Jay told me he didn't like the song, it wasn't soulful enough. The Techniques were only offered the song after producer Jerry Ross offered it to Bobby Hebb who turned it down. Jay said although the Techniques received the credits for "Apples Peaches Pumpkin Pie " they were not in the studio when it was made. Jerry Ross didn't think they were good enough! Session musicians and vocalists were used instead, including Ashford & Simpson and Melba Moore. Jay and the Techniques are mainly remembered for "Apples Peaches Pumpkin Pie" but had other songs including "Keep The Ball Rollin" and "Baby Make Your Own Sweet Music."

Barry Pearson & Steve Bardsley with Jay Proctor © Steve Bardsley

Jay explained in the 1960's groups like his were actually a rarity because they were multi-racial, that is having both black and white members, with Jay and George Lloyd being the two black members of the Group. The music genre of Jay and the Techniques was somewhat unusual, in that it was neither full on soul or pop music, perhaps hence why Jay and Bobby Hebb both weren't keen on "Apples peaches Pumpkin Pie" when they first heard it. The song is not an out and out Northern Soul stomper either, perhaps more of a youth club track, yet is a floor filler on the Northern Soul scene. The record is also unusual, in that unlike most Northern Soul records it was actually a big hit when first released as Jay and the Techniques debut song in 1967, it won a gold disc and reached No 6 on the American Billboard Hot 100 chart, "Keep the Ball Rollin" also won a gold disc.

When in New Jersey, Jay Proctor kindly gave me and signed a re-release 45 RPM of "Apples, Peaches, Pumpkin Pie " on the Smash label and which has "Keep The Ball Rollin" on the flip side. Most Northern Soul fans will also know that Jay and the Techniques released "Baby Make Your Own Sweet Music" on the Smash label in 1968, do they know though it is a cover of the original recording by Johnny Johnston and the Bandwagon recorded on the Epic label earlier in the same year?

Jay told me that the song "Apples Peaches Pumpkin Pie" was both the best and the worst thing in his musical career, although a big hot and money maker, he believes it was responsible for the Band being offered bubble gum soul type songs to record, this rather than real soul records and so it in effect deprived him of the opportunity to record the more soulful type of records he always preferred.

JACKIE MOORE

Meeting Jackie Moore in Las Vegas has to be one of the greatest privileges I have ever had. Jackie's record "Precious" sold over a million copies and won a gold disc in 1970, she also had a hit in 1973 with "Sweet Charlie Babe" on the Atlantic label which was written by Bunny Sigler. It was through her 1973 Northern Soul classic on Atlantic "Both ends against the middle" and the 1979 Disco monster "This Time Baby" on Columbia which helped make her such an idol of mine.

Steve Bardsley and Jackie Moore © Steve Bardsley

Jackie told me amazing things in Vegas, like how in 1975 David Crawford wrote the disco classic "Young Hearts Run Free" for her, but then suddenly without explanation after visiting Candi Staton gave the record to Candi. Jackie said she had ideas of why this happened, but with a glint in her eye and a cheeky grin said she best not go into it.

"Young Hearts Run Free" became a massive disco hit, Jackie obviously disappointed she didn't get to record it, it should have been hers. Jackie however had no hard feelings or regrets, she knew her time would come, kept working hard and this paid off big time, she became a disco diva after recording her disco version of the 1978 record by the O'Jays "This Time Baby".

Jackie's version of "This Time Baby" went massive on the disco scene in 1979 and was No 1 on the American dance music charts, it was No 49 on the UK popular music charts and a big hit all over the World, it is still today one of, if not my all-time favourite disco record and which I treasure on the 12" disco single, along with Jackie's autograph which she signed on a Tropicana Hotel napkin as well as signing my copy of Kev Robert's "Northern Soul Top 500".

The photograph of Jackie and I in this book was taken at the Tropicana Hotel, Las Vegas in 2018, where I was so happy to finally meet her in person and spend time with her talking about both her Northern Soul and Disco releases. Jackie was so pleased her version of "This Time Baby" was sampled for the massive 2005 club hit "Love On My Mind" by the Freemasons featuring Amanda Wilson and so "This Time Baby" lives on. Jackie was so pleased to share time with me and all those on the Las Vegas Soul Trip who appreciated her music and she was such fun to be with.

I was devastated to hear just a year after having met Jackie in Las Vegas that she had passed away.

RIP Jackie Moore, I'll be playing your Northern Soul and disco classics until I join you in Soul heaven.

FRANKIE GEARING (THE STEINWAYS)

How time flies, it is now over 10 years ago since I met Frankie (Frances) Gearing in Orlando, Florida. What a great lady, a Northern Soul legend, former member of the Laddins, the Steinways, the Glories and Quiet Elegance who toured with the Temptations. I was fortunate to meet, talk with and see Yvonne (Frankie) Gearing perform at the Radisson Hotel in Orlando in 2011, she was on the bill with Tony Galla, Spyder Turner, Jock Mitchell, the Embers, Jake and the Soul Searchers, Eugene Thomas of the Epitome of Sound (RIP) and Detroit Soul, could it ever get better than this? I was able to get a Flyer from this event signed by all who performed at the Radisson Hotel in Orlando and it hangs proudly behind my bar (see photo), what a piece of soul memorabilia it is.

Frankie Gearing & Steve in Orlando, Florida © Steve Bardsley

Frankie told me she got her big break replacing David Coleman when he left the Laddins.

With Frankie now upfront the Group became The Steinways and recorded "You've Been Leading Me On". Frankie told me she has had a life-long love of music and started her own Group "The Co-Eds" while still at high school, she then shocked me revealing she became engaged to Dennis Edwards, although they never did marry, I just had to ask her "were you leading him on? The Glories were prolific from 1967 to 1969 recording eight singles on the Date label including "Sing Me A Love Song", "I Stand Accused", "I Love You Babe But (Give Me My Freedom)", "No News" and my favourite from the Glories "I Worship You Baby", "My Sweet Baby", "Dark End Of The Street" and "Try A Little Tenderness", Frankie being very proud of every one of them. The Glories "Date" singles command good money nowadays but there is always the fantastic CD released in 2005 *"Special Singles for the Glories, a date with Frankie Gearing"* which features them all and so is a must for any soul lover.

In 1972 after touring with the Temptations the Glories (Frankie Gearing, Delores Brown and Mildred Vaney) were noticed by Willie Mitchell and formed a group called Quiet Elegance, Delores left and was replaced by Lois Reeves, who was one of the Vandellas and Martha Reeves Sister. From 1972 to 1977 the Glories went on to release 8 records on the Hi label, which were mainly love ballads other than the funky "Mama Said" and their last single in 1977 "Roots of Love". I was surprised to learn during this time the girls went on tour with Engelbert Humperdink as his backing group. Quiet Elegance called it a day in 1977. Frankie continued performing as a solo artist recording her last Album "Just Frankie" on the "Beale Street" label in 1980, she finished up with the singles "Tears On My Pillow", Bluer Than Blue" (backed with "Spinning Top") and "Say You Love Me" in 1982. Frankie was a little embarrassed performing "I Worship You Baby", live in Orlando at the Kev Robert's Soul Trip as she forgot some of the words, it didn't really matter though as the UK Northern Soul loving audience took over and sang them for her. It delighted Frankie the audience knew the words to her song. It's moments like this that make the Soul Trips so special.

EUGENE THOMAS (EPITOME OF SOUND)

Another amazing memory, from the Kev Roberts Soul reunion of 10 years ago in Orlando, Florida, is seeing Eugene Thomas perform "You Don't Love Me" live. It's also another sad one, as Eugene who was the lead singer of the Epitome of Sound passed away just a year ago, so many soul artists are no longer with us. What is fascinating is how we are still learning about Northern Soul and the artists that made the records.

Johnny Redpants Warren, Eugene Thomas (R.I.P) and Steve Bardsley
© Steve Bardsley

It was generally thought prior to the 2011 Soul reunion the song "You Don't Love Me" from 1967 and recorded on the little known Sandbag label by the Epitome of Sound, was in fact blue eyed soul (in other words the lead singer was white).

In fact Kev Robert's says on page 23 in the first issue of his book "The Northern Soul Top 500", "I suspect a blue eyed soul effort here". Kev contacted the past owner of the Sandbag Record label Mike Szymanski looking for the songs writer and producer Robert Paladino, wanting him to appear at the 2011 Soul Trip, he was put in touch with Robert who obviously knew who the lead singer really was and revealed the vocals were in fact by Eugene Thomas and so were definitely not blue eyed soul as had been thought for so long. Eugene Thomas was then of course also invited to attend and perform at the Soul Trip and what a performance it was, one of the best ever. The flip side of this marvellous Sandbag label 45 is "Where Were You" and it also features Eugene Thomas as the lead vocalist, it is superb too. "You Don't Love Me" was a Wigan Casino anthem and has become increasingly popular (and expensive) in recent times, in 2000 Kev listed it as being No 7 the Northern Soul all-time top 500 records, I expect it is seen by many as being in the top 5 nowadays. Eugene Thomas was a pleasure to meet, such a modest man and he really appreciated how "You Don't Love Me" is loved by Northern Soul fans, he was never aware until 2011 that it was, it came as a big surprise to him.

When I spoke to Eugene he was really looking forward to performing the song for those who had come from the UK and Australia to Orlando, USA for the Soul Trip. We first met Eugene the night before the live soul revue, where he gave an impromptu rendition of "You don't love me" to unsuspecting soul fans, it had many soul fans in tears and the Sunday night "official" performance was no different. If Eugene thought he was going to get away with performing the song just once he was very much mistaken, but he was absolutely delighted to sing it again when urged on by the Northern Soul fans. If anyone happened to take a glance at Rob Paladino during Eugene's performance they would have seen one of the proudest guys on earth, this really was the stuff that memories are made of, as they say "you just had to be there". This was without doubt one of those magic moments which can never be repeated!

ROBERT PALADINO (EPITOME OF SOUND)

Robert Paladino is the writer and producer of both "You Don't Love Me" and "Where Were You" released on the Sandbag label in1967 by the Epitome of Sound. Robert actually performed himself in Doo-Wop and jazz groups in the 1960's and wrote songs for the Megatons, a four piece group which included his Brother Mike Paladino, the Megatons would later become a five piece band called the Epitome of Sound with Eugene Thomas, the only black member as their lead vocalist.

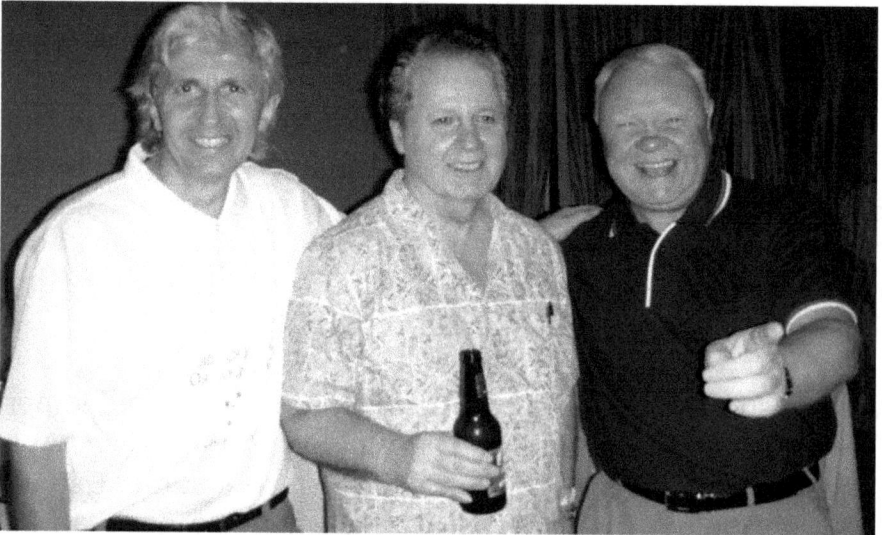

John Warren, Robert Paladino and Steve in Orlando © Steve Bardsley

In Orlando Robert was delighted to tell me he composed both "You Don't Love Me" and "Where Were You" using a guitar with three missing strings and then with this gave the guys in the Megatons a rendition of both songs, which they loved and wanted to record, which they did as the Epitome of Sound on the Sandbag label, they were in fact the first group and perhaps the last that the Sandbag label ever signed. The story of the Epitome of Sound, courtesy of Robert Paladino is a fascinating but unfortunately a short one.

"You Don't Love Me" was very nearly not recorded by them at all, others had heard the demo, they liked it and wanted to buy the rights to it and record the song for themselves, these including Alvin Cash of the Crawlers and Jay Proctor of the Techniques, yes the "Apples, Peaches Pumpkin Pie" group which feature earlier in this chapter. Fortunately Robert refused all offers from those wanting to buy the song and so it was recorded by the Epitome of Sound. The record was a hit and reached No 11 on the charts. The newly formed Epitome of Sound were an instant success with a hit under their belts and a bright future ahead. Unfortunately things went wrong very quickly, the Sandbag label had financial difficulties and no more records could be sold or produced, the radio stations stopped playing the record and the Epitome of Sound were out on a limb. The group broke up shortly afterwards and went back to being the Megatons. The Epitome of Sound was no more, that is until 1974 when the record started to be played on the UK Northern Soul scene, remarkably the real identity of the band was "covered up" and those on the scene were told the record was by Moses Smith not the Epitome of Sound.

An original "You Don't Love Me" on the Sandbag label is now rarely found and if it is will cost a fortune, there have been bootlegs including the one supposedly by Moses Smith and also official re-releases of "You Don't Love Me". The latest official release which has the blessing of Robert Paladino is by the New Zealand band Jamie and the Numbers featuring lead singer Jamie Musuva, I was fortunate enough to get one of these from the Author of this book, Johnny Warren and it is an excellent version.

Jamie and the numbers have also previously covered other Northern Soul tracks including very credible versions of "Magic Touch" by Melba Moore and "If This Is Love I'd Rather Be Lonely" by the Precisions.

That's about it for now, although I have mentioned less than half of the soul artists I have had the pleasure to meet, I have run out of time and space in this Book. Author Johnny Warren has asked me to do a Chapter for Book 3 and include the artists I have not covered here. Time and God willing I may write a Chapter for Book 3 and if so hope to include: Jerry Williams, Lenny Curtis, Larry Clinton, Spider Turner, Sonny Turner, Sidney Barnes, Jock Mitchell, Tony Galla, Timothy Wilson, Willie Clarke, Detroit Soul, the Younghearts, the Inspirations, the Spellbinders, Laura Lee, Sandy Sheldon, the Soul Shakers, the Escorts, the Persuaders, Freddie Scott, Jimmy Raye, Sonny Turner, Jodi Mathis, Connie Questell, Tommy Hunt, Jackie Gore, Chris James, Lonnie Cook, Ray Charles and Wilson Pickett. There are some great stories to be told!

In signing off I say many thanks to Johnny Warren, Kev and Sam Roberts who have reached out, not only to soul lovers but also to the U.S. artists, many who never realised their records were revered in the U.K. It's people like Johnny, Kev and Sam who have helped ensure many artists, musicians and producers have now been made aware how popular they and their music was and indeed still is on the 'Northern Soul' scene. I can personally vouch this means so much to them, even though in many cases they never made much, if indeed any money from their musical and recording careers.

It's now time to give back, to finally give something to those responsible for making the soul records we so much love, as without them there would be no Northern Soul scene and so to them we must remain eternally grateful. I hope Johnny's series of "Our Soul Journeys" books will help those in need and I thank him for allowing me to be a small part of that. I always remind myself that no matter how much of a 'Northern Soul' fan I or anyone else believes they are, we all need to appreciate we can never own 'Northern Soul', it will always own us. The reality is the best we can do is not to "Keep the Faith" but spread it around.

Chapter 24

John Warren The Runaway Train

I am simply on a runaway train of trying to get these books published before I pass on stories of other passionate like minded soul music lover's. Hopefully it is not for ages, because I am in fighting fit form and the best I have been in for many a year. I am currently riding my bike playing my harmonica. https://www.youtube.com/watch?v=m2ugXKoeBK

I am truly really enjoying trying to write! And it's heartwarming that so many other kind soul lover's also want to give their time to write . I cannot do it without them and hopefully we can make a difference but it will not happen overnight but I am confident that it will happen and all we can do is try! Some of you might hear of soul artists in need of help, or having recently passed on and not having a tombstone, and laying in a pauper's grave. If you do, could you contact me please and if we are able to help we will. I really would like more younger people who like & love soul music as much as we do to get involved and contribute and write, talk about how they feel soul music will evolve in the decades ahead and what soul genre's really rocks their boat! Up to today sadly no one under 30 years has offered to write, and I have asked quite a few so if you are younger & reading this please get in touch because it would be really appreciated. What would your thoughts be on the crazy record prices we see? Also when do they feel the supply and demand shifts, as it has to logically when we all progress in age & the demand might not be there anymore, and the younger crowd might not have the disposable income to pay the record prices that they are currently! More collections will be up for sale and selling them is a tough call when they are your "babies".

Do people feel it will go the way off Doo-wop, and die as a genre especially the uptempo genre we so much love that is labeled northern soul & rare soul, when we all die & some off us get to stomp with the Angels! I personally do not go out as much to hear the genres that I once loved, especially the top 500 as it does not inspire me as much after hearing it for over 40 years. When I was 17 it was naturally fresh but it is not the same now I am 64 having heard it so many times. What really excites me today is to go to a venue and my ears prick up to a new song that I have not heard before, but sadly here in Queensland Australia that rarely happens, and so on the rare times I do venture out I often hear the same records I have heard for many decades, when there are so many that seem to have been forgotten, with instrumentals like " Lady Lady Lady" Boogie Man Orchestra, & "Girl When You Wake Up" by Liberty. Instrumentals you do not seem to hear as much as you once did! One song that stuck in my brain and kept me awake after I left St. Ives all nighter way back was an instrumental song called "Exodus" .

With vocal songs the list could be many pages long. It took ages for Santiago "Feeling Good" on a Philadelphia label called Bam-boo, a 1975 Blackpool Mecca song that was not played much and is on two different label designs, to then get the demand it has today, which my good mate Dennis Locantore from New Jersey played bass guitar on it. Some other songs like Clara Ward "In The Right Direction", Johnny Bragg "They're Talking About Me", to name just a few you rarely hear! Some songs are put in the handbaggers not to be played basket and one of them is the superb song from The Poppies "There's a Pain In My Heart", but I would bet any money if it was dropped in a set anywhere it would get better dance floor reaction than maybe Don Varner "Tear Stained Face", or Larry Clinton "She's Wanted" (in Three States')!

But much respect to the people here in Australia & around the world who put on soul nights, it can be a thankless task, trying to keep everyone happy with the different thought processes of people in general, especially the grumpy old men syndrome is not easy. The grumpy old men syndrome seems to be creeping into the soul scene as more and more, as many of us age towards seventy & even older, like the original Twisted Wheelie's who attended the Brazennose Street Wheel in Manchester & other less talked about venue's like Bletsoe Allnighter, not forgetting some of the other pioneering venues in the 1960's & 70's, venues like Wilby, Market Harborough, Earls Barton, Kelmarsh, Kettering North Park, Nags Head Wollaston, all venues in my old stomping ground of Northamptonshire.

Naturally there are people who mostly like the top 500 and then ones who like newer stuff as I do, but in reality most songs are rare like Joan Procter (sic), her real name is Joan Proctor on Scenic, a Philadelphia label with "Just My Pride" and "Lazy River" a lovely double sider to name just one. That impressive lady DJ Jayne Hulme from Barnsley has been playing it a lot lately. Rare does not necessarily equate to being expensive. Some go on about playing original vinyl only to the point they make my ears bleed, but ultimately respect to all, as I think that obnoxious word called Covid, has taught us that life is very precious. If it's an original 45 RPM only night fine, but because of some of the songs and because of their rarity at some venues you might not hear them at all! So if none of the DJ's has an original, then maybe playing a re-issue does not matter as much as would the paying public and a lot of the dancers really care?

The book series also would like to have more lady writer's, but I do understand the discrimination that some of them on the scene suffer, which could put some of them off writing. So if you feel you have an interesting lady soul journey then please tell me and I'll put it in one of our books. I have also noticed for over a decade that some ladies are being discriminated against when they have a go at DJing, they are given really poor time spots, a shame because so many I have seen excel in their song choices & passion.

Many years ago at a Sydney allnighter Elaine Griffin from Queensland was for me a stand out, we are blessed in Australia having so many lady soul DJ"S who impress.

Due to Covid & because soul fans in most countries could not get out and hit a venue because of all the lockdowns, a lot more talented DJ'S of all sexes have come out of the woodwork, which is a good thing as it keeps the ones who are established on their toes ! But maybe some should retire with grace, and if not maybe just film themselves and they would see their expiry date is long gone, because some look more than bored. I suppose eating the same meat (playing the same songs because maybe you feel you have to! might resonate in their persona and is why they look truly bored). It is always better to go out on a high and there is a plethora of DJ"S in the wings for the better time slots. To be fair some of the older DJ"S in Australia such as Steve Bardsley and Vince Peach can get away with it, they retain passion and their song choices often lean to the less expensive or forgotten songs, which helps keep their sets fresh. Vince has been a DJ on PBS radio in Melbourne for 4 decades and has a following of younger soul fans, his Cherry bar night attracts a lot of university students. Steve Bardsley is one of my favourite DJ's, he is an entertainer, was a radio DJ and knows a few tricks, like instead of headphones using the mixer LED's to cue a record, he though always tells me the best DJ in Australia is Vince, high praise indeed. Not all are like Steve and Vince though, what other profession can a person with a basic skill set go out buy some rare records and then wangle his little willie for his own egotism, without doing the apprenticeship? It's lucky such DJ's are the minority and fortunately for every egotistical DJ there is a multitude of passionate DJ's young and old who really do make the scene epic.

So if you want to have a go and spin a few records try it, because it's fun when it works, but always remember you're only as good as your last set and it does not necessarily have to be rare.

Try not to be pressured on the rarity, as a lot of the dancers really don't care what the value of a record is. A good record is just that, simply a good record and I bet if you asked some of the crowd what is rare a lot might not even know or care. Some supposedly original 45's may look real, but sometimes what is supposed to be real can look just too new and is often just that NEW. So the people banging on about "It's originals only here mate" maybe have been had! Some dealers have been aware of this for many years and in many countries. Simon Soussan and others pulled such tricks way back in the 70's, so it is very logical that with the technology and printing processes of today it's more likely than ever that there is an abundance of impressive Mint - condition counterfeits in circulation, they just might not be "originals" mate! Ian Levine did it to prove a point with the Four Vandal's "Wrong Side of Town', showing you can make a tailor made song which sounds like it was made in the 1960's. There are also thousands of underplayed cheaper records and with Covid, some DJ'S have experimented playing some that might not have been given much play before Covid, as there is no pressure to fill a dance floor when it is a virtual internet soul night! Some record sellers have noticed how some of the 45's which have sat on their sales site's for years and are cheap are suddenly starting to sell, there is new demand for them. So many records though are naturally rare, for the simple fact they are over 50 years old and with time and natural wastage not so many have survived, especially in good condition, never forget condition is king when selling records!

Also due to Covid so many more soul lovers & record collectors have got their tunes out and played them on the internet, some of them maybe having some of the best collections on the planet. These are often people who have stayed under the radar for decades & just do what they truly love and that is collect records, continuing to feed their expensive addiction, just as they did over 40 years ago, when some would eat baked beans all week so as to be able to feed their record collecting addiction and buy another record.

If you are reading this and you live in one of the many countries that are yet to be represented in a Soul Journey book, then I personally would like to read what is happening in your neck of the woods and feel many other readers would too! It also might encourage more soul music lover's to travel & check your country soul music event's out once Covid has ended.

For example I personally have never been to Japan, which has a massive market for some of the soul genres and a great following. In Book 2 we have a lovely Chapter by one Japanese soul fan Izumi Sawamoto, and hopefully we will get to hear from other diverse countries where soul music is played. Currently the books are heavily subscribed by Australian's writers and it would be great to normalise it with other countries. I hope to get out and visit Japan myself once this total madness of Covid is resolved, sadly I feel may be many more years before it has truly played out and died, but I hope I am wrong! So please contact me by email at rushden88@hotmail.com or Facebook as "Johnny Redpants Warren" if you would like to contribute as a writer, because I hope to bring out one book per year, that is providing interest dictates it and as long as I still have the energy to stay on this runaway train, which has afforded me so many new friends. I appreciate that I have met so many people through it, many I may not ever have met otherwise in a lifetime. I also plan in the future to try and bring the books out in several different languages, especially Japanese, German & French to name a few, because book sales to these countries are few at the moment, perhaps as they are in the English language only.

There are so many here in Australia I would like to see write a chapter, such as Keith Sutcliffe from Narre Warren in Victoria and another truly mad lad who we all love on the Australian soul scene, Howard Yates, who incidentally was married to George Wallace's Sister from Edinburgh. Most of us maybe have a chapter that might be of interest, but too many on the same topics of Wigan Casino, Blackpool Mecca & The Twisted Wheel would start to get boring. So if I don't ask you it is simply because of that reason. So I will endeavor to hopefully keep these books interesting by getting writers to touch on a plethora of diverse & interesting topics. One I am personally interested in are the soul artists who joined up and went to Vietnam and sadly never returned, or if they did return it was not as the "Same Man". So I will try to research and hopefully do that in Book 3 which is planned for 2022. So if you feel you have something to relate that would be of interest please contact me.

We try to stay away from writing too much on dark topics such as drugs, sex & violence, we know it went on, but we will let others maybe write about it in their books if they so wish! We also try to limit the expletives but appreciate in some contexts they may be necessary.

I have bought & sold records for nearly 25 years on EBay as Johnny Redpants Warren, but now with the fees & the expectations of some on condition & the manic dramas on postage problems and the import duties and taxes, it is not the fun it once was. One year ago in 2020 I could post up to four records for $12 Aud but now it's $29 and can take up to 6 weeks for a parcel to be received. Recently some of us here in Australia have found our imported 45's have arrived damaged (melted), due possibly to sitting in hot climates waiting for connecting flights, but more than likely because the postal services are treating parcels with industrial microwaves, which they will obviously not admit too! So I have decided not to post overseas anymore until this dilemma is sorted out, as I don't need the drama and it's sacrilege how pieces of art are continually being destroyed. Quite a lot of Australian music sellers are having similar problems. I really do miss buying from the USA, but do not do as much these days due to the high postage costs, especially when buying small lots (blind) not knowing what you are buying.

There is nothing more exciting than making a cup of tea, opening a parcel and getting a rare record like the Appointments ``Stepping Closer''' a mis- press on Red Coach, they sound a bit like the Carstair's on the same label! Or something I had never heard of like Chuck Henley ''Broken Arrow'' when it popped through the door buried amongst some common pop records. Getting bargains does not happen often nowadays, but in June 2021 I found Andrea Henry in a lot of 20 records bought for 1 cent each, which I then sold to a good lady DJ friend in New Zealand. Many years ago you would often find bargains on a daily basis like The Moments great 45 ''You Said'' on Deep, which I bought for $9.99 and then three months later I found another for $50. Back then I used a sniper program called Auction Sniper which won me so many 45's cheap. Like three Ralph Graham ''She Just Sits There'', written about the Vietnam war on the New York label Upfront, it's a great double sider which was buried with his other 45's on the Sussex & RCA label's.

For me, I also love reading books on music and one that stands out from last year is Richard Gilbert's ''I Searched For Soul And Found the Stars'', which he kindly sent to me and ironically the lad is living in Higham Ferrers, Northants just a few miles from my old home of Rushden, Northants, where I lived till I emigrated to Australia in 1987. Emigrating for me personally has been a great decision, I really thrive in a warmer climate and here in Scarborough Village, Queensland it's generally 22-35C all year round. We are currently in the middle of winter and have had days as warm as 28C. When I am out and about it still amazes me how many living here are originally from the UK and when I mention keywords like Wigan Casino, Twisted Wheel, or northern soul their ears prick up and then we have a chat about it for ages. This confirms what a major influence soul has made on so many lives & how fortunate we were to have been born in that era of the 1950s-60s, and so experienced venues like the Twisted Wheel (Manchester), Blackpool Mecca, Wigan Casino, Cleethorpes, The Catacombs (Wolverhampton), The

Torch (Stoke), Va VA's (Bolton), Tiffanys (Coalville), Samantha's (Sheffield), The Ritz (Manchester) & one my big favorites St Ives near Huntingdon. There are naturally so many more, the list is endless of great soul nights way back then! I have to smile thinking back at how I used to rush to go and hear Brian Rae in tho oldie's room in 1976.

I personally feel very blessed to have lived and discovered in 1973 the music genre which has formed the soundtrack of my life and the comradeship it has given me. It's amazing when I meet soul brothers and sisters from way back when visiting the UK, it's also very heartwarming to share a dance floor with them here in Australia. Dancing spiritually for me is truly better than sex, I do mention of course that I am mad.

One part of doing the books that really excites me is being able to speak to people who are Soul music Icons, the star's, the singers & the band members and the thing I generally notice is how humble they are. The tales they tell me in confidence often cannot be repeated in a book, especially those about organized crime and links to the mafia in the USA, which were prolific way back then in the music industry with payola. I would love to do a chapter on it, but in reality it would not be the smartest move, so it might not happen. We had hoped to do a chapter by Henry Stone's son, but Jan Lisewski R.I.P, was organising this, so sadly it might not happen, but it would have been a fabulous chapter.

One person I ring regularly is Michael Paladino who was the drummer in the Epitome of Sound, he is now 82 and still lives in New Jersey, he is without doubt one the funniest men I ever had the pleasure to communicate with. He has struggled with health issues, especially a bad hip and hopefully he will get that sorted soon. He related to me all his walking sticks have a specific name: Citizen Kane, & Sugar cane etc. When he goes out it is a talking point introducing his cane to a younger lady and her dog. The world truly needs more characters like him.

407

Michael often sings down the phone when I ring him because he still practices many song's every day and boy the lad can still sing. I tried to sing to him & then whistle down the phone but he was not impressed and said do not give up your day job Johnny. Mickie as I call him does some fabulous comedy skits. One that makes me howl with laughter is "The Winston Churchill, addressing the British Royal Navy, and telling them he doesn't care how they do it, but they must sink the Bismarck". He truly is an amazing comedy talent. He always has loved the ladies and he relates how back in the day all he had to do was shrug his shoulders, while playing his drums, and then he had one of his ladies for the night. Yes I did say ladies for the night as more often than not there are more than one . He told me he kept a diary and in it, he had 298 names and two skunks, "skunks" I asked. He said yes to the two that I married, ha ha, another joke, he exclaimed! I hope the skunks are not reading this as they might do what the mafia failed to do on several occasions, as messing with their dames' is truly a death wish! Mickie relates so many funny stories of his escapades of meeting a mafioso dame and how one night a few of the mafioso came in with shotguns, he luckily got out of the bathroom window, and another experience was when they knocked on the wrong room. He says he was often asked how he was such a ladies man and beyond the fact he had the look, he also had the brain to know, you got to get to their head, make them laugh, to get to their nether region's & how very true when we meet some batting leagues above our batting positions. Mickie told me how when he was drumming for Frankie Valli & the Four Seasons he got to room with Franke. He also got to play for John F. Kennedy & his wife Jackie, in New Jersey before he became the President of the USA.

To put a smile on a person's face is something I try to do every day, in particular when I meet someone new. I sometimes introduce myself to them as "Mad John" which I truly like to be and I love watching their reaction. I also like to sometimes start talking in Thai, French or German languages which I have a limited understanding of and sometimes they call my bluff when they speak back to me. I have a sense of humour, which I personally find some Australians can struggle with, they look upon me as truly mad and some live in their ivory towers in Scarborough Village, which is very niche. The look on their faces often depicts they are not happy, even if they have their name proudly displayed on the number plate of their newest Mercedes, so go figure. Inner peace & happiness can come from within, and not needing material things can truly be a Nirvana state of mind. Since I developed Aspergilloma (a fungus ball) growing in my left lung 4 years ago, I have taken control of it & my life by treating it with CBD oil and also started whistling every day, as that exercises my lungs. There has been a dramatic improvement and I really enjoy whistling "Joe 90" or "The Snake" as I will never be good enough to whistle a tune like Silky Hargreaves, but maybe one day! I have also taken up playing the harmonica in the last 3 months, I love the blues and the fabulous harmonica playing of Little Walter, it will probably take me a lifetime to get proficient, as I would like to combine my limited singing ability with whistling and playing the harmonica to those living in old people's homes, this as my dear dad John Warren did, many decades ago. Dad used to sing his many favourite tunes like Frank Sinatra "My Way" which is still a big favorite of mine and other songs like Tony Bennett's "I Left My Heart in San Francisco". While recently attempting to play my 48 hole harmonica (a Swan brand) on the beach at Redcliffe Queensland, a hundred high school kids and their teachers came along and gave me a massive applause. I asked a few of them how long they thought I have been playing and a few said 20 years.

They were thunderstruck when I told them 3 months, which pleased me and yes I also have an ego. Maybe it is a previous life I am channeling into, but I really feel it's an instrument I have long forgotten from the deeper recesses of my mind and I am kind of addicted too. I have started playing it while I ride my bicycle, but up hills & down dales it is not that easy, it is though kind of an adrenaline rush.

My downhill speed on my bicycle has been 39 km/h and 32 km/h on the flat. I wave at the local police and they wave back. Bob Dylan also rode a bike playing a harmonica and a thought which occurred to me is, was "Blowing in The Wind" inspired by the fact that on a windy day the harmonica can play on its own?

It is heartwarming that my young adult children also like music but unfortunately not the genre I love. My son John Warren Jnr, has recently bought a record player and is buying LP's. He has recently joined me for a few local soul nights here in Scarborough Village but after 90 minutes he has had enough, but it is pleasing he tries. I tend to bounce around a bit when I try to write due to the combination of dyslexia and bipolar, neither are conducive to good prose.

Spiritualism And Soul Music

I believe Soul Music and spirituality are very intricately related, with spirituality often being the inspiration for the creation of music, and music so often is creating the desired atmosphere for a spiritual occasion, this may be why so many dancers are in a trance like state and if you watch the old footage from the Wigan Casino it is very easy to spot the ones "In The Zone"!

Soul music can ultimately be one of our most powerful gateways to connect to our spiritual nature -- our divine source -- the unseen, as well as to the universe around us and those other divine beings that inhabit it with us.

In a soul venue, there might be several spiritual mediums but most tend to naturally stay under the radar. It personally fascinates me when I am watching dancers & it's very easy to pick the ones who have the incredible gift of being a spiritual dancer. If you were to take photos of them and then go and check to see if you can see the "Orbs" you might be enlightened! An "Orb" is a transparent ball of light energy that is connected to spirits. Orbs can be spotted in photos or even videos and if you watch the Netflix series the Vikings, there are at least two in there that I noticed, maybe there are more ! You will only see what your mind will allow you to see & being spiritually blind is what it is! In book one there is a photo of me on a dance floor at The Rock Foundation 30 year anniversary all-dayer that I held for my 50th birthday, you can see an "orb" in it. There are photos where I am surrounded by orb's, a bit like a bubble machine has gone off near me, which makes me truly blessed by them wanting to come through. So when I say the experience is better than sex, it is in the context of the inner peace you feel when you are "Out on the floor". I also experience this when I play my harmonica and then I play out of my skin with a skill set that is truly not mine!

Out on the floor on my 50th " In the Zone with my "Orb"
© **John Warren**

411

In Book 1 I touch on a story that happened to me when I had the privilege to DJ at Prestatyn soul weekender many years ago, this when Benny Troy and the Volumes to name just a few were performing there. I had just flown into the UK from New York from the New Jersey soul trip, so I was on a musical high and arrived at those prestigious chalets and thought how do I get warm? I rarely drink but had to purchase a bottle of whiskey which helped me survive the weekend. How damn cold and grim that holiday camp was & it should have been described as a "Stalag Camp".

I had been kindly given a couple of DJ spots and went on the main stage for a Saturday 8.30-9.30 spot, all was going reasonably well until I played Lee Roye "Tears" for my daughter Ethan Elizabeth Warren R.I.P & the very next 45 Joanne Courcey's "I Got the Power" would not play. I tried to press the Technics decks button twice but no luck, so with shaking hands I picked up the headshell and then dropped the needle onto the record 30 seconds in, this blunted the needle. Fortunately I always carry a spare headshell so I faded "I Got the Power " out and went to my ending song the Bobby Gentry acetate "I Walked Away" and was very glad to walk off that stage with my tail between my legs. When you feel like you're representing your adopted country Australia you really do not like to mess up as badly as I did on that particular night. I was then asked by a few of my mates what the hell just happened! I had just walked over to the South Yorkshire crew who I have spent a lot of time with, this on my trips over to the UK over the year's way back then. My dear mate Nell Goddard was going through a tough time in his life so I went over to him and said "are you alright mate" and then I put my hand on his shoulder, and said "you are not on your own" 'he replied "I know John" with him looking at the circle of friends around him, at that point his four inch pint beer glass peeled, it was full of beer and then Nell Goddard started shaking and said "what is that all about John" which I replied I told you, Nell you were not on your own, I was referring to his "spirit guides".

There were a lot of people there who witnessed this just in case some might think I am truly delusional. I always carry the last photo taken of Ethan, my daughter when she passed away nearly 22 years ago and I keep it in my 45 cardboard record box when I DJ and occasionally things like that would happen. It's very liberating to communicate to a loved one "In Spirit "!

The affirmation of the "Proof of Existence is so very profound! Most people can build those lines of communication if they so wish. About a year ago I was talking to Marianne Chesnovsky-Walker from Philadelphia, the wife of Ronnie Walker the famous soul singer who passed over 2 years ago, she messaged me one day very excited, she had done her daily ritual saying good morning to Ronnie's photo, which is near a grandfather clock that had not chimed for many decades and suddenly it chimed. Just further proof to anyone who needs a sign and a message. I am still here and I am not going anywhere until we are reunited and when you walk towards the light. Recently when I rang her, I asked if it had chimed since and she said it had not. Many of these spiritual events happen to me regularly, recently I could not find my sunglasses and being stubborn spent an hour looking, I gave up, rode my bike and bought a new pair. When I returned there was my old pair in the middle of the bedroom floor. Recently I accidentally had my razor cover fall down behind a heavy cupboard and I thought it could stay there & when I got up a few days later it was sitting on the top of the bedroom cupboard. Then a few weeks ago I was in a rush to attend a record shop opening in Redcliffe Queensland on a Saturday from where I was recently banned for talking too much! I proceeded to put my washing on the line and I had unlocked my back screen door. I had left the key in the lock, I tried to turn it but it would not budge, a message in my head said the wrong key! so I took the key out & put the front door screen key in and it locked. So I took this as a message to be delayed and rode there a bit slower. The list is endless of these bizarre experiences which I then try to comprehend, the message of and the meaning that is being sent to me. There is always a message there, it is just being able to decipher it. Many years ago at the Perth Australian national at the Sunday all-dayer, a lad from Perth came up to me very distressed and wanted a word so I picked a quiet spot, and he related that recently he had come off his motorbike and was in a bad way and all he wanted to do was go to sleep and he then said he heard a voice "keep awake son" which he tried to ignore as he was so banged up, but he looked up on the curb and he then saw his mother sitting next to him, so he stayed awake and the ambulance arrived, incidentally he still kicking and a good lad. His parents had died many years before in tragic circumstances!

Soul music is spiritual in its essence and many music artists if you read their books, like those by Barry White, Marcia Hines to name a few touch on it and Ruby Andrews mentions it briefly in our Book 1. I had the great pleasure to interview her by phone for several hours when doing her chapter, she mentions how she was an Indian Squaw who drowned and even in this present life she fears water. Ruby Andrews relates how she was regressed by Shirley Maclaine *for Shirley's television show.*

"Music should be healing; music should uplift the soul; music should inspire. There is no better way of getting closer to God, of rising higher towards the spirit, of attaining spiritual perfection than music, if only it is rightly understood."
Hazrat Inayat Khan

Naturally, we are all born spiritual, if we want to "**See**" and when we do our lives may truly become enriched by that "Proof of Existence "and then we never fear death and also when we lose someone very close to us, it can help that there is a line of communication still available to us, if we would like to study and get in tune to this. Also the unexplained moving of objects by higher powers to make us aware they are always there for us when we need them and will guide us if we let them, as often the book has already been written. Maybe it is up to us to follow that chapter path or not, as it is our own free will if we so wish. Maybe we truly are the masters of our own destiny. But our own freedom will also allow us to change what might be destroying us from evolving spiritually. It may be the love of wealth or an addiction that stops us from evolving, so we may not have to return again in another life form to repeat the lessons we failed before, because we are all born imperfect! I am often inspired by the disabled who often accept their lot with acceptance that "It is what it Is". So I try to "Live in The Second" has what happened before and what happens after might not be as blessed as this exact moment! I notice people with dementia and Alzheimer's are also living in the moment as sadly their memory is often just in the here and now. For me to be able to hit a dance floor and bring through an "orb" is very enlightening. The levels of spirituality which people are at may often be reflected in how many past lives may have been experienced. Also thought provoking is we all are born imperfect and when you watch a baby or younger child they often have that gift "Of Sight" but this will often fade around 5 years of age!

Twenty years ago I took my children to China, and we went down the Pearl River on the way to a fish restaurant. The tour guide related, we don't waste anything here in China & pointed out the fish they had caught and which were being fed. He explained we feed all our food waste to them including our body waste. Sabrina my daughter then aged 12 and John Warren Jnr then aged 10 were not impressed, but it got much worse when the guide showed them the delightful looking food and said with much pride it's dog, cat & fox. I asked them what they were going to eat and they adamantly said Rice dad, saying "we are Aussies dad, we don't eat those animals".

I have digressed as I tend to do. One of my weaknesses is I tend to waffle and if I ever ring you, then trying to get a word in it's not easy as Duncan McAllister from Newcastle often reminds me! Do I like the sound of my own voice? Maybe I do, as I am as imperfect as the next person with an ego. This week a local record shop opened in Redcliffe at an old service petrol station and I just got my first ban for talking too much. Apparently I had upset a couple of customers which made me chuckle. Upsetting Australians is not hard to do, try telling them a joke, like why do Aussies wear thongs! The answer is because they have not worked out how to tie shoelaces. Do they get the joke often no!

Back to the tale from China, we all started eating, me with my rice and vegetables and yes dog cat or fox was not for me either, although I did try snake once in a youth hostel in Brunswick, Georgia in the USA, this in 1978 one the most fascinating hostels I have ever visited "The hostel in the forest " was set up by a lad who on his travels ended up there because of one of their legendary cyclones. On a Saturday we would all go on a run and for a reward we are served by him, the dish grits and fatback bacon. Another thing I remember from those days of over 42 years ago was the smell of the sulfur from the lake which was pumped to our shower blocks.

Sorry to have gotten off the point of spiritualism, but some may have needed a "Time Out", as some of you will surely be thinking Johnny Red Pants is truly mad, and yes I am different. Some of us spiritual disciples truly are looked upon as that way inclined by non-believers. We started eating our meals in China and the family was staring at me, and I thought maybe there was a bit of egg on my face but no it was that it was the adept way I was using the chopsticks, like a natural & very similar to how I recently picked up a harmonica and played it as if I had done it many times before. Sabrina Warren commented, "Dad you've been practicing", but I had not. Maybe there was another regressed life I had sadly forgotten.

Some of you I am sure would have experienced "Déjà vu" as I have on my travels, getting off a bus in a strange land and knowing what is around the corner. It's such a fantastic, enlightening feeling to discover that I most probably have been here before! So many levels of spiritual awareness really thrill me like astral travel. Some of you reading this might be fascinated and you can always personally message me and have a chat. If you lose a loved one I am always here to help, just reach out and I will be happy to help if possible. It is a heavy topic but I will try to KISS (keep it simple spiritually)!

"Music is a moral law. It gives soul to the universe, wings to the mind, flight to the imagination, and charm and gaiety to life and to everything." -- Plato

This is like the train I am on doing these books. I feel it is my spiritual path and even though the train has stopped at many stations, I have not wanted to get off & really do not think I ever will. So hopefully there will be a few more books in the years to come. I really hope so, but that is up to you the reader and the purchaser of the books, as everything has a limited time frame and the books are no different. Some of you may be in need of spiritual guidance and will be of a higher level than me and can influence me like my teacher Daniel, a homeless man who has traveled for years living that way. Daniel, who I only met recently is from Wiltshire and is 71 years old and his is a spiritual path after giving his wealth away.

It is his calling and also his way of growing to the next level for him personally, my gut feeling is this could be one, if not the very last of his lives walking "Hell on Earth"! With Covid & when we were in a lockdown they tried to put him in Mont Komo, a posh hotel on the beach in Redcliffe Queensland with 3 meals a day for free and he declined. He tells me that when he is bedded down for the night at the chemist warehouse at Redcliffe,

417

the smile on his face at night that he gives to people on the way to the posh restaurants that are in abundance near his outside bedroom, confuses them a lot ! He truly inspires me, because I see so many very wealthy people here and some of their faces are full of doom and gloom and some wind me up by their lack of inner happiness. He truly believes his guide is Michael the archangel. Last week in April 2021 we were chatting away and a violent drug and drunken man came at us with a bottle and we both noticed our lack of "fear" and the man quickly noticed our eyes and realised he would lose and so quickly "walked away". Being dyslexic, writing is very problematic, but with Grammarly it is doable. Due to bio polar disorder I can tend to bounce around which can be confusing, but again it is part of my own journey and I would not change a thing! I also noticed in Ian Levine's book how he bounces around and that for the reader this can be difficult, which I do struggle with, because writing for me is not easy. I recently joined the Australian Queensland writers association, which I am enjoying immensely. I am very privileged to stand up and talk "open mic" in front of many other published writers for about 30 mins at a time and I do really enjoy public speaking, as I can talk "underwater". I am learning lots of skills like building a manuscript and formatting as this will help keep the Books costs down and then I will have more funds to donate to the artists in need, at some point sadly there will be very few left, so we will then progress to the very respectful looking bench tombstones like has been done in the past for Darrell Banks by some kind soul lovers from around the world.

https://www.findagrave.com/memorial/14594141/darrell-banks

Book 1 of Our Soul Music Journey is starting to get into libraries in Australia, which I am very proud of and it is in my local Moreton Bay region library, where they have kindly bought two books and I also hand-signed a free one.

The demand for it is good at the moment, I really wish Jan Lisewski was here to see it, but he can "in spirit" as I really feel his presence. In Book 1 spiritualism is touched on by Ruby Andrews and Marc Bolan, and many thanks to Gloria Jones who allowed me to print the Marc Bolan piece & the superb photos. When I sent it to her for her approval before I published it, she wrote back to me "It's like Mark has written the piece from the grave ", which I feel he had done. I had got the message, Marc Bolan was very troubled in how he had passed over.

I really hope that "soul work" has helped him! If words are the limited language of my mind, soul music is the limitless calling of my soul intertwined in the evolution of continually trying to grow and be a better person. I was born imperfect and as I reach my end in this life I hope to have evolved a bit more. There is a close link between music and the spirit and many artists and many fans have this gift and for me, I didn't really understand, only getting this gift late in 1999 when I had reached 42. My daughter Ethan Elizabeth Warren passed on Friday, August 13th, in the Royal women's hospital in Brisbane & thanks to Robert Paladino's love there is a song in her memory now called " Ethan's Theme" which also honors "apple ', Johnny boy Pryor's brother, who was nicknamed 'apple' and this is why the artist is credited as "The Apple Heads" on the flip side of "Cause my Lover's Gone" which was released in 2018 on Red Pants records, incidentally some of which remain unsold and Robert Paladino has for sale!

Robert Paladino has also written a song called "Bring Back that Soul Music", which the late Eugene Thomas recorded on, although I liked & loved Eugene, you could tell his heart was not in the track and when I rang & asked Eugene Thomas (R.I.P) why? He told me he did not like the song and me being a straight shooter I told him you should maybe have told Robert that! But hopefully someone will release it soon. Bobby Wilson, the son of the late great Jackie Wilson showed interest, but it didn't happen.

I know Jamie & the Numbers also like it so maybe she will make the song happen in the near future!

Eugene Thomas was the lead singer of the Epitome of sound with their iconic song "You Don't Love Me "on Sandbag records. I had met Eugene at a Soul Trip in the USA in Orlando, Florida and the photo taken of him and I below shows two people connected spiritually. We are like moths attracted to a light and we tend to attract similar energy & vibration when we meet like-minded people. .

John Warren and Eugene Thomas Orlando USA © Steve Bardsley

Naturally a few wolves in sheep's clothing pop up and a few of Lucifer's workers but we weed them out quickly. Eugene was religious, he would send me a personal message in that vein every day. I am sure there are many reading this who also were privileged to have Eugene message them with his "joy and happiness". I rang him occasionally, he often mentioned he wanted to sing in the UK one last time. I truly miss Eugene who passed from Covid in April 2020.

In June 2020 that lovely man from New Zealand, Simon Bayliss played ' 'YDLM" to Jamie of the Numbers, she loved it, so the cover was released in September 2021 in memory of Eugene Thomas. It's a 500 press, a great cover version faded out with lovely words from his dear mate Robert Paladino, who also wrote fine words on the cover. There are also some collector signed ones, I am privileged to have been given a test press. Simon has made a deal to bring an Album out in the UK by a label called Superfly of Jamie & the Numbers, on which they perform fine cover versions of the Precisions ''If This is Love '' and 'Melba Moore's ''Magic Touch''

Spiritualist's Raj , Clarissa , and Johnny Pink Hair Scarborough Qld 2021

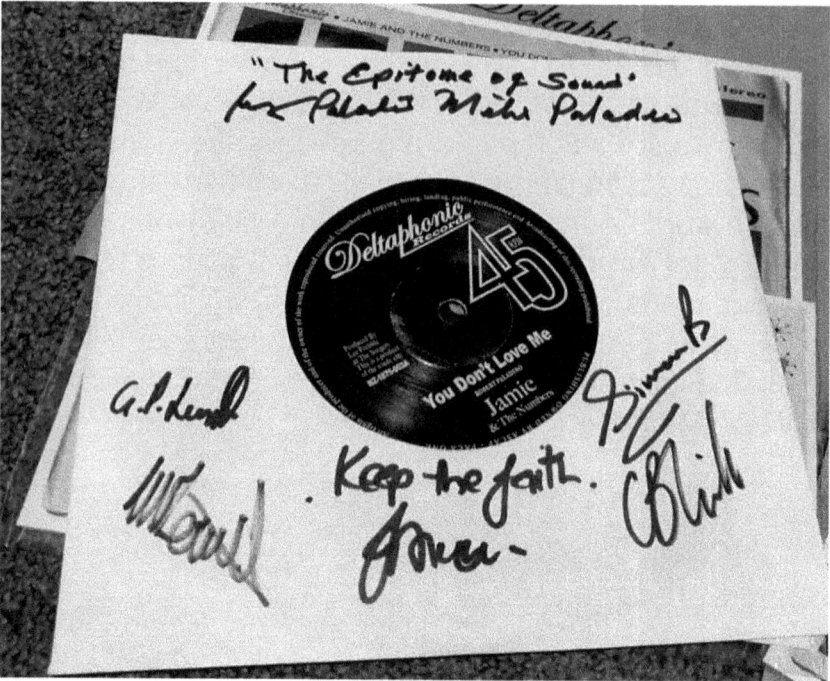

Signed photo of Jamie & The Numbers "You Don't Love Me"
© Simon Bayliss

Jamie has also done cover versions of the Cure & The Jam. Simon Bayliss also has kindly written his own chapter for this book. On Ethan's passing, I searched for answers as people often do, to try and make some kind sense of "why" and in a spiritual church in Hervey Bay Queensland, my spiritual journey started thanks to one of the world's best mediums Jason McDonald from Brisbane. He told an elderly lady next to me that Bill & Fred were "alright now" and you must let go of your grief! He related a very distinct movement of their necks saying "they are alright now". There were tears of joy from the lady, who explained things to me later when I got her a cup of tea. Apparently Bill, her husband & Fred the co-pilot were shot down over Singapore in 1942 and were beheaded by the Japanese. She explained that her tears of joy were from heaven. Jason McDonald is extremely talented in his gift, it is hard to get him to do a reading as he is booked out many months ahead.

That was a personal Eureka moment of how there is a higher power and my journey of "Proof of Existence" 'started this way, it was truly a great moment in time. To live knowing that Karma is the big word, that what goes around does truly come around, before then I was a very weak person, I was caught aged 8 stealing from Woolworths a batman suit. I was a real thief and had been up to it for years, the store detectives called my Dad who gave me the belt to my bare back side and I will always be grateful to my best Dad, John Warren Snr, who passed sadly eleven years ago for his unconditional love and for giving me this wake up call, I so badly needed. Did I listen? Well no! because I was an arrogant little twat and continued to live my life doing things I am now truly ashamed of! But I will try to evolve, to be better, day by day and year by year until I go home and I hope I get in the queue to the small door (heaven) and that I am allowed in. There might be some going down the line shouting no pushing at the back and ironically some reading this will be sent to the right and the big door, which is sadly the gates of hell but in their lives they had choices and hopefully I have appeased my soul and will be allowed into heaven.

I still want to be an "Ordinary Joe " and having my name on the book can perceive EGO, which is one thing I truly don't want. Ironically Simon Bayliss's daughter Ellie has sung a fine version of the Terry Callier classic with those iconic lyrics. There hopefully will be a limited release of that on a 45, Hopefully sometime in 2022.

My Biggest 45 Record Find

I purchased **The Bobby Paris 57 acetates** collection in 2006 when I luckily had a USA eBay account, this was when only USA bidders were allowed.
"Night Owl" on Cameo Com/Promo", "I Walked Away" on Capitol Northern Soul, Detroit Soul, Motown, and Related Items Produced by the legendary Bobby Paris.

This Collection includes mainly acetate (some with demo-style lyric sheets) and a few 45's including a commercial copy of "Night Owl" on Cameo and a commercial and a promo copy of "I Walked Away" on Capitol. (On an 8-inch acetate (proof copy) on Capitol and an 8 inch edited version on acetate.)

https://www.popsike.com/NORTHERN-SOUL-Bobby-Paris-Detroit-Motown-Acetates-45s/4864924466.html

I have since sold all of them to my good mate Barry Motown Simpson who has kindly written for this book.

John Warren with the Bobby Paris acetates © John Warren

Queensland Soul Scene

I discovered the soul scene here in Queensland by default in 1999 when I arrived in Scarborough, north of Brisbane and brought a computer and typed in the words Northern Soul. I had to look more than once to see there was a big scene here in Australia and then contacted Pete Feven in Adelaide and he put me in touch with Hillary and she kindly invited me to a barbeque they were holding. When I arrived Larry Santos "You Got me Where You Want Me" was being played. I felt like I was home, sometimes you do not realise how much you miss something as profound as this music until you lose it, as I had for many years.

I only had 30 records that I brought with me when I emigrated, the rest I left in the attic in Moor Road Rushden, which were stolen by a roofer called "Rex the Robber" when he put a new roof on my parent's house where my dear mother who is 83 still lives. So I started collecting again a year later but even then I called myself tight and would not pay most of the crazy prices.

The most I have ever paid was $1000 for Ronnie McNeir's "Sitting In My Class". So I started to go on eBay and worked away buying records a lot cheaper, sourced through some contacts and also started buying bigger lots because to open a box and find a new gem is what thrills me and still does 22 years on. The last record I found like this was in 2020, a Herbert Hunter "I Was Born To Love You" for $6 on eBay. But these days finding a cheap gem is very hard. I will try to do a Queensland soul scene chapter in Book 3, but I would prefer somebody else do it! The soul scene here started in 1974 at the Breakfast Creek hotel by that good lad Brian Williams and now in 2021 there are many events put on and respect to all who do, because it's hard work ! Luckily for me near where I live in Rock Street, Scarborough Village there is a niche venue that holds about 60 people and is run by "Sounds Of Soul".

Steve & Elaine Brophy have started a monthly Saturday afternoon- night event and because I live nearby, I can attend regularly. A recent article written by Gary Williamson failed to mention the "Soul In the City" which he does a fine job of putting on with Ainslie White, he stated it was started by Steve & Elaine Griffin, so I politely correct the fact that Brian Williams and myself were also involved in starting it many moons ago. In fact it was myself and the Griffin's who discovered the Polish Club venue for the event.

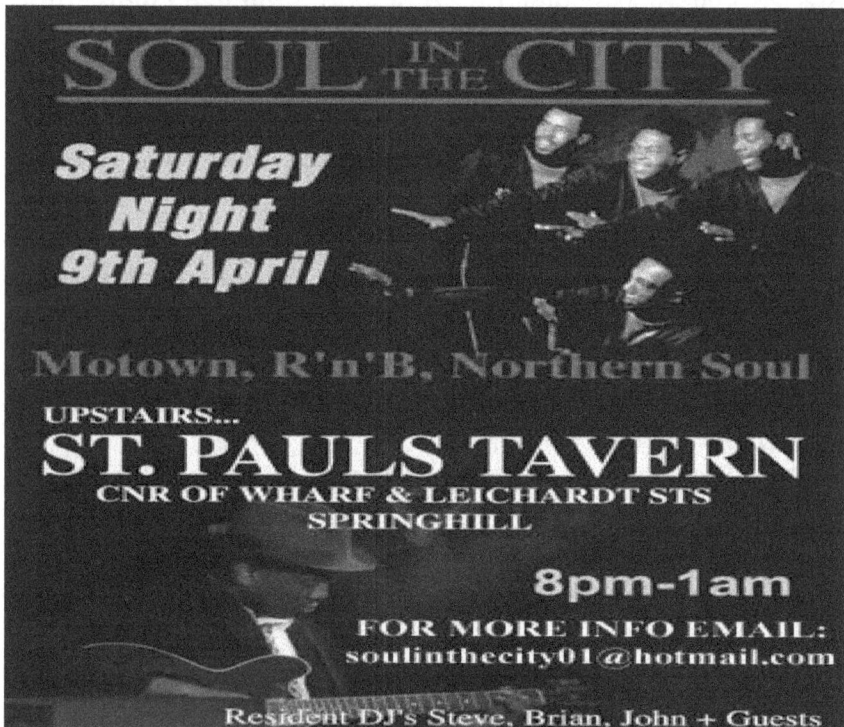

Original Soul in The City Poster Brisbane © Brian Williams

The website Soul In The City. I also commissioned & paid Keith Miller to do it and was happy to hand that and the baton over to Garry Williamson when "I Walked Away". Hopefully more in Queensland offer to write in the future as at this point there has been none with West Australia, way out in front donating their time and their soul journey stories!

426

LIFE ON KIBBUTZ BEIT GUVRIN
SOUTH JORDANIAN VALLEY

Very recently I had another "Lightbulb Moment" about a moment in time come 10 years ago when I was living on the kibbutz "Beit Guvrin'," a non-religious kibbutz formed in 1949 by Turkish holocaust survivors near Hebron. I lived there for 6 months and shared a room with a lad called Mike from New York and one day he was trying to impress Yvonne & Brigitta, two Swedish ladies I shared a room with, they were two attractive ladies from Stockholm and there was something he wanted to show them. He noticed I had heard, so I also was invited "to look". After fruit picking the next day off we went, he said do you get scared and I truthfully said no, but how wrong I was. Jim was an archeologist and had researched where we were going and had done it many times before. We entered a cave robber's tunnel through a pothole. Jim had a helmet torch, I went last and you held on to the feet of the person in front of you. It was dark and very tight, very claustrophobic and eventually we came into a massive opening where there was a ledge and a massive drop of hundreds of feet. Over the far wall were lots of boxes cut into the rock for pigeons to nest.

Off we went down this ledge path until it was eroded away and you could see in the near distance where it resumed, Jim says "we rock climb", this with a sheer drop which he did in a nanosecond, and then the two lassies did it effortlessly. It was then my turn, I got halfway and froze and I will never forget that primal fear I had that day. The ladies were cursing for the chicken shite they thought I was, but Jim noticed I was in real trouble and talked me in, to do what I had to do, or fall to my death. I experienced true fear! I never went again with them which I regret, but in 1982 they started excavating and after my "lightbulb moment "I googled and found out those cave robbers tunnels lead to Beit Guvrin-Maresha National Park in central Israel, 13 kms from Kiryat Gat, encompassing the ruins of Maresha, one of the important towns of Judah during the time of the First Temple and Beit Guvrin, an important town in the Roman era when known as Eleutheropolis.

https://www.israel-in-photos.com/bet-guvrin-national-park.html

Archaeological artifacts unearthed at the site include a large Jewish cemetery, a Roman-Byzantine amphitheater, a Byzantine church, public baths, mosaics, and burial caves. So little did I know that this was originally discovered in 1902 and I was one of the first to visit it sheerly by chance meeting mad Mike from New York. I feel like I would like to return and maybe write about life on a kibbutz and if you are under 35 and reading this, because 35 is the cut-off age for volunteering, I suggest you put it on your bucket list as the whole experience is very enlightening. Arriving on that kibbutz was by chance I had flown from Athens in Greece to Tel Aviv Israel and then went to a kibbutz agency, who sent me to Beit Guvrin in November 1980. You are expected to work six days a week Monday to Saturday for minimal pay, it's basically about the experience. You are given a dormitory style bedroom which you share with two others, usually of the same sex. You get up to work at 8am and are taken by van to the job you are designated for, which is different some days, but most are jobs like picking oranges. At 10am you stop and go back to a communal style eating area with so much food to choose from, which you can eat as much as you wish. There were only 19 volunteers from various countries when I arrived. Being a non-religious kibbutz some of the younger members would try to engage with us, saying ' 'There Is No God" because their families had not survived the holocaust, which was a hard one to try and debate with them. But these younger people would also be very kind and take us out to visit things like Bethlehem and Manger Square, which we did on Xmas eve.

After work around 1-2 pm we would come back and play soccer and volleyball. It's a very idyllic lifestyle on this kibbutz, although only a small one of 300 members, but it still had its own doctor and school.

Every Friday night we went into a communal room to watch the latest movie. One particular week it was "Chariots of Fire" and early in the movie when the Jewish lad wins the race the words come out " We are God's Chosen people" , and the whole room stood up which kind of confused me as they were non-believers. Then two weeks before Xmas I thought I had won the lottery as 12 Swedish ladies arrived, and we men were heavily outnumbered, so my mind overplayed thinking of all the scenarios that might happen. Did they? Well true to form back then NO. I was given the responsibility of mixing the drinks for the New Year's Eve party, when you stay on a kibbutz there is always an abundance of cheap alcohol, so I got a plastic dustbin and filled it with everything and anything. Everyone got so very drunk except me as I like to just watch and observe. When the New Year struck it was time for everyone to kiss, everyone was that drunk men were kissing men, but remember I was still sober so I declined as men are not my thing, but it was funny observing it all transpire. I was sharing a room with Tom from Manchester and Mike from New York, but Tom was a snorer which really grated on my nerves and when I get tired I can be very cranky, so for his safety I moved in with Brigatta and Yvonne, but they were concerned when they got undressed, I am respectful, so I would shut my eyes and count 1-10 but cut out most of it and opened my eyes and usually I got a right nice eyeful, which I got used to. We often when the sabbath kicked in every week traveled around Israel together. They had boyfriends back home in Sweden so I was like a brother. Hitchhiking was always easy with me hiding in the bushes, while they pedaled their wares. At checkpoints the Israeli army conscripts would get us rides in Mercedes or they would not be let pass through, which they were not too happy about. One time we thought we would go and check Massada out and got a lift from Jericho to Ein Gedi by a reluctant German businessman in his Mercedes and then had a float in the dead sea. One time we went to Massada youth hostel in a bus that was returning to the depot, the driver put me in the back off the empty bus, and had the girls in the front near him, but he was on the tannoy to another driver for party time with them, but when we arrived I told him bad luck it was not happening. The girls were adventurous types and wanted to sleep out in the Negev desert, but we only had two sleeping bags and it gets incredibly cold there, so to keep warm we had to do the body rub which was technically my very first three-some. I have an inner tuition for danger and they noticed around midnight, I went very quiet and they got the message! and what transpired was that the Israeli army was doing night maneuvers. We were lucky because we were in a large hole and we saw the torches flash past us, it could have ended so badly. So I did not get any sleep and the next day declined to go up the cable car to the top of Masada and instead slept against a metal pylon. I woke up to hear a large crowd of Asian tourists laughing and taking photos of me which confused me. What had happened? Well pigeons had been shitting on me. So many happy memories with those two ladies. One night for a laugh they wanted to paint my face with makeup and I was up for anything and then they then took photos. I hope they do not turn up on Facebook one day. Anyone reading this who is young should go and check a Kibbutz out, you will not regret the experience.

When in Israel I visited so many great places, the Sea of Galilee, Jerusalem and the Church of the Holy Sepulcher, Yad Vashem the holocaust museum, which has left an eternal effect on me having spent a whole day there in what is an incredibly sad place. I enjoyed Eilat and the beach resort and also Jericho and so many more interesting place's. Hebron was also fascinating and the fact there are some Israeli families living amongst the Palestine people, when you go there you hear the words welcome to Palestine. The Mayor of Hebron kindly invited a few of us to his house for Turkish coffee. I also wanted to go to Lebanon, so I got a bus to Kibbutz "Qirat Shimona " when the driver asked where I was going he pointed to a landmine sign, but that was not going to deter me. I skirted the sign gingerly and safely got to the border where two Irish United Nations peacekeepers were laughing and saying we are not letting you in as you don't have a Visa.

I had to return the way that I had come hoping not to find a landmine. About 3 weeks after the Swedish ladies had arrived, one who was a real player and was there for all sundry who would like to party, there were 3 members who had been there 7 years, they were from Birmingham UK and all were house painters. They had some weed and we could hear them all having a good time with her, which is fine, but we had to get up early the next day and as they were in the next room the noise was too much so we had to sort it out. Jim knocked on their door, a golden rule is never goes first and in a nano second he was king hit, his nose was broken and then it was on. The kibbutz had soldiers with Uzi submachine guns to protect us, so quickly they arrived and it got sorted very quickly! When we went to work the next day the three brummie lads were gone and I was quickly installed as the house painter as they were building new houses.

My six months on the Kibbutz went quickly and when I left I was given a certificate which I still treasure. Incidentally talking of painting, when I back packed to Australia with Seamus Vickers, we both quickly got a job painting for Robert Case Painters and when they found out I had restored old buildings they gave me the hospital job at Botany Bay where Captain Cook had landed and then the Boathouse at Concorde hospital in Sydney to restore for the Queens upcoming visit in 1987.

AUSTRALIAN RECORD LABELS

There are many collectors here in Australia & around the world who collect soul music genres & many other genres on small and major Australian record labels. Some Australian collectors here to name a few are Frank Driscoll, George Coumbis, Nigel Loveless & Kev Core and they each have a wealth of knowledge. Hopefully, one of them might like to write a chapter in a future book, as it is of worldwide interest in my humble opinion! In recent times some of the top prices were being paid for the 1960s of other styles and genres of Australian music by lesser-known bands such as the Missing Links, the Creatures, the Marksmen, the Pink Finks, and the Wild Cherries. Their singles were worth $100's depending on condition, and among them was what was considered the ultimate prize of Australian vinyl - the rare, self-titled album by the Missing Links. Another rarity is a single given away at the Crystal Ballroom in St Kilda by the Boys Next Door, later known as the Birthday Party, fronted by a young Nick Cave. This phenomenon continues despite most of the music having been re-released on CDs. The collector seeks the 1st release in the original sleeve in the way philatelists want the first issue of a stamp. This is what is known as the "Trophy Mentality". Serious collectors, and investors, get a kick out of having something few others have, it's not really about the music.

Valuable Australian punk singles include:

Radio Birdman, Burn my Eye (EP). 1976 Recorded at Trafalgar Studios. $650.

The Saints, I'm Stranded (Mail-order single). 1976 Fatal Records. $650.

Boys Next Door, Happy Birthday/Riddle House Crystal Ballroom Giveaway 7" with foldover picture cover. $250.

The Thought Criminals, Hilton Bomber EP (Doublethink Records DTDT -1) from Sydney 1978, with cover and insert. $1750.

Victims, No Thanks To The Human Turd EP with hand-colored cover and insert. From Perth 1978. $750.

Young Identities, EP (Savage Music SM-02 / PRS-3672) from Brisbane 1979, with original fold-over picture cover. $1000.

Fun Things, EP (EMI Custom PRS-2783) from Brisbane 1980, with original picture cover. $1200.

The Chosen Few, The Joke's On Us! EP Self-released by the band on Few Records. From Melbourne 1978. Needs to be complete with an original fold-over cover and lyric insert. $850.

Other Australian treasures include:

Barry Gibb & the Bee Gees, Sing and Play 14 Barry Gibb songs. Leedon Records, 1964. $1500.

Brian de Courcy presents My Favourite Kinda People. W&G compilation LP. $135.

The Twilights, Once Upon A Twilight. Rare Pop-up Cover. $400.

Extradition, Hush. Sweet Peach. $1000 plus.

Madden and Harris, Fool's Paradise. Jasmine Records. $1000 plus.

Lobby Loyde and the Coloured Balls, Ball Power. $200.

Syrius, self-titled. Spin Records. $400

Kahvas Jute, Wide Open. Infinity. $700

The prices naturally fluctuate and this is only a guide, but for any Aussie music lovers reading this book, check the charity shops which sadly mostly have LP's and rarely have 45's. In Redcliffe, Queensland, close to where I live two shops have opened in recent months. Australian 45s are so rare due to the simple fact that supply and demand dictates, being a small population they pressed fewer numbers and also because of the licensing. I have been fortunate to have had one issue copy of Fia Karin who does a version of the Dana Valery classic "You Don't Know Where Your Interest Lies " on Spin record label. Some that sell well but not as hard to find are Bev Harrell's "You Baby", a great version of the Jackie Trent classic on Aussie HMV is also available on a picture sleeve E/P. Then there is the popular Doug Parkinson's version of the classic 'I'll Be Around". Also so many rare ones like Gloria Scott "A Case Of Too Much Love Making" and Marcia Hines "You Gotta let Go".

Hopefully in a future book someone will elaborate on this interesting subject matter.

LOCKDOWN IN AUSTRALIA

We have been fortunate up to today, which is the end of November 2021 that the lockdowns in my State of Queensland have been limited, and we are very fortunate to have had only 7 deaths so far. Queensland has a population of over 5.1 million people and the state government is the Australian Labor Party with the leader being Annastacia Palaszczuk. So fortunately for us soul lovers generally we have been able to go to soul nights, with the occasional event canceled or where masks had to be worn or dancing was not allowed, as was the case recently at Elaine & Steve Brophy's Scarborough Village soul night, held in a niche venue called Showcase Beers. Check it out at the link below .

https://www.facebook.com/showcasebeers/

This is a very well-run beer bar, it holds around 60 people and there is a monthly event which is always fully attended by some lovely soulies. With my health improving I plan to get out more and if we don't see eye to eye please stay out of my way, as I just want to dance and play the fool because life's so short and the grains of sand are going through the glass way too quickly. In December I went to the Polish Club and it was brilliant, run by Gary and Nardia Williamson & Ainslie and Linda White who do a grand job. It used to be put on upstairs when myself, Steve and Elaine Griffin and Brian Williams ran it back in the day & then Gary kindly joined us. It was a lot of hard work lugging equipment up the stairs, but I fondly remember those nights. I left doing it over 11 years ago for personal reasons. These days it's held downstairs in the big ballroom, what a venue it truly is with a big stage and a wooden dance floor. I have to mention the bar staff and one lady who has been doing it for all those years and is much loved. The beer naturally is Polish and many soul music lovers may have been more than a bit drunk after attending. I will never forget the day I got to meet one of those special people you tend to meet on your life's journey, Duncan

McAllister and his lovely lass. He played records that we were not conversant with, we had a great night and he went on to DJ and attend so many Australian national events with the last one being in 2019 at the Gold Coast, Queensland. Sadly there has not been a national soul event since with the next one planned for 2022, god willing in Sydney booause the last two years have been canceled due to covid. With Covid here in Australia we have state governments and we had lockdowns on cases as low as a few, especially here in Victoria and here in Queensland. I have felt for the soul lovers of NSW & Victoria who had lockdown's simply because of an arrogant state government leader. I personally don't trust politicians. They start out with good intentions but often get corrupted along the way, and kick the can down the road and sadly worldwide children and grandchildren are going to have to bear a heavy climatic and financial burden in the many decades to come, this due to decisions made over Covid !

It is heartening to read that at the end of July 2021 people in other countries are getting out to soul events, and DJing and dancing again, and I pray that continues as there is no set rule book in this calamity that is Covid. Another soul afternoon & evening chill-out event run here in Queensland that I must mention is Sub Rosa, Fortitude Valley, Brisbane run by a great mate of mine of many years Brian Williams which was gaining a good following with a recent one having some interstate DJ's from Melbourne Victoria. Sadly it recently closed and Brian Williams is currently looking for a new venue.

Covid And The Impact On The Soul Scene

These are my own personal thoughts and not those of the other writers in this book. Covid has been disastrous for most artists that I have met, not being able to perform their beloved skill set . For me selling records and them arriving warped and melted I have touched on already .Not being able to go out and be with like minded soul lovers is something which has had a worldwide impact. I have an interest in Virology and Immunology and took an active interest from when Covid first started in Wuhan China in 2020 . It quickly became apparent there was "Something Fishy Going On" the blame was being laid at China's door for a specific reason and to detract from who was really behind this Plandemic. I have to be careful in my wording and not be too specific, all you gotta do is join the dots, this is not hard as long you don't do it through the propaganda sites controlled by those who have a massive financial and vested interests, to keep this agenda going, this for reasons some you off you do understand and more are waking up too. For some it will be "Too Late "and for me that is sad.

I have been vilified by some, but spiritually I don't pick up your rubbish and I have only met about 2% who claim to be spiritual who have gone along with this scam. My own personal family has been divided perhaps like many of yours and for me that is incredibly sad and some of mine are getting covid after being jabbed. The British government has spilled the beans about the fact that once you get double jabbed, you will never again be able to acquire full natural immunity. In its **Week 42 "COVID-19** vaccine surveillance report, the U.K. Health Security Agency admitted on page 23 that "N" antibody levels appear to be lower in people who acquire infection following two doses of vaccination. It explains this antibody drop is basically permanent.

What does this mean? We know the vaccines do not stop infection or transmission of the virus (in fact, the report shows elsewhere that vaccinated adults are now being infected at much HIGHER rates than the unvaccinated). What the British are saying is they are now finding the vaccine interferes with your body's innate ability after infection to produce antibodies against not just the spike protein, but other pieces of the virus. Specifically, vaccinated people don't seem to be producing antibodies to the nucleocapsid protein, the shell of the virus, which are a crucial part of the response in unvaccinated people. In the long term, people who take the vaccine will be far more vulnerable to any mutations in the spike protein that might come along, even if they have already been infected and recovered once, or more than once. The unvaccinated, meanwhile, will procure lasting, if not permanent, immunity to all strains of the alleged virus after being infected with it naturally even just once. Read it for yourself (Page 24).

When you take interest in the Spike Protein & Graphene Oxide we become very alarmed and because of the love of our fellow man we shout it from the trees, but we get labeled conspiracy theorists but sadly history repeats. Living with Turkish Holocaust survivors 40 yrs ago in Israel, taught me a lot and books like Adolf Hitler's "Mein Kampf" and George Orwell's 1984" are a playbook in all this! Mind control as I take a great interest in watching human behavior while playing my harmonica, and have never ever seen so much anger and depression, also I have noticed a pattern which I noticed years ago when I lived with drug addicts in Amsterdam, that is what I used to term the walking dead or a zombie style of lack of life. No one is actually free regardless of if you are jabbed or not and our civil rights, that our ancestors fought and died for over the centuries, have been eroded on this totally trumped up virus . I have never been more ashamed of my adopted country Australia and how we have now got the term "Prison Island"' which is very ironic when you understand how this colony was formed. But a lot of brave people are fighting back because their backs are against the wall. That great Australian Anzac spirit is returning with a gusto and hopefully the lads lying in graves in far off lands, who died for our freedom, will stop turning in them! So hopefully the civil rights movements here will take Australia back from these despots and when there is a Nuremberg 2.00 they are held to account. We all know who they are worldwide, and they have fear and a lot of us do not. We will die glad that the world is free, because we have no choice for all of us because "This is End Game".

I put this in writing because if I am wrong I will be one the **happiest** persons walking this planet, but I truly doubt I am wrong and the reality makes me writing this as **sad as it gets**! I also have interest in common law and won several cases of mine over the years because I stand up for what I believe, passively and I find masking children is child abuse under "common law earth."

People are losing their jobs because all they want to do is work and are pro-choice, but then I can empathise with so many worldwide who have mortgages and bills to pay and take jabs under duress. One very evil politician here just spoke out saying we are a "mob" well he is about to learn his past about to come back to haunt him, and the power of the people will make him hold him to account! **Vaccinating Children** really messes with my head, and I truly feel for those generations to come, who are going to sadly pay a heavy price for their parents, who did not do their job and that's protect those they claim to love dearly, and did not even do some basic due diligence and research the impacts of their monumental decision.

Speaking obviously comes with risks but I have no fear and you always have to be true to yourself and accept what will be! I have also noticed many behavior changes, aggression, confusion and personality changes so profound in some we thought were our friends! Shedding of the spike protein is a problem for those of us who chose to be cautious and not accept any of the current vaccines, you might notice runny noses and bleeding, to help I personally use Dandelion tea and rinse my mouth with coconut oil.

VigiAccess was launched by the World Health Organization (WHO) in 2015 to provide public access to information in VigiBase, the WHO global database of reported potential side effects of medicinal products.		
Vaccine or Drug Name	Total ADRs	Years
Mumps vaccine	711	1972-2021
Rubella vaccine	2,621	1971-2021
Ivermectin	5,705	1992-2021
Measles vaccine	5,827	1968-2021
Penicillin nos	6,684	1968-2021
smallpox vaccine	6,891	1968-2021
chloroquine	7,139	1968-2021
tetanus vaccine	15,085	1968-2021
Hydroxychloroquine	32,641	1968-2021
Hepatitis A vaccine	46,773	1989-2021
Benzylpenicillin	51,327	1968-2021
Rotavirus vaccine	68,327	2000-2021
Accutane	70,719	1983-2021
Vancomycin	71,159	1974-2021
Hepatitis B vaccine	104,619	1984-2021
Polio vaccine	121,988	1968-2021
Meningococcal vaccine	126,412	1976-2021
Ibuprofen	166,209	1969-2021
tylenol	169,359	1968-2021
Aspirin	184,481	1968-2021
Pneumococcal vaccine	234,783	1980-2021
Influenza vaccine	272,202	1968-2021
Covid-19 vaccine	2,457,386	2020-2021

www.vigiaccess.org
Updated Nov. 12th 2021

This will explain a lot!

150,000 people attended the World Peace Rally, with our next event being held in Brisbane on November 20th,2021 the biggest protest ever seen in Brisbane, a real moment in time and anyone who attended would understand! "A change is going to come "

I end this here, as there is no one so blind as those that can't See.

Whistling & learning to play the Harmonica

My love in the last few years has been whistling, mainly to assist with my lung disease. It was also a love of my beloved father John Warren Snr and I often feel when I do practice that I bring him through. I am slowly improving, last week at an open mic of the Queensland writers night I ended my talk with a rendition of Frank Sinatra's "My Way" a song my dad did with aplomb, and many people used to comment he was as good a cover artist as you would hear. In his later years my Dad sang at many old people's homes and that is something I would also like to emulate when I am proficient enough. John Warren, my Dad, was a very talented singer who should have done very well. My Dad sang locally around the Northamptonshire area in the 60s-80s. I sadly cannot sing, but I continue to try, but my whistling is slowly taking shape, and I whistle constantly on my rides and walks and I feel my lungs are feeling the benefit of all that lung exercise. I have just bought a harmonica in July 2021, and am inspired by the blues, especially the wonderful Little Walter, so I am going to try to practice every day for hours as I really like going around riding the streets and getting known as "The Harmonica Man'. Bob Dylan used to also ride a bike practising and I often wonder how he got the inspiration for "Blowing in the Wind ". I started out on a 48 reed Swan which I personally find easier to learn on than a 10 reed blues one. Children seem to love it when I show them how to do a train coming.

I also find it very rewarding when the disabled many trapped in their wheelchairs, seem to come alive full of joy when I attempt to play! Harmonica's are not expensive and so much fun so if you are bored or want to exercise your lips and lungs. I would also strongly recommend them for mental and memory recall. I stopped playing the ambulance sound as I went down the road as cars were stopping and then they saw me adding to their confusion.

Record Fairs In The USA

I have been fortunate to attend three in New Jersey, Chicago, Orlando and LA and have spent all day and not found any 45's above a $50 value, so the myth they are still there for the picking is not the reality for me. I also searched record shops in those cities and also came up with very little. When I flew into LA I hooked up with Steve & Antony (Gabby) Beeby who grew up close to me in Higham Ferrers, Northamptonshire and they attended the rock foundation soul event in 1974 and I touch on it in Book 1, when they disappeared around that year because they had emigrated to California. Then decades later I was in a queue at the bar at the soul trip USA, in New Jersey, when Gabby heard my accent as I stood with just a few people in front of him. When I turned around he said, it is you, you are the lad who let me in the club when I was only 12, after I had asked to come in as my brother and sister were stomping away inside. I replied "get in there lad and get out on the floor". So here we were reunited through the love of this great music and he said if you are in LA, come to check us out and I have been three times, as they are great company and really do look after me. The very last time I visited them was about 10 years ago.

I did not have much sleep due to family turmoil and when we got in the car to go record searching as we had done many times before I got a message in my head and said to Gabby you are going to do very well today. So off we drove 50 kilometers into the heart of the ghettos. We would go to places like Compton and Paramount. Who could ever forget those salubrious suburbs where white honkeys are welcomed with glee. So our very first appointment was a young couple whose grandmother had left them over two hundred 45's which they brought out. They were in no sleeves and were in a plastic beer crate so this did not look good. The Beeby's glanced at me, this will be a waste of time and then the 2nd 45 out of the beer crate was a Motown demo and the treasure trove kept going on 45 after 45 starting with The Inconquerable's "For Your Love" & "Wait For Me" on the tiny label Floidavier, but what made this so unique is it was on yellow vinyl which is incredibly rare. When we left the house they were crying and I kid you not Gabby was very emotional hugging me and saying "This is Our Biggest Find in decades``. Incredible days like this are etched in my mind forever. We had a few lucky days searching together over the years and I hope and feel I am their lucky talisman, so I truly hope we get to do it again.

They also don't suffer from that wasted emotion called fear and they're smart, they put their money in their socks and are built like the proverbial brick shit house. They are so very generous and gave me a suitcase of the standard cheaper 45's like "Hand it Over", "Open the Door to Your Heart " and "I Have Faith in You" to name just a few. I never got to see Gabby DJ, he was the resident DJ at the famous Hollywood Crush bar for over 10 years, with his clientele being Rod Stewart who he went on to privately DJ for Tom Cruise & Peter Falk, and many more. Hollywood celebrities. Gabby and Rod Stewart would go for a beer and chat about English Soccer and on one of those night's Gabby said why do you not bring out a Motown & Soul album, which Rod then went and did when he brought the Soul book album out. Steve Beeby is my age and he recently has had a few young children and when I last spoke to him he seemed a bit fed up with what is happening in the USA and was considering emigrating. If you are reading this mate, I truly hope it all works out & we get to meet up again somewhere one day really soon!

The Dreaded Soul Police

DDJD (Dreaded DJ Disease) was touched on in Book 1 of the "Our Soul Music Journey" series, a tongue-in- cheek reference to those who become obsessed with being a DJ and who sometimes seem to believe they are more important than the artists who created the very records they play. I think we have all seen this type of DJ, they are not hard to spot. Another type which personally frustrate me are the Soul Police, the self-appointed rulers of soul, who bang on about the rules they demand we must abide by if we want to be part of "the scene", they are driven by old fashioned and purist thought processes, which are fine if you really want soul not to be about the actual music, but about rituals creating a protected species called :Northern Soul". I personally feel a lot of the younger people do not get the magic we heard sadly, even including my own adult children. When I speak to the artists we love and hear their tales of woe, how they did not make a dime and how now in later life many of them suffer from not being in the best of health. You also hear some lie in a pauper's grave which is beyond sad. The artist's relate they are often despondent on how it all played out for them musically, and they don't own a copy of their own records and If they did own copy, over the years they would have had to sell them to survive.

Some also mention artists covering classic's like Jamie & the Numbers from New Zealand with their 3 covers of some of the classic's. Maybe when these younger artist's do cover these songs it highlights them to people of their own generation and it might make some a bit inquisitive and the royalties might flow back. I often look at a great dancer like Shawn Chapman, who kindly did a DJ spot at my 50th and then watch how he DJ'S with passion and some on the other side of the coin, you will get the bored looking DJ who you can read the body language of easily, it shows he does not truthfully appreciate the record he is playing, but needs to feed is ego and there prevails a "look at me and my rare records" attitude. I once even heard a DJ talking about a record he had played, not about the music, or the artists, but saying "there's only six in the world and it's worth this much" that was truly beyond sad. Where else can someone with a lot of money buy rare records and then stand up on a stage in front of hundreds of people to feed their egotistical personalities, but thankfully they are very easy to spot and in the minority! Sadly we are not going to be here forever and it will be beyond sad if this incredible music, mostly undiscovered by the masses because maybe it is too good, follows us to our graves when we pop our clogs. Hopefully the future is bright and like a wheel it revolves around and continues for many decades to come and I like most of you reading this truly wish that eventuates!

Northern soul in its essence is a very highly emotive subject matter and it can bring out the best and the very worst in people, people with very diverse careers and educations. The coined phrase "Keep the Faith" has been used for ion's, but I personally prefer "Keep the Faith and Spread the Faith". After all these decades the music has not aged, so technically may still be around in many decades to come, I truly hope so.

Soul Trip's USA

I met so many fabulous soul music artists at the three events I attended in New Jersey, Chicago & Orlando and here are a few of the photos I proudly cherish!

Martha Reeves & John Warren in Detroit © Barry Simpson

Francis Nero, John Warren & Lorraine Chandler © Barry Simpson

Signed DJ Shirt with Signatures from Chicago Soul Trip USA © John Warren

Soul DJ Shirt Orlando with artist's signatures © John Warren

In Chapter 22 Paul Stuart Davies does a short introduction about the Gloria Jones school in Sierra Leone and about Kim Weston, some of the profits of the book will be going to them, hopefully Paul will do an in depth chapter on them in Book 3. I will now end with this chapter and if you read any of the books and find them worthy of a review, please do. You may have noticed Book 1 has no reviews, this is because I had to republish it with Amazon after my original publisher Jan unexpectedly passed away. Amazon in their wisdom does not port reviews across to a 2nd edition so you lose any reviews. I spent 15 hrs ringing and emailing Amazon attempting to sort this out. Unfortunately Amazon's executive customer department were uncooperative, this is one the reasons this book will be published with several other publishers including Ingramspark and I have also purchased the ISBN and barcodes to retain full copyright.

" The music business is a cruel and shallow money trench , a long and plastic hallway, where thieves and pimps run free and good men and women die like dog's!" **Hunter S. Thompson**

Book 1 with the revised cover available on Amazon
© Steve Bardsley

We at "Soul Music Journeys" wish you a healthy and a prosperous year in 2022, best regards John Warren.